LORD CHATHAM
And America

By the same author

LORD CHATHAM
A War Minister in the Making

LORD CHATHAM
Pitt and The Seven Years' War

O. A. SHERRARD

LORD CHATHAM
AND AMERICA

GREENWOOD PRESS, PUBLISHERS
WESTPORT, CONNECTICUT

Library of Congress Cataloging in Publication Data

Sherrard, Owen Aubrey, 1887-1962.
   Lord Chatham and America.

     Reprint of the ed. published by Bodley Head, London.
     Bibliography: p.
     Includes index.
     1. Pitt, William, 1st Earl of Chatham, 1708-1778.
I. Title.
[DA483.P6S52 1975]   354'.41'0610924 [B]   75-2700
ISBN 0-8371-8031-7

Contents

Contents

Preface

THIS BOOK is the third and last volume of my *Life of Lord Chatham*. It deals with the period from October 1761 when he resigned the Seals as Secretary of State to May 1778 when he died. It has not taken exactly the form which I originally intended, and so perhaps a word of explanation may not be out of place. When the first volume appeared in 1952, a critic, not finding it to his taste, suggested that in the second and third volumes I might consider deeply whether Pitt was not 'the man most responsible for confusion in domestic affairs between 1760 and 1778'. That was a view which had been presented to me many years ago, and which at one time I partly believed. But after studying the evidence for some twenty-five years, I have changed my mind; I no longer believe it. As, however, it is not an uncommon view, I thought it as well to begin this volume by setting it out and have used it as a sort of inverted text for what follows. The result has been to give the book a more polemical flavour than I had meant, and perhaps to stuff it too full of quotations. I am sorry if this should give offence to the critic in question, or indeed to anyone else; but as the book represents what I believe to be the truth it had better stand. In any event I hope the critic, if he happens to come across the book, will agree that whether my conclusions are right or wrong, at least I have given the point 'deep consideration'.

As in my other volumes, the bibliography is not intended to be exhaustive, but is limited to works from which I have quoted directly or indirectly.

Introduction

ON THE fifth of October 1761, while the Seven Years' War was still raging, Pitt resigned the Seals as Secretary of State, and with the resignation entered on the third and final period of his life —a period at once magnificent and sombre when, in spite of the burden of years and the mounting load of infirmity, he strove to guide the country into the path of wisdom at home, and to save her from calamity abroad. At the time, and for many years after his death, the world recognised that, given the chance, he and he alone might have warded off disaster. But the one chance he had came too late, and darkness fell on him and humiliation on the country. Recently, the pendulum has swung the other way, and historians have begun to lay at his door the futility of the age, holding him responsible for the weakness and waywardness of shallow ministries, and, by implication, for all the losses and disquiets of the times. From such an interpretation I profoundly dissent, and pray that this book may help to redress the balance.

If it is to do so, it should begin by setting out the indictment. Here it is in words other than mine: 'It was his [Pitt's] intractable incalculable nature, his genius tinged with madness, which, at least as much as the immature, unbalanced, passionate obstinacy of George III, produced the chaos of the first ten years of the new reign, and during the next fatal ten years placed the Government in incompetent hands. He would take no account of other people, nor pay any regard to their wishes or feelings; he objected to Bute taking office, but when Bute declared that "he would be a private man", Pitt objected to his being "*the* Minister behind the curtain". Even now a leader has to put up with colleagues whom he might prefer to do without. . . . In 1760, the King, with his "friends" or servants, filled the place of the party organisation, and had a clear right to be represented in the Cabinet; but Pitt would not have it. This produced the first difficulties; after that he would not lead the Opposition, though they were ready to follow him, and in critical moments he would make the proscription of those who had had any share in the Peace Treaty, or the obtaining of

9

office for Lord Temple or of the Great Seal for Pratt, into a
cardinal point. Next it was he, more than the King, who destroyed the Rockinghams by his unreasonable refusal to co-operate
with them—he withheld from them the strength they required.
And after everyone had surrendered to him, and he got an even
freer and fuller chance than in 1756, he found himself deprived by
his previous actions of colleagues far preferable to the shifty
Charles Townshend or the inexperienced Duke of Grafton. In
the end his nerves broke down, and the Government and country
were thrown into confusion.'[1]

Even if we ignore the implied assumption that all unreasonableness was on Pitt's side; even if we ignore the false antithesis
between Pitt's objection to Bute in office and Pitt's objection to
Bute as Minister behind the curtain; even if we ignore the suggestion that Pitt was deprived of desirable colleagues solely by his
own previous and apparently unprovoked actions, and the still
more startling hint that his nervous breakdown was a matter within
his own control—even ignoring all these points, the charge is
heavy. Is there nothing to be said on the other side? I think a great
deal; but each point must be dealt with in its own place, when the
facts have been set out. Only one is ripe to be discussed at the
moment—Pitt's objection to Bute's presence in the Cabinet as the
representative of the King. The facts are given at length in my
previous volume[2] but can be briefly recapitulated.

At an early date, the future George III had told Bute that he
intended to make him Minister when he ascended the throne.
On being consulted, Pitt had made no secret of the fact that he
did not wish to act with Bute, who, in his opinion, was not suited
for the job. It would have been strange if a man in Pitt's position
could not express his views on such a subject, and dishonest if,
on being asked, he had given any but his true opinion. The views
he expressed were not peculiar to himself; they were shared by
most of his colleagues, and have been endorsed by every suc-
ceeding generation.

Whatever Pitt and his colleagues thought, two days after his
accession, George III appointed Bute a Privy Councillor, and
from that moment had his own representative at all Cabinet
deliberations. Pitt, like his colleagues, raised no objection nor did

[1] Namier: *England in the Age of the American Revolution*, pp. 181–2.
[2] See *Lord Chatham: Pitt and the Seven Years' War*.

he make any protest—except at the slights, perhaps unintentional, heaped upon himself by Bute and the King to the detriment of public business. Some four months later, Bute became Secretary of State. His appointment was made without Pitt's knowledge, still less his approbation. He said afterwards that if he had been consulted, he would have repeated his previous opinion that it was not for the good of the King's service for Bute to hold office. But here again, he accepted the *fait accompli*. When the news was broken to him, he remarked briefly: 'The thing is done, and I have all duty and submission to the King'. For the next six months, he worked with Bute, who on the whole supported his policies, until friction arose over the terms of peace to be offered to France and shortly afterwards a difference of opinion on the question of war with Spain. On these two points Bute swung over to the side of Pitt's opponents in the Cabinet and, somewhat to the dismay of his new allies, declared that 'Mr. Pitt and my Lord Temple could not stay', that, in fact, it was 'impossible' to keep them.[1] A fortnight later Pitt had been jockeyed into resigning. That is the short story of Pitt's objection to Bute taking office and the King being represented in the Cabinet. We are told that it 'produced the first difficulties'. What difficulties? And in what way? Must Pitt, who had been uniformly successful, necessarily defer to the counsels of others? And if he disagreed with his colleagues, was he wrong to resign? And if he resigned, must he be held responsible for the difficulties which ensued? Unlike his critics, he himself believed that he was smoothing the path of his successors, and told the King that 'he thought his remaining in office would only create difficulties and altercations in His Majesty's Council.[2] Nor was he alone in that view. 'I think it no matter of dispute', wrote a member of Parliament at the time, 'that public business cannot be carried on with any degree of decency, or any probability of success, if the Minister is of one opinion, and all the rest of His Majesty's servants of another.'[3] What would have happened, if he had stayed on, simply to be over-ruled and out-voted—a mere clog on proceedings? He would, beyond reasonable doubt, have been sent about his business, since, in Bute's words, it was 'impossible' to keep him, and in the King's

[1] Newcastle to Hardwicke, 21st September 1761. Add. MSS. 32,928.
[2] Newcastle to Bedford, 6th October 1761. Add. MSS. 32,929.
[3] *The Conduct of a Right Honourable Gentleman in resigning the Seals of his office justified*, etc. By a member of Parliament, 1761.

words, 'let that mad Pitt be dismissed'.[1] The origin of the trouble was not Pitt's objection to Bute's presence in the Cabinet or in office, but Bute's opposition to Pitt's policy and his determination to drive him out. The facts, in short, do not support the first charge, which can hardly be sustained. The facts must also in due course speak to the other charges. So to our story.

[1] George III to Bute, 19th September 1761. Sedgwick, p. 63.

I

THE PROFFERED BRIBE

(i)

PITT'S RESIGNATION was a world-shaking event. Bute was only too well aware that no one would hear the news unmoved. Some might be glad; but most would be sorry, and the cry of disappointment might well deafen, and even destroy, the author of his fall. How was Bute to allay the probable consternation? How avert the possible wrath? It would need cunning, but should not be beyond the powers of a man who had graduated in the stratagems of a petty court, nor of a vindictive man worked up to the pitch of telling his friends that 'he looked upon Mr. Pitt as his enemy for the time to come, and it was all the same to him whether he met him on foot in the streets, or riding in a coach-and-six'.[1]

The scheme he chose was not without its artfulness; he would blacken Pitt's reputation in that one trait which blazed brightest in the public eye—his 'disinterestedness'. The plot was laid with skill. When Pitt entered the Closet to resign the Seals, the King, though uncompromising on the political issue, was exceedingly gracious on the personal plane. He could not, he said, have approved Pitt's policy of immediate war with Spain, even if backed by the full weight of the Council; but he was none the less sorry to lose so able a servant, and would be very glad to mark his appreciation 'by such honours or emoluments as it was proper for him to bestow.'[2] Pitt, who felt an exaggerated reverence for majesty even in so questionable a shape as George III, was overwhelmed with emotion. Such bounty, such goodness, such condescension was something he had not expected; it was too much for him, and he burst into tears. But the ground had been salted, and he had hardly bowed himself obsequiously out of the presence, before Bute was dangling the bait before him. What would he like? What would be agreeable to him? Pitt's mind was still in a

---

[1] Devonshire's Diary, 7th October 1761. Chatsworth Collection.
[2] *The Border Elliotts.*

turmoil; the King had been so amazingly gracious that Pitt hardly knew what to answer. Beggars, he said, ought not to be choosers; any mark flowing spontaneously from the King would make him happy. Bute was in a hurry; he wrote next day, in the King's name, and 'with more than ordinary desire to succeed', to offer Pitt his choice of the Governorship of Canada or the Chancellorship of the Duchy of Lancaster, with a salary in either case of £5,000 per annum; if neither appealed to him would he make his own suggestions.[1] His answer was anxiously awaited. Until the fish was hooked, the conspirators had their qualms, hinting their hopes and fears to each other in breathless whispers. As Hardwicke wrote to his son, if Pitt would only accept, 'that would do a great deal. But of this *ne verbum quidem*.[2] Pitt put both suggestions aside; considering the office from which he had just resigned, he could hardly accept any other post; but would be doubly happy if the 'monument of royal approbation and goodness' could include those dearer to him than himself. Bute jumped at the hint and promptly informed Pitt that Hester was to receive a peerage, which would descend to his sons, whilst he would be given a grant of £3,000 per annum for his own life and that of any two others he cared to name. He named Hester—who became Lady Chatham—and his eldest son, John.

The award was niggardly in all conscience. Six months earlier Holdernesse had been given £4,000 a year simply for resigning to make way for Bute. But, niggardly or not, it was sufficient for Bute's purpose, more especially as despatches had just come from Lord Bristol (our Ambassador at Madrid) which suggested that Pitt had misread the Spanish situation. The very next day two paragraphs appeared in the *Gazette*, artfully juxtaposed, the one containing the soothing syrup from Spain, the other announcing Pitt's retirement and, contrary to the usual practice, setting out at length the awards made to him. 'I am glad you like the *Gazette*', Hardwicke wrote. 'I hear it operates'.[3]

It did indeed, giving official imprimatur to a supposition that England's idol had feet of filthy lucre. The City, which on the rumour of Pitt's fall had meant to demand his restoration,[4] hastily

[1] Bute to Pitt, 6th October 1761. Chatham, Corr. II. 146.
[2] Hardwicke to Royston, 6th October 1761. Add. MSS. 35,352.
[3] Hardwicke to Royston, 12th October 1761. Add. MSS. 35,352.
[4] 'I hear some of them are rash enough to say they will have their Minister again', Bute to Newcastle, 6th October 1761. Add. MSS. 32,929.

changed their minds and substituted a petition to Parliament for wider streets in place of a proposed vote of thanks to Pitt.[1] Walpole, with one eye on his literary fame, wrote to his cronies that 'virtue is ar. errant strumpet',[2] that in four days Pitt had 'tumbled from the conquest of Spain to receiving a quarter's pension from Mr. West', and much other fustian about being 'the dupe of Pitt's disinterestedness'.[3] Even parsons assured each other, with fewer flowers of speech but more honest indignation, that 'whatever Mr. Pitt may be, or may not be—I care not. He may have been a good Minister, or not, for what I know. But I am sure he is a very inconsistent and shameless man'.[4] Indeed a terribly bitter cry rose throughout the country that the people had been betrayed—sold for a 'long-necked' Lady Cheat'em and a pocketful of guineas. The humbler sort were sick at heart, believing that their champion had made a corrupt bargain to forsake them; while the higher sort indulged in sneers and self-congratulations. 'I am truly happy', Bedford assured Newcastle, 'that you have got rid of all your difficulties, and that it has been effected in a way which must entirely cut up all Mr. Pitt's ill-gotten popularity by the roots'.[5] Sackville, who knew from Minden days all about dereliction of duty, supposed that Pitt had been moved by a 'conviction that he cannot hope to steer the ship safe into port, and so takes the present pretence of leaving her, that if she sinks, it may be laid to the unskilfulness of the next pilot, and not to his own mismanagement of bringing her into such troubled waters',[6] while Melcombe, a toady and a turncoat, rejoiced to think that Bute was 'delivered from a most impracticable colleague, His Majesty from a most imperious servant, and the country from a most dangerous Minister'.[7] So soon had men forgotten that Pitt had stood in the breach at England's darkest hour, when all others had despaired and none would come to her rescue.

Undoubtedly Bute had been clever. He was disposed to pat himself on the back: 'the storm', he said with some confidence, 'seems blowing over. . . . Secure of my own heart, depending on those who, with me, wish nothing but happiness and glory to

[1] Walpole, *George III*, I, 66.
[2] To the Countess of Ailesbury, 10th October 1761.
[3] To Conway, 12th October 1761.
[4] *Memoirs of a Royal Chaplain*, p. 358.
[5] Bedford to Newcastle, 11th October 1761. Add. MSS. 32,929.
[6] Sackville to Irwin, 6th October 1761. H.M.C. Stopford-Sackville MSS.
[7] Melcombe to Bute, H.M.C. Various Collections, Vol. VI, p. 50.

their King and country, I shall go on without dismay or hesitation.'[1] But he had over-reached himself because he had not visualised the tornado he was letting loose. It was too violent to last. Before long the more sober and the more charitable, remembering that the labourer is worthy of his hire, began to think the reward hardly commensurate with the service. It was a shame, said Burke, who was no friend of Pitt's, that any defence was necessary; it was impossible for the King to let him go unrequited and the sum seemed to have been regulated rather by Pitt's moderation than by the King's liberality. The idea spread, and was put in a popular form by Delaval, who called Pitt a fool for taking so little; if he had told the City he was a poor man with a wife and family to maintain, they would have subscribed half a million. The *coup de grâce* was given by Pitt himself, who was as much surprised at the uproar as Bute could be. He wrote a letter to Beckford, briefly detailing the story of his resignation, and declaring that the 'public marks of His Majesty's approbation' were 'unmerited and unsolicited', but a source of pride to himself. He was writing, he said, in the interests of truth, not 'to court return of confidence from any man, who, with a credulity as weak as it is injurious, has thought fit hastily to withdraw his good opinion from one who has served his country with fidelity and success; and who justly reveres the upright and candid judgment of it; little solicitous about the censures of the capricious and ungenerous'.[2] His letter, which was printed in the *Public Ledger* on 17th October, fell like a bomb-shell on the conspirators. They loaded it with abuse—it was 'astonishing', 'most extraordinary and unwarrantable', 'not to be paralleled in history', 'offensive' to the King who was 'much provoked at it', 'the work of a heated brain, carried away by passion'. None the less they studied it carefully in the hope of extracting some comfort. They found it in the fact that he had assigned his resignation solely to the difference of opinion on the subject of Spain; and concluded, much to their satisfaction, that this 'would give great advantage against him'.[3]

But if Ministers could examine the letter only from a hostile angle, the commonalty received it with heartfelt relief. So great

---

[1] Bute to Bedford, 10th October 1761. Bedford Corr. III. 50.
[2] Pitt to Beckford, 15th October 1761. Chatham Corr. II. 158.
[3] Hardwicke to Newcastle, 17th October 1761. Add. MSS. 32,929.

was their eagerness to be reassured that the *Public Ledger* was sold out in a matter of minutes, and by one o'clock copies were fetching five guineas apiece.[1] Pitt was restored to his pedestal in a twinkling. As Newcastle mournfully observed 'all is fire and flame in the City', the letter 'had brought back all his old friends'.[2] They showed their repentance in too noisy a fashion, especially at the City's great annual festival. Pitt had been invited to the Lord Mayor's dinner and, with an uneasy premonition, was reluctant to accept, but was over persuaded by Beckford. The crowds lining the streets, and indeed the guests in Guildhall, gave him a tremendous ovation, far exceeding that given to the King and his newly-wedded Queen. George never forgave the insult, unintentional though it was.

(ii)

It may be well, here, to turn from outward manifestations to the inward views of the two protagonists, Bute and Pitt. Bute, for all his chicanery, was, according to his lights, an honest man. He was wrapped up in his pupil, George III, devoutly hoping that his reign would be honourable and glorious. If it was to be so, the foundation must be peace. But, impatient as both he and the King were to attain this prerequisite, he was acute enough to realise, not only that it was difficult to bring war to an end, but that, in spite of war-weariness, the country would reject any peace not commensurate with its victories. Bute had no clear idea of the real objects of the war, but as the inevitable result of Leicester House days his outlook was Tory; he believed in a maritime and colonial war, and looked askance at entanglements on the Continent. In that respect he stood where Pitt had stood before he had attained office. But Bute went further. Pitt had always recognised the need to 'have regard' to Hanover, which was to be redeemed at the end of the war; and it was only the chance of the Prussian and Hessian treaties which he inherited from his predecessor that made him hope to avoid the need of redemption, and, by preserving Hanover inviolate, to promote what he picturesquely called the conquest of America in Germany. To Bute, on the other hand, devoid of Pitt's strategical genius,

[1] Hardwicke to Royston, 17th October 1761. Add. MSS. 35,352.
[2] Newcastle to Hardwicke, 20th October 1761. Add. MSS. 32,929.

all movements towards the Continent were suspect, and even the need to 'redeem' Hanover was diminishing in view of George III's professed dislike for his Electorate and his determination never to visit it. Nor again did Bute appreciate Pitt's aim of making England mistress of the seas, which so strongly influenced his attitude towards the terms of peace. In Pitt's eyes it was essential to leave no loophole through which France could creep back as a strong maritime power. To Bute's lack of vision, the conquest of Canada was sufficient—almost too dazzling a reward —and the disappearance of the French fleet was to be avoided as likely to promote international jealousies. In all this there was a fundamental cleavage between the two which was bound sooner or later to make its presence felt. The first hint came during the abortive peace negotiations with France, and it finally broke surface when Pitt proposed to make war on Spain. Bute, starting with a bias against Pitt's 'German' war, revolted at the thought of extending the Continental entanglements. It was on this point that his wavering allegiance to Pitt foundered, and his defection may truly be ascribed to strategical ignorance darkened by ingrained prejudice. So much for the background.

With Pitt's resignation a wholly different problem arose, to which Bute reacted sharply, not because of political differences, but through fear. He was not in the least interested in Pitt's welfare or Pitt's claims; it was a matter of great indifference to him whether Pitt were rewarded or not. What made him desperately afraid was the belief that Pitt would go into opposition, when, with his acknowledged popularity in the country and his influence in Parliament, he could make Bute's path insupportably difficult. Bute not only feared what Pitt might do, but was jealous of him with an angry sense of inferiority. All he could oppose to Pitt's genius was cleverness, and to the power and pull of his personality, the reluctant obsequience given to a Favourite. Hence the plot against Pitt's 'disinterestedness'. It was a fork with two prongs; on the one hand, the reward should in itself be a moral brake on Pitt, if he wished to oppose; on the other hand its acceptance would blast his popularity, and so, as Bute hoped, take the sting out of his opposition if he indulged in it. Hence, too, Bute's hurry; Parliament was due to meet on 3rd November and the mine must explode before that date.

(iii)

Had he known Pitt better, had he even believed Pitt's statements, he might have spared himself much trouble. Pitt had no intention of going into opposition, though he might be driven to it. His attitude was governed by his views of the Constitution and by what Legge described as his 'visionary notions'. The British Constitution is not a hard and fast rule written on tables of stone, or even on parchment, nor is it bound by the laws of logic. On the contrary, it is unwritten and illogical, but it has one fundamental virtue—it is a living thing, with the capacity to grow and change and reconcile illogicalities in practice. It is also, like all life, elusive; it can die and be lost. Pitt gave it his heartfelt allegiance, always showing himself solicitous for its safety, and always trying ceaselessly to reconcile its contradictory elements. Hence his 'visionary notions'; hence also much of what his contemporaries dubbed his impracticality, and later historians his insincerity.

For Pitt, the Constitution's last great change had occurred at the time of the Glorious Revolution, some seventy years before George III's accession. On that change Pitt took his stand. He looked back at the later Stuarts with loathing; they had been tyrants, intent on reintroducing Popery. With his burning love of liberty and his deep devotion to the Protestant religion, Pitt could not abide them, and as William III had been our deliverer, Pitt 'revered the memory of King William and would die by the principles of the Revolution'.[1] But even this revised Constitution had not properly reconciled its two divergent elements—the Crown and Parliament. In Pitt's eyes, the Government was the King's; the Ministers were his servants; and their appointment and dismissal rested with him. In theory at least, he could choose whom he would, but, in practice, it was becoming more and more difficult for him to choose anyone who was not acceptable to Parliament. This undefined relationship between King and Parliament led to two divergent views—the Tory view which emphasised the King's prerogative, and the Whig view which emphasised Parliament's rights. Pitt was uneasily poised between the two; he had an immense and almost unbalanced reverence for

[1] West to Newcastle, 21st April 1760. Add. MSS. 32,905.

the idea of royalty, while at the same time he was an uncompromising champion of the House of Commons. In foreign affairs, the attitude of the two parties was to a large extent reversed; the Tories, out of half-remembered loyalties to the Stuarts and half forgotten animosities against the House of Hanover, preferred colonial enterprise, while the Whigs were absorbed in Continental politics in order to protect the King's electorate. Pitt was heart and soul in favour of colonial enterprise, though not without a dutiful regard to Hanoverian needs.

So much for party platforms. Coming down to realities, there was for practical purposes only one party, the Whigs; for ever since Walpole had shattered the Tories, they 'had ceased to be a serious political factor'.[1] As a consequence the Whig party became too large; its plethora of would-be leaders produced numberless factions, united only in an ardent desire to replace existing Ministers, and divided hopelessly over the method of cutting up the skin. Pitt as a young man and an ambitious politician, had no option, if indeed he had any desire, but to enter Parliament as a Whig. He entered it as a member of a faction—the Cousinhood—but did not take long to weigh up the demerits of 'faction', and thereafter he set himself against it. Promptly he was faced with a problem. If the Ministry was the King's and therefore to be treated with respect, and the Opposition merely wrangling factions and therefore to be distrusted, where was the place for that true opposition which Pitt perhaps more vividly than anyone else, recognised as imperative? There must be an opposition in the sense of an alternative government, and some method of bringing it in when the necessity arose. The absence of what is now known as Her Majesty's Opposition was something that puzzled and troubled Pitt, more particularly as one of his 'visionary notions' was a growing belief in the collective responsibility of the Cabinet, and consequently their collective dismissal in the case of failure.

As he was never allowed to develop his visionary notions, they must be approached with caution. It is unlikely that he ever formulated a complete theory, if only because he was always more interested in doing than describing. But his words, and still more his actions, show certain consistent and unmistakable trends, from which deductions can reasonably be drawn. He accepted without reserve the sovereignty of the King; the Government was

[1] Sedgwick p. xxiv.

his; the Ministers were his servants, and if they disagreed among themselves, he was the final court of appeal. More than that, his choice of Ministers must be free and unfettered; he could be advised, and undesirable candidates could be warned off, but the final choice was his in an absolute sense; he must not be forced, and the prospective Minister must await his summons. Lastly the Minister must have what Pitt called the King's countenance; until he obtained it, he should not seek office; when he lost it, he should leave office. So much for the one side. On the other, Pitt was more vague. Parliament consisted of Lords and Commons. Pitt looked up to the Lords with the mixed feelings of a snob, convinced of his own superiority, but consumed with a secret envy; and perhaps for that very reason was the more violent and determined in his championship of the Commons. They must never be ignored; they must never sink to the condition of a mere rubber stamp, to countersign and confirm the edicts of the peerage. He did not like to think of the members as being in the pockets of great lords, and brooded, without much result, over the boroughs, 'the rotten parts of the constitution'. The existence of pocket boroughs, and so of factions, grew more and more distasteful to him, until in the end he urged an enlargement of county representation, as being less open to corrupt influences. But whatever its composition, Pitt believed that, with the backing of the King and with a right policy, it was possible for any Minister—certainly for Pitt himself—to win the confidence and support of the Commons. In his first abortive Ministry he had electrified the world by 'throwing himself on the Tories', that pitiful remnant whom nobody regarded; they were to be the nucleus of that alternative government which today would be called Her Majesty's Opposition, and which under Pitt's leadership was to come into office. They were a small body, but Pitt had no serious doubt that as his policies developed and proved successful, they would be joined by many others, until before long he would have a following which could challenge even Newcastle himself. His dream was shattered by the Coalition into which he was forced in a moment of weakness and much against his will. From that moment he recognised regretfully that he could never collect his own following; the budding alternative government was lost beyond hope, swamped in a House elected on the Newcastle ticket, which Pitt had no longer the right, nor indeed the opportunity, to filch from his own colleagues. All he could hope to do was to retain the loyalty of his Tories. Consequently his interest in the Commons waned, and one may suppose his interest in the Lords increased. Joining the coalition was Pitt's first great mistake; but for it, as the leader of a compact party in the Commons he might well have restrained that hankering after a peerage which led to his second great mistake.

But that was in the future. His conduct in the last months of 1761 followed precisely his general views of the Constitution. Ever since the accession of George III, he had been slipping from what he regarded as a Minister's proper position. He had been losing the support of his colleagues, though that was troublesome rather than fatal. Far more important, he was losing the King's countenance. The first serious sign of ill-omen appeared at the Cabinet meeting on the 14th August, when the draft of his letter to Bussy was discussed. Pitt, exasperated beyond endurance at the carping criticism of his colleagues, had threatened to appeal to the King, with more than a hint that, if the King disapproved, Pitt would resign. The Cabinet gave way, though with a bad grace. A few weeks later, there was a fresh storm over the question of war with Spain. On this occasion the Cabinet did not give way, and Pitt did appeal to the King, setting his views out in a written memorandum. When the King rejected his advice, Pitt resigned. Under his theory of the Constitution, he had no option, having lost the King's countenance.

What he would do next could hardly be in doubt. The immediate cause of his resignation was not a question of principle, but a question of method and timing. As a statesman he was certain that Spain would shortly declare war; and as a strategist, he knew the tremendous advantage of getting in the first blow. His colleagues did not deny the possibility of war, nor were they unwilling to fight, if it were necessary; but hoping against hope that the cloud would pass, they were unwilling to precipitate matters. 'I would be behindhand in nothing', said Granville, 'but in the actual striking the blow',[1] and with one accord the Cabinet approved precautionary movements of the fleet.[2] There, however, they stuck; let us wait and see, they said in effect. This was not a

[1] Hardwicke's Notes of the Cabinet Meeting, 2nd October 1761. Add. MSS. 35,870.
[2] Newcastle's Minute of the Cabinet Meeting, 2nd October 1761. Add. MSS. 32,929.

fundamental clash of principle or policy, though it was a mani-
festation of the differences and disputes in the Council; and Pitt,
disappointed at what seemed to him infirmity of purpose and
'measures of procrastination and weakness',[1] impatient also at
this new check to his plans, and irritated by the antagonistic
attitude of his colleagues, took what was for him the final step.
He appealed to the King, as in ancient days men had appealed to
Caesar. When the King rejected his advice, he knew of no further
appeal. Great Commoner as he was, he did not look to what
Hardwicke called the 'Mobb' for support against the Crown. His
colleagues had the King's 'countenance' and he had lost it. They
still remained the King's Government and there was no point of
principle on which he could oppose them, nor any reason for
thinking that, if he did, the King would recall him to his service.
His course was therefore clear—to resign from office; and from the
back benches to support the King's government in so far as he
could. The time might come when he would be bound to oppose
on principle; but that time was not yet, nor was it to be artificially
created. He made his attitude amply clear to the King and to the
Ministers, telling the King that 'out of office, he would do everything in his power to support His Majesty',[2] and the Ministers
that he was unlikely to be much in the House, did not mean to
disturb the Administration unless he were misrepresented or
attacked, and would give all the backing in his power to votes for
supplies whether of men, money or ships.[3]

[1] Temple to Denbigh, 13th October 1761. H.M.C. Denbigh MSS.
[2] Newcastle to Bedford, 6th October 1761. Bedford Corr. III. 48.
[3] Hardwicke to Newcastle, 13th October 1761. Add. MSS. 32,929.

II

THE NEW BROOM

(i)

WHEN PITT met his Cabinet for the last time, he ended his farewell speech with a graceful compliment, saying that 'he saw with pleasure such an union and such a conjunction of the greatest and most considerable men in this kingdom as, he hoped, would carry on the King's business with success'.[1] He said much the same thing to the King three days later, declaring that 'it was some comfort to him that he left the Seals in the hands of one from whose firmness and good intentions he was convinced His Majesty might draw great advantage'.[2] But on both occasions, while emphasising his satisfaction at their concord and aims, he glossed over his poor opinion of their capacity. To his friend Elliot he was less reticent, painting 'in strong colours the inability of the Council, most of whom now for the first time began to think for themselves'.[3] What most impressed, and indeed depressed, him was the solid phalanx of the Whig magnates, whose 'influence and authority were so widely spread and so artificially woven' that there was no resisting them. And yet, not one of them was fit to govern—not even Hardwicke, 'a slow man whom the law had made'; not even Mansfield, 'a man of fine parts whom the law had unmade'.[4] Pitt owned that he felt 'most gloomy apprehensions for the public', but we may suppose he was sustained by the knowledge that he left behind him a marvellous inheritance. His colleagues had received at his hands the dying flickers of England's most successful war; and though peace was still beyond the horizon and Spain might yet give trouble, it was hardly to be supposed that they could go far wrong; or that, if they did, they would fail to summon him back to put matters right. England had little to fear from the war, and much to hope from the peace, when the recent abortive

---

[1] Minute of Cabinet Meeting, 2nd October 1761. Add. MSS. 32,929.
[2] *The Border Elliotts.*   [3] *Ibid.*   [4] *Ibid.*

24

negotiations were renewed, as soon they must be. Meanwhile, in war time all must be united, and Pitt would give what help he could.

Pitt was right about their want of ability, but wrong about their union and good intentions. He forgot, or perhaps never realised, that he himself had been their bond of union—first by their need of his successes, and then as the object of their common enmity. His disappearance opened the door wide both to their mutual jealousies and to their divergent plans. With his overshadowing figure out of the way, Newcastle and Bute faced each other in naked and ill-matched rivalry—Newcastle with his age, experience and serried ranks of followers, Bute with his comparative youth, ambition and the King's unwavering favour. There were only two points on which they were agreed. Both expected Pitt to go into opposition, and both knew that he must be confronted in the House by a man of weight. But there agreement ended. Each was anxious to have the goodwill of the new leader and each therefore pressed for his own nominee. Newcastle suggested George Grenville who in himself was dull, prosy and precise, while his ambition at the moment was to become Speaker—a post for which he was eminently fitted, not least because it would muzzle his verbosity. True, he was also Pitt's brother-in-law, but the beams from Pitt's glory which had been reflected on him, had only kindled a mounting flame of jealousy; he had shown his feelings more than once and was doing so again now by failing to follow the example of his brothers, Temple and James Grenville, who had both resigned with Pitt. In addition to this bias which seemed so apposite, he was a man of ability, a Minister of experience and a respected member of Parliament. Bute could scarcely object to him, being on good terms with him, and addressing him familiarly as 'my dear George'. But Bute had other uses for him; he wanted him to take Barrington's place as Chancellor of the Exchequer, in order to keep an eye on Newcastle. It was a thought which drove Newcastle to distraction. He poured out his woes to Hardwicke: 'the moment Mr. Grenville is Chancellor of the Exchequer, it is to him and to him only, to whom the King and his Minister will apply; and it is he who will have singly the King's confidence. Besides, Mr. G. Grenville is too considerable in himself, and too well supported to make an agreeable Chancellor of the Exchequer. I know myself, I am sure I should not pass one easy moment in the

Treasury, after that was done. It is cruel to put me to such a test'.[1]
When Grenville, perhaps at Bute's suggestion, perhaps out of
fear of Pitt, perhaps, though less probably, from what he described
as 'a delicacy of mind',[2] refused to accept the Seals, Newcastle
saw him drawing closer to the Exchequer, and felt that
his own position as First Lord of the Treasury was becoming
desperate.

Bute, on his side, wanted the Seals for Fox. But Fox, though no
one could deny that he was possibly the only man in the House who
could stand up to Pitt, seemed particularly ineligible. As Stone
shrewdly remarked, to go 'from the most popular man to the
most unpopular man in England would give such an advantage to
Mr. Pitt as would put it out of Mr. Fox's power to be of any service
upon this occasion'.[3] Added to which, the King detested Fox as
a bad man 'void of principles'.[4] Bute struggled, but was forced to
admit, no doubt with an inward reservation, that 'the scheme
about Mr. Fox would not do'.[5] In the end they compromised.
Lord Egremont, Grenville's brother-in-law and an inconsiderable man, succeeded Pitt as Secretary of State, while Grenville was
given the leadership of the House, though without promotion,
still remaining Treasurer of the Navy. Nor was Fox forgotten.
His own conduct made it easy to bargain with him. Though once
Cumberland's henchman and a bitter opponent of Leicester
House, he had not scrupled on George III's accession to turn towards the rising sun. His spur was ambition to secure a peerage
for his wife—an ambition forgivable for the tenderness in which
it was rooted, though marred by the bad faith with which it was
pursued. For some months he had been making ineffectual
approaches to Bute through the young Lord Shelburne. On Pitt's
resignation, he changed his methods and became menacing,
partly because he was affronted at having Grenville placed above
him, and still more because he was hurt to the quick at Pitt's
Hester obtaining precedence over his own Caroline. He declared
that unless he obtained some 'salve to honour', he would be
forced into thorough-going opposition. Bute was startled into
action and a bargain quickly followed. Fox agreed to support Bute

[1] Newcastle to Hardwicke, 26th September 1761. Add. MSS. 32,928.
[2] *Grenville Papers* I, 414.
[3] Newcastle to Hardwicke, 26th September 1761. Add. MSS. 32,928.
[4] Sedgwick p. 198.
[5] Newcastle to Hardwicke, 26th September 1761. Add. MSS. 32,928.

unofficially but effectively in the Commons, and to 'enter into no
sort of engagement with anyone else whatever', i.e. with neither
Pitt nor Newcastle; while Bute, on his part, promised that
Caroline should have her peerage before the end of the next session.[1]
The bargain gave Bute a notable addition of strength as against
Newcastle. Yet the two between them had produced only a makeshift Ministry, with none of the signs of strength or stability. Their
common bond was still hostility to Pitt, which indeed riddled the
whole of the ruling hierarchy. Pitt was an element so disturbing
to their mediocrity that old and young alike instinctively eschewed
him. The coming men followed blindly in the footsteps of their
elders. Rockingham, barely thirty-one and with little or no firsthand knowledge, dismissed Pitt's letter to Beckford as showing
'the violence of his temper and no true patriotic spirit', and used
his whole influence as a territorial magnate in an attempt to
prevent the York Corporation from according Pitt a vote of
thanks;[2] Shelburne, who as a young man of twenty-three had
recently been appointed A.D.C. to George III, put on paper that
'I can see nothing for my life in Mr. Pitt's character, which can be
called a *sine qua non*', and hoped that Bute would keep clear of
him;[3] while Royston, Lord Hardwicke's eldest son, chose this
moment to turn pamphleteer in disparagement of Pitt, and when
Newcastle counselled prudence, retorted that 'Mr. Pitt was never
on such bad ground before, and if no use is made of it, we shall
smart for it when repentance can do no good'.[4] Such was the
attitude of the younger men and future leaders, who were aping
faithfully the attitude of their elders.

(ii)

Just as there was manoeuvring over 'men', so there was
friction over 'measures'. Pitt's resignation had not altered facts;
it had merely removed the one man who had a policy, leaving the
wishful thinkers in control. Broadly speaking, now that Pitt and
Temple had gone, the Cabinet was composed of professed pacifists who were as quarrelsome as such gentry usually are. They
were all genuine in wanting peace, but not one of them knew on

---

[1] Fitzmaurice I, 116–7.
[2] Rockingham to Newcastle, 29th October 1761. Add. MSS. 32,930.
[3] Fitzmaurice I, 108, 110.
[4] Royston to Hardwicke, 16th October 1761. Add. MSS. 35,352.

what terms or by what methods. Worse still, they had no clear conception of the war, regarding it not as a connected whole, but as a series of disjunctive phenomena. 'If we have war with Spain', Bute told Newcastle, 'we must give up the German war'—much as though it were a piece of wilful extravagance. Newcastle observed that 'giving up the German war is easier said than done'[1] which would suggest that his experience had flowered into wisdom, had not he, on his side, been equally ready to discard the 'maritime' war. 'Lord Bute', he decided, 'wants to have the popularity of carrying on the war in popular places; and the merit of easing the nation of the exorbitant expense upon the Continent. I am afraid this will not do'.[2] What Newcastle wanted was 'a reasonable peace'; failing that, in his view the one war which above all others must be kept going, was the German.

Newcastle and Bute were thus diametrically opposed, and to make matters worse Bute was fooling Newcastle to the top of his bent. He recorded his true opinion, or at least his inward wishes, in a letter to George Grenville, which has survived only in Grenville's Jingle-esque *résumé*. He had thought Newcastle's conduct during the last reign, 'odious' describing it as 'pusillanimity in the Closet, foreign system, foreign ideas, sole access [to the King], power of calling people rascals and Jacobites'. Since George III's accession the position had improved, for realising that his influence had waned, Newcastle no longer insisted on his own way, and would certainly resign when peace was made. In the circumstances Bute 'thought it better to let this old man tide over a year or two more', though under the threat of 'immediate punishment', if he tried any tricks.[3]

The near approach of Parliament made some compromise between this ill-assorted couple necessary, if only for the purpose of preparing the King's Speech; but no decision could be more than a temporary makeshift, since each was pursuing his own line. The growing disunion in the Ministry led to bewilderment and division among the people. 'Since the Great Commoner laid down the reins of administration', wrote Symmer, 'it does not appear who

[1] Newcastle to Hardwicke, 26th September 1761. Add. MSS. 32,928.
[2] Newcastle to Hardwicke, 14th October 1761. Add. MSS. 32,929.
[3] *Grenville Papers* I, 395–6.

has taken them into their hands'. With no strong guidance from above, opinions were divided: 'the City and the trading part of the nation adopt Mr. Pitt's measures and support his personal interest or rather popularity. They are not only for continuing the war with France till she be brought lower, but are for humbling the haughty power of Spain. . . . On the other hand, the cooler part of the nation and the landed interest in general are sick of the war; are willing to have an end put on any reasonable terms; and are by all means for avoiding a war with Spain'.[1]

The confusion was not due simply to Pitt's fall, or to the divergence of views between Newcastle and Bute, but to the change of personality at the head of the Government. Morale invariably flows from the top downward, and in all those qualities of leadership which create unity, in all those methods of action which inspire confidence, in all those virtues which compel respect, Bute and Pitt were poles apart. The difference began to be felt at once. Pitt had been strong, incisive and successful. Bute was inexperienced, conceited, and for all his good intentions, fundamentally untrustworthy. It seemed impossible for him to avoid playing fast and loose with everyone—both because he was naturally deceitful and no less because he was void of plans. Not knowing his own mind for two minutes together, his decisions were often contradictory. Thus, amongst his earliest official actions, he instructed Mitchell to give Frederick 'the strongest assurances that the change in the King's Ministry will produce none at all in His Majesty's measures with respect to the general affairs of Europe', and that fresh forces were being raised 'to push the war with all possible vigour and activity as well by land as by sea';[2] while at the same moment he was declaring roundly to Newcastle that if, as appeared likely, the supply of Hessian recruits dried up, 'there was at once an end of the war', and probably the Prussian subsidy as well.[3] In precisely the same way, he emphasised to Newcastle the King's desire to settle amicably all outstanding disputes with Spain, while telling his brother, James Stuart Mackenzie, that 'strong measures and strong declarations is to do everything'.[4] As with policy, so with the day-to-day dealings with his colleagues. He asked Hardwicke

---

[1] Symmer to Mitchell, 20th November 1761. Add. MSS. 6,839.
[2] Bute to Mitchell, 9th October 1761. Add. MSS. 6,819.
[3] Newcastle to Hardwicke, 14th October 1761. Add. MSS. 32,929.
[4] Newcastle to Hardwicke, 20th October 1761. Add. MSS. 32,929.

to draw up the King's Speech on certain agreed lines, compli-
mented him to his face on his draft and then proceeded behind
his back to re-write it in a different tone. 'I am not apt to be
captious', Hardwicke commented, 'but . . . those performances
used to have much better quarter from Mr. Pitt'.[1] Indeed, the
magnates lost no time in deciding that Pitt had been little more
than King Log compared with Bute's King Stork. 'My Lord Bute',
Newcastle lamented, 'has got rid of his rival, Mr. Pitt, who dared
to contradict him, and he will make everybody else as insignificant as he can. . . . Pitt will say we are right enough served'.[2]

If the magnates were jumpy and on edge, the leaders in the
Commons were hardly more serene. Fox and Grenville were
mutually jealous and uncertain of their relative positions. On the
whole, Fox was the less unhappy of the two, because his ambitions
were restricted and were in part to be fulfilled, but it was none the
less a fact that his standing in the House was equivocal and his
pride hurt. Grenville's position was no less equivocal and far
more galling. Owing to his defection from the Cousinhood, he
had lost the goodwill of his family, who were 'most hostile and
outrageous against him', not only politically but personally, going
so far as to shut the door in his face.[3] He felt the snub keenly, and
probably also felt angry with himself for having refused the Seals;
if he was to be ostracised by the elect, he might as well have
accepted the full compensation offered by the mammon of
unrighteousness. As it was, with Fox hovering on his flanks, his
hole-and-corner leadership, void of the usual 'marks of credit and
power', tasted sour in his mouth; it was challenged by his
subordinates—Charles Townshend in particular—and, combined
with the family squabble, formed 'the great motives of his
present uneasiness'.[4]

It was thus no happy Ministry which met Parliament early in
November. Yet, whatever the turmoil behind the scenes, the
façade was imposing. The King's Speech, in its final dress, was
vigorous in its reference to the war, and encouraging in its
reference to our allies. It seemed, as Barrington (the Chancellor of
the Exchequer) had said, that there was not 'any disposition
anywhere to change the system of the war; or to make peace on

[1] Hardwicke to Newcastle, 23rd October 1761. Add. MSS. 32,929.
[2] Newcastle to Devonshire, 9th October 1761. Add. MSS. 32,929.
[3] Hardwicke to Newcastle, 17th October 1761. Add. MSS. 32,929.
[4] Newcastle to Devonshire, 31st October 1761. Add. MSS. 32,930.

improper conditions'.[1] What then could Pitt find to cavil at? They awaited his reaction with bated breath.

Pitt defined his attitude in a series of speeches remarkable for their moderation and the breadth of view displayed. He justified himself, as Burke declared, 'without impeaching the conduct of any of his colleagues, or taking one measure that might seem to arise from disgust or opposition'.[2] Indeed, he went much further, admitting that his opponents had acted out of conviction, and hoping that as their views on Spain 'had been supported by so many of rank and abilities and had been adopted by His Majesty',[3] they might prove right and his own fears wrong. Nor did he fail to pour out a flood of wisdom on matters of strategy, the conduct of the war and the aims of the coming peace.

His first speech was on 13th November in the debate on the Address. He rose, he said, reluctantly. He had no wish to justify himself, and would prefer to let his conduct be judged by the facts. As to Spain, he would wait until the Ministry had published the advice he had given to the King. He had resigned because that advice had been rejected and because he would not be responsible for measures he was no longer suffered to guide. His main object in speaking was to support the war in Germany. It distressed him to think of the world hearing that the German war had been arraigned in so many speeches without a single Minister saying a word in its favour. He would speak up for it, though he could speak only as a private man. The war in Germany had robbed him of sleep often enough, but if our troops were now withdrawn, it would rob him also of his honour. It would do worse. If the French were at liberty to quit Germany, they would frighten us out of our conquests, just as in 1756 their threat of invasion had frightened us out of Minorca. If we abandoned our allies, God would abandon us. England was equal to both wars, the American and the German; they could result in nothing but conquest, and all owing to the German war. 'America had been conquered in Germany'.[4] The cost had been great; we had spent a hundred millions, but the man who would throw away the fruit rather than spend twelve million more was too narrow-minded to govern a kingdom; he should stand behind a counter. They must not be

---

[1] Barrington to Mitchell, 5th October 1761. Add. MSS. 6,834.
[2] *Annual Register*, 1761.
[3] Sackville to Irwin, 16th November 1761. H.M.C. Stopford-Sackville MSS.
[4] Walpole, *George III*, I, 76.

too strict with the Treasury, who would certainly 'save what money they could and be good economists'.[1] When it came to the peace, they should refuse any concession on the Newfoundland fisheries. As there was no prospect of making peace at the moment without some such concession, there would have to be another campaign, fear of which was no doubt the justification of those from whom he had differed; but the effort must be made: 'the exclusive fishery was a *sine qua non*'.[2]

The magnates heard the speech with mixed feelings. They had convinced themselves that 'Mr. Pitt was to make a flaming oration' but hoped that his conduct would be 'looked on in the light it deservedly bears'.[3] They found it difficult to rid themselves of their preconceptions. Walpole described the speech, not very accurately, as 'guarded, artful and inflammatory',[4] and Sackville, while admitting the ability—Pitt 'was modest, humble, stout, sublime and pathetic, all in their turns'—insinuated that he was not sincere—'Garrick never acted better'.[5] But the most telling because the most naïve comment came from Newcastle: 'certain it is that Mr. Pitt's speech takes with the bulk of our friends, who expected nothing but fire, flame and personal abuse. Sir Francis Poole says it has softened *for the present* his resentment to him for his abominable conduct on my Lord Mayor's Day'.[6]

There was virtue in those words 'for the present', since the benefit of Pitt's moderation was ephemeral. Though a few politicians turned towards him—notably Charles Townshend—it was more out of discontent with Bute than attraction towards Pitt. In general, as the Whigs recovered from their astonishment they came to the conclusion that Pitt had been muzzled by his pension; and revelled in the thought that they could now safely indulge in twisting the lion's tail and even in giving it a vicious jerk. Nor were the Tories much better disposed; they too had been shocked by the pension and in their bewilderment were inclined to revert to their older convictions;[7] they or 'the soberer part of them' were supposed to be 'sick of Mr. Pitt's measures of war, more especially

[1] Barrington to Newcastle, 13th November 1761. Add. MSS. 32,931.
[2] Royston to Hardwicke, 13th November 1761. Add. MSS. 35,352.
[3] Rockingham to Newcastle, 14th November 1761. Add. MSS. 32,931.
[4] Walpole, *George III*, I, 77.
[5] Sackville to Irwin, 16th November 1761. H.M.C. Stopford-Sackville MSS.
[6] Newcastle to Hardwicke, 15th November 1761. Add. MSS. 32,931.
[7] Rigby to Bedford, 12th October 1761. Bedford Corr. III, 52.

Continental, and of the immense expense', and were succumbing to the loaves and fishes doled out by Bute.[1] Indeed, Bute was perhaps unique in still retaining a *soupçon* of fear, which in his case was due, not so much to Pitt himself, as to the rift in his own Ministry. He and Newcastle were not well together, and had recently taken to wrangling or, to use Devonshire's quaint expression, 'had got into a sort of piqueering, the one saying "you are Minister for you have got both Houses of Parliament", the other "you have the King".'[2] Into this queasy atmosphere there had floated rumours that Temple certainly, and Pitt possibly, were angling for a reconciliation with Newcastle, and it occurred to Bute that, if a militant Pitt were added to a snappish Newcastle, his own position would be precarious indeed, especially if the war flared up again. In the circumstances, he wanted Pitt's stock to fall, but could do little openly to vilify the statesman for whom he had notoriously obtained a pension; he must leave that task to others.

Perhaps he hinted as much, for his wishes were soon gratified. On 9th December (1761) Parliament debated the vote for the army in Germany. It was a matter which gave great scope for attacking Continental measures and all who supported them. Both Rigby, a creature of the Duke of Bedford, and George Grenville seized the chance to trample on every one of Pitt's toes. Rigby snapped his fingers in the King of Prussia's face, calling him a 'little Prince', so negligible a potentate that we were not obliged to keep faith with him. Grenville aimed more directly at Pitt. The only reason he could find for maintaining the German War was that we were too far in it to recede, but it should never have been begun. Then he indulged in a species of irony. Of course, if we had really conquered America in Germany, the merit was Pitt's and Pitt's alone, but if, on the contrary, 'our successes might have been obtained without the German war, and we now found the peace prevented, our measures cramped and our trade oppressed by the expense of it, there was then no great merit due to the advisers of it'.[3] He droned on with his indictment, but lacking Pitt's colourfulness or Charles Townshend's lightness of touch, he made it flat-footed and pedestrian—a series of semi-rhetorical

[1] Hardwicke to Newcastle, 17th October 1761. Add. MSS. 32,929.
[2] Devonshire's Diary, 1st November 1761.
[3] John Cavendish to Devonshire, 10th December 1761. Chatsworth Collection.

c

questions and desiccated answers. 'Did the war in Germany beat
the French Fleet? No, Sir Edward Hawke. Did the war in Germany take and preserve Quebec? No, but the fleets and armies'.
And so through the whole gamut.[1]

Pitt had warned both Ministers and King that if he were
attacked, he must and would defend himself. He did so now, and
with a gentleness which was not reciprocated. Let us try, he urged,
to avoid recrimination; let us be as brothers together, not
apportioning blame, but seeking a solution. It was not he who had
entered into Continental measures; he had found them already in
existence when he had been called to the King's service. Indeed,
he had opposed them while they were in the making; but when
he found them established, he had accepted them as facts and
made the most of them. What he had tried to do was to see where
his predecessors had gone wrong, and then, borrowing their
majority, to develop their plans on sounder lines. And what had
been the result? France had paid heavily and obtained nothing
but shame, while we had annihilated her power, both east and
west. Perhaps he had done it the wrong way; perhaps Grenville
would have done it some better way. But well done, or ill done,
economically or extravagantly, it had been completed, and our
job now was to set the seal on it. If at this point we neglected our
allies, if we relaxed our efforts, 'all France would illuminate,'
standing as she did at the gates of Holland, and able to be masters
of the whole Continent—whilst we should destroy all prospect of
future alliances, and lose Prince Ferdinand whom Providence had
raised up as a rampart against the French in Germany. Continental
measures as managed in the past had been millstones round our
neck, but as managed now, round the neck of France.[2]

The time had not yet come when the German war could be
dropped, and the vote was therefore passed. But the baiting of
Pitt was delight to Bute's soul. 'Dear George', he wrote exultantly, 'millions of congratulations upon your very great, very
able and manly performance; this will do, my dear friend, and
shows you to the world in the light I want, and as you deserve'.[3] It
is a curious commentary on the lack of magnanimity in lesser

[1] Newcastle to Devonshire, 9th December 1761. Add. MSS. 32,932.
[2] Walpole, *George III*, I, 82; West to Newcastle, 9th December 1761. Add.
MSS. 32,932; John Cavendish to Devonshire, 10th December 1761. Chatsworth
Collection.
[3] Bute to Grenville, 10th December 1761. *Grenville Papers*, I, 418.

minds that Bute could apply the epithet 'manly' to Grenville's speech, and Newcastle could record, with obvious satisfaction, that 'my friend Sir William Baker, who is a very good judge . . . thinks Mr. Pitt acted a most abominable part'.[1]

[1] Newcastle to Devonshire, 9th December 1761. Add. MSS. 32,932.

III

SPAIN

(i)

PITT WAS not Bute's only, or his greatest, problem. He might be troublesome, but his wings had been clipped; for fallen Ministers, even when they command the allegiance of the mob, are rarely popular in the House. Much more pressing was the problem of the war. Bute and the Cabinet had now, as Pitt said, to think for themselves, and their thoughts were flying, like splintered glass, in all directions. 'There is nobody in the House', said Symmer, 'distinguished enough to take the lead, or that has authority sufficient to interpose and moderate the violence of others'.[1] Hitherto individual Ministers had indulged their fancies in the comfortable, if unacknowledged, assurance that Pitt was there to guide their thoughts and distil some sense even from their follies. He was there, too, to carry out their decisions, and, best of all, to shield them against popular indignation. Now they must fend for themselves; and having neither brains to conceive nor hands to perform, they strayed in all directions. There was only one point which they had in common. All wanted peace. But, while some, like Bedford, were ready to snatch it on any terms, others, like Grenville, thought it should be commensurate with the victories won. How to obtain it was another matter altogether, 'Mr. Pitt, having', as Bedford remarked with a spiteful distortion of the facts, 'in the last act of government he has been able to effect, broke off all negotiations with France'.[2] That, of course, meant that the war must go on; and all recognised that, without Pitt, it was likely to go on haltingly. 'I know nobody', Newcastle sadly admitted, 'who can plan, or push the execution of any plan agreed upon, in the manner Mr. Pitt did; but we must do the best we can'.[3] Miscarriages must be expected; and they, as Bedford

---

[1] Symmer to Mitchell, 11th December 1761. Add. MSS. 6,839.
[2] Bedford to Newcastle, 7th October 1761. Add. MSS. 32,929.
[3] Newcastle to Hardwicke, 15th November 1761. Add. MSS. 32,931.

angrily confessed, would be 'matter of triumph to Mr. Pitt's advocates'. He chafed at the thought and in his efforts to wriggle away from it was for ever changing his opinion of what should be done. At one moment he was sure that 'too great vigour cannot be exerted in carrying on the war':[1] at another that it must be given up altogether: 'for God's sake, my dear Lord, don't lose a moment in renewing the negotiations for peace. . . . Now Mr. Pitt is out, don't let us madly follow his plans'.[2] Bedford was the most ardent advocate for immediate peace, and if the others differed from him, it was only in doubting if the time had yet come. But all, Bedford included, differed from each other in their views of how to conduct the war, the widest breach being between those who wanted to 'contract your war in Europe',[3] and those who were appalled at the thought of 'abandoning the Continent'.[4] Whatever their preference, all kept a wary eye on Pitt, settling their plans more with the object of silencing 'Mr. Pitt's noisy friends in the City'[5] than in accordance with the needs of strategy.

But however the members of his Cabinet might wrangle among themselves, the final responsibility rested with Bute. He had taken over the conduct of affairs at a moment of crisis, and had done so very deliberately, even if not altogether willingly. The premiership was something which George III wanted for him, and which in some degree he coveted for himself; but he would much have preferred to wait until the war was over. There had been a time when he and his young pupil had dreamed dreams of the golden age which was to come when George III ascended the throne, when righteousness and peace would kiss each other, and England become again 'the residence of true piety and virtue'.[6] When those happy days dawned Bute would be proud to be Minister, but for the realisation of that dream there must be peace. Peace dominated their thoughts; the longing for peace had coloured the King's first address to his Council; the search for peace had occupied the first year of his reign. But all had been in vain; the bright vision had faded; the negotiations with France had failed. And then, suddenly, out of the blue had loomed up not peace but the prospect of war with Spain and Pitt had been the

[1] Bedford to Newcastle, 11th October 1761. Add. MSS. 32,929.
[2] Bedford to Newcastle, 30th November 1761. Add. MSS. 32,931.
[3] Bedford to Newcastle, 11th October 1761. Add. MSS. 32,929.
[4] Newcastle to Hardwicke, 20th October 1761. Add. MSS. 32,929.
[5] *Ibid.*   [6] George III to Bute, June 1757; Sedgwick, p. 6.

protagonist. Nothing could be less like the dove of peace than Pitt; he might perhaps be an eagle, but never, no never, a dove! So Bute's idealism, woolly as it was, had joined with his enmity to push him into the ranks of Pitt's opponents. He had leagued with them; he had ousted Pitt, and had taken upon himself the conduct of affairs, firmly intending to bring peace to a distracted world, and veiling his eyes determinedly against awkward possibilities.

His trouble lay in the fact that while he knew his goal to be peace, he had no idea how to set about reaching it. The convictions of a lifetime persuaded him that England's destiny did not lie on the Continent; the German war was a mistake and the Prussian alliance wrong. If the war must be continued it should be continued overseas. But was the game any longer worth the candle? Pitt's triumphs had been so widespread that England, like Alexander the Great, had no fresh worlds to conquer; and France had shown herself so accommodating that anyone less rapacious than Pitt must surely be satisfied. Peace was by no means unattainable—could be attained tomorrow, if only Pitt and the mob would be quiescent and Frederick and his claims were out of the way. But how was he to restrain either Frederick or Pitt?

Without delay and on his own initiative he took certain steps, —to be described hereafter—but before they could fructify, whether for good or ill, the great hazard crashed down upon him. Pitt's fall had an instantaneous effect in every direction, and not least upon Spain. Up to that date the interminable negotiations had been tediously polite. Fuentes, the Spanish Ambassador, had instructions to speak gently, to emphasise 'his disposition to accommodate everything', and to play down any reference to a possible break.[1] But when the news of Pitt's resignation reached Madrid (26th October) Wall, the Spanish Prime Minister, finding it something 'to be rejoiced at',[2] promptly displayed a 'surprising change' in his discourse and an 'unlooked-for alteration' in his sentiments. Lord Bristol, our Ambassador, wrote in haste and some alarm to Egremont describing 'the haughty language now held by this Court, so different from all the former professions made to me by the Catholic King's commands, and so diametrically opposite to the most solemn and repeated declarations I had received from the Spanish Secretary of State'. His interviews

---

[1] Newcastle to Hardwicke, 20th October 1761. Add. MSS. 32,929.
[2] Wall to Fuentes, 26th October 1761. Add. MSS. 32,930.

with Wall, which had hitherto been so soothing, had now become extremely disconcerting. Instead of pacific utterances, Wall roundly asserted that England's conduct was unwarrantable; that we were intoxicated with all our successes; that we had treated France's reasonable concessions with undeserved contempt, and clearly meant to crush first France and then Spain in order 'to satisfy the utmost of our ambition and to gratify our unbounded thirst of conquest'.[1]

Here was a check which Bute was very unwilling to face, though Newcastle, with his greater experience, had no hesitation in drawing the obvious conclusion: 'I suppose,' he said, 'we must take it for granted that Spain will break with us'.[2] Bute, however, still clinging to the hope that his plans might prosper, if given time, and still unwilling to admit that Pitt had been right, decided to keep Bristol's report dark for the moment and to resist any parliamentary probings.

(ii)

It was difficult, for the public were taking an interest in Spain. Newcastle, whose ear was usually close to the ground, recorded that 'the dread of a Spanish war is very great in the City', and added, with his usual touch of fatalism, that 'if it should happen, the stocks will tumble to nothing'.[3] There was a growing demand for fuller information, and the probability of pressure for it in Parliament, which the Cabinet, against the advice of Grenville, decided to resist.[4]

The subject was one in which Pitt was bound to take a lively interest. Spain had been the immediate cause of his downfall, and Spain alone could provide his justification. Of course war, if it broke out, would vindicate him completely, but at what expense! Far better would be a vindication springing out of the papers. And the need was growing, since the hostility, initiated by Bute's pamphleteers and introduced into the House by Grenville, was rising. On the 10th December, for instance, during a debate on the 'German' war, there was a regular broadside from a newcomer, one Colonel Isaac Barré, brought into Parliament by Shelburne,

---

[1] Bristol to Egremont, 2nd November 1761. Add. MSS. 32,930.
[2] Newcastle to Hardwicke, 15th November 1761. Add. MSS. 32,931.
[3] Newcastle to Devonshire, 3rd December 1761. Add. MSS. 32,931.
[4] Devonshire's Diary, 10th November 1761.

so it was said, 'as a bravo to run down Mr. Pitt'.[1] In a maiden speech of uncommon vigour, Barré dubbed Pitt a dangerous, profligate and abandoned man who had thrust himself into office on the shoulders of a deluded people.[2] His impertinence had provoked more astonishment than indignation, though the full effect was marred by the fact that Pitt was not present. The next day (11th December) Mr. Cooke, member for Middlesex, moved for the Spanish papers. Grenville, acting on the Cabinet's decision, resisted the demand, and as he was speaking against his convictions, managed adroitly to turn the debate from the papers to the more popular subjects of the King's prerogative and Pitt's insistence on his right to 'guide'. Others followed his lead, whooping and barking after their prey. At last Pitt rose to defend himself. He did so with dignity and restraint. He had never, he said, wished for dictatorial powers; on the contrary whenever he proposed anything outside his own department, he had always acted through the appropriate Minister. If he believed that the Spanish papers would tend to make anyone 'sole Minister', he would oppose their publication, but he did not believe it. There was nothing to be gained by holding the papers back. Hesitation would merely encourage Spain in her claims; and delay in producing them, which might be useful if Spain were prepared for war and we were not, could only be hurtful when the contrary was the case. The Spanish claims must be resisted; they had no justification; 'whoever admitted a cockboat of Spain to the right of fishing in Newfoundland, or even negotiated about it, should be impeached'. If she were foolish enough to declare war, she would be committing suicide. Indeed, it would be far better for us to fight her than to allow so weak, so feeble, so insolent a power to aid and abet France by covering her trade, lending her money and supplying her with arms. It was not proper for him to disclose what he had learnt as a Minister, but the papers would show how 'amusive' and misleading had been the news from Spain published in the *Gazette*. Yet it was of no consequence to establish on which side truth lay. The fact remained that if war came we should have lost our opportunity; while, if we reached an accommodation with Spain, she would feel less obliged to England who had bowed to her demands than to France who would be credited

1 Walpole, *George III*, I, 87.
2 Newcastle to Devonshire, 10th December 1761. Add. MSS. 32,932.

with extorting from us all the advantages which Spain might receive.[1]

When he sat down, Barré, egged on by Rigby and Fox, attacked him with greater virulence than ever. But, as Walpole said, 'the whole apostrophe wore the air of an affront more than of a philippic', and while Pitt maintained silence, the House as a whole felt a touch of shame at this railing at a man 'who had gained the hearts of his countrymen by his services'.[2] Some felt more than shame; 'I am furious', wrote John Cavendish to his brother, 'you know I never was partial to Pitt, but I am scandalised that such a creature as Shelburne should dare to turn loose an Irish ruffian in the House of Commons to affront a man of Pitt's age and rank'.[3] Yet neither shame nor fury bore any fruit; the motion for papers was rejected without a division; Barré was graciously received when next he went to Court; Bute informed Newcastle that he had determined 'never to sit at a Council Board with Mr. Pitt again'; and Bedford declared that his favourite object was 'the keeping Mr. Pitt down now that he is down'.[4] So low had Pitt fallen in the estimation of the country's rulers.

(iii)

Though the demand for the Spanish papers had been staved off, Bute had still to settle England's foreign policy. His attitude was vague and fluctuating. Yet, for all his lack of decision, he had certain leanings which were not inadequate as the basis of a firm, even if mistaken, policy. He had been imbued—to some extent by Pitt himself—with the Tory preference for a colonial and maritime war. The Continent meant nothing to him, nor, being blind to the future, was he obsessed, as Pitt was, with the necessity for 'laying France on her back'. If anything, he was disposed to accept Bedford's belief that harshness towards France would bring a jealous Europe about our ears. Now that Canada and the West Indian Islands had been conquered, he saw no reason to continue the war. His main object, therefore, after dislodging Pitt, was to prevent a break with Spain, to get out of the Con-

---

[1] Walpole, *George III*, I, 92–4; Devonshire's Diary, 11th December 1761; West to Newcastle, 11th December 1761. Add. MSS. 32,932.
[2] Walpole, *George III*, I, 96.
[3] J. Cavendish to Devonshire, 12th December 1761. Chatsworth Collection.
[4] Newcastle to Devonshire, 18th December 1761. Add. MSS. 32,932.

tinental entanglements and secure peace with France. For these ends he was prepared to make great sacrifices—not necessarily at England's expense. He would desert Frederick without a moment's compunction, ignore the cries of Hesse and Hanover, and offer very lenient terms to France. What held him back was fear of the contrast which people might draw between the terms he would accept and those Pitt would have demanded. Apart from that, he like Pitt, found it more difficult to get out of a war than to wage it; and, unlike Pitt, he had no warlike strategy by which peace could be enforced. He was indeed an amateur in strategy and statecraft alike, and he was following, and anxious to emulate, a master of both.

It was at this point that his deficiencies began to show themselves. One of the greatest was a tendency towards wishful thinking. Bute had a good conceit of himself, and it irked him to find Pitt so much more successful in the paths of war and so much higher in the popular esteem. Even the sunshine of the King's favour could not assuage his pangs of jealousy. For all his pacifism, he was not wholly indifferent to martial glory, and at the outset, knowing that the war must go on, he was tempted to set himself up as a rival to Pitt. Newcastle might be humble enough to confess that 'outwar Mr. Pitt we cannot',[1] but Bute had no such diffidence. It was in part at least this desire to outshine Pitt at his own game that led Bute to assure both Frederick and Ferdinand that the war against France would be pushed with all possible vigour; it was the same desire, combined with his own lack of inventiveness, which induced him to carry on with Pitt's plans for the coming campaign. Nothing at first was altered. On the contrary, Bute even insisted, against the wishes of his colleagues, and indeed against his own convictions, on taking a firm line with Spain,[2] and actually told Bedford that 'vigour appears more likely to prevail on a very tricking enemy than supplication'.[3] The King's Speech was drafted in strong and decided terms, and all seemed warlike, though Newcastle, calling to mind Bute's known desire for 'getting out of the war in Germany', was disposed to think it was mainly bluff.

Be that as it may, it was not long before Bute's dream of out-Pitting Pitt received a number of rude shocks. The first came from

[1] Newcastle to Devonshire, 15th October 1761. Add. MSS. 32,929.
[2] Newcastle to Hardwicke, 20th October 1761. Add. MSS. 32,929.
[3] Bute to Bedford, 10th October 1761. Bedford Corr. III, 50.

the Landgrave of Hesse who declared that he was quite unable to recruit his losses. Bute, irresolute by nature, at once began to think of returning to his first love and dropping the Continental war—an idea which Newcastle found extremely distasteful.[1] Then came, in quick succession, two unexpected blows,—Frederick's loss of Schweidnitz in Silesia and of Colberg in Pomerania—which made Bute doubt whether Frederick would be any better able than the Landgrave of Hesse to rebuild his armies. He made urgent enquiries of Mitchell, who confessed that he had no idea how the Prussian losses—not less than 25,000 men—could be made good, but trusted to Frederick's skill, having been himself 'an eyewitness to the successful execution of many projects which at the time appeared impossible'.[2] Here, for all Mitchell's optimism, was further ground for caution. Then, as a final blow, came Wall's changed tone, which left no shadow of doubt that war with Spain was inevitable. Bute had nothing of Pitt's constancy in the face of a set-back, and his career as a war Minister was becoming too realistic to be pleasant. All he had done by it was to make his own policy more difficult. Now he must get back to the right path and drag in peace somehow—by the heels if necessary.

His method was typical. Backstair intrigue had made him master of Leicester House and St. James's Palace; it would no less make him master of the courts of Europe. As with all such intrigue, secrecy was the keynote—secrecy not only against the public, but against his allies, his officials and his colleagues. Alone he would do it. As a first step, he decided to re-open negotiations with France, and without a word to his colleagues, commissioned Viry, (the Sardinian Ambassador), to approach Choiseul through his opposite number in Paris, the Bailli de Solar. So confident was Bute, that even before Viry had had time to act, he was hinting to Newcastle 'without explaining himself, but yet significantly enough, that he had some small hopes, and *not without foundation*, that we should soon hear from France for renewing the negotiations of peace'.[3] Alas for his hopes! Choiseul's first reaction was unpropitious. Having Spain in his pocket and being heartened by Pitt's fall and Frederick's reverses, he showed himself cold and non-committal, even expressing doubts whether the overture

[1] Newcastle to Hardwicke, 14th October 1761. Add. MSS. 32,929.
[2] Mitchell to Bute, 25th November 1761. Add. MSS. 6,809.
[3] Newcastle to Hardwicke, 15th November 1761. Add. MSS. 32,931.

was sincere. He had no intention of responding before Spain had broken with England and was standing openly at his side.

(iv)

Bute's diagnosis was wrong from beginning to end. Just as the soft approach to France met with rebuff, so did the firm attitude towards Spain. Wall responded in kind, and by the end of the year matters had reached a crisis. Fuentes left England on 1st January (1762) and three days later Bute himself was forced to declare war—a war which, according to Walpole, was 'conceived rashly, adopted timidly, and carried into practice foolishly'.[1] All the world now knew that Pitt had been right, and while some hoped that he would be recalled to cope with the situation, others, in their alarm, blamed him for not having made peace while the going was good.[2] But these hopes and fears found at the moment only private expression, for Parliament was not sitting to give them voice. When it did meet, on the 19th January (1762), Bute in the House of Lords, was forced to offer the Spanish Papers which only a month earlier had been refused. They were presented ten days later (29th January) in a manifestly incomplete and unsatisfactory form. Yet partial and selective as they were, a careful reader could not fail to note that they exonerated Pitt from all charges of harshness towards Spain, on the showing of both Egremont and Wall,[3] and that the outbreak of truculence on the part of Spain coincided exactly with her knowledge of Pitt's resignation. Up to that time Spain had been withstanding the French demand that she should enter the war immediately, partly because she was not ready, and even more because she feared Pitt. With his disappearance she no longer felt the need to hide her intentions. To that extent it might even be argued that Pitt was responsible; had he remained in office, he would have declared war on Spain; because he fell, Spain declared war on us, or, as it was ironically said, 'against Mr. Pitt'.[4]

In the Commons, Lord North tried to shut Pitt's mouth by accusing him of 'abdication', and disparaging 'his intelligence, activity and discernment'.[5] Pitt defended himself with the for-

---

[1] To Mann, 4th January 1762.
[2] Symmer to Mitchell, 1st January 1762. Add. MSS. 6,839.
[3] *Papers relative to the Rupture with Spain*, pp. 31 and 63.
[4] H.M.C. Weston Underwood MSS.   [5] Walpole, *George III*, I, 104.

bearance which now seemed habitual. It might, he said, be a matter
of pride to him, but not of satisfaction, to find that he had not
misjudged the intentions of Spain. But this was not the time to
apportion praise or blame. It did not signify what any man's
opinion had been three or four months ago—'perhaps neither very
right nor very wrong'. Now, we were at war and must be united.
Our position was difficult but not calamitous; we still had 'such
troops, officers and fleets as no nation can produce and which
providential success for five years has rendered great'; we were
equal to all our enemies and nothing could hurt us but jangling
and faction.[1] 'No speech', said Barrington, 'ever had more effect
or conciliated more'.[2]

But relieved as they might be, the Whig magnates were too
much absorbed in the implications of their new war to be very
mindful of Pitt's speeches. Spain, unfortunately, had on her
western boundary an equivalent to Hanover, and was proceeding,
in true French style, to embarrass England by threatening Portugal. If Portugal succumbed, we should lose our lucrative trade
with her and also the use of her ports; if she resisted, we should
be obliged to protect her from invasion. Either way, our resources
would be unbearably strained, and at the prospect Bute swung
round again to the idea of dropping Germany. He hinted as much
at a Cabinet meeting, called on 6th January, ostensibly to consider
'the most effectual methods of distressing and attacking the
Spaniards'. The decision on that point took no time, for, fortunately, Pitt had roughed out the method when he was stressing the
need to break with Spain. The Cabinet merely adopted his schemes.
That concluded, Bute 'threw out' his hint about Germany only
to find himself opposed by Newcastle 'with great force and
warmth'. Devonshire followed, with views which might have
come straight out of Pitt's speeches, condemning any such move
as dishonourable towards our allies and dangerous to ourselves.
Bute thereupon backed down, declaring that 'he did not mean to
come to any resolution at present'.[3] Yet that was precisely what
he had done. He had made up his mind to desert Frederick.

His plans were forwarded by a quaint fantasy of Newcastle's.
The now openly avowed union of France and Spain stirred

[1] West to Newcastle, 19th January 1762. Add. MSS. 32,933.
[2] Barrington to Newcastle, 19th January 1762. Add. MSS. 32,933.
[3] Devonshire's Diary, 6th January 1762.

nostalgic memories in the old man's mind. Surely there was only one means of keeping the arrogant House of Bourbon within bounds; and that was by a revival of the 'old system'. If the liberties of Europe were to be preserved, we must go back to tried and trusty ways; we must renew the triple alliance of England, Holland and Austria, such as it had been in Marlborough's days. Beyond doubt, if we put the matter to her properly, Maria Theresa would recoil from the spectre of Franco-Spanish domination, and, given the proper inducement, would revise her policies, denounce her treaties with France, and even abjure her hatred of Frederick. Buoyed up with these convictions, Newcastle turned with ardour to the old game of carving up Europe—on paper. 'Some care' must of course, be taken of Frederick, though he must make 'very considerable concessions' in order to satisfy Austria and release her for more urgent work elsewhere. Holland must come into the picture to keep France busy on the north; while Austria and Sardinia should be encouraged to seize and share the Bourbon possessions in Italy.[1] In Newcastle's opinion, no one could possibly resist the allurements of the 'old system'; it was all so neat and tidy.

Certainly Bute could not, especially as it had the merit of forwarding the breach with Frederick. He entered whole-heartedly into the scheme, and forthwith drafted instructions to our ambassadors. 'I have received', Newcastle wrote in triumphant accents 'dispatches from Lord Bute to Sir Joseph Yorke and Mr. Mitchell entirely conformable to my ideas. . . . It is upon the idea of sounding the trumpet against the united House of Bourbon, and endeavouring to get Holland, the Court of Vienna, the King of Sardinia etc. to take part. I never saw abler letters in my life'.[2]

The task which Bute entrusted to Yorke was to induce Prince Louis of Brunswick to broach these 'salutary views' to Maria Theresa, with the object of either 'alarming her by the threatened invasion of Portugal and the danger to her Italian dominions, or flattering her ambition with the prospect of increasing them'.[3] Prince Louis did as he was desired, though with some reluctance and not much hope. The upshot was such as might have been expected. Maria Theresa rejected the advances with scorn. The

[1] Newcastle to Hardwicke, 10th January, and to Yorke, 15th January 1762. Add. MSS. 32,933.
[2] Newcastle to Devonshire, 10th January 1762. Add. MSS. 32,933.
[3] Bute to Yorke, 12th January 1762. Add. MSS. 32,933.

only effect was to engender suspicions in Frederick when rumours of the transaction came to his ears.

Meanwhile Bute proceeded steadily with his project of deserting Frederick. He had already raised a number of points in connection with the renewal of the subsidy—points of no real substance but admirable as delaying tactics—and now, without breathing a word to either Mitchell or Frederick of his approach to Maria Theresa, he insinuated that the reverses Frederick had suffered must have turned his thoughts 'to the way of accommodation', and the need to limit his wishes to what his sword could enforce. 'It would', said Bute, 'be highly agreeable to His Majesty to hear that any step was taken towards a negotiation with the Queen of Hungary', the more so as the war with Spain and the impending invasion of Portugal had added so greatly to England's burden both in money and men.[1] As chance would have it, Bute could not have chosen a more unpropitious moment. While he was penning his letters, news was on its way from St. Petersburg which entirely altered the whole situation. On 5th January 1762, Elizabeth of Russia, Frederick's unforgiving enemy, died and was succeeded by his fanatical admirer, the Grand Duke Peter.

The news reached Germany on 21st January and London a week later. The reactions of Frederick and Bute were characteristic—and diverse. 'I cannot help fearing', said Mitchell, on the first rumour, 'that the King of Prussia's lively imagination, which generally carries him too far, may, on this occasion, lead him to abandon all thoughts of peace, if ever he had any'.[2] It did. He sent ingratiating messages at once to 'son ancien ami', the new Emperor and, as a gesture, released all his Russian prisoners. At the same time he told Knyphausen in London that although he could hardly expect anything reasonable from the English Ministers while they continued to squabble amongst themselves, yet everything conceivable must be done to impress upon them how disastrous it would be if they let France bind all the great powers to herself, if they abandoned the Continent, and 's'ils ne font pas dans le moment présent jusqu'à l'impossible pour détacher entièrement la Russie de la dite ligue formidable'.[3]

The English Ministers felt no particle of Frederick's urgency

[1] Bute to Mitchell, 8th January 1762. Add. MSS. 6,820.
[2] Mitchell to Bute, 21st January 1762. Add. MSS. 6,809.
[3] Frederick to Knyphausen, 29th January 1762. Add. MSS. 32,934.

or optimism. Hardwicke, it is true, ventured to say that the
Czarina's death seemed '*prima facie* to be the principal thing in
the Chapter of Accidents to help us', but he was snubbed by
Bute's friend, Melcombe, who retorted, 'Help us? Which way? If
to make peace, well; if to continue the war, not so well'.[1] Bute
himself was occupied at the moment by two problems—how to
prevent Bedford from moving prematurely in the Lords for the
recall of the troops from Germany, and how best to present the
Spanish papers to Parliament. The news from Russia he welcomed
as likely to damp Bedford's ardour; 'after this', he remarked,
'the Duke of Bedford will not be so wild as to persist in making
his motion'. Actually, Bedford did persist; but having as he
thought disposed of Bedford, Bute returned to the Spanish Papers.
His object, he told Newcastle, was to present them in such a way
that he could 'conclude with some vote of censure upon the
measures of Mr. Pitt and my Lord Temple'. The suggestion shocked
Newcastle, who tried to remonstrate, but gave up when, as he
said, 'I found my Lord Bute began to suspect me of partiality and
management for Mr. Pitt, which I did most solemnly disclaim'.[2]

Yet the news could not be ignored. It seemed to be good news
so far as it went and might help to produce the peace for which
Bute was longing. He studied it from that angle, and being far too
self-confident, blundered into a situation which damaged England's foreign policy at the moment, and affected it still more
disastrously in the future. Without waiting to hear from Keith,
our Ambassador at St. Petersburg, he discussed the news, in a
long conversation, with Prince Galitzin, the Russian Ambassador.
Except for a short paragraph in a letter to Newcastle,[3] he made
no record of what passed, but Galitzin promptly and rightly sent
an account to the new Czar, who as promptly informed Frederick.
According to Galitzin, Bute said that he was despatching a special
representative to Russia to persuade the Czar to work for a
general peace, and for that end to retain his troops in Prussia so
as to force Frederick to make 'considerable concessions to the
House of Austria', adding that 'it was not the intention of
England to make eternal war to please the King of Prussia,
England wanted just to save him'.[4]

[1] Hardwicke to Newcastle, 28th January 1762. Add. MSS. 32,934.
[2] Newcastle to Hardwicke, 28th January 1762. Add. MSS. 32,934.
[3] Bute to Newcastle, 6th February 1762. Add. MSS. 32,934.
[4] Mitchell to Bute, 3rd May 1762. Add. MSS. 6,809.

The effect on the Czar was instantaneous and unmistakable. He flatly refused to receive the special representative,[1] and completely altered his demeanour towards Keith, so much so that Keith, wholly ignorant of the reason, became first puzzled, then unhappy and finally anxious to return home.[2]

Frederick, as might be expected, was furious, and indeed for some weeks was unable to refer to the matter without losing his temper. He exonerated Mitchell, recognising that he had been kept in the dark, but inevitably became reserved and uncommunicative. Mitchell was as puzzled and unhappy as Keith had been, but relying on his long-standing and real friendship with Frederick, pressed to be told the reason. For some time he was fobbed off, but at last, on the 2nd May, was enlightened.[3] Bute was now forced to explain his words away which he did by denying Galitzin's account. His denial seems to me a masterpiece of *suggestio falsi*, though it has been described as transparently sincere.[4] He had spoken to Galitzin, he said, in the terms of the orders which he had sent to Keith, and anyone could see how totally improbable it was that he should hold a language to the Russian Minister, 'I do not say different, but so absolutely contrary to the orders which I had just sent'.[5] The denial would be complete, if it were not that the words of which he was accused were in no sense 'absolutely contrary' to Keith's orders. The essence of those orders was the promotion of peace, and it had long been a commonplace with English Ministers that peace was impossible unless Frederick could be induced to make 'considerable concessions' to Austria.[6] At the meeting, as we know on Bute's own showing, he and Galitzin discussed the restorations of certain of Frederick's provinces which had been occupied by Russia. It would have been easy, and not unnatural, for Bute to hint that in order to bring some pressure to bear on Frederick, the Czar should not be in too great a hurry to evacuate them. If he did so hint, Galitzin's report was accurate enough, and is not to be shaken by Bute's carefully worded explanation. Keith declared emphatically that Galitzin's account 'was certainly and literally

[1] Keith to Mitchell, 19th March 1762. Add. MSS. 6,825.
[2] Keith to Bute, 19th March 1762. Add. MSS. 32,935; and Jenkinson to Grenville, 10th April 1762. *Grenville Papers* I, 420.
[3] Mitchell to Bute, 3rd May 1762. Add. MSS. 6,809.
[4] See Corbett II, 292; and Buckinghamshire Corr. I, 49.
[5] Bute to Mitchell, 26th May 1762. Add. MSS. 6,820.
[6] See e.g. Newcastle to Yorke, 8th January 1762. Add. MSS. 32,933.

D

true',[1] and indeed it is as unusual as it would be reprehensible for an Ambassador knowingly to mislead his own Government. The conclusion seems inevitable that whatever Bute actually said, he had been guilty of a formidable gaffe. Frederick accepted his excuses, but the old relations had been irreparably damaged; the old confidence never returned, the trust henceforward was shot with suspicion. As the harvest was to be gathered when Pitt returned to power, it has seemed necessary to deal at some length with the sowing.

[1] Keith to Mitchell, 23rd August/3rd September 1762. Add. MSS. 6,825.

IV

EXIT NEWCASTLE

(i)

BUTE'S INDISCRETION was in a sense merely incidental. From the moment of Pitt's fall, Bute had been searching for an excuse to stop Frederick's subsidy, for financial as well as political reasons, and during the last months of 1761 had raised one difficulty after another about the form which the new subsidy treaty should take. Frederick had grumbled, but to Bute's dismay had accepted all his suggestions. In January (1762) the outbreak of war with Spain gave Bute a fresh excuse for delay. He wrote impressing on Frederick 'the expediency and indeed the necessity' of his trying to negotiate with Austria now that this 'great additional burthen of expense' had fallen upon us,[1] and asked pointedly what means he had for carrying on the war if peace could not be secured. Just at that moment came the news of Elizabeth's death, which in Frederick's eyes so radically altered the situation that he could not believe Bute would require any answer but would at once take every possible step 'to improve this great event'.[2] He waited expectantly and impatiently, and when it was explained to him that Bute regarded the great event as simply improving the prospects of peace, he could hardly contain himself. He dashed off a short note to George III 'breathing', as Newcastle plaintively observed, 'war more than ever—that the present disposition of Russia was the most favourable for the King and himself—that by pushing on the war the King would decide his command over the seas; and the King and His Prussian Majesty would defeat the greatest combination of powers against them that ever was known. That the war with Spain was a lucky incident',[3] Frederick would have been singing to deaf ears in any case, but he managed to ensure that the ears should also

---

[1] Bute to Mitchell, 8th January 1762. Add. MSS. 6,820.
[2] Mitchell to Bute, 21st January 1762. Add. MSS. 6,809.
[3] Newcastle to Hardwicke, 22nd February 1762. Add. MSS. 32,935.

tingle. Forgetting his own skill in intercepting and reading despatches from other countries, he indulged his irritability by writing a letter to Knyphausen in which he declared that Bute and his colleagues were throwing away such golden chances that they 'ought to be sent à la petite maison, to Bedlam'.[1] Bute read the letter, and the offending word eclipsed whatever hope of the subsidy yet remained. In his pseudo-regal manner, Bute expressed himself as 'extremely displeased with the King of Prussia', and took it out of Knyphausen by telling him that 'the great event in Russia. . . . made the measure of the subsidy *doubtful*'.[2]

In one sense everything played into Bute's hands. Frederick had acted as he had expected Bute to act; he had sent Baron Goltz hot-foot to St. Petersburg with full powers to conclude a treaty of friendship with the new Czar. At first Goltz was ordered to work in conjunction with Keith, but, as suspicion followed hard on disappointment, Goltz's instructions and his attitude altered. He began to avoid Keith and when they met offered politeness instead of information. Keith's bewilderment confirmed Bute's determination to break with Frederick, more especially when it was whispered that Frederick was to help in establishing the Czar's old claim to Schleswig, in return for a guarantee of Silesia. That could only mean trouble in Denmark; all Europe would soon be in flames. And at such a time to be talking of Bedlam! Bute gave a further turn to the screw. He told Mitchell that Frederick's letter to George III, so far from giving the information required, was nothing but 'a pompous exposition of mere hopes of better fortune, a declamatory exhortation to the King and a heroism ill suited to the broken and almost ruined state of his own affairs'. The King would have to think again before asking Parliament to grant the subsidy.[3] Bute's patent ill-will progressed through complaints against the Prussian Ambassadors, which Mitchell was to make to Frederick 'in their full sense and without any softening',[4] to complaints against Frederick himself. His treatment of the King, Bute asserted, was 'reserved', 'unfriendly', and 'unjustifiable'; worse than that, while the King had made it a condition that the subsidy should be used to procure peace, Frederick

[1] Newcastle to Hardwicke, 22nd February 1762. Add. MSS. 32,935.
[2] *Ibid.*
[3] Bute to Mitchell, 23rd February 1762. Add. MSS. 6,820.
[4] Bute to Mitchell, 30th March 1762. Add. MSS. 6,820.

apparently wanted it for the 'pernicious use...of fomenting new troubles in Europe'. That being so, the King would require further intelligence 'before he can determine to give any at all'.[1] By this time Frederick was not only passionately angry, but deeply concerned at what he believed to be Bute's double dealing at Vienna and St. Petersburg, and had consequently given up hope of the subsidy and was concentrating on friendship with Russia. Before reaching this conclusion he had consulted Pitt privately, not only on the question of money but on a proposal to work up an agitation in England against Bute, and had found him despondent. He sympathised with Frederick, he regretted the course Bute was adopting, but with a loyalty which Bute would not have understood, did his best to support what he regarded as the King's policy, emphasising the difficulties with which England was faced and the possibility that a change of public sentiment might yet force a withdrawal of the troops from Germany. It would be best if Frederick would try to conform.[2] Frederick bowed to his opinion so far as stirring up trouble in England was concerned, but went on to complete his treaty with Russia (5th May 1762). The break with Bute was complete and was merely papered over by Bute's tardy explanations of the Viennese probings and the Galitzin conversation.

(ii)

Bute had thus gained one object—at what price history was to disclose. He had two others in view, which were interconnected. He wanted to conclude peace with France and he wanted to oust Newcastle—in that order. Newcastle had to go so that Bute might become the nominal as well as the actual head of the Government. It was a step demanded by his vanity, and no less by his lack of Pitt's capacity to endure an uncongenial colleague. Pitt, for all his invective, for all his haughtiness and extravagant moods, had the magnanimous spirit of true genius. He chafed at incompetence and indeed would never forgive it; but he bore no personal rancour. By contrast Bute was domineering with the arrogance of a small mind too uncertain of itself to brook rivals. Newcastle sensed the difference. In the old days, being overawed

[1] Bute to Mitchell, 9th April 1762. Add. MSS. 6,820.
[2] Knyphausen to Frederick, 22nd January 1762. Add. MSS. 32,933.

by Pitt, he had given vent to his petulance in private, but now finding Bute's arrogance different in kind and harder to bear, he showed an unexpected tendency to make tart answers. 'My Lord', said Bute, discussing the Prussian subsidy, 'you don't know the thoughts of numbers of your own friends upon this point. They say that we have worked Mr. Pitt out and are now following his extravagant measures'. 'And my Lord', Newcastle retorted, 'I will tell your Lordship what they say—that Mr. Pitt went out because we would not declare war against Spain, and as soon as he was out, we did the same thing'.[1] But the bitterest pill which Newcastle had to swallow was the sudden realisation that Bute was trying to get rid of him—Bute, whom he had once welcomed as an ally for the overthrow of Pitt! He became full of self-pity, complaining that 'he had been a Minister forty years and served two Kings, but never had had such language held to him, and that he imagined his Lordship meant to turn him out'.[2] It was too true, but the time had not yet come. Newcastle still had his following in Parliament, which Bute needed to confirm whatever peace he might settle with France. And so the sentence of death was delayed, pending the negotiations for peace.

(iii)

The negotiations did not keep step with Bute's impatience. He was casting his net in every direction—Vienna, Madrid, Paris—but the catches were worse than tin cans or old boots. Vienna's answer was 'unpolite, brusque, and indecent'.[3] At Madrid the Dutch Ambassador 'executed his commission very clumsily' and was snubbed.[4] In Paris, Choiseul was slow to accept the Sardinian channel which Bute had chosen, and made it quite clear that only the advent of another Pitt would induce him to offer as good terms as the year before.[5] Indeed, he was not prepared to offer terms at all; he had had enough of that method, and now insisted on Bute's showing his hand first. It was easy for Choiseul to adopt a high tone, for, as Hardwicke shrewdly surmised, 'France will

---

[1] Newcastle to Devonshire, 13th April 1762. Add. MSS. 32,937.
[2] Devonshire's Diary, 1st February 1762.
[3] Hardwicke to Newcastle, 21st March 1762. Add. MSS. 32,936.
[4] Yorke to Newcastle, 2nd April 1762. Add. MSS. 32,936.
[5] 'Il faudroit avoir à traiter avec un second Pitt, pour oser négocier sur de pareilles propositions'—Choiseul to Ossun, 17th November 1761—quoted Rashed, p. 119.

think we are knocking at every door for peace, and will stand upon the higher terms'.[1]

Nevertheless Bute struggled on and it may be helpful to consider his motives. Originally his only motive had been a desire for peace, but experience had damped his ardour, and the extension of the war to Spain and Portugal had had a further sobering effect. He became thoroughly scared, not so much at the military as at the financial aspect. He was not a financier himself, nor was he popular in the City, and, more embarrassing still, he had no faith in his own First Lord of the Treasury. He could, therefore, look for advice only to George Grenville and such Treasury officials as he could suborn to spy upon Newcastle and expose the emptiness of the Exchequer. From what these not disinterested advisers told him, he had convinced himself that England could not maintain all her many wars for more than a year at most, and he was fortified in this view by Newcastle's evident reluctance to look too far ahead. Not unreasonably, in the circumstances, he came to the conclusion that unless peace could be made with France within twelve months England must be bankrupt, or as he preferred to say, ruined.[2] Hence his eagerness to push ahead with the negotiations; hence also, one may believe, his flabbiness in standing up to Choiseul—much must be surrendered, not to lose all. But he was not without his share of patriotic pride, and it irked him when Choiseul too obviously assumed the upper hand. At such times he would flare out as violently as Pitt had ever done, and declare that Choiseul's letters were 'insolent to the last degree' and should not be answered.[3] But the anger was impotent and fleeting; it subsided like bubbles in soda water. At other times he was oppressed by an uneasy feeling that a peace negotiated under such duress might, and perhaps must, be unpopular; and then his natural timidity made him anxious to cover up his tracks. Just as once he had wanted to be 'made Secretary of State at the instigation of you great people' in order not to offend public opinion, so now he wanted to ensure that any possible odium should fall on the Whig magnates.[4] For this purpose, he thought it expedient to let some of the Ministers know what he was doing, and chose Devonshire as his first confidant, confessing

[1] Hardwicke to Newcastle, 21st March 1762. Add. MSS. 32,936.
[2] Hardwicke to Newcastle, 14th April 1762. Add. MSS. 32,937.
[3] Devonshire's Diary, 3rd March 1762.
[4] Devonshire's Diary, 23rd February 1762.

to him that negotiations were in train. He added that Choiseul was to be told that 'no Ministry now Mr. Pitt was out could make a much worse peace than he had proposed'[1]—presumably he meant worse for France and was thus leading Devonshire to understand that he would go a long way towards meeting French demands. Thereafter the small group known as the King's Ministers (Bute, Egremont, Newcastle, Hardwicke, Devonshire and Grenville) were gradually let into the secret, and all had been informed by at least the beginning of March. But the progress of the negotiations was slow, partly because of Choiseul's tardiness, partly perhaps because Bute was waiting for good news from Vienna and Madrid, but most of all because of his own lack of experience.

The fact is that the time was not ripe. Bute should not have attempted to reopen negotiations so soon after they had been broken off. Nor should he have pressed on with them in the early months of 1762, when the whole position had become extremely fluid. But his fears spurred him on. He ignored the fact that Spain's intervention could hardly fail to buttress Choiseul's resolution, and he flung away the counters which Fortune so plentifully put into his own hands. The first was the Czarina's death, which, as Yorke reported from his watchtower at The Hague, 'has confounded the French who were not prepared for it.'[2] But Bute, unlike Frederick, frittered away his chances. Then came news of further victories. Pitt's plans for the coming campaign had not been cancelled and soon bore fruit. By the middle of February (1762) Rodney and Monckton had captured Martinique, Grenada and St. Lucia, and the news arrived in England on 22nd March. Choiseul, certain that the islands would fall, had written them off in advance, and though in private speaking of 'la perte affreuse de la Martinique', in public affected to treat the loss as a trifle. It was a view which Bute had to accept, reluctantly one may suppose, and very unlike Pitt who, warmly rejoicing at this 'most important stroke', hoped that 'short-sighted silly man, if it [he] does not know how to improve, at least may not be able totally to reject the proffered blessing'.[3]

Yet that was precisely what Bute's fears forced him to do. He

---

[1] Devonshire's Diary, 8th January 1762.
[2] Yorke to Mitchell, 20th February 1762. Add. MSS. 6,836.
[3] Pitt to Warburton, 31st March 1762. Egerton MSS. 1,955.

had already gone a long way towards rejecting everything which might hamper his purpose. On the 7th March he handed his peace proposals to Viry without consulting or even telling his colleagues. The reason was obvious. Grenville and Egremont had been trying to stiffen his backbone, and it was part of his tragedy that he believed it necessary to be pliant and yielding.[1] He was prepared to give way all along the line, accepting the French views on outstanding points, and making no fight for Frederick. Wesel and Guelders, captured by the French, must no doubt be mentioned in the treaty, but no article about them was to be regarded as a *sine qua non*. Peace, in short, might be concluded at once, were it not for the French insistence on settling our disputes with Spain, and even that might have been overcome had not Egremont been so 'very *fiers* upon it'.[2] Having thus burnt his boats, Bute summoned his colleagues to confirm his action.

They were a Cabinet of professed pacifists. The only apparent exceptions were Egremont, whose overfat body was more weighty than his brains, and Grenville, who still cherished in his cold heart some cinders of patriotism caught from Pitt; and who, while willing, like a good student of economics, to give up Frederick and the German War as too expensive, yet shrank from yielding up our conquests without compensation. The majority, however, feared to take a strong line, lest Choiseul should feel affronted and break off negotiations. They were too apprehensive to conceive that he also might be anxious. Yet Choiseul's difficulties were not hard to guess. At the outset he had been slow to respond to Bute's overtures because he was waiting for the added ballast of Spain, and Spain was not yet ready. Later, he had been galvanised into action by events in Russia. If Peter III made friends with Frederick, the Continental war might end suddenly, and France might be forced by her allies into a premature peace, or else have to face a Britain freed from entanglements in Europe. Neither prospect was pleasing. Hence, as 1762 progressed, he became more eager to come to terms with England, but found, to his chagrin, that Spain, having just put on her armour, had no intention of taking it off until she had won for herself Minorca, Gibraltar, and, in the first flush of enthusiasm, Portugal as well. She had not realised, as others had, that 'les

---

[1] Devonshire's Diary, 23rd February 1762.
[2] Newcastle to Hardwicke, 8th March 1762. Add. MSS. 32,935.

Espagnols ont une idée chimérique de leur puissance',[1] and being by no means anxious to talk peace at this early hour, worried Choiseul by her haughty intransigeance. Truly his lot was not a happy one. But of this the English Ministers had no inkling. Bute summoned his inner Cabinet on the 26th March, and told them that the time had come to renew negotiations openly and drop Viry. The suggestion, as no doubt he intended, was an apple of discord, Hardwicke and Grenville agreeing, Newcastle and Devonshire opposing. When the wrangling had gone on long enough, Bute proposed by way of compromise that no further secret letters should be written, but that Viry, instead of being dropped, should be supplied with an unsigned memorandum of England's conditions, for open presentation to France. All agreed, and Bute was content; his responsibility had been sensibly diminished. On the 29th March the matter came before the full Cabinet who formally decided that 'this is a proper time to make an offer to France of renewing the negotiation with that power'.[2] So Bute went cap-in-hand to Choiseul.

(iv)

Meanwhile the war was progressing favourably. Bute had seen enough of Pitt's methods to be cautiously hopeful, and Spain's entry even stimulated him. Borrowing Pitt's schemes and relying on Anson for the details, he despatched Pocock and Albemarle to reduce Havana, and Draper and Steevens to capture Manila. The expeditions were to prove brilliantly successful, but they served to emphasise the split in the Cabinet. Bedford, on purely pacifist grounds, opposed them tooth and nail. Newcastle, as ever, havered; in themselves, and especially as they had Pitt's imprimatur, he thought them good; but as likely to deflect effort from Germany, he objected to them, declaring that they were 'expensive, hazardous and uncertain'.[3] The German war was the touchstone. Newcastle and his friends swore by it as the only gateway to peace; Bute was against it as the precipitous road to ruin. His convictions were fortified when Spain threatened Portugal. All were agreed that our oldest ally must be protected; but the added

[1] Solar to Viry, 16th April 1762. Quoted Rashed, p. 140.
[2] Cabinet Minute, 29th March 1762. Add. MSS. 32,999.
[3] Newcastle to Hardwicke, 12th February 1762. Add. MSS. 32,934.

expense was the last straw, and, in Bute's eyes at least, put a final 'paid' to the German war and Frederick's subsidy. He maintained that we could not possibly face the expense; nor was he shaken by Newcastle's affirmation that we could, at least for the current year—a limited assurance which, if anything, merely confirmed his apprehensions.

It appeared that finance, as understood by Bute, was to determine strategy and decide the time and terms of peace. But finance was the function of the Treasury, and Bute's incursions into its realm angered Newcastle, who could not endure contradiction based, as he knew it was, on advice given secretly by his own underlings. Finding other arguments in vain, he fell back on a plea which Pitt had used more than once, that the ship should not be spoilt for a ha'porth of tar: 'after we had loaded the nation with an additional debt of seventy millions sterling', he said, 'I would risk 700,000 more to the King of Prussia rather than leave His Majesty [i.e. George III] without one single friend or ally in all Europe'.[1] It was a powerful argument, the full force of which England was to feel only too soon. But Bute was now in full cry; he had won over the waverers—even Mansfield was 'violently against giving the money'[2]—and on the 9th April wrote an imperious letter to Mitchell, ordering him to protest at a number of Frederick's actions real or imagined—his secret negotiations with the Czar, his guarantee of Schleswig, his reserve towards the King—and to hint broadly that the subsidy would not be forthcoming.[3]

By a stroke of ill-luck Newcastle chose the very next day—10th April—'to lay before the Cabinet the state of the expense that would attend the war in Portugal'. He asked them to approve a Vote of Credit for two million pounds, including some half million for Portugal, but found himself strenuously opposed. Grenville in particular argued 'with great warmth' that the cost of Portugal could and should be met out of savings in other directions, and went on to attack the burden of the German war; he would not agree to a total of more than one million. It seems to have been recognised on both sides that the Vote was a trial of strength: 'we shall', said Elliot, 'fight our Portugal against your

---

[1] Newcastle to Devonshire, 13th April 1762. Add. MSS. 32,937.
[2] Newcastle to Hardwicke, 6th April 1762. Add. MSS. 32,936.
[3] Bute to Mitchell, 9th April 1762. Add. MSS. 6,820.

German war'.[1] Newcastle with a presentiment of failure thought
of retirement, acutely conscious that his friends were slipping
away, and doubtful of Pitt's support, who, when sounded, had
simply replied that all depended on facts, if two millions were
necessary, the Treasury view should be supported; but if less
would do, so much the better. From which the hapless Newcastle
could deduce nothing but the existence of a secret intrigue to
give Bute the Treasury and Pitt the direction of foreign affairs![2]

The debate on the Vote of Credit took place on the 12th May.
Pitt's speech was temperate and wise. Portugal, he said, must be
helped as a matter of justice to an ally, but our aim should be to
set her on her feet, not to carry her on our shoulders. Then,
looking further afield, he foresaw and forewarned the country
against Napoleon's future Continental system. Portugal he declared
must also be helped for the sake of her ports. The Bourbon
Powers were trying to shut them against us, and if they succeeded,
would go on to debar us from the whole of Europe. We should
lose the immense advantage of our trade, which more than
compensated for the whole cost of the war. Certainly, the war was
expensive. That was an old cry. Every year, for the past three
years, we had been told that the money could not be raised; but
the event had proved otherwise, and would again. We could well
afford the money; the only difficulty was to find the appropriate
Fund. No doubt there had been extravagance, no doubt there had
been some frauds. They should not be excused or screened, but
neither should they be exaggerated or allowed to exert undue
influence. To contract expenditure when possible was right and
wise; to contract military operations wrong and foolish. He
deplored the division into parties—one for Portugal, another for
Germany. For himself, he agreed with both sides; Portugal was
part of the Continent, and the Continental plan alone could bring
us 'a speedy, a sober and well-understood and permanent peace';
any other would be 'inglorious and precarious'.[3] He most sincerely
wished for unanimity in the Administration; 'if they fall out, the
nation is undone'. He deplored also the cloud that had arisen
between us and Frederick. 'For God's sake', he cried, 'remove it'.
Don't let us risk losing two mighty powers—Russia and Prussia—

[1] Devonshire's Diary, 19th April 1762.
[2] Newcastle to Devonshire, 7th May 1762. Add. MSS. 32,938.
[3] West to Newcastle, 12th May 1762. Add. MSS. 32,938.

now united in our interest against 'this wicked Bourbon Compact'·
Don't let us quibble over finances. Let us have our Vote—he
could have wished it was larger—and then we could negotiate
from strength; then the King 'at the head of well compacted
alliances and backed with money' could treat with the enemy, with
good hope of obtaining a glorious peace.

The Vote was passed for one million, and Newcastle prepared
to resign. He had already told the King of his intention, and had
received the cold answer 'Then, my Lord, I must fill up your
place as well as I can'.[1] Indeed the King was pleased, holding
Newcastle to be a man full of 'dirty arts', unmindful of his
country's good and intent only upon jobs; a far better man
—Bute—was available for his place.[2] But Bute was not so happy,
he 'hesitated and was afraid'.[3] Newcastle might be woolly but he
was a cushion to fall back upon; and his cohorts were needed in
Parliament for what Bute had in mind. Bute was loath to give him
a hastening kick. But none was needed; Newcastle recognised the
position: 'My Lord Bute's schemes for foreign affairs', he noted,
'are very different from ours'; different, too, from Pitt's who
'though he had all that popular nonsense about him, he mix't it
with real system'.[4] And so on the 26th May, disillusioned, downcast, disgraced, but not as Walpole said 'disgracing himself'.[5]
Newcastle laid down office, a poorer and perhaps a wiser man,
and was succeeded by Bute.

[1] Walpole, *George III*, I, 132.
[2] Sedgwick, p. 93.
[3] Devonshire's Diary, 9th May 1762.
[4] Newcastle to J. Yorke, 14th May 1762. Add. MSS. 32,938.
[5] *George III*, I, 133.

V

BUTE AND PEACE

(i)

BUTE HAD now reached his zenith, which, unlike Prospero's, did not 'depend upon a most auspicious star'. Sixteen months earlier Pitt had said that 'there had been often favourites, but the nation would never suffer them to be both favourites and Ministers'.[1] He was right. Bute would have been better advised —as, indeed, he had wished—to keep Newcastle as a screen; but Fate and Newcastle had decided otherwise. Now, by assuming the nominal lead, he lost the actual power, slipping back from being Master of England to being Mayor of the Palace. He had never been popular out-of-doors, and now became doubly unpopular. To the people at large he was not only a 'favourite', he was a cuckoo in the nest—a Scot, and their dislike of the interloper was heightened by their love for the dispossessed; they wanted Pitt back again, and all they had got was the dismissal of Pitt's one-time partner. Their reaction was violent: 'the new administration', Walpole noted, 'begins tempestuously. My father was not more abused after twenty years than Lord Bute is in twenty days'.[2]

Bute shrank from the animosity he aroused; he had no confidence in himself, and was puzzled to know where to look for support. Grenville must succeed him as Secretary of State, there was no alternative; but Grenville was an uneasy bedfellow, more obstinate than wise. Still more baffling was where to find a Chancellor of the Exchequer. Newcastle's disappearance left the Treasury in the hands of Barrington, who, to his infinite surprise, had been created a stop-gap Chancellor barely twelve months earlier.[3] No one had regarded him as competent, but that had not

[1] Devonshire's Diary, 21st January 1761. [2] To Mann, 20th June 1762.
[3] 'The same strange fortune which made me Secretary at War five years and a half ago has made me Chancellor of the Exchequer. It may perhaps at last make me Pope. I think I am equally fit to be at the head of the Church as of the Exchequer'. Barrington to Mitchell, 23rd March 1761. Add. MSS. 6,834.

mattered so long as Newcastle's experience was available. Now, with the inexperienced Bute as First Lord, it became important. Having no faith in Barrington, Bute transferred him to the post of Treasurer of the Navy, but could hit on no successor. It was the King who solved the problem. Still convinced of Bute's worth and unconquerably sure that Bute's diffidence was the offspring of a passing fit of fever, he laid it down that a good Chancellor was unnecessary; all Bute need do was to appoint 'an honest quiet man' as a figurehead, and relying for advice on one of the junior Lords of the Treasury, be his own Chancellor.[1] Willy-nilly, that was what Bute had to do, but his idea of an honest quiet man was as inconsequent as the rest of his conduct. He chose Sir Francis Dashwood, who was certainly easy-tempered and courageous, and perhaps not dishonest, but otherwise was a rumbustious debauchee, expert in riotous horseplay, but no economist either in theory or in practice.

Two thoughts were uppermost in Bute's mind—to push on with the peace and to placate opposition. The desire for peace became an obsession, and so warped his judgment that he began to regard friends as enemies and gains as losses. He could find no virtue in Frederick; he could see no guile in Choiseul. English victories, which in spite of everything *would* supervene, gave him no pleasure—they delayed the peace; French successes—they had one when they temporarily recaptured Newfoundland—gave him no pain, they could be ignored. When in March Martinique fell, Bute was ready to give it back without equivalent; when in June Ferdinand won the battle of Wilhelmstal, Bute was embarrassed;[2] when in September a despatch announced the capture of Havana, Bute wished it could be suppressed. Clearly he was in no fit state to negotiate. Choiseul was equally on tenterhooks, but kept his head far better, betraying his eagerness not by yielding points but by paying half-compliments to Bute and Egremont. He would, he said, negotiate only with them, since he could rely on their honesty; and he compared them with Pitt, much to the latter's disadvantage.[3]

What shattered Bute's nerve was the ferment in the country. The unrest was only too evident. He had not been Prime Minister

[1] Sedgwick, p. 109.
[2] 'You cannot imagine how comically *some people* look. What a mixture in their countenances.' Hardwicke to Royston, 1st July 1762. Add. MSS. 35,352.
[3] Choiseul to Solar, 13th May 1762. Bedford Corr. III, 81.

a fortnight when the *North Briton*, that notable forerunner of the more notable *Letters of Junius*, brought out its first number. 'Weekly papers', said Walpole, 'swarm, and like other swarms of insects, sting'.[1] Time merely increased the uproar. By the end of July it was 'growing very universal';[2] by the middle of September 'coffee houses were ringing with the most atrocious language; and the Exchange was prostituted to the posting up of papers that were a disgrace to the police of any civilised nation'. So at least it appeared to Symmer.[3] To Bute it appeared more frightening still. Loyalty to the King compelled him to push blindly on, but as the months passed he realised with a sinking of the heart that he stood in the position into which he had once deliberately thrust Pitt—he was alone, unsupported by his colleagues—'hardly meeting with anything but cruel abuse and base ingratitude'; and even his one asset, the King's favour, merely rendering him 'the object of envy and resentment.'[4]

As he had begun in secret, so when his colleagues refused to follow him, he reverted to secrecy. 'I saw', he told Egremont, 'from the beginning that the peace was too complex to be made, except by a perfect confidence between the French Ministers and the King's. I will speak plainly, I mean by Ministers your Lordship and myself'; the other Ministers were a stumbling block on which 'I am persuaded, a negotiation begun and carried on in a very unusual manner will certainly break'.[5] With occasional help from Egremont, he entered into private understandings with Choiseul, and even private schemes to hoodwink the rest of the Cabinet. It was thus that he yielded up St. Lucia; it was thus that he settled the boundaries of America; it was thus that he accepted Florida as a *quid pro quo* for Havana; it was thus that he failed Frederick over the captured German cities of Westphalia.

The fact that he did not trust his colleagues made outside help essential, and side by side with his secret approaches to enemy countries, he began testing and tempting political opponents. He had not been ready to lose Newcastle, whose resignation at this early stage had been much less acceptable to him than to the King. 'The more I know of this fellow', said the King coolly,

[1] To Mann, 20th June 1762.
[2] Royston to Hardwicke, 1st August 1762. Add. MSS. 35,352.
[3] Symmer to Mitchell, 10th September 1762. Add. MSS. 6,839.
[4] Bute to George Townshend, 2nd November 1762. Add. MSS. 36,797.
[5] Bute to Egremont, 26th July 1762. Add. MSS. 36,797.

'the more I wish to see him out of employment'.[1] But Bute could not be so indifferent. Newcastle had been, after Bedford, the most pronounced pacifist in the Cabinet, and the least likely to be shocked at Bute's surrenders. More important, he had the cohorts in Parliament, and might, if he went into opposition, ruin everything. Bute therefore did his best to soften Newcastle's fall, making him tempting offers of titles and rewards, as he had previously made to Pitt. But Newcastle, though he left office a much poorer man than he had entered it, was invulnerable; unlike Pitt, he was still wealthy, and there were no further honours or rank to which he could aspire. Having failed to bribe, Bute attempted to flatter; he sent Bedford and Lyttelton to praise his behaviour and press upon him their 'earnest advice' that he should continue to give no disturbance.[2] He sent Viry to talk of friendship and honourable employment.[3] Even the King was enlisted to speak him fair and deprecate opposition.[4]

Newcastle held himself aloof—not proudly but confusedly. He was very uncertain what course to adopt. He had been told, and probably believed, that no opposition could be effective without Pitt's help, but he was not sure of Pitt's attitude towards him or of his towards Pitt. What was clear was that the longer he remained in the wilderness, the more bitterly he felt his position. Indeed, it was difficult. Originally he had intended to remain neutral, but as time went on, he found himself growing restive. The cause no doubt eluded him, but was, in fact, the emptiness of retirement. His life had left him no leisure for outside interests, and now having nothing to do, he brooded on opposition.[5] But how to set about it? He was acutely aware that he lacked what he called a 'point'. He also knew, though he was reluctant to admit it, that he had no quarrel, other than personal, with Bute, who was only doing what he himself would have been glad to do at any moment during the past three years. His previous attitude towards peace hampered him sorely. Nor had he any knowledge of the latest developments, which might conceivably have given him a lead. The thought provoked him to the quite unreasonable complaint that the way in which he was kept in ignorance was

[1] Sedgwick, p. 94.
[2] Newcastle to Devonshire, 10th June 1762. Add. MSS. 32,939, and Note dated 24th August 1762. Add. MSS. 32,941.
[3] Devonshire's Diary, 29th July 1762.
[4] Newcastle to Hardwicke, 4th September 1762. Add. MSS. 32,942.
[5] Devonshire's Diary, 28th July 1762.

'pretty odd and I believe scarce ever known before'.[1] But if he could not make up his mind to fight Bute, neither could he screw himself up to be reconciled to him. He remained a wavering uncertain figure, edging slowly into opposition, half reluctantly, half willingly. The other magnates who were nominally of his party, were equally uncertain and as passively discouraging. Devonshire showed his displeasure merely by asking the King's leave to absent himself from Council; Hardwicke maintained a disapproving reserve; Mansfield paid increasing attention to the law. They wanted to oppose, but found themselves shackled, being all tarred with the same brush—jealousy of Pitt and their own past pacifism. Hence, their attitude though not actively hostile, gave Bute no encouragement, and the mere lack of encouragement was frightening. To add to Bute's fears, the Cabinet itself was showing less and less inclination to stomach his surrenders and ignore the mounting tale of victories. Grenville was becoming stubborn, Egremont touchy, and even Granville occasionally flared into wrath.

Yet Bute had no option but to keep doggedly on, and in spite of obstacles, in spite of fears, he decided in September (1762) to send a plenipotentiary to Paris, with orders to finish off the negotiations and sign the Preliminaries. His choice was Bedford —admirable from his own point of view, but a further irritant to the people at large. The simmering discontent boiled over at the end of the month when news arrived of the capture of Havana. Regarding this victory as simply a fresh obstacle to peace, Bute wished to ignore it, but this was more than the rest of the Cabinet would endure. They insisted on compensation, and Bute, finding himself torn between fear of offending Choiseul and fear of losing his colleagues, searched round for a plan by which he could 'involve the whole Cabinet in what risk there might be in consenting to the preliminaries',[2] and at the same time plunged ahead with a scheme for 'widening the foundations of Administration'[3] which he had long had in mind. For the former purpose he sent a peremptory summons to Devonshire to attend a Council meeting at which the final terms of peace were to be settled; but Devonshire, alive to his intentions, excused himself, which so angered the King that he dismissed him from his post as Lord Chamber-

---

[1] Newcastle to Hardwicke, 16th June 1762. Add. MSS. 32,939.
[2] Rigby to Bedford, 29th September 1762. Corr. III, 125. [3] Sedgwick, p. 144.

lain in a grossly insulting manner, and subsequently with his own hand struck his name out of the list of Privy Councillors. Rockingham and one or two other magnates resigned in protest.

So, open war was declared, not altogether to Bute's liking; for the King had been acting on his own initiative.[1] Bute meanwhile was pursuing his efforts to 'widen the foundations of Administration'. There was only one direction in which they could be widened; the only resource left to Bute was Fox. Yet Fox presented problems. The King had always disapproved of him, and the only justification he could now find was that 'we must call in bad men to govern bad men'[2]—a sad falling off from his one-time upright intentions and a pitiful comment on the slough into which Bute was leading the country. As Fox must be endured, Bute at first pondered the possibility of appointing him joint Secretary, with Newcastle, in the hope that mutual jealousies would make the pair of them less formidable and more accommodating,[3] but gave up the idea when Fox frowned on it and Newcastle showed no inclination. Nor were the King and Bute alone in feeling hesitation; Fox felt it no less. For many years he had been Cumberland's man; and decency, if not gratitude, demanded that he should pay some heed to his opinion. But Cumberland had already told him, 'Mr. Fox, I shall not be obliged to any friend of mine that supports this administration which I do not approve of'.[4] The hint had been broad enough, and Fox had since responded by taking little part in Parliament. What was now being asked of him would mean breaking with Cumberland. It would also mean something even more distasteful: it was now many years since Fox had renounced ambition for wealth, and he was not anxious to leave his Aladdin's Cave at the Pay Office, merely to sweat in a dusty arena. For all reasons he would give little and his price would be high. Yet he had his price; indeed he was the only man among the potential leaders who could be bought. Pitt was beyond even the attempt, and the magnates had no chink in their armour. They were immensely wealthy; they were full of honours; they had no hopes or wishes which Bute could fulfil; nor had they any reason for gratitude. It was different with Fox; wealth he had in plenty, but he panted for an earldom. Bute now promised him a peerage, if he would take the Seals and steer the Preliminaries of

[1] Sedgwick, p. 152.
[3] Sedgwick, p. 142.
[2] *Grenville Papers*, I, 452.
[4] Devonshire's Diary, 30th July 1762.

Peace through the House. The Seals Fox would not take; that was asking too much; he would do the dirty work, if he were, like another Pooh-Bah, sufficiently 'insulted', but he would do no work which carried no special reward. All he would undertake was the temporary 'management' of the House. That was enough for Bute, and so the bargain was struck. It involved a further step. Though Fox had refused the Seals, they could not be left in Grenville's possession. He must be muzzled, for he had not only been pressing for better terms from France, but had demanded that the Preliminaries should be discussed in Parliament before they were signed.[1] Such a course seemed to Bute fatal; it would open the door for Pitt, whose views would certainly be adopted by the country at large, and might well win over the House; Bute's secret promises to Choiseul would be swept aside; his intrigues would go for nothing, and, in his view at least, the peace would be lost.[2] At all costs the Preliminaries must be signed before Parliament met, and meanwhile Grenville's untimely activities must be curbed. He was accordingly told that he must give up the Seals and change places with Halifax, sinking to the position of First Lord of the Admiralty. In breaking the news, Bute not unnaturally showed 'great marks of uneasiness', and tried to soften the blow by hinting that he wanted to retire and put Grenville in his place. He had not done so, he said, only because the bare suggestion had so completely upset the King, that he had sat for hours together, leaning his head upon his arm without speaking.[3] Whatever Grenville may have thought of this picture,[4] it is of more than passing interest, letting a flood of light on to Bute's embarrassments as well as the King's determination. Bute was finding that power was less delectable, and the lack of popularity more disturbing, than he had supposed. Even loyalty to the King was not so uplifting now that it was found to involve the need for a sullen tenacity in the face of opposition. As for the King, he was growing up and rapidly developing a will of his own, that stubborn will which not only carried him inflexibly along his chosen

---

[1] *Grenville Papers*, I, 483.

[2] 'The articles once brought into debate and discanted on by so numerous an assembly, will put it out of the power of this, or any other Administration, though as well inclined (a thing not likely) to continue the negotiation, or make any peace'. Bute to Bedford, 24th October 1762. Add. MSS. 36,797.

[3] *Grenville Papers*, I, 485.

[4] Grenville greatly resented his disgrace. 'Mr. Grenville,' wrote the King, 'is, I find, in open war with every man, because he will not forgive the change of his office'. To Bute, 6th January 1763—Sedgwick, p. 182.

path, but dragged unwilling Ministers in his wake. On this occasion, it steeled Bute, in spite of his lively fears, not merely to disgrace Grenville, but also to make a peace which, in his heart, he can scarcely have believed to be adequate. On the 3rd of November, Bedford signed the Preliminaries at Fontainebleau. On the 18th the news reached England. It came in time for the meeting of Parliament which had been postponed till the 25th for that very purpose.

(ii)

Meanwhile, what of Pitt? Throughout the summer both sides had been ready to use him as a bogey. Thus Viry had admonished Devonshire that 'if agreement could not be made with the Duke of Newcastle, Lord Bute would be forced to come to Mr. Pitt'.[1] His words would have carried more weight, if Devonshire had not himself, only the day before, hinted at a possible junction of Newcastle and Pitt, in order to startle the King.[2] If, however, they made use of him *in terrorem*, they were shy of seeking him as an ally. Yet, as time went on, the uncertainties of the peace constrained Bute, and the hankering after opposition constrained the magnates, to knock at his door. Bute held off as long as possible; he could hardly have forgotten Pitt's reiterated opinion that it was not for the good of the King's service that he should hold office. Indeed, it was not until he found himself deserted by his colleagues, and thought an Opposition was rapidly taking shape, that he ventured to throw out feelers. When he did, he offered 'great terms', if Sackville is to be believed,[3] but aroused curiosity rather than interest in Pitt, whose comment was that he 'had seen persons whom he never expected within his doors, and had given answers that would not be agreeable'.[4] It was still in his eyes not for the good of the King's service for Bute to hold office.

Like Bute, the Whig magnates were in no hurry to approach him. It is true there were moments when Newcastle, if left to himself, might have welcomed Pitt, but the moments were fleeting and by no means typical. The others were much more reluctant. Devonshire was against 'letting in Mr. Pitt'[5] because

---

[1] Devonshire's Diary, 29th July 1762.   [2] *Ibid.*, 28th July 1762.
[3] Sackville to Irwin, 17th October 1762. H.M.C. Stopford Sackville MSS.
[4] Conversation with Nuthall, 5th November 1762. Add. MSS. 32,944.
[5] Hardwicke to C. Yorke, 9th September 1762. Add. MSS. 35,352.

he feared that Pitt would be for 'violent measures';[1] and Hardwicke was oppressed by the thought that, if opposition were
successful, 'Mr. Pitt would be at the head of the new administration'.[2] The truth is that they were in an utterly false position,
which made them half-hearted in their hostility to Bute and
insincere in their proffered friendship to Pitt. They were playing
the old, old game of Whig Factions, intent on huffing each other,
not on changing policy. They had no real quarrel with Bute;
like him, they had no particular objectives in the war; like him,
they yearned for peace. What they desired was simply a return to
power, and what nonplussed them was how to obtain it. There
was no place for them in the politics of the day. On the one side
was Bute, the Favourite, with the King's ear and the policy after
which they hankered; on the other was Pitt, the natural leader of
the opposition, without the King's favour and with a policy
which they had rejected. Bute had cast them off as they had cast
off Pitt. How, then, could they creep in again? By themselves
they were helpless; their past rose up in judgment against them
and slammed the door. The only key to open it was Pitt, and when
they thought of him conscience warned them that he would
surely be 'much offended' with them because of 'the altercations'
which they had had with him in council the last year.[3] And behind
his indignation loomed the 'violent measures'. If they could
return to power without Pitt, it would be their aim to pursue
peace simply as the end of a war which they disliked. They might
differ among themselves in the degree to which they would go in
bargaining with France, but they would all differ from Pitt in
principle. He alone looked beyond the mere cessation of fighting
to the objects for which the war had been fought—the safety of
the colonists, the mastery of the seas, and the increase and security
of trade. Those were points which the magnates seem never to
have noticed; they never mentioned them and certainly would
never fight for them. As they had no real quarrel with Bute, so
they had no real sympathy with Pitt; they wanted, as they always
had wanted, to get his services without paying his fees. Their
prospects of success were deservedly small, and they hung back
reluctant.

In the end Fox's defection and Devonshire's dismissal frightened

---

[1] Diary, 31st July 1762.   [2] *Ibid.*
[3] Hardwicke to Newcastle, 23rd October 1762. Add. MSS. 32,943.

them into making the effort. Perhaps too they had caught a glimpse of Bute's letters which, at this moment, were 'full of swords, scabbards and factions'.[1] Whatever their motives, they thought their best approach would be through Cumberland, partly because Cumberland was known to dislike Bute,[2] partly because Pitt was reported to have said that 'no one in this country is fit to be at the head of affairs, but the Duke of Cumberland'. Any such remark, if made, was clearly no more than an *obiter dictum*, and was recognised as such by Newcastle who thought it sprang 'more from his dislike or contempt of others than any predilection at present for the Duke'.[3] None the less it offered a ray of hope to men who were otherwise hopeless.

They asked Cumberland for his help, but Cumberland felt himself hobbled by his rank; he could hardly 'beat up for volunteers or send for Mr. Pitt', but he agreed to make known his views, if Pitt should ask him. 'We must now' said Newcastle busily, 'consider how to convey this to Mr. Pitt'.[4] They conveyed it by two separate emissaries, his solicitor, Nuthall, who saw him on the 5th November, and Thomas Walpole who visited him on the 13th. As a result, an interview between Pitt and Cumberland was arranged. Newcastle was delighted. Hitherto he and his associates —Hardwicke, Devonshire and Rockingham—had been at a loss; they were daunted by what he described as 'the difficulty of determining what to do; the inclination in many to do nothing, and in some perhaps to do or attempt too much'. But now Cumberland's prudence, firmness and wisdom would settle everything, including especially the necessary restraint on Pitt 'if he should be disposed to go too far, by an improper attack upon the peace'.[5] It is curious to note how correctly Newcastle could describe the divergence between Pitt and himself and yet fail to realise its significance. Pitt had no such blindness. At the interview with Cumberland he emphasised the points he had already made to Nuthall and Walpole. Bute must of course go. What Pitt had said of him from the beginning was now obvious to all; it was impossible to put up with a man who insulted the nobility, intimidated the gentry and trampled on the people. Whatever

[1] Sedgwick, p. 156.
[2] Newcastle's Note, 3rd October 1762. Add. MSS. 32,943.
[3] Newcastle to Hardwicke, 30th September 1762. Add. MSS. 32,942.
[4] Account of conversation, 2nd November 1762. Add. MSS. 32,944.
[5] Newcastle to Devonshire, 16th November 1762. Add. MSS. 32,945.

Pitt could do to end Bute's 'transcendency of power', he would do. But he must do it in his own way. There was no point in pushing out Bute to put in Newcastle, whose policy was the same. If the King thought fit to recall Newcastle, Pitt would, if he must, serve with him, but only on the same lines as before, that is, at the head of those Tories 'who had acted with him upon revolution principles and had supported his administration'. His real wish, implied rather than declared, was, as Newcastle despondently remarked, 'to come in upon his own terms and with his own people', a wish which he qualified by saying that he would not force himself on the King against his will.

So Pitt made his attitude clear. He rejected Bute utterly. He had found him a lop-sided man, with far too much influence over the King and far too little aptitude for government. Newcastle was little better; he was stubborn towards his own colleagues, weak and wavering towards England's enemies. With neither would Pitt willingly take office again, only to be flouted, foiled and finally discarded. As for himself, he was a lonely man; Bute had come between him and the King, Newcastle between him and the Commons. Without royal favour or parliamentary influence, there was little he could do at the moment, but the time might come when the King would awake to facts and feel the need of his services. If that time came, he would be ready to take up the burden with his handful of faithful followers.

Cumberland was not dissatisfied. Believing that Pitt had been flinging out ideas to which he had no intention of adhering, he remarked simply that 'it was the man', and assumed that all would come right.[1] Newcastle knew better. Pitt had been heard to say, not long before: 'Nothing will be done. . . . The Duke of Devonshire is at Bath, my Lord Hardwicke at Wimple; the Duke of Newcastle will do nothing without those two. Is this an appearance of doing anything?' Newcastle was forced to admit, much against his will, that 'Mr. Pitt reasons as every man of sense will do, and must do'.[2] The Whigs would attempt nothing and Pitt's time had not yet come.

Newcastle accepted the position with querulous fatalism, noting that Fox's threats and offers were having their effect on the Whigs, that some of his best friends were beginning to shrug their

[1] Newcastle to Devonshire, 20th November 1762. Add. MSS. 32,945.
[2] Newcastle to C. Yorke, 25th October 1762. Add. MSS. 32,944.

shoulders, and that daily they were becoming more disinclined to attack the peace, which, whatever its terms, they regarded as 'absolutely necessary for the nation'.[1]

(iii)

Whilst the Whigs were thus returning consciously, if slowly, to the point from which they had never departed, Fox had been taking every possible step, not merely to ensure approval of the Preliminaries, but to obtain an overwhelming majority. He meant to pay handsomely for his peerage. Being a past master of the art of corruption, he made the widest use of the normal baits, and on this occasion even descended to bribes in cash.[2] His progress was palpable, and filled the Whig magnates with increasing perplexity. Their threat to oppose the Preliminaries had never been more than a sprat to catch Pitt, and had been thrown out the more half-heartedly because they were sure that Pitt, if caught, would carry his opposition beyond the point to which they were prepared to go. Must they still keep up the pretence when all prospect of success seemed to be dead? They thought not, and when Pitt showed no desire to dilute his fiery indignation with their tepid disapproval, they pushed the Preliminaries into the background of their thoughts and concentrated instead on a grievance which filled their whole horizon, though it was next to invisible to the country at large—the affront to their caste by the King's treatment of the Duke of Devonshire. Here was something on which they could expatiate with deep and genuine resentment, not untouched by fear. By any criterion the King's

---

[1] Newcastle to Devonshire, 20th November 1762. Add. MSS. 32,945.

[2] Sir Lewis Namier's criticism of the story in Walpole's *Memoirs*—George III, I, 157—of the issue of £25,000 in one morning for the open purchase of votes, is well known. He not only corrects the amount, but casts doubt on the whole transaction, asking what contemporary evidence there is to support it. I do not know what sort of evidence is expected or is likely to be forthcoming; the offer and acceptance of a bribe is not usually broadcast; but there is corroboration in Almon's *History of the Late Minority*, published in 1765, and also in his *Anecdotes of Lord Chatham*. Almon could not have borrowed from Walpole, and as the two stories differ in detail I doubt if Walpole borrowed from him. There is further corroboration, nearer the time, in Wilkes's *North Briton* of 12th February 1763, No. 37, and in his *Letter to the Electors of Aylesbury* of 22nd October 1764. There is also something that looks very like a reference to it in Ruffhead's *Considerations on the present crisis* (p. 37) published in 1763. Fox was not afraid of bribery either in word or deed, and I see no reason why he should have boggled at cash. I am inclined therefore to believe that the story, however exaggerated, is founded on fact, though I hasten to add that the form of bribe offered by Fox does not seem to me very important.

conduct had been outrageous, and who could tell what it porten-
ded. There were other similar causes of discontent, such as the
'elevation of Mr. Fox' and the absorption of government by 'a
sole Scotch minister and favourite'.[1] But they recognised that, for
the present at least, none of these matters would serve as the
foundation of a parliamentary opposition. In short, they did not
dissent from Bute's view that 'the happy conclusion of peace has
drawn the teeth of faction'.[2] They were void of ideas; they were
bankrupt of policy; and when they heard that Pitt had promised
the Tories not to speak in the debate on the Address, Newcastle
concluded, with feelings almost of relief, that 'as things stand, and
till we can know a little more than we do of our strength, I think
we must look about us a little before we do anything'.[3] So the
Whigs adopted *dolce far niente* as the motto of their opposition. Had
Bute realised it, he might have ridden out the storm without Fox,
and Fox could have saved himself a world of obloquy.

A fortnight or so before Parliament met, Pitt went down with a
more than usually severe attack of gout—a fact which greatly
encouraged Fox, and confirmed the Whigs in their *non-possumus*
prognostications.

[1] Hardwicke to Newcastle, 15th November 1762. Add. MSS. 32,945.
[2] Bute to Lowther, 17th November 1762. H.M.C. Lonsdale MSS.
[3] Newcastle to Devonshire, 20th November 1762. Add. MSS. 32,945.

VI

THE PRELIMINARIES

(i)

WHEN BEDFORD returned from Paris with the Preliminaries, Granville, the Lord President, was at death's door, but rallied his dimming spirit to laud 'the most honourable peace this nation ever saw'.[1] The ineluctable mystery of death lends oracular weight to last words, though perhaps at times they are as little understood by the speaker as by the hearers. Granville's 'last words' were true, but superficial. After so victorious a war, the peace was bound to be honourable. It was more important that it should be adequate, and on that point Granville was silent. Yet that was a point on which the public were deeply concerned and over which they had been showing signs of growing uneasiness. Rumours of concessions were too persistent; they provoked doubts—sometimes expressed in sober sadness, as by the old man from Bath who wanted to 'discover some small degree of attention to our interest';[2] sometimes wittily and wickedly, as by Wilkes when, in the *North Briton*[3] he made Bute lament, 'O, that I must be doomed to watch over the caprices of furriers, sugar-boilers, cod-merchants, planters, rum-distillers, freighters, importers, and haughty East India directors!' Had the House represented public opinion Fox might have been anxious, for public opinion was becoming daily more noisy and unfavourable. By the time Parliament met (25th November) feelings were running high indeed. The populace made Bute's passage to and from Westminster so stormy that the Guards had to be summoned, and George III in an agony of apprehension offered to do anything, even to recalling Pitt, if that might prove 'the best means of preserving a life I so much value, and which I look on as of so great consequence to this ungrateful people'.[4]

In contrast to the seething mob without, and the quakings of his heart within, Bute had drafted the King's Speech in proud and

---

[1] Ballantyne, p. 364.   [2] *A Select Collection of Letters*, etc., I, 56.
[3] No. 24. 13th November 1762.   [4] George III to Bute, Sedgwick, p. 168.

ringing tones. Except for a few epithets applied to the war, and here and there a touch of jauntiness, it might almost have come from Pitt's pen. It gave a triumphant list of victories; it praised the valour of British arms; it spoke of vigorous measures and of enemies compelled to accept peace. More particularly it defined the objectives at which that peace had aimed: 'There is', Parliament was assured, 'not only an immense territory added to the empire of Great Britain, but a solid foundation laid for the increase of trade and commerce; and the utmost care has been taken to remove all occasion of future disputes between my subjects and those of France and Spain, and thereby to add security and permanency to the blessings of peace'. Nor was that all. The good things of life were to overflow on to our friends; 'while I carefully attended', the speech continued, 'to the essential interests of my own kingdoms, I have had the utmost regard to the good faith of my Crown, and the interests of my allies'. It was thus that the coat was trailed before all who might dare to oppose.

Here it may be as well to set out briefly the terms of the peace so confidently recommended. Out of the many possessions which she had lost, France was to cede to us, formally, Canada, Nova Scotia, Cape Breton and Mobile in America; Grenada, the Grenadines, St. Vincent, Dominica and Tobago in the West Indies; and Senegal in Africa. Out of the many conquests England had made, she was to restore to France St. Pierre and Miquelon in America; Guadeloupe, Marie Galante, Desirade, Martinique and St. Lucia in the West Indies, and Goree in Africa. Belleisle was to be traded for Minorca, and in India the position was to be restored as it had been at the end of 1748. France was to demolish the fortifications of Dunkirk and in return was to be given the right to fish on the banks of Newfoundland and in the Gulf of St. Lawrence.

Spain was to exchange Florida for Havana—to which Manila was subsequently added—give up her claim to fish on the Banks of Newfoundland, accept the jurisdiction of the Court of Admiralty in prize cases, and allow the English to continue cutting logwood in Honduras, provided the English fortresses there were first demolished. Though it was not stated in the Preliminaries, France was to compensate Spain by the cession of Louisiana.

So much for England. As for her friends and allies, France was to restore in their original condition all conquests made by her in Hanover, Hesse and Brunswick; and Spain was similarly to restore all conquests in Portugal, the King of Portugal being 'expressly included in the present preliminary articles'. Immediately after the signing of the Preliminaries, France was to evacuate Ostend and Nieuport; and after their ratification she was to evacuate 'the fortresses of Cleves, Wesel and Guelders and in general all the countries belonging to the King of Prussia', who, incidentally was not expressly included in the present preliminary articles. Both sides were to betake themselves out of Westphalia and the Empire, and neither side was to furnish men or money to their allies, though France specifically reserved the right to pay any debts or arrears of subsidy which might be outstanding—and in fact were pretty considerable.

Finally—or more correctly, firstly—and certainly ironically, it was agreed that 'as soon as the Preliminaries shall be signed and ratified, sincere friendship shall be re-established between England, France and Spain'.

(ii)

The Address was voted without trouble. A few days later the Preliminaries were presented, and it was decided to discuss them on 9th December. As Pitt was still prostrate with gout, an attempt at postponement was made, in order to ensure his attendance, but Pitt's probable absence was a bonus which Fox was not prepared to forgo. He brought his well-oiled machine into operation and the motion was decisively rejected—243 votes to 74—a preliminary canter which added greatly to his confidence. He could now await the event unmoved. It was otherwise with the Whigs. They were utterly at sea—loth to oppose, yet afraid to abstain. As Onslow said, the Whigs must divide against the peace if they were not to lose 'all their ground, all their popular cry'; and yet, if they did, 'might not that throw things more than is to be wished into the hands of Mr. Pitt'.[1] Onslow supposed that Pitt would 'certainly be strenuous in his opposition', but others, and more particularly the Whig leaders, were not so sure. They had no faith in themselves and were looking not trustfully but suspiciously, at Pitt, inclining on the whole to Walpole's opinion, that even Pitt himself did not know what he would do till he was in the middle of his first speech.[2] If Pitt did not know, how could they?

[1] Onslow to Newcastle, 30th November 1762. Add. MSS. 32,945.
[2] Walpole to Mann, 26th September 1762.

It was thus a curiously apathetic House which assembled on the 9th, the greater part cool and unconcerned, with the indifference of the bribed; the lesser part despondent and bemused. There was only one man who could vivify those dry bones and he was not in his place. The debate opened languidly, and was continuing on the same languid lines, when of a sudden the mob outside gave a triumphant shout which startled and flustered everyone within. There was no mistaking the message of that shout; it meant that Pitt, the Great Commoner, was coming to give voice to the views and wishes of the people of England—that people who had responded so purposefully to his call and were now, as they believed, so wantonly being deprived of the benefits he had secured. Pitt would see justice done; Pitt would put all to rights. The doors opened, and the people's champion appeared—a man wan and emaciated, a man twisted and tortured with pain and swathed in flannel to get some relief, a man unable to walk unaided, who crawled to his place with the help of crutches and the assistance of pitying hands. Fox and his battalions, blind to the courage of his endurance, smiled contemptuously at the trappings of his illness. To them he was a figure of fun.[1]

Walpole and the Whigs had doubted if he knew his own mind; but Pitt, if he was bowed with pain, was still completely master of himself. He knew exactly what he wanted to say, if only his strength would hold out; he knew exactly what he proposed to do. The Preliminaries, he had told Wilkes, were 'the great object which decides the fate of this country', and as he very strongly disapproved of them, he would declare his sense of them in public, provided it was possible for him to rise from his bed.[2] But in declaring that sense, he was under no illusions, nor was he buoyed up by fictitious hopes. There was no prospect of changing or defeating the Preliminaries. It was not for Parliament to make peace. Parliament could advise and Parliament should approve, but the making of peace was the King's prerogative. Here, the terms had been agreed and the Preliminaries signed. The House was presented, artfully enough, with a *fait accompli*. Advice was no longer of use, and ratification was inevitable. There was no doubt, said Pitt, of the Government's victory on the main question.[3] But if he must give up hope of changing the terms, no one

---

[1] Walpole, *George III*, I, 176-7.   [2] H.M.C. MSS. of Colonel Macaulay.
[3] Almon, I, 441.

could deprive him of his right to criticise their deficiencies, nor turn him from his duty of pointing out their dangers.

Though Pitt had managed to leave his bed, he was desperately ill and desperately weak. He could barely raise himself in his place to make his speech, and could remain standing only with the support of friends. His condition was so pitiable that a House, whose ears were plugged with gold against his words, could not deny the witness of their eyes, and were fain to let him sit from time to time. Even sitting he needed stimulants, and neither his physical strength when standing nor his recumbent position when sitting gave scope for those striking gestures, those lightning glances, those modulations of voice, which his enemies called theatrical and his later detractors insincere, but which in fact were legitimate and vastly effective artillery in the battle of Parliament. As a speech his effort was voted a failure, 'unmeasurably dull, tedious, and uninteresting,'[1] but its bare bones still stand as a record and a prophecy. Pitt and Bute had approached the peace from opposite ends. There was no single point at which their policies coincided. Bute was living for the ephemeral present. Pitt was looking mainly to the past and the future. In the past France had been the tyrant of Europe, and England's rival—at sea, in the colonies and in trade. Pitt had wanted a peace which would be permanent, leaving no room for future rivalry in either trade or war, and no chance of revenge—a peace that would be safe, not only for his own generation but for his children's children; a peace, moreover, that would do justice to friends and allies, not only for their own sakes, but for the sake of Europe. That he had wanted too much is possible; that he did not understand economic laws is likely—they are little enough understood two centuries later—but at least he had a clear idea based on the knowledge then available. For him, the war had been inextricably bound up with colonies and trade. We needed colonies, not only as markets for our manufactures, but even more as sources of commerce; for merchants, not manufacturers, were the financially important element of the times. A sugar island, a spice island, a fishery, a forest of logwood were to Pitt much what an oil-bearing district is to a modern statesman. It was essential to gain and hold them, if we were to have our share of trade, if we, instead of France, were to supply 'almost all Europe with the rich

[1] Walpole, *George III*, I, 178.

commodities which are produced only on that part of the world'.[1]
The Preliminaries as Pitt saw them, gave neither security nor
trade in any degree commensurate with the victories won, while
they left France in a position to rebuild her resources and at the
appropriate time give rein to her desire for revenge.

His arguments, deprived of oratorical force by his state of
health, were further obfuscated by the need to touch upon
constitutional points, and the desire to justify himself. The Whigs
might think they could influence the peace, but Pitt knew better.
He began, therefore, by admitting the King's prerogative, and so,
by implication, giving up all claim to prescribe the terms. At the
same time he stressed the right of Parliament to advise, thus
indirectly condemning signature before Parliament had been
consulted. The peace had been made; it was irrevocable; and it
was bad, not because it was unfavourable in itself, but because it
fell lamentably short in every point of national importance, both
present and future. For all her losses, France had been allowed to
keep fast hold of the key points, and so retain the means of
recovery; while England, for all her acquisitions, had jeopardised
the future by throwing away her friends. Canada had been
ceded in its fullest extent, and that was good because it gave
security to the English colonies; but from the commercial point
of view, Canada was a long-term investment; the existing trade
was extremely small and its future speculative and remote. What
we needed was an immediate and assured supply of merchandise,
which we could have had, if we had retained even one of the
important French sugar islands. But, no! in the division of the
West Indian islands all that were really valuable—Guadeloupe,
Martinique and St. Lucia—had been restored to France without
equivalent; and the other rich island, Cuba, the key to all the
treasures and wealth of South America, had been exchanged for the
barren wastes of Florida. What was true of the West was true of
the East; in India we had conquered everywhere and had given
back all our conquests, gratis and for nothing. 'No nation had
ever lost an opportunity so happy, so almost accomplished, of
fixing its ascendant and commerce'.[2] As in America and Asia, so
in Africa. In the war we had secured the trade in slaves and gum
by the capture of Senegal and Goree, and by the peace we were
likely to lose all by yielding the island of Goree, so 'essential to

[1] Almon, I, 450.   [2] Walpole, *George III*, I, 182.

the security of Senegal',[1] And looming over everything were the fisheries. They should be ours alone; their retention was a *sine qua non*, since they were not only exceedingly profitable in themselves, but also provided an admirable nursery for seamen. For those reasons Pitt had never imagined that France would easily be persuaded to give them up, and precisely for those reasons he would have been willing to continue the war for one or two further campaigns; it would have been worth while. In the earlier negotiations he had struggled to carry his point, and had been over-ruled, as he had been in many matters; but in yielding he had insisted on conditions which would have limited the damage done. Those conditions had been scrapped. His Majesty's servants had 'lost sight of the great fundamental principle that France is chiefly, if not solely, to be dreaded by us in the light of a maritime and commercial power;' and by their concessions had given to her 'the means of recovering her prodigious losses and of becoming once more formidable to us at sea'. It was lamentable. No less lamentable was our desertion of the King of Prussia, and that at a time when the old balance of power in Europe had been fundamentally altered, first by the sudden rise of Russia—moving in its own orbit and still to be attracted to one camp or the other— and then by the unexpected growth of Prussia as the rival of Austria. The desertion of Frederick was 'insidious, tricking, base and treacherous'. It was worse; it was insulting because 'a malicious and scandalous distinction' had been drawn between him and our other allies. Their possessions were to be restored immediately and in their pristine condition; the Prussian possessions were to be evacuated only, and that at the latest possible date —after ratification—and left to be scrambled for, with the dice loaded in Austria's favour. We were casting aside our greatest ally with every mark of contempt, whilst our enemies were keeping their Family Compact safe and untouched. 'The peace was insecure, because it restored the enemy to her former greatness. The peace was inadequate, because the places gained were no equivalent for the places surrendered'. Pitt could see in it only 'the seeds of a future war'.[2]

Having made his almost solitary protest,[3] Pitt left the House.

---

[1] Almon, I, 451.   [2] *Ibid.*, 461–2.
[3] 'Nobody beside him spoke a word against the Preliminaries worth remembering'. Hayes to Neville, 10th December 1762. Bedford Corr. III, 168.

F

He had spoken for three and a half hours, and was now utterly exhausted and 'in the greatest agony of pain'.[1] Besides, there was no point in staying. But the life of the debate left with him, and at midnight a vote of 319 to 65 showed that Fox had amply earned his peerage. The minority might have been larger, had not Newcastle, too fearful to force a division in the Lords, advised his followers in the Commons not to divide even there.

(iii)

When all was over, the minority, both those who had voted and those who had abstained, were full of recriminations. As though to confirm the accuracy of Pitt's prophecies, Newcastle wrote three days later: 'I always feared attacking the peace, and you know it.'[2] Most of those who held office expected to be turned out, and some hurried to make their submission. None of them wanted to be conspicuous; indeed Legge, having 'lost some part of his courage', went so far as to admit that he was 'afraid of being the Leader Designatus'.[3] Inevitably they tended to whitewash their own infirmity of purpose by denouncing Pitt. 'Mr. Pitt', Newcastle asserted roundly, 'has a great deal to answer for',[4] while others complained that, but for his impolitic declaration that he was 'a single man', the minority would have been much larger.[5] Though they denounced him amongst themselves, they were still angling for his support, mainly in order to have 'some leader and some plan',[6] but, as ever, with a strong undercurrent of dislike and distrust. 'I cannot say', wrote Hardwicke censoriously, 'that I am much edified with Mr. Pitt's discourse',[7] the discourse being one in which Pitt had told his neighbour, Thomas Townshend, that though he declined to enter into a coalition with Newcastle, he would support him in Parliament on 'all great occasions'.[8] Hardwicke's reaction was not encouraging. Indeed there was nothing in the attitude of the Whig magnates to tempt Pitt back into an alliance with men who had thwarted him con-

[1] Almon, I, 462.
[2] Newcastle to T. Walpole, 12th December 1762. Add. MSS. 32,945.
[3] Newcastle to Devonshire, 12th December 1762. Add. MSS. 32,945.
[4] Newcastle to Hardwicke, 1st January 1763. Add. MSS. 32,946.
[5] Countess Temple to Temple, 17th December 1762. *Grenville Papers*, II, 21.
[6] Newcastle to Devonshire, 23rd December 1762. Add. MSS. 32,945.
[7] Hardwicke to Newcastle, 25th December 1762. Add. MSS. 32,945.
[8] Newcastle to Hardwicke, 25th December 1762. Add. MSS. 32,945.

sistently during his own administration and finally united with Bute to turn him out.

Whilst Pitt was recuperating and the Whig magnates were making wry faces, Fox and Bute took steps to consolidate their advantage by smashing every vestige of opposition. They found a ready accomplice in the King, whose first reaction on hearing the result, was to declare that Colonel Fitzroy and Mr. Robinson —two household officials who had voted with the minority— 'can't be too soon dismissed'.[1] Before December was out, he had deprived Newcastle, Rockingham and Grafton of their Lord Lieutenancies, and was no doubt pleased when Devonshire, whom Fox wanted to protect for old times' sake, resigned of his own accord. Then came the deluge. Fox had planned the procedure in detail, laying down that 'those out of Parliament' should be dismissed 'immediately'; the rest 'just before the holydays'.[2] So it was. 'Execution day', as Walpole called it, was 20th December,[3] when numbers of Newcastle's friends and adherents were deprived of posts, places or pensions. Other execution days followed, for the massacre was far-reaching and fierce. Newcastle would not be comforted; he lamented loud and long—with plenty of reason, and yet perhaps not altogether justifiably, nor yet entirely without thought of self. It may be that in some cases Fox's motive was revenge, and probably in others he made mistakes, but in general his object was political, even in the case of seemingly humble dependants. In a long life of patronage, Newcastle must have been kind to some persons who could not repay him, but far the larger number of his beneficiaries were expected to, and did, serve his political ends whether in Parliament or as agents or voters in the constituencies. The method of election then in vogue gave a tremendous pull to the man in possession, and Fox proposed to be that man. He meant, as Hardwicke assured Newcastle, 'to disarm you of any remains of power and influence.[4]

The ferocity of this wholesale massacre gave rise to feelings of indignation which have not altogether subsided to this day. It seemed, and still seems, brutal to deprive civil servants of their

---

[1] Sedgwick, p. 173.
[2] Fox to Bute. Quoted Ilchester, II, 215.
[3] Walpole to Mann, 20th December 1762.
[4] Hardwicke to Newcastle, 25th November 1763. Add. MSS. 32,953. See also George III to Bute, 18th January 1763, Sedgwick, p. 187.

jobs merely because of the manner of their appointment, and
utterly callous to stamp on inoffensive pensioners. Yet if Fox went
much too far, almost running amok, he was taking a step which
was to prove of Constitutional importance. His action was the
obverse of what Pitt had tried to do in 1756. In those first hopeful
days, Pitt had felt, in a groping and uncertain fashion, that the
political system was inadequate, and that there ought to be some
alternative government other than a mere repatterning of the
Whig factions, something, in short, in the nature of what today
is called Her Majesty's Opposition.

In accordance with his 'visionary notions'[1] he had tried to set
up a new Cabinet and a new party, and his action, tentative as it
was and frustrated by events, was the first move towards the change-
over from eighteenth-century politics to the modern system.
Fox was now making the second move, though he had no 'visionary notions' and merely wished to crush his opponents. His step,
unlike Pitt's, was negative; instead of bringing in fresh blood, he
simply drained off the old. But the result was much the same. Just
as in 1756 Hardwicke had found Pitt's plan of administration 'a
most extraordinary one indeed' because it included none of the
old Cabinet,[2] so now, after Fox's massacre, Wilkes, with a touch
of exaggeration, found it 'remarkable, though not in the least
astonishing' that except for Fox himself, not one of the old
ministers remained.[3] Fox had managed to consolidate an exclusive
governmental party which was superimposed on the existing
system. Hitherto the King had appointed his Ministers as he
thought fit, and had expected Parliament to support them irre-
spective of their party label. Henceforward the King would continue to choose his ministers, but only from a favoured circle; the
rest, shattered by the massacre, were to remain in outer darkness.
As 'the rest' included the powerful Whig magnates who had so
long dominated the scene, it was unlikely that they would sink
without a struggle into the insignificance which had formerly
overtaken the Tories. The chances were that they would
react, and as soon as they did, Fox's massacre, which was
meant to destroy 'faction', would become the birthpangs of
a two-party system. It did so, rapidly, if not altogether con-

[1] See my *Pitt and the Seven Years' War*, Chap. X.
[2] Hardwicke to Yorke, 31st October 1756. Add. MSS. 35,357.
[3] *North Briton*, No. 30, 25th December 1762.

sciously, for two reasons, neither of which had applied in Pitt's case.

The first was the impact of the massacre on Newcastle. When Pitt introduced his 'extraordinary' plan, Newcastle had been content because he had assumed that sooner or later Pitt would require his help. Now he had no such hope, and consequently fell at the outset into a state of stunned reflection that 'people are everywhere so cowed and intimidated by those acts of violence, and the apprehension of still greater, that no man dares *now* say one word'.[1] As he began to recover, he began to desire 'an active resentment in my friends',[2] and then proceeded to clamour for a full-blooded opposition, which, sweeping Bute aside, would force the reinstatement of 'all our friends of all sorts', and a Whig administration 'supported by the Whigs'.[3] It was an idea which Wilkes had already adumbrated in the *North Briton*, when, after lamenting that 'the Tory faction' was now triumphant and 'the friends of liberty and the revolution' had no countenance but from the nation, he went on to a defiant declaration that opposition had become 'the duty of every honest man and every sincere lover of his country'.[4] The reaction to Fox's violence was bound to be strong. The question was whether it would be effective.

The second reason sprang out of Bute's lack of popularity. There was no disputing the fact that he was immensely unpopular, and the pamphleteers took infinite pains to let him know it. His supporters had to find some counterblast, not merely to the scurrilities, which could be answered in kind, but to the more serious objections based on Bute's standing in the country. They found it very simply in the King's prerogative, believing that Bute's best protection was to be hidden beneath the royal robes. They argued that as the King admittedly had the right to appoint his Ministers, the people had no business to oppose them. Any such opposition shackled the independence and infringed the prerogative of the Crown. The Whigs retorted that a Minister was the servant not only of the King but also of the nation, and therefore accountable to the people as well as the King; and hinted as broadly as they dared that when, as in the case of Bute, a Minister becomes unacceptable to the people, the King should

---

[1] Newcastle to Hardwicke, 1st January 1763. Add. MSS. 32,946.
[2] Newcastle to Hardwicke, 5th January 1763. Add. MSS. 32,946.
[3] Newcastle to Devonshire, 31st January 1763. Add. MSS. 32,946.
[4] *North Briton*, No. 30, 25th December 1762.

dismiss him.[1] Here was an up-to-date version of the old Whig and
Tory conflict. The gulf between the two was exceedingly troublesome, and would remain so until a *modus vivendi* between King
and Parliament had been discovered. Until that happy time, the
prosperity of an administration would depend on the good sense
of the King and the Minister. Bute and George III were not
remarkable for good sense, and the conflict raged.

(iv)

When political feelings were running so high, Pitt's attitude
became a matter of importance; he could so obviously throw
immense weight into whichever scale he preferred. Unfortunately,
while in one sense it was easy for him to decide, in another it was
exceptionally difficult. He had told the King, when he resigned,
that he would do his best to support his Government. That
intention still remained; the Government was the King's and as
such commanded the allegiance of all good men. But Pitt drew
a sharp distinction between the King's Government and the
King's Ministers. He had never said that he would support
Bute; he had never approved of him and never would. He was
still as firmly convinced as ever that Bute's 'transcendency of
power' was not 'for the good of the King's service', and indeed,
was wholly to be deplored. For every reason, Bute must go, and
the only question was how to get rid of him. There were two
methods—he could be forced out of office by public opinion, or
he could be defeated in Parliament—but neither was simple and
both had serious drawbacks. Pitt undoubtedly regarded the former course as the more desirable. Bute was an inefficient Minister,
but, far more disquieting, he was also a favourite; and as Pitt was
never tired of emphasising, the nation would never suffer a man
to be both a favourite and a Minister. Sooner or later, the nation
would spew him out—a consummation clearly presaged by the
restless turmoil in the country. The pity of it was that the gutter
press, by giving the wrong reasons, was debauching the people's
indignation. Instead of concentrating on the evils of arbitrary and
irresponsible power, it was harping on Bute's Scottish nationality
and wallowing in innuendoes of illicit amours with the King's
mother. However profoundly Pitt might approve the object, he

[1] Almon, *A Review of Lord Bute's Administration*, p. 75 ff.

could not but regret the means. Such writings would lead to bitterness in royal circles, and promote hatred and enmity between the two halves of the country. The mills of public opinion might grind exceeding small, but they made an intolerable mess in the process.

Yet if, instead of trusting to public opinion, Pitt turned to Parliament, he found a fresh crop of difficulties. He could not reconcile it, either to his promise to the King or to his own conscience, to oppose merely for the sake of opposing. The King's government must go on; its day-to-day functions must be helped, not hindered. Opposition was manifestly factious unless it was based on large questions of principle, and even then must be honest and heartfelt. Such questions—great occasions, as he called them to Thomas Townshend—were rare, and as a means of dislodging Bute open to Hardwicke's criticism that 'an attendance now and then upon great occasions only will not answer the purpose of an opposition'.[1] Something more was necessary, which Pitt was reluctant to give—reluctant because of his promise to the King, because of his hope that public opinion would solve his problem, because of his doubt how far the Whigs would see eye to eye with him on such great questions of principle as might arise.

But perhaps there was a still greater obstacle. Pitt was bound to look beyond the mere fact of Bute's downfall. What would happen when Bute had disappeared? It was a baffling question which Pitt was not the only man to ask. The Whigs also were greatly agitated by it. They were only too sure that Bute's downfall meant the return of Pitt to power, and as that was the last thing they desired, their approach to him was hobbled by doubts. Though ready to admit that he was indispensable for the success of their opposition, they would not contemplate more than putting him at their head 'to a degree',[2] and a degree that was none the greater for being unspecified. Their hesitations were many and various, but all reached the same conclusion—a hope that Pitt would be the wave to carry them on to fortune, and a fear that, unlike a wave, he might after reaching the shore, fail to recede and be swallowed up again in the ocean. Pitt had little doubt of their wishes and less of his own impotence. He had foreseen something, though not all,

[1] Hardwicke to Newcastle, 25th December 1762. Add. MSS. 32,945.
[2] Newcastle to Devonshire, 31st January 1763. Add. MSS. 32,946.

of his present position when he had been jockeyed into the coalition with Newcastle.[1] That coalition had effectively strangled the party he had been trying to create for himself, and he had never been able to recover the lost ground. On the contrary, he had slipped farther back. The nucleus of his own party had been the Tories, who had followed him faithfully so long as he was in office. After his resignation, it was not unnatural for them to turn to Bute's half-Toryism rather than to Newcastle's uncompromising Whiggism, especially bearing in mind Pitt's own decision to support the Government; and, serving under Bute's banner, it was not surprising that they were now leaning towards doctrines of which Pitt disapproved. He was not therefore indulging in high-flown rhetoric when he said that he had been 'out-Toryed by Lord Bute and out-Whigged by the Duke of Newcastle'.[2] He was merely stating facts. To attack Bute in Parliament now, meant a final break with the Tories and a definite junction with the Whigs; he would be absorbed in Newcastle's party and, judging by the past, could look forward to nothing but frustration. Nor, in such circumstances, was there any reason to suppose that the King would recall him to office, and without 'the King's countenance' he was not prepared to serve; he would not force the King, even if he could. But should Bute be driven out by public opinion, Pitt thought it not unlikely that the King might 'be convinced of the error of his measures',[3] and look to Pitt himself to calm the popular ferment. When that happened, the Tories would come back to him; 'he would certainly have them again' though they might not yet be sensible of it.[4] With them as a nucleus he could once more set about creating his own party, and at its head, strive for prosperity at home and security abroad.

In short, all lines of argument led to the same conclusion: it would be best to leave Bute to the expulsive force of public opinion. In the meantime Pitt must remain 'a single man' and 'unconnected', attending the House on matters of importance but without joining the Whigs in any set scheme of opposition.

[1] See my *Pitt and the Seven Years' War*, p. 246.
[2] Thomas Walpole's conversation with Pitt, 13th November 1762. Add. MSS. 32,945.
[3] Newcastle to Devonshire, 11th August, 1763. Add. MSS. 32,950.
[4] Rigby to Bedford, 10th March 1763. Bedford Corr. III, 218.

(v)

The gout which tortured Pitt in the debate on the Preliminaries was no passing disorder. An 'unlucky jaunt' into Wiltshire had given rise to a series of violent attacks which continued on and off for the best part of six months. No doubt they helped him to his decision to attend the House only on 'great occasions'; certainly they induced a melancholy, and at times even a jaundiced, outlook on public affairs. Like any retired colonel in a bath-chair, he could now and then complain that 'there was no more stuff or spirit left in the nation, the desire of getting or keeping prevailing throughout',[1] but underneath there was vastly more than mere querulousness. He felt, and felt deeply, that Bute had betrayed the country, that the terms of peace prevented England from becoming 'what favouring Providence seemed to intend it to be'; and that all his efforts and all his toil for England's honour had been brought to nothing by the machinations of selfish men. Now there was nothing for him to do but 'avert my mind from this contemplation, devoutly wishing that the progress of our country's decadence may not be so rapid as my mind forebodes'.[2] From gloomy thoughts such as these he turned with increased appreciation to the exquisite joys of home. Buried in his small village and in the bosom of his family, he could forget that he had been 'driven into retirement'; he could become absorbed in 'small but endearing occupations'; and with Hester at his side 'find much delight in the little sage discourse of the diminutive philosophers who surround us'. It would have been 'a happiness too large and too perfect for a mortal man', had it not been for the disappointments in the great world outside.[3]

His absorption in domestic bliss gave the Whigs a breathing space in which to make up their minds. Did they need Pitt, or could they do without him? Before the fiasco of the Preliminaries, Onslow had declared that the rank and file wanted Newcastle and Devonshire as their leaders and would enlist under Pitt's banner only *faute de mieux*.[4] After the fiasco, Pitt was for the moment thrown entirely aside. Symmer wrote his contemptuous epitaph:

[1] T. Walpole to Newcastle, 1st January 1763. Add. MSS. 32,946.
[2] Pitt to Richard Lyttelton, January 1763, Chatham Corr. II, 208.   [3] *Ibid.*
[4] Onslow to Newcastle, 30th November 1762. Add. MSS. 32,945.

'the explosion of this bomb proved to be but the bursting of a bubble',[1] and the Whig magnates began searching for new gods. 'We are endeavouring', said Newcastle, 'to persuade Mr. Legge and the Attorney General to take the conduct upon them, to whom our friends should resort for advice; and my nephew Charles Townshend may be at the head, if he pleases; and he will be sounded upon it'.[2] Alas! the new gods, when they were sounded, proved as deaf as Baal, and so by slow and reluctant steps Newcastle reached his decision that Pitt must 'to a degree' be put at the head. All that remained was to find the herald who should break the news to him, and explain the one condition—how trifling!—which Newcastle laid down—'that all our friends of all sorts should be reinstated; that there should be a Cavendish, and a Pelham and Lord Villiers in the Treasury; and that the administration should be Whig and be supported by the Whigs'.[3] No Tories for Pitt on this occasion!

But while Newcastle was thus sidling towards Pitt, Hardwicke was slipping away. Truly his position was puzzling. Life was no longer as clear-cut and simple as it had been in the years of Whig domination. In those days he had risen from obscure origins to be Lord Chancellor, and then, satisfied with his own honours, had centred his ambitions in his family. In particular, he longed to see his favourite son, Charles, now the Attorney General, follow him up the path which led to the Woolsack. But in the new political world which Bute was creating, he seemed to be losing his way. How could he any longer square his hopes for Charles with his old loyalties? Those old loyalties demanded that he should support Newcastle in his opposition to the peace, and in his hankerings after Pitt. Yet family ties demanded that he should do nothing to alienate Bute, and nothing to benefit Pratt who was Pitt's choice and Charles's rival in the Chancellor stakes. His uncertainty was worse confounded by Newcastle's hesitation and his own pacifism. Did he really object to the peace? Did Newcastle? Would it really pay either of them to offend Bute? What prospects had Pitt and how far was he committed to Pratt? And be Pitt's prospects what they would, might it not be better for the Hardwicke family to be off at once with the old love, never

---

[1] Symmer to Mitchell, 31st December 1762. Add. MSS. 6,839.
[2] Newcastle to T. Walpole, 12th December 1762. Add. MSS. 32,945.
[3] Newcastle to Devonshire, 31st January 1763. Add. MSS. 32,946.

more than lukewarm, and on as soon as possible with the new? Inevitably Hardwicke hedged, and as a first step turned the Preliminaries into a family affair in order to lessen the risk by spreading it. In the Lords, he joined with Newcastle in criticising the terms, but without pressing for a division; in the Commons, Charles made a mildly critical speech, and left without voting. John did nothing but listen, while Royston went over to the majority. After the Preliminaries, Hardwicke did his best to damp down Newcastle's inclination towards Pitt. He agreed that everyone thought Pitt's help essential, but asked what hope there was of getting it. Pitt was coy, and who could guess at his motive? Perhaps it was 'an aversion to join us; a desire to keep his connexion with the Tories, or some management for the Court, or partly all three'. Hardwicke did not know, but he was sure that such conduct was useless for opposition, and so perhaps the Whigs had better lie low for the time being.[1] Newcastle was not slow to read the signs, nor perhaps to interpret them. 'I have every day', he commented, 'more reason to fear that Lord Hardwicke's sons are all against me'.[2] Charles's ambitions were breaking the Whig solidarity; he and his family were following a private path of their own to what they hoped was a land bursting with coronets and woolsacks.

(vi)

Such was the position when Parliament met after the Christmas holidays—Bute and Fox were in the ascendant, Pitt in retirement and the Whigs in pieces. There was little business done. The Government were waiting for the definitive Treaty of Paris which, possibly because of Pitt's attack, was still hanging fire. It was not signed until 10th February (1763). But the pause was fruitful, since it enabled Halifax to come to an agreement with France for the immediate restoration of the captured Prussian towns in return for a guarantee of Dutch neutrality.[3] This was a commendable effort on the part of Halifax to retrieve some of Bute's errors, and, for all that it had little effect.in pacifying Frederick—whom Bute chose this moment to call the 'scourge of mankind'[4]—it did assist the Prussian negotiations with Austria which led to the

---

[1] Hardwicke to Newcastle, 2nd February 1763. Add. MSS. 32,946.
[2] Newcastle to Devonshire, 5th February 1763. Add. MSS. 32,946.
[3] Halifax to Mitchell and Bedford, 15th January 1763. Add. MSS. 6,821.
[4] Bute to Lowther, 3rd February 1763. H.M.C. Lonsdale MSS.

Treaty of Hubertsburg. With the signature of that Treaty on the
15th February 1763 the Seven Years' War ended.

The return of peace brought its own problems. Some of them,
such as the administration of our new possessions, were too
complicated to be dealt with out of hand; time would be needed
to evolve a system. But there were other problems which demanded prompt attention, as, for instance, the reduction of the
armed forces and the pressing question of finance. Bute was to
tinker with both before the session ended.

Early in March the army estimates were submitted. The Whigs
felt that they would be on popular ground in pressing for large
cuts, especially in America. What need could there be for big
armies in a continent cleared of the enemy? Judge, then, of their
'amazement' when they heard that Pitt was actually coming to
town 'to support every part of the Court plan'.[1] It pained them
to forgo their point—grounds for opposition were desperately
hard to find—but clearly no view on military matters could be
sustained against Pitt's authority. Perforce, they toned their
speeches down, to avoid 'giving him any disgust or cause of
discontent'.[2] It was a gesture which, however reluctantly given,
was not to be without its effect.

In Pitt's eyes, the army was no fit subject for political manœuvre; its numbers, its location, its equipment and training
must be decided on national grounds. We had suffered too often
in the past from premature disarmament, and must be cautious
now—a warning given with all the greater conviction because
Pitt believed that the peace, so recently signed with such a beating
of ministerial drums, was 'hollow and insecure and would not
last ten years'.[3] History was to show, in his own lifetime, how
nearly exact his estimate was. Feeling so strongly on these points,
he not only supported the Government's proposals, but wanted
to go farther. Stronger forces were desirable in many directions,
as for instance Minorca and Gibraltar. In particular he insisted
that more troops should be allotted to America.[4] Why he singled
out America has not been recorded. His wishes ran counter to
Government and Whig opinion alike, but, as so often in Pitt's case,
were prophetic. Even while he was speaking, Pontiac, the most

---

[1] Newcastle to Hardwicke, 3rd March 1763. Add. MSS. 32,947.
[2] Newcastle to Devonshire, 5th March 1763. Add. MSS. 32,947.
[3] Walpole, *George III*, I, 195.
[4] West's *Paper*, 23rd March 1763. Add. MSS. 32,947.

subtle and far-seeing of Red Indian chiefs, hoping to drive out the English as the English had driven out the French, was secretly sending the wampum belt and the blood-stained tomahawk from village to village, to summon the tribes to war. His great blow against the paleface, timed for that very May 1763, was for over two years to strain Amherst's exiguous forces almost to breaking point.[1] The strain might have been less if Pitt had been given his way. So much for the army estimates.

Three days later (7th March) the Budget was opened by Sir Francis Dashwood—the 'honest quiet man' of Bute's choice. (*See p. 63*). His appointment as Chancellor of the Exchequer was more than a mistake; it was a shame. No period more surely demands financial skill than the transition from war to peace, and Dashwood possessed no spark of it. He was a roistering man-about-town, with no morals and not many virtues, except a quizzical good humour and a careless courage. Until Bute sought him out, his one ambition had been to excel in the more immodest forms of lewdness. And now this dunderheaded black sheep was called upon to settle the country's finances disordered by seven years of war. He had no glimmering hope of success, and his failure was heightened by his unsavoury reputation, though mitigated for us by his naïve admission that people would call him the worst Chancellor that ever appeared.[2] He fathered three measures— perhaps none of them legitimate offspring of his own brain— which brought him into conflict with Pitt. He raised a government loan for three and a half million pounds by private treaty, giving unduly profitable terms to a favoured few; he allowed Bute and Fox to fill with their own friends vacancies in regiments about to be disbanded, so increasing the number of officers entitled to half pay; and he included in his budget a tax on cider. Pitt disapproved of all three; the first was corruption unadulterated; the second was not only bad economy but hard on existing half-pay officers; and the third extended or seemed to extend the laws of excise to private houses. Pitt's speech was comparatively mild, for under proper conditions he preferred excise to customs,[3] but when George Grenville came to Dashwood's help, he retorted with all the acrimony of severed friendship, 'belabouring him',

[1] Parkman, *Conspiracy of Pontiac*, I, 203.
[2] Walpole, *George III*, I, 198.
[3] West's *Paper*, 23rd March 1763. Add. MSS. 32,947.

as Rigby said, 'with ridicule and wit and misrepresentation,
beyond what I ever heard him do before.'[1] The Whigs were
delighted; they became spirited and gay; so potent was the effect
of 'putting themselves under Pitt's management'.[2] It seemed not
impossible that Dashwood and Grenville between them had united
Pitt and the Whigs. Temple thought so; he told Newcastle in high
glee that 'what he had been about unsuccessfully for six months, is
now come about as it were of itself; that nothing could be better;
that his wishes and desires were fully answered'.[3] There were
dinner parties at which Pitt and Temple sat down with the Whig
magnates, and plans and stratagems were discussed. Even when
the Commons had passed the bill, the fight continued in the Lords.
Pitt was full of encouragement; 'he thought the opportunity was
a good one, especially if the Cyder Lords continued warm;' and
urged the signing of 'a well-drawn protest, strong in argument'.[4]
The Lords were sufficiently stirred and on 30th March 'for the
first time divided upon a money bill'.[5] But without success; Bute
won the day by 62 votes to 38.

Failure seemed likely to shake the new-formed Opposition to
pieces, for it was at best a brittle thing. The Lords squabbled over
the protest which Pitt had suggested. A few signed, but more
refused, and justified themselves by recalling how Pitt had differed
from them on the army estimates and had 'overruled that point by
his own single opinion to the dissatisfaction of numbers'. Hardwicke went further, reviving the old grievance about the Habeas
Corpus Bill[6] which Pitt had introduced in 1758 'against the opinion
of all of us, and without communication with any of us'.[7] It was
no easier now than it had been for Pitt and the Whigs to run in
double harness; their views and aims were too divergent. But
before they had time to fall apart, the unexpected happened. On
the 8th April (1763) Bute resigned.

[1] Rigby to Bedford, 10th March 1761. Bedford Corr. III, 218.
[2] *Ibid.*
[3] Newcastle to Hardwicke, 11th March 1763. Add. MSS. 32,947.
[4] Rockingham to Newcastle, 26th March 1763. Add. MSS. 32,947.
[5] Phillimore, II, 638.
[6] See my *Pitt and the Seven Years' War*, p. 258.
[7] Hardwicke to Newcastle, 1st April 1763. Add. MSS. 32,948.

VII

THE WILKES AFFAIR

(i)

THOUGH BUTE'S resignation took the world by surprise, it was
not a sudden resolve; it had been maturing for some time.
According to Walpole, Bute had two reasons: 'he pleads to the
world bad health; to his friends, more truly, that the nation was
set at him'.[1] In other words, in accordance with Pitt's expectation,
England had extruded the Minister who was also a Favourite. But
there was a further reason, more deep-seated and perhaps ultimately
more important—a subtle change in Bute's relations with the
King. Those relations had always been over-emotional and un-
wholesome, and Bute had been perspicacious enough to realise
that they might alter when George married.[2] The danger materialised in the shape of Princess Charlotte of Mecklenburg-Strelitz.
When she arrived in England (7th September 1761), as the
Queen-to-be, she was a cheerful, high-spirited girl of seventeen,
with no pretensions to beauty and no interest in statecraft, but
with a pretty mixture of submissiveness and self-will which George
found altogether entrancing. George took to marriage joyously;
and Bute, noting the fact, was foolish enough to be jealous.
Worse still, trying to bring the girl under his control, as formerly
he had brought the Dowager Princess,[3] he interfered in matters
that were no concern of his, such as the visits of the Queen's
brothers, or her purchase of a new Court dress.[4] The two became
mutually antagonistic, so much so that even when the Queen had
reason to thank him, she would do it indirectly through the
King,[5] and then run away to disparage him to her ladies-in-
waiting.[6] Charlotte's influence, albeit nothing but the prejudice

[1] Walpole to Montagu, 8th April 1763.
[2] Sedgwick, p. 4.
[3] 'The Queen, her brother and the brothers of the King were taught to feel their
total want of credit'. Walpole, I, 110.
[4] Devonshire's Diary, 31st December 1761 and 5th April 1762.
[5] See e.g. Sedgwick, p. 90.
[6] John Yorke to Royston, 3rd May 1763. Add. MSS. 35,374.

of a teenager, was bound to have its effect; Bute noted before long that though he still received ardent letters from George, he 'never saw the King but in a morning' and 'was only treated as a Minister'.[1] Charlotte in fact, was a disruptive force. By absorbing the King's leisure she was loosening Bute's hold on him, and not the less surely because she was acting without premeditation. This change in the atmosphere at Court, coming on top of the ferment in the country, the coolness of his colleagues and the growing opposition in Parliament, emphasised for Bute the loneliness of his position and added to the strain of responsibility which had already affected his health. He wished to relieve that strain. He may, too, genuinely have thought that, with the return of peace, government could, as he said, 'be managed by a child',[2] and that it was no longer incumbent on him to shelter the King from an infuriated people. On the contrary, with his disappearance the storms of popular resentment would die down, and, in such troubles as might arise, it would still be possible for him to stretch out a guiding hand from behind the curtain. For though Bute wanted to retire, he had not lost the itch to be a schoolmaster; he had made up his mind that if he must forgo the splendours of rule, he would not give up its satisfactions; he was still to be the dominie in the closet.

Bute had broached the idea of retirement more than once. At the first hint, in the previous September (1762), the King had been overwhelmed with dismay (*See p.* 68), but familiarity was having its usual effect; though the King still felt qualms, he was able to see some advantage. On the day itself, West told Hardwicke that 'it was observed by some ladies yesterday at the Queen's drawing-room that his Majesty never appeared more easy nor in better humour—that he looked like a person just emancipated. This', Hardwicke added, 'falls in with what I observed in his appearance today'.[3] Surely, if slowly, the King was coming into his own! Indeed, as he became accustomed to the idea of Bute's departure, he began to take a lively interest in Bute's successor, and even to have decided views of his own. Bute could see no alternative to Fox. The King struggled against the suggestion with a feeling of moral nausea, but was at last forced to accept. 'From the moment he comes in', the unhappy George wrote, 'I

[1] Devonshire's Diary, 5th April 1762.
[2] Bute to Dr. Campbell, 30th January 1763. Quoted Sedgwick, p. lxi.
[3] Hardwicke to Newcastle, 8th April 1763. Add. MSS. 32,948.

shall not feel myself interested in the public affairs and shall feel rejoiced whenever I can see a glimmering hope of getting quit of him'.[1] Fox came to his relief by refusing the offer. He had done the job required of him in Parliament and now wanted his reward; he must be given his peerage at once and left in peace to grow rich at the Pay Office. He had his wish—possibly the more easily because of the King's horror at the thought of promoting him— and henceforward was known as Lord Holland. But with Fox out of the running, Bute had perforce to find someone else. Still playing the part of England's evil genius he chose George Grenville to be First Lord and Chancellor of the Exchequer. Halifax and Egremont remained Secretaries of State, and Sandwich was brought in to fill the vacancy which Grenville had left at the Admiralty.

(ii)

When the world heard that Bute had resigned, it expected him to send 'the keys of St. James's and Buckingham House to Mr. Pitt'.[2] No doubt Pitt shared that expectation. But there was never a hope of it; in Bute's words, the King had determined on three things: '1st, never upon any account to suffer those Ministers of the late reign, who have attempted to fetter and enslave him, ever to come into his service while he lives to hold the sceptre. 2ndly, to collect every other force to his Councils and support. 3rdly, to show all proper countenance to the country gentlemen acting on Whig principles; and on those principles only supporting his Government'.[3] One point in this statement was of particular interest; 'country gentlemen acting on Whig principles' was a phrase invented by Pitt to describe his own Tory followers. It appears that so far from being invited to St. James's, he was to be stripped of all semblance of a party. But to return.

For five days the Opposition held their breath, and then Wilkes published a defiant notice, giving tongue to their doubts and disappointments. Bute, it seemed, was not bowing to the country's wishes, nor giving place to the country's darling; he was merely, in Protean fashion, changing his form, turning from a Scot into a 'triple-headed Cerberean administration'. As such Wilkes

<hr />

[1] Sedgwick, p. 200.
[2] Walpole to Mann, 10th April 1763.
[3] Bute to Bedford, 2nd April 1763. Add. MSS. 36,797.

and the *North Briton* would continue to fight him. On the 19th April Parliament rose, and on the 23rd Wilkes let fly his first broadside—No. 45 of the *North Briton.*

Wilkes was a queer character who has, in his own words, been 'much misrepresented', mainly because he was one of those politicians whom Bute's advent seemed to have let loose—the politicians without morals. Dashwood (now Lord le Despenser), Sandwich, and Wilkes were all libertines of the first water. As such, they were in marked contrast to the older generation. Hardwicke, Newcastle, Fox and Pitt, however much they differed in standing, ability, or sense of honour, were all respectable members of society. Pitt's private life was beautiful in its devotion; Newcastle atoned for his folly and Fox for his villainy by tenderness at home, and Hardwicke loved his family perhaps too well. But Wilkes had no such cover for his sins. He was now thirty-five, and his life hitherto had been less meritorious than merry. Its outline can be quickly sketched. He was the younger son of a distiller, and at nineteen his parents, as they thought, had settled him in life by pushing him into marriage with a colourless woman ten years his senior. She had some money, and Wilkes used it to set himself up as a landed proprietor at Aylesbury. There he became acquainted with Temple, at whose house he met Pitt. Apart from visiting Temple, his main preoccupation was to avoid his wife, and by 1756 he had not only succeeded in shedding her but also in running through a good part of her fortune, without acquiring anything in the process but the reputation of a rake. The next year he entered Parliament as member for Aylesbury, not because he had any bent in that direction, but because Temple and Potter were looking out for bright young men to support their party. His advent was welcomed by Pitt; it would, he said, give him an opportunity for 'displaying more generally to the world those great and shining talents which your friends have the pleasure to be so well acquainted with'.[1] But for the next four years, possibly to Pitt's regret, Wilkes remained too silent in the House, and a great deal too scandalous out of it. With Pitt's resignation, however, he woke to more serious life. He was no orator, but he could write, and he proposed to oust Bute and restore Pitt with his own unaided pen. It was a magnificent gesture, and was to have extraordinary results.

[1] Pitt to Wilkes, 20th July 1757. Add. MSS. 30,877.

Wilkes's relations with Pitt were to go through several phases, and perhaps were never altogether easy; the two were at once too much alike, and too utterly dissimilar. Both were strong individualists; both had genius, hampered in Pitt's case by pain and in Wilkes's by pleasure; both in their several ways were patriots; and both had the dangerous gift of swaying the crowd. But the great gulf of morals divided them; Wilkes was essentially lewd and vulgar, Pitt aristocratic and chaste. The difference showed itself in all departments of life and perhaps most strikingly in their sense of humour. Wilkes possessed a sparkling wit, full of verbal felicity, which at its best was inimitable, but was too often bawdy and profane and almost always flippant. Pitt could be terribly sarcastic, but was lacking in that puckish humour which the French call *espièglerie*, that lambent play of fancy which dazzles the eyes and tickles the ribs of our understanding; Pitt's jokes were involved and pedantic. His strength lay rather in the majestic and grand, and even more in sincerity and fervour. Wilkes could appreciate Pitt's oratory and Pitt's achievements without reserve; but Pitt was never entirely happy with Wilkes's 'shining talents'; he found amusement in them, no doubt, but was apt to be a little embarrassed, a little shocked. On one occasion Wilkes asked him to procure an appointment for his brother. In replying, Pitt wrote: 'Be assured, I should be extremely glad to promote your desires', and then, when the letter was finished, inserted as an afterthought 'always meaning your virtuous ones'.[1] The afterthought was revealing, not only of Wilkes's characteristics but of Pitt's uneasy reaction to them.

Political papers in the mid-eighteenth century were mostly scurrilous rags. Pitt heartily disliked them, and when he heard that Wilkes was proposing to bring one out, did his best to stop him: 'he expressed himself very warmly against all kinds of political writing, as productive of great mischief'.[2] But Wilkes was not to be deterred. Though he was by no means above exploiting the prejudices of the day, he wrote wittily and well; the paper was popular from the first, and was soon seen to be driving Bute's pamphleteers out of the field. No doubt this had its influence. The Opposition members, according to Wilkes, 'all *soon* warmly espoused the *North Briton*'[3] an exaggeration which

[1] Pitt to Wilkes, 16th October 1759. Add. MSS. 30,877.
[2] Wilkes's Notes in the *History of the Late Minority*. Brit. Mus.　[3] *Ibid.*

may be pardonable but was not wholly accurate. Hardwicke at least never espoused it. Whether Pitt was entirely reconciled is not so clear, but certainly he followed Temple, Devonshire and others, in accepting the gift which Wilkes was offering. He went further, discussing the draft of some of the papers with Wilkes himself. Possibly, too, it was at his suggestion that Wilkes consulted a solicitor, Charles Sayer,[1] on each paper before it was published.

Whoever suggested caution, the need for it was emphasised when in November 1762 the authors, printers and publishers of the *Monitor*, another opposition paper, were arrested. Wilkes, with a mixture of daring and contempt, began his next *North Briton* with Jinglesque consternation—'Almost everyone I meet looks strangely on me—some industriously avoid me—others pass me silent—stare—and shake their heads. . . . Liberty is precious—Fines—Imprisonment—Pillory—not indeed that they themselves—but—then in truth—God only knows'.[2] None the less he began now, if never before, to look to his guard. Amongst other things he examined the form of warrant which had been used. So did Temple; so did Pitt; so did Pratt. The men had been arrested under a 'general warrant', so called because it described them by their actions instead of their names. Such warrants were obviously convenient when the names of the wanted persons were unknown or uncertain; they were issued as occasion demanded by the Secretaries of State, and were not without respectable precedent. Pitt himself had issued two, though Pratt had warned him that they were illegal. He had thought himself justified in taking a risk to meet wartime emergencies, but he could see no ground for using them to suppress pamphlets in time of peace. Such action threatened the liberty of the press, without which Britons, for all their boasting, would be slaves. Only a few weeks earlier Pitt had castigated Warburton for suggesting a general law to prevent literary abuses. Now he repeated his castigation, declaring that 'the sacred liberty of the Press, unshackled by any general preventive law, in any case possible for the wit of man to imagine' was one of the 'objects which lie nearest to my heart'.[3] Looking at general warrants with eyes thus sharpened, Wilkes, Temple, Pitt and Pratt came to the conclusion that they were not only

---

[1] See Wilkes to Churchill, 15th June and 2nd December 1762. Add. MSS. 30,878.
[2] *North Briton*, No. 27.
[3] Pitt to Warburton, 9th November 1762. Egerton MSS., 1955.

illegal but unjustifiable. This, to a man of Pitt's temperament, meant a desire to abolish them. The problem was how to bring the matter to an issue. One hopeful prospect lay in the possibility that Wilkes might be arrested under just such a warrant. Hitherto he had been relying on his privilege as a member of Parliament to save him in any such contingency, but now the four of them hit on a new plan. It was arranged that if and when Wilkes was arrested on a general warrant, he should inform Temple who would at once apply for a writ of habeas corpus, not to the King's Bench as was the more usual procedure, but to Pratt's Court of Common Pleas. On Wilkes's appearance, Pratt would release him on the ground that the general warrant was illegal. So the matter would come before the public.[1] How it would develop remained to be seen, but the springe would have been set.

(iii)

Though Bute had just been driven from office, the King's Speech at the prorogation of Parliament, probably written by Bute himself,[2] was not conciliatory. It lauded Bute's work and ended on a somewhat truculent note, charging members of Parliament to promote concord and obedience to law in their constituencies and 'to discourage every attempt of a contrary tendency'. Wilkes happened to be present when Pitt and Temple were discussing the Speech, and he embodied their views in his next *North Briton* the famous No. 45. Possibly for that reason, the paper was among the more able and temperate of the series. It began by arguing that the King's Speeches were admittedly drawn up by the Ministers; and went on to lament that Bute should have put into the King's mouth statements which were simply untrue. Then followed a strongly argued criticism of the actions for which Bute had been responsible, more particularly the desertion of Prussia, the terms of peace, and the tax on cider. As a leading article in an opposition paper, the effort had much to commend it; but, while imputing the blame to Bute, it did, in so many words, say that the King had been 'brought to give the sanction of his sacred name to the most unjustifiable public declarations' and that the honour of the Crown had been 'sunk even to prostitution.'

[1] For the arguments supporting this theory, see my *Life of Wilkes*.
[2] See Sedgwick, No. 306, p. 218.

George, who was just beginning to stand on his own feet, and whose morals were much sounder than his mind, gathered this charge of falsehood to his bosom, and took it hardly. To punish Wilkes as he deserved became with him first a passionate desire and then a deeply entrenched obsession. For some years, beginning from this moment, this desideratum was to be the decisive factor in politics.

It fell to Grenville's lot to uphold the King's outraged dignity. Everything except the King's wrath suggested caution. Grenville had only just taken over the reins, and with a weak team and strong opponents, his prospects looked bleak enough without challenging popular papers. No one had confidence in him, not even the King. Barely eleven months had elapsed since George had stated categorically that 'he is very far out if he thinks himself capable for a post where either decision or activity are necessary; for I never yet met with a man more doubtful or dillitory'.[1] Bute had chosen him now, and the King had accepted him, *faute de mieux*. Others were less ready. Bedford refused bluntly to take part in an administration 'which I know cannot last',[2] and Charles Yorke declared that 'Mr. Grenville's conduct in the House had shown he could not do the business'.[3] Those were the views of men closely associated with Bute. His opponents were equally emphatic. Apart from Wilkes's strident attacks, Pitt wrote, perhaps with a touch of chagrin but none the less truly, that 'the task he [Bute] has transmitted to his successor is indeed an arduous one. How equal he shall be to it, is less fit for me than for another to conjecture. I will only say that the period of this country's decadence seems begun'.[4]

Grenville recognised that it might be difficult to suppress the *North Briton*, and when not stampeded by the impatience of the King, proceeded with a proper sense of responsibility. On the 25th April the paper was submitted to the Law Officers of the Crown (Charles Yorke, the Attorney General, and Sir Fletcher Norton, the Solicitor General) who, on the 27th gave it as their opinion that the paper was 'an infamous and seditious libel'.[5] Halifax had already drawn up and signed a general warrant for the

[1] Sedgwick, p. 104–5.
[2] Bedford to Bute, 7th April 1763. Bedford Corr. III, 227.
[3] Devonshire's Diary, 9th April 1763. Chatsworth Collection.
[4] Pitt to Newcastle, 9th April 1763. Add. MSS. 32,948.
[5] *History of the Minority*, p. 147.

arrest of the 'Authors, Printers and Publishers of a seditious and treasonable paper intitled the North Briton No. XLV',[1] and was holding it up only pending the receipt of the Law Officers' opinion. Now that it had come, he handed the warrant to the 'Messengers' without noticing, or at least paying heed to, the difference in the description of the libel; and yet that difference was one of those apparently trifling matters from which great events can spring. The Messengers, thus armed, set off on a merry game of catch-as-catch-can, which resulted in their rounding up forty-eight persons, many of whom had nothing to do with the matter. From these forty-eight they heard of Wilkes. His appearance on the scene raised a fresh problem. He was a member of Parliament; could he, by any chance, be covered by privilege? Very correctly the Secretaries appealed once more to the Law Officers. As this was a ticklish question involving a possible clash with Parliament, Charles Yorke would have preferred to give a verbal answer, but the Secretaries, wisely enough, insisted on an opinion in writing. Yorke gave it on the 29th, laying down that 'the publication of a libel, being a breach of the peace, is not a case of privilege'.[2] Hardwicke saw this opinion the next day and though he did his best to support it out of his vast knowledge of legal precedents, was obviously scared: 'the point of privilege,' he wrote to his son, 'is always delicate, and therefore we used to avoid giving opinions in writing'. He hoped that Charles's opinion would not be produced and urged that the Secretaries should be told to consult the Speaker.[3] But by that time it was too late; the mischief had been done, and was not to end till it had literally cut Yorke's throat. For, relying on Yorke's opinion, the Secretaries had already sent out the Messengers to arrest Wilkes.

Early on the morning of the 30th they arrived at Wilkes's door. He demanded to see the warrant, and noting with delight that it was 'general', kept them in play until he had been able to send the agreed message to Temple, and then, in high spirits, allowed himself to be carried off to the Secretaries. There, buoyed up by the thought that he would very shortly gain a resounding victory over them in the Courts, he indulged in a display of scintillating *gaminerie* which nearly drove the choleric Egremont mad and reduced the more suave Halifax to silence. But all good things

[1] *Wilkes's Papers*, p. 25.
[2] *History of the Minority*, p. 148.
[3] Hardwicke to Charles Yorke, 30th April 1763. Add. MSS. 35,353.

must come to an end; and as the writ of habeas corpus which Wilkes was momentarily expecting, had so far failed to materialise, Halifax at last signed a warrant committing him a prisoner to the Tower. In this warrant Halifax, probably without thought, certainly without *arrière-pensée*, discarded the words of the general warrant—seditious and treasonable—and used instead the words of the law Officers' opinion—infamous and seditious.[1] It was one more twist in the tangled skein, and as things turned out, an error from the Secretaries' point of view. Meanwhile, Temple had not been as dilatory as he seemed. He had gone post-haste to the Court of Common Pleas and had obtained the necessary order from Pratt. But either because the clerks of that Court were not used to writs of habeas corpus, or perhaps because it was a Saturday and the clerks were off for the week-end, the actual document addressed to the Messengers was not forthcoming until late that evening. By that time Wilkes was safely under lock and key; the Messengers were *functus officio*, and a new writ had to be obtained addressed to the Lieutenant of the Tower.

When Wilkes finally came before Pratt, he was still under the impression that the point at issue was the legality of general warrants, and under that impression made a short and confident speech in which he proudly declared that 'the liberty of all peers and gentlemen and, what touches me more sensibly, of all the middling and inferior class of people, who stand most in need of protection, is in my case this day to be finally decided upon'.[2] So he believed; but Pratt knew better. The only warrant before the Court was the warrant for Wilkes's commitment to the Tower, and that was in order: 'we are all clearly of opinion', said Pratt giving judgment, 'that the warrant is good.' It would have gone hard with Wilkes had that been all; but there remained his privilege as a member of Parliament. Such privilege extended to everything but treason, felony and a breach of the peace. Had Halifax kept to the words of the general warrant —'seditious and treasonable'—it might still have gone hard with Wilkes; but he had adopted Yorke's words—'infamous and seditious'. Pratt was clear that a libel, even if infamous and seditious, was neither treason, felony nor breach of the peace. He discharged Wilkes on that ground, and in so doing unwittingly crossed swords with

---

[1] Wilkes's *Papers*, p. 30.
[2] *History of the Minority*, p. 168.

Yorke whose opinion had taken a contrary view. The crowd cheered Pratt's judgment with the wildest enthusiasm, but Wilkes himself was not so pleased. 'What', he wrote, 'must his grief have been, when he heard the Chief Justice narrow the bottom, and confine the principle of his discharge to the privilege of Parliament?'[1]

Wilkes was not the only man to be perplexed. Pitt, Temple and Pratt had equally to lament the apparent failure of their hopeful scheme in the matter of general warrants. If, at this point, the King had been less touchy or more forgiving, the course of English history might have been different; but the King could not swallow what seemed to him a further affront. He gave immediate and stringent orders that Wilkes was to be prosecuted for libel at the earliest possible moment, and that 'the opinion of the twelve judges' was to be obtained on the question of privilege.[2] With those orders he made certain that the squinting, slippery, unpredictable Wilkes would not be allowed to fade into obscurity, but would be pushed on into becoming the centre of several tremendous questions—the legality of general warrants, the limits of parliamentary privilege, the liberty of the press, and the function of juries in cases of libel—in a word, into being the protagonist of Pitt's new conception of civic rights and duties against the hidebound legalism of the Yorke family and the King's indignant sense of the royal prerogative.

[1] Wilkes's notes in the *History of the Minority*. Brit. Mus.
[2] Egremont to Charles Yorke, 7th May 1763. Add. MSS. 35,430.

VIII

THE WRITTEN OPINION

(i)

THE STAGE had now been set, and both sides at once commenced hostilities. The Secretaries lost no time in informing Wilkes that 'notwithstanding your discharge from your commitment to the Tower, His Majesty has ordered you to be prosecuted',[1] and Charles Yorke, in pursuance of that order, filed an information against him in the Court of King's Bench, where Mansfield presided. At the same time, Temple, who had openly espoused Wilkes's cause, was summarily dismissed from his Lord Lieutenancy.[2] These moves clearly indicated war to the knife; gloves and Pratt's verdict alike were to be discarded, and all was to be settled by *force majeure*. Wilkes retorted by refusing to appear in Court, on the plea of privilege,[3] and by suing the Secretaries for false imprisonment; while Temple replied by financing the printers so as to enable them to bring actions against the Messengers for unauthorised arrest. The public at large followed these legal battles with a tumultuous and at times embarrassing interest, which each side interpreted in accordance with its own wishes. 'I think', said Barrington, 'I never knew all persons above the degree of mob more united than at present in lamenting the violence with which government is attacked',[4] while Onslow noted with joy that 'the many thousands that escorted Wilkes home to his house [were] of a far higher rank than the common mob', and were indulging in heart-warming slogans, such as 'Whigs[?Wilkes] for ever. No Jacobites'.[5] Whatever the truth about the status of the crowds, there was no doubt anywhere that public opinion was profoundly stirred. A very big storm was evidently brewing, and Grenville, that finicky precisian, was not the man to ride it. One

---

[1] Egremont to Wilkes, 7th May 1763. Wilkes's *Papers*, p. 47.
[2] Halifax to Temple, 7th May 1763. *Grenville Papers*, II, 55.
[3] Speech, 15th November 1763. Wilkes's *Papers*, p. 53.
[4] Barrington to Mitchell, 13th May 1763. Add. MSS. 6,834.
[5] Onslow to Newcastle, 6th May 1763. Add. MSS. 32,948.

week of turmoil was enough. The Government decided to seek for support, and on the 13th May Egremont went on a fishing expedition to Hardwicke. In typical eighteenth-century fashion, they approached each other crab-wise; all was hint and suggestion. The King, said Egremont, was extremely hurt and provoked by the Wilkes affair. Hardwicke admitted that he was not surprised, but 'avoided giving an opinion upon any point'. The conversation then drifted off to 'the general state of things', and both agreed that 'the present violent and disturbed situation and fermentation' was much to be lamented. Slowly they approached the main point. Egremont breathed a wish that the basis of Government might be broadened; nothing would give him so much pleasure; it would be for the benefit of King and public alike. When Hardwicke regretted that certain persons seemed to have been proscribed, Egremont hoped that there was no proscription so fixed as to be irrevocable. True, there were two individuals who stood in a special category. He believed the King would run great risks rather than accept Pitt and Temple; indeed 'whoever should venture to propose it would pass their time very ill'. The fact was, the King had never got over their triumph at the Lord Mayor's show (November 1761); it remained vividly in his memory; he was for ever talking of it, and the bitterness he still felt had been 'particularly revived and aggravated by the countenance given to Wilkes'. Hardwicke's friends stood in an altogether different position; and though Egremont could not bring himself to say so openly, he gave broad hints that there would be no insuperable difficulty about taking them in. Hardwicke made discreetly vague answers, and so the conversation ended.[1]

(ii)

Possibly Hardwicke would have preferred to be more forth-right, but there were impediments. The storm that was brewing was not simply a war between Government and Opposition. There were wars within wars. Wilkes meant different things to different persons, and those differences cut across each other and clashed. To the King he was simply a foul-mouthed slanderer who deserved to be horsewhipped but who, to the King's intense annoyance, had so far eluded punishment; he must not be allowed to escape

[1] Hardwicke to Newcastle, 13th May 1763. Add. MSS. 32,948.

finally. To Grenville he was a dangerous customer who must be quashed for 'the honour of the Crown, and of both Houses of Parliament, as well as the authority of the whole legislature',[1] or in other words he was Grenville's potential destroyer and as such must be dealt with cautiously. But at least King and Government were united in detesting him. On the other hand the Opposition were as uncertain and as full of hesitations as they had been over the Preliminaries; and the main cause of their distraction was the Yorke family. Charles Yorke, in his capacity of Attorney General had given a written opinion on the point of Wilkes's privilege which Pratt's verdict had flatly contradicted. The rivalry between the two was strong, and so far as Yorke was concerned contained more than a dash of rancour. He was afraid of Pratt's abilities, and he resented his candidature for the Woolsack which Yorke had been brought up to think of as his own almost by right of birth. Pride, jealousy and vexation would not allow him to accept Pratt's decision as right, still less as final. But how to reverse it was a problem. It might be possible to overthrow it in the King's Bench; but any such attempt would certainly involve 'setting the two great Courts in Westminster Hall at variance',[2] and in the existing state of public opinion might whip up still further what Newcastle was already calling a great flame and universal alarm.[3] No doubt the certainty of the clash and the uncertainty of the upshot made Yorke the less eager to press on with Wilkes's prosecution. His reluctance was described by Newcastle as 'wise and manly',[4] but possibly his real reason was more personal. The Wilkes affair, when all was said and done, did involve privilege, and that was a matter, as Hardwicke had insisted,[5] for Parliament rather than the Courts. When he came to think of it Yorke found Parliament the more attractive milieu. Amongst other advantages, Pratt was not a member, and Yorke, as Attorney General, would have no one of authority to gainsay him. Nor would a decision in the House create jealousies between the Courts. In Parliament Yorke could more confidently expect to overthrow Wilkes, even if he were supported by Pitt. But would he be? Pitt's attitude, as usual, was a matter of intense interest.

---

[1] Grenville to Lord Strange, 15th October 1763. *Grenville Papers*, II, 134.
[2] Newcastle to Rockingham, 24th May 1763. Add. MSS. 32,948.
[3] Newcastle to J. White, 15th May 1763. Add. MSS. 32,948.
[4] Newcastle to Hardwicke, 2nd June 1763. Add. MSS. 32,949.
[5] Hardwicke to C. Yorke, 30th April 1763. Add. MSS. 35,353.

Pitt had no doubt about the part he should play, but he disliked the *mise-en-scène*. The element of constraint in his intercourse with Wilkes and a certain moral fastidiousness prevented him from becoming a whole-hearted partisan. In general, he showed himself 'very cool and moderate',[1] or, as Hardwicke preferred to say, 'much more prudent' than others.[2] None the less, he recognised, in the Wilkes affair, the makings of one or more great constitutional issues, which demanded solution. There was, to begin with, the momentous question of general warrants, which might at any moment flare into life. Apart from that, Pitt believed that Wilkes was entitled to privilege; he doubted whether No. 45 was a libel, and thought that the attempt to condemn it as such would 'in a high degree infringe the liberty of the press as to censuring the transactions and advice of the Ministers'. More than that, he maintained that if Wilkes were prosecuted for libel, his guilt or innocence should be settled by a jury and not by a judge, since the latter would most assuredly be prejudiced in the King's favour. In thus laying down that—to use the jargon of the age—in libel actions 'the jury were judges of the law as well as fact', he was subscribing to a tenet which prevails universally today, but was anathema to the legal luminaries of his own times. His attitude was therefore doubly irritating to Hardwicke, first because it contradicted Yorke's written opinion and secondly because it depreciated the importance of judges for which Hardwicke, as the embodiment of the law, had the deepest respect. 'My apprehension', he told Newcastle, 'is that he [Pitt] will set himself up as a peremptory judge of Constitutional Law, as he did in the case of the Habeas Corpus Bill in 1758, when he laid it down as a maxim, that the lawyers are not to be regarded in questions of liberty. For my own part', he continued, 'I did not give way to him then, nor will I do so now'.[3] It is evident that, while Wilkes represented for Pitt a constitutional and political problem, he was in Hardwicke's eyes little more than a menace to his son's advancement and a challenge to the law's authority. As such he must be put down.

Hardwicke went to work with his usual mole-like subtlety. At the outset, the Opposition had been 'in the highest spirits', and under Temple's guidance had made up parties to visit Wilkes in

[1] Newcastle to Hardwicke, 2nd June 1763. Add. MSS. 32,949.
[2] Hardwicke to Newcastle, 8th June 1763. Add. MSS. 32,949.
[3] *Ibid.*

the Tower; they were, as Newcastle said, 'very warm indeed'.[1] Left to himself, Newcastle would probably have been infected with their enthusiasm; but Hardwicke, acutely aware of the difficulties lurking in Yorke's opinion, hurried to distil doubts into his ear. He assured him, with all the weight of his unrivalled legal experience, that No. 45 was certainly a libel; and however artfully phrased was certainly aimed at the King personally. He emphasised that while privilege might possibly extend to Wilkes, more probably it did not; and in any event was a matter for the Speaker and the House of Commons, and should not be bandied about while Parliament was up. What, too, was all this loose talk about general warrants? Newcastle, as he must surely remember, had signed a number of them himself. How then could they be called unprecedented, and what sort of figure would Newcastle cut if they were now judged to be illegal? It was easy for Hardwicke to frighten Newcastle who had for so many years relied on his advice; and he was merely recording the expected when he told Charles that 'I could perceive my last night's conference with the noble Duke had produced a good effect'.[2] The ball had been set rolling. Newcastle grew daily more irresolute and Hardwicke more incisive. The doubts which he was deliberately injecting were qualified, however, by the obvious weakness of Government. A change of administration was not only probable; it was becoming inevitable; and therefore Hardwicke deemed it essential for Opposition to preserve an appearance of solidarity. Pitt must not be driven too far, since he must needs be included in any future Ministry, if it was to be stable. Egremont's visits had led Hardwicke to believe that he might have a hand in forming the new ministry. What he hoped to do was to create another Newcastle –Pitt coalition, much as he had done in 1757, but with just this difference, that Newcastle and his friends were to be paramount, while a firmly controlled Pitt was to contribute the popularity which was now considered desirable.[3] Hardwicke's object was clear, however difficult of attainment; the Wilkes affair must be played down sufficiently to protect Charles but not to save the Government; and Pitt's influence with the magnates must be diminished but not destroyed.

[1] Newcastle to Devonshire, 2nd May 1763. Add. MSS. 32,948.
[2] Hardwicke to Charles Yorke, 2nd May 1763. Add. MSS. 35,353.
[3] Hardwicke to Royston, 5th August 1763. Add. MSS. 35,352.

(iii)

Meanwhile Pitt was feeling hopeful. He was not yet aware of Yorke's written opinion or of Hardwicke's machinations. So far as he knew, the Opposition were united and very much alive. It was no doubt a pity that the Wilkes affair had a twofold aspect, and that the Opposition seemed too much taken up with the less important part; but Pitt himself had no difficulty in assessing the respective values of the two halves and keeping them separate. The libel, if there was a libel, was a matter of law, to be decided in the Courts; Pitt was not much concerned with what that decision would be.[1] Whatever it was, the constitutional points remained, giving ample scope for parliamentary action. The more Pitt considered those points, the more important they appeared. From every angle they touched on liberty—the liberty of speech in Parliament, the liberty of the press, the liberty of every individual—and liberty was the palladium of the people. In defence of such a cause Pitt was eager to march in step with the Opposition, many of whom were as eager for his guidance,[2] but he soon sensed that there was an element of resistance. Very rightly, he assumed that it came from the Yorke family, and was centred in Charles, who was still a member of the Government and, as Attorney General, deeply implicated in the legal aspect. Nor did Pitt overlook the fact that Charles was Pratt's rival. In Pitt's eyes, Pratt was incomparably the better man, the better lawyer, the better friend; but the issues were so important that great sacrifices must, if necessary, be made, to lead the Yorke family back into the fold and induce Charles to resign. Charles clearly would do no such thing, unless assured that his resignation would not put him at a disadvantage in the race for the Woolsack.[3] Early in June, therefore, Pitt had a long conference with him, in the course of which he offered, in the event of his having any say

[1] Newcastle to Hardwicke, 2nd June 1763. Add. MSS. 32,949.

[2] Cf. 'Mr. Pitt without whom (and your Grace knows I am not partial) no administration can now be formed that will be either easy, useful or durable'. White to Newcastle, 24th May 1763. Add. MSS. 32,948. And 'my determined plan was to preserve and cement harmony and a good understanding between his Lordship [Temple] Mr. Pitt and us'. Rockingham to Newcastle, 3rd June 1763, Add. MSS. 32,949.

[3] 'He flung out his suspicions that Mr. Yorke stood off, in order . . . to have the preference given him by the King to my Lord Chief Justice Pratt '. Newcastle to Devonshire, 11th August 1763. Add. MSS. 32,950.

in the matter, 'to accommodate the affair of the Great Seal' in Charles's favour, provided Pratt were given some 'other marks of distinction'—for example, a peerage.[1] It was a notable concession, in which one may suppose Pratt had acquiesced. Yorke received the offer coldly; maybe he thought himself safe whatever Pitt and Pratt might do. Nor was there greater cordiality when the subject of Wilkes came up. Pitt expressed his view that the point in which Yorke was directly concerned—the prosecution for libel—was purely personal and legal, and would have no political consequences. Yorke disagreed; as he was bound to do, bearing in mind his intention to use Parliament not only for the overthrow of Wilkes, but still more for the reversal of Pratt's verdict. Pitt was inevitably discouraged, but being still ignorant of Yorke's written opinion, did not give up hope entirely. Indeed he was less despondent than Newcastle.[2] He took such opportunities as came his way to explain his attitude—his indifference to Wilkes personally, his dislike of political pamphlets, his desire to reach agreement with Yorke, and his interest in constitutional points— but the Whigs, with curious perversity, continued to misunderstand him. His offer to Yorke was somehow twisted into a deep-laid but inexplicable scheme 'to play my Lord Chief Justice Pratt against my Lord Mansfield',[3] a thought which increased Hardwicke's irritability.[4] The breach was widened in July when the claims of the printers came into court. Charles had been specially chosen by the King to conduct the defence,[5] and he lost the case. Pratt allowed the jury to find what was called a 'general verdict', and the jury promptly awarded the printers exorbitant damages, to the noisy delight of the spectators and indeed of the City generally. Charles was 'much mortified at his defeat',[6] and not the less so because it was in Pratt's court. But he was also worried. By nature he was a mixture of indecision and obstinacy, and this rebuff made him wonder if his previous attitude of waiting on events had been wise. Would it perhaps have been better to break

[1] Newcastle to Devonshire, 11th August 1763. Add. MSS. 32,950.
[2] Cf. 'This affair of Wilkes, I am afraid, may produce differences . . . amongst some of our most material friends; I mean Lord Hardwicke and his family, Lord Temple and Mr. Pitt'. Newcastle to Devonshire, 23rd June 1763. Add. MSS. 32,949.
[3] Newcastle to Hardwicke, 30th June 1763. Add. MSS. 32,949.
[4] Cf. 'I chiefly fear him upon the affair of Mr. Wilkes, and that his constant inclination to concur with and support my Lord Temple may make him fly out'. Hardwicke to Newcastle, 1st July 1763. Add. MSS. 32,949.
[5] See Egremont to Charles Yorke, 3rd July 1763. Add. MSS. 35,636.
[6] Newcastle to Devonshire, 13th July 1763. Add. MSS. 32,949.

with a Government which seemed to be falling and to join the Opposition openly? He might perhaps now have taken the plunge had not wounded pride rebelled at the thought and the memory of his written opinion made him obstinate. Probably, too, he was encouraged in his obstinacy by his father, who was now receiving frequent visits from Egremont, and felt increasingly confident that he would play a leading part in the reconstruction of the Ministry.[1] In any such business, he would of course look after Charles's interests; there seemed to be no pressing need for him to eat humble pie.

The continued aloofness of the Yorke family, indeed its growing estrangement, forced Pitt to look more closely at his own situation. He was as well aware as anyone that the Government were tottering; he had warned Yorke of it at their conference in June,[2] and it would have been false modesty on his part not to admit, at least to himself, that he might shortly be recalled. He had no intention of accepting office unless the King were 'convinced of the error of his measures'[3] and he himself were given the lead. But what in the circumstances would his prospects be? He knew, from reiterated statements, that the Opposition thought him 'necessary',[4] but he also knew that he was regarded with suspicion, if not positive dislike, by most of the Whig magnates. As he turned the matter over in his mind, he realised more acutely than ever the ill-effects of his previous coalition. It had deprived him of his own party, so that he was now, as he said, 'naked', a fact which Hardwicke noted with some satisfaction,[5] and none of the magnates was disposed to forget. His lack of a following meant that he must depend upon others, and in whatever direction he looked, he saw little hope of a lasting alliance, or even wholehearted support. The trouble did not lie simply in personal likes and dislikes, it sprang from diversities of view. To a statesman such as Pitt, with his wide outlook and his burning patriotism, 'measures' were far more important than 'men', and he would no doubt have been willing to accept uncongenial colleagues; but at a time when political parties were non-existent or at least

---

[1] Cf. Hardwicke to Newcastle, 1st August 1763. Add. MSS. 32,950, and to Royston, 5th August 1763. Add. MSS. 35,352.
[2] 'From appearances at Court, and the preparations made in many great offices, he judged that some alterations would soon take plaçe'. C. Yorke to Newcastle, 14th June 1763. Add. MSS. 32,949.
[3] Newcastle to Devonshire, 11th August 1763. Add. MSS. 32,950.
[4] *Ibid.* [5] Hardwicke to Newcastle, 8th June 1763. Add. MSS. 32,949.

H

ill-defined, and each man formed his own faction, men and measures tended to be indistinguishable, so that uncongenial men usually meant uncongenial measures. The men with whom Pitt might have to work were most of them identified with policies which Pitt abhorred. There was for instance the Austrian party, headed by Cumberland, whose aspirations were at variance with Pitt's belief that we must cling to our alliances with Prussia, Russia and the protestant princes of Germany, if we were to face successfully the united House of Bourbon, supported as it now was by Savoy. Then there were all those who had voted for the peace. In Pitt's eyes the peace was at the bottom of all our trouble. It had left inflammable material in every direction, so that if we wished to be secure, we must send new squadrons to all parts of the world —a procedure which would never be supported by the pacifists, of whom Bedford was the chief; and we must incur fresh expenses when we hardly knew how to pay old debts—a course which would alienate economists such as Grenville. Then again there was the problem of Ireland which was seething with discontent, and the settlement of the American colonies, old and new. Those —and there were too many—who contemplated the use of 'power or force' had nothing in common with Pitt, who believed in healing measures, in the efficacy of moderation, in the need for restraint and wise guidance. Under Bute's and Fox's régime all the old landmarks seemed to have gone, all the old loyalties to have been destroyed. How many of Newcastle's Whigs had deserted him for Fox? So many that Pitt thought it best to discard the old labels and speak only of Revolution Principles. How many of his own Tories still remained true to him? So few that they could no longer form the basis of his party. If he came back, he would recover some of them no doubt, perhaps more than he thought, but in the main he would have to rely on the Whig magnates —Newcastle, Hardwicke, Devonshire and Rockingham.[1] Pitt was far from thinking such an arrangement ideal, for the party would clearly not be his; once more he would be leader on sufferance. But it seemed inevitable, and it was this inevitability which made the defection of the Yorkes so ominous. They were the nearest approach to backbone in a flabby group. No

---

[1] 'His party for the basis of an administration (was) the Whigs' party, to which the Tories and country gentlemen might accede if they would accede to the principle; but he was not for an administration on a Tory bottom, to which particular Whigs might be invited'. Yorke to Newcastle, 14th June 1763. Add. MSS. 32,949.

reliance could be placed on the others. Devonshire, it is true, commanded a measure of respect, but, though he did not know it, he was a dying man with barely a year to live, and was growing weary of politics; Rockingham was young and inexperienced and had never been Pitt's admirer; Newcastle was notoriously unstable, and would be without a rudder if Hardwicke were to withdraw. Any or all of them might leave him in the lurch; none of them was likely to understand him. Perforce he spoke of himself as firmly united with them but he summed up his inward doubts by emphasising once and again, his apprehension of being 'left to play a solo' with only Temple to support him, and perhaps not even Temple[1]—a possibility which Newcastle foresaw: Lord Temple, he confided to Devonshire, seemed willing to 'accept nothing but what should make him considerable in himself, and not to be looked upon only as necessary to gain or keep Mr. Pitt'.[2] Jealousy can be contagious, and jealousy of Pitt was spreading from Grenville to his elder brother!

All this bred doubt. Pitt was tossing on a sea of indecision, when the King suddenly lost patience with his Ministers. They had failed to calm the popular ferment ; they had failed to suppress Wilkes; they had failed to win over Hardwicke or split the Opposition. They were as incompetent as they were powerless and to make matters worse were squabbling among themselves. Some change must be made if law and order and the King's reputation were to be maintained. George was still only twenty-five and a little apprehensive now that Bute was no longer at his elbow. Not knowing how to handle the situation, he fell back on a system of sulks, refusing to speak to his Ministers, and demanding ten days in which to decide what he would do with them.[3] Finally he ordered Bute to sound both Pitt and Bedford. The negotiations moved haltingly, as Pitt would have nothing to do with Bedford and Bedford distrusted Bute. They might conceivably have come to nothing had not Egremont's sudden death on the 21st August made fresh arrangements imperative. Bedford was dropped, and on the 25th Bute had a long conference with Pitt. At his request, Pitt described at great length his views 'as well with regard to things and measures as persons'.[4] Bute apparently found no fault

[1] Newcastle to Devonshire, 11th August 1763. Add. MSS. 32,950.
[2] *Ibid.*
[3] *Grenville Papers,* II, 83–88.
[4] Newcastle to Hardwicke, 28th August 1763. Add. MSS. 32,950.

with what was said and passed on the information to the King, with the result that Pitt was summoned to an audience at Buckingham Palace on the 27th August.[1]

(iv)

Before dealing with that audience we must go back for a moment to Wilkes. His release, on Pratt's verdict, had paved the way for a compromise, had either side been willing. But neither was. The King was full of the unreasoning passion of youth; he had been insulted and his good opinion of himself hurt. Wounded *amour-propre* is always painful, and perhaps most of all to the august. As already recorded, he ordered Wilkes to be prosecuted. Wilkes, on his side, was very much *tête montée*: it is difficult to snap one's fingers modestly at kings and governments. On reaching home he found that his papers had been seized, and promptly wrote to the Secretaries a letter, which he subsequently admitted to be 'unbecoming', demanding their return; he also began legal actions for damages against Halifax and Egremont and the Under Secretary of State, Wood. Having thus answered force with defiance, he found time heavy on his hands; Parliament was not due to meet for some months, and his law suits were subject to the law's delays, intensified by every artifice Government could invent. What he wished to do was to continue his weekly papers, but no printer was bold enough to accept his work. Accordingly in a evil moment for himself, for Pitt and the Opposition, he erected a private printing-press in his own house. Its output was small and expensive, and in the end proved to be explosive. He published a couple of pamphlets dealing with his wrongs; he published the complete series of *North Britons* in book form; and in between whiles he struck off a few copies of a production known as the *Essay on Woman*. This notorious piece of obscenity consisted of Pope's *Essay on Man* altered so as to give an indecent turn to practically every line and was embellished with notes purporting to be by Dr. Warburton, Bishop of Gloucester.

By this time Hardwicke's efforts to damn Wilkes were having their effect. 'I cannot help looking upon this affair of Wilkes as big with very mischievous consequences' he had said;[2] and

[1] Hardwicke to Royston, 4th September 1763. Add. MSS. 35,352.
[2] Hardwicke to Newcastle, 8th June 1763. Add. MSS. 32,949.

Newcastle passed on the thought to Devonshire: 'the affair of Wilkes is a very unfortunate one'.[1] Devonshire agreed; 'as to Mr. Wilkes's affair', he wrote, 'your Grace knows I never approved of it, and it certainly is the most untoward point in our situation'.[2] In short, Wilkes who was in such bad odour with the Government, now found himself being cold-shouldered also by the Opposition. His 'affair' was having the unique distinction of shaking Government and Opposition alike. But whilst he was rejoiced to worry the Government, he took the Opposition's disparagement amiss and towards the end of July showed his displeasure by decamping to France. Harmless as this move seemed, it was in fact disastrous. It left the citadel undefended, and the enemy promptly moved in.

From the moment of his release, the Government had been moving heaven and earth to circumvent him, and just about this moment they got wind of his private edition of the *Essay*. From what they heard of it, they felt sure that it would prove his heel of Achilles, if only they could obtain a copy and publish it to the world. How to obtain it was a problem, but they found a fitting agent in a needy and disreputable parson of the name of Kidgell. Wilkes had given strict injunctions that only twelve copies were to be printed, for the private delectation of his boon companions; but, in fact, the head workman, Curry, had printed an extra copy for himself. It was this copy which Kidgell believed he could secure, especially now that Wilkes was out of the way. Curry was plied with every sort of temptation but at first proved reluctant. Towards the end of August, however, the prospect grew brighter, and on the 23rd Kidgell's go-between wrote to him 'I believe I shall be able to secure the sheets for good'.[3] This letter was written three days after Egremont had died, and four days before Pitt's audience with the King, to which we may now return.

(v)

After his bout of silence, the King informed Grenville that he proposed to make a change. As might be expected Grenville protested strongly. He stressed the point that the new Ministers would demand 'the King's abandonment of the peace, and those

[1] Newcastle to Devonshire, 23rd June 1763, Add. MSS. 32,949.
[2] Devonshire to Newcastle, 2nd August 1763. Add. MSS. 32,950.
[3] Faden to Kidgell, 23rd August 1763. Add. MSS. 22,131.

who made it . . . the sacrificing his servants in Mr. Wilkes's affair, though acting by His Majesty's commands; and the repeal of the Cyder Tax'.[1] It is worth noting that of these three objections, the only really live one was the Wilkes affair. The peace had been signed and no one proposed to overthrow it; even Pitt went no further than a wish to 'ameliorate' it[2] by renewing the alliance with Prussia and taking such steps in the colonies as might prevent the rupture with France which he thought implicit in its terms.[3] As for the Cyder Tax, Bute himself had half promised its repeal before he had resigned.[4] But the Wilkes affair was different. It was a sore point, very fresh and throbbing, and the thought of its excoriation may well have shaken the King. He had long been vacillating, and now, for whatever reason, he changed his mind again, welcoming Grenville back as his Egeria. He had hardly done so when Egremont died in an apoplectic fit. The suddenness of his death shocked the King, throwing him once again into a state of agitated uncertainty which on this occasion lasted five days. The upshot was that on the 26th he told Grenville he had definitely made up his mind to call in Pitt. Again Grenville protested but this time in vain. On Saturday, the 27th, Pitt was received in audience. He remained three hours, and left with instructions to return on the Monday, fully persuaded by the King's manner and behaviour that he was engaged in 'the formation of an administration'.[5] He spent the Sunday at Claremont, giving Newcastle a full account of his interview and summoning Temple, Devonshire, Rockingham and Sir George Savile up to London, to support him with their advice. On the Monday, he returned to the palace and was with the King an hour. When he left, in his own words, 'I carried with me lights of a very different tendency from those which I imagined I had reason to expect. . . . In a word, the thing is over'.[6] Pitt had been rejected and Grenville restored to favour.

What took place at those two momentous interviews will never be known for certain. They were big with a fate as then undreamt of, for on them depended whether Grenville or Pitt should settle the course of American history. Only two persons were present—

[1] Grenville's Diary, 19th August 1763. *Grenville Papers*, II, 192.
[2] Grenville's Diary, 28th August 1763. *Grenville Papers*, II, 199.
[3] See e.g. Newcastle to Devonshire, 11th August 1763. Add. MSS. 32,950.
[4] Almon, I, 466.
[5] Pitt to Devonshire, 28th August 1763. Chatsworth Collection.
[6] Pitt to Newcastle, 30th August 1763. Add. MSS. 32,950.

Pitt and the King—and their versions are greatly at variance. Pitt claimed that on the Saturday he had put forward his views, mainly on 'measures' though partly on 'men' at some length, but with moderation, and showing 'great complaisance and douceur to the King'.[1] The King, on his part, had listened graciously, seemed to be impressed, and, beyond saying that his honour must be consulted, had offered no criticism. Something must have happened on the Sunday, some outside influence must have caused him to change his mind. Casting round for what that something might be, Pitt fastened on the man who had frustrated him once, and was soon to become in his eyes a sort of King Charles's head. He fancied 'that it was my Lord Bute who broke it off at last; that he could not well account for it; that he supposed the Ministers had frightened him; and perhaps they might have something in their power to produce against him'.[2] This theory, though mentioned in Grenville's Diary, carries no conviction; it is quite out of keeping with Bute's character, which was remarkable rather for obstinate perseverance than timidity. Apart from this vague suggestion, all that Pitt could say was that 'if the King shall assign any particular reason for it, he [Pitt] will never contradict it'.[3] So much for Pitt's version. The King's version was quite simply that Pitt's demands were extravagant. Hardwicke, trying to reconcile the two, hinted that the King had wished to split the Opposition by taking in Pitt and Temple alone, much as he had previously in Egremont's talks tried to split them by taking in Hardwicke alone, and in each case had broken off negotiations when he found that they were all firmly united. But, ingenious as this theory was, Pitt would have none of it; during the two audiences he had perforce mentioned many persons, but had pointedly refused to draw up a list and had named not more than five or six for particular places. 'To do Mr. Pitt justice', said Newcastle—though the need for justice is not very clear—'he never once insinuated that his negotiation miscarried, or that the difficulty arose from any objection made to any of the persons who were named to His Majesty by Mr. Pitt. On the contrary, that there was no objection made to any one of those persons'.[4]

In attempting to assess the relative values of these two versions,

---

[1] Hardwicke to Royston, 4th September 1763. Add. MSS. 35,352.
[2] Newcastle's Notes, 28th September 1763. Add. MSS. 32,951.
[3] Hardwicke to Royston, 4th Spetember 1763. Add. MSS. 35,352.
[4] Newcastle's Notes, 28th September 1763. Add. MSS. 32,951.

certain points must be borne in mind. To begin with, we know them only by hearsay. Pitt's is derived from Newcastle and Hardwicke who almost equalled Boswell in their ability to remember conversations; their accounts, so far as they go, are undoubtedly a true record of what Pitt said. The King's is derived mainly from Grenville's Diary which is known to be prejudiced and often unreliable. Secondly, Pitt had no reason for concealing or distorting the truth. He had of course been rebuffed, humiliated if you will; but it was not the first time. Why should he wish to palliate the fact? And how could he do it? The King's case was different. With or without justification, he had changed his mind. That change had to be explained, and the less justifiable it was, the more need to make Pitt responsible.

Where all is obscure and where the ultimate consequences were so stupendous a further suggestion may perhaps be forgiven. In all versions, the King is said to have emphasised that his honour was concerned. How, is not stated, and various opinions have been put forward. But in fact, at that moment the King felt his honour to be far more concerned with Wilkes than with anything else.[1] What had Pitt said about the Wilkes affair in those two audiences? We do not know but it hardly mattered whether he said much or little or nothing. His views were known, and had aggravated the King's dislike. They were a pill which the King would have to swallow if Pitt returned. Pitt had hardly left the room when Grenville came in and, on his own showing, 'resumed the conversation of the former day'[2] i.e the peace, the Wilkes affair and the Cyder Tax—and on this occasion he would have been able to quote the assurance received from Kidgell, fore-shadowing Wilkes's downfall. Is it too fanciful to suppose that Kidgell's hopes were the straw that swung the balance? At least the King told Grenville on the Sunday that he wished to turn all his thoughts toward two points—easing the financial burdens of his people and 'restraining the general licence which prevailed'.[3] Perhaps Wilkes and his *Essay* had more influence on American history than on English. It is an ironical thought!

---

[1] Cf. 'That [the Wilkes affair] seems to affect the King more than any point of much greater consequence'—Newcastle to Devonshire, 21st December, 1763. Add. MSS. 32,954.

[2] Grenville's Diary, 27th August 1763. *Grenville Papers*, II, 196.

[3] *Ibid*, 28th August 1763.

IX

THE ESSAY ON WOMAN

(i)

PITT'S AUDIENCES, though they led to nothing, were not without their influence on the Whig magnates. They had been surprised and not a little disconcerted. Hitherto they had convinced themselves that Pitt had been proscribed by the King, and that consequently any change of government would bring, not him but them, back into power; he would trail in their wake. They looked on him as a tool—dangerous like a charge of dynamite, but a tool none the less--useful for the contribution he could make in the House so long as they were in opposition, and perhaps still more for the popularity he would bring to their support when they were again in office. Their troubles sprang mainly out of what they regarded as his presumptuous arrogance, his inexplicable preference for Pratt over Yorke, his insistence on choosing the grounds on which the Government were to be attacked, and his attempt to impose conditions which 'might tend to make him absolute master'.[1] He must be taught his proper place. That was the burden of Hardwicke's talk at the very moment that Pitt was seeing the King. It was Rockingham's underlying thought when he received Pitt's summons to London. 'I imagine', he wrote to Savile, 'it will rather fluster you, as it has done me'. Was this the time and was Pitt the man to cure the present ills? Rockingham was by no means sure.[2]

The audiences and Pitt's account of them upset all their conclusions. The former showed that Pitt was no longer proscribed; the latter that he had done them ample justice in the Closet. It should have reconciled them to him. To some extent it did. 'We are all highly pleased', wrote Newcastle with evident relief, 'with the honest and honourable part that Mr. Pitt has acted toward the

---

[1] Newcastle to Devonshire, 27th August 1763. Add. MSS. 32,950.
[2] Rockingham to Sir G. Savile, 29th August 1763. H.M.C. Savile Foljambe MSS., p. 144.

public and his friends'.[1] Shelburne resigned his post at the Board
of Trade as a protest at Pitt's rejection, and several of the magnates
paid friendly visits to Hayes. Rockingham had 'a very pleasant
interview',[2] and Hardwicke a conference lasting two hours which
was 'very amicable and with great good humour on both sides'.
Hardwicke not only realised that the proscription was off, but
believed that 'this negotiation must be resumed either sooner or
later'[3]—a belief which clearly made it wise to remain on good
terms with Pitt, in whose hands apparently their future lay. He
expressed his belief to Pitt, who with his ingrained truthfulness
and perhaps a lack of guile, begged leave to differ; he 'thought the
negotiation would never be resumed'.[4] Except that 'never' is too
long a time, Pitt was right. He felt dejected. The country, he said,
'is lost beyond the possibility of being restored, the moment now
thrown away was in my judgment the last which offered the
smallest gleam of hope. May it never be my fate again to hear anything of taking a share in the affairs of a nation devoted to confusion and ruin'.[5] It was a passing phase, but like his restless search
for the causes of his failure, it served to underline his conviction
that recent events had made the Opposition's task more difficult.[6]
His despondent, questioning attitude, his brooding over his
failure and his reluctance to contemplate the future, reawakened
the old suspicions in the magnates' minds. They recalled that he
had offered concessions to the King in the matter of 'men'. What
was that but a bid 'to gain the King to himself and in concert with
my Lord Bute'.[7] Surely he was double-crossing them? Pitt
unwittingly added fuel to the fire. He heard that Bedford who
had recently become President of the Council, was 'violent
for driving my Lord Bute out of the kingdom, because he had
introduced Mr. Pitt to the King'. Pitt flared into wrath. What
right had Ministers to force a man out of the kingdom 'without
any legal accusation or condemnation?' What crime was there in
introducing Pitt to the King? And Bedford, of all people, Bedford,
who had himself recommended Pitt to the King, Bedford the
author of the Peace of Paris, and Pitt's abhorrence! But while

[1] Newcastle to Charles Townshend, 8th September 1763. Add. MSS. 32,950.
[2] Newcastle to Legge, 7th September 1763. Add. MSS. 32,950.
[3] Hardwicke to Newcastle, 2nd September 1763. Add. MSS. 32,950.
[4] *Ibid.*
[5] Pitt to Newcastle, 12th September 1763. Add. MSS. 32,951.
[6] See T. Walpole to Newcastle, 21st September 1763. Add. MSS. 32,951.
[7] Newcastle to Devonshire, 24th September 1763. Add. MSS. 32,951.

Pitt's indignation was as justifiable as it was genuine, the magnates construed it into evidence of the cloven hoof.[1] Clearly he was hand in glove with Bute, or at least wanted to be; his actions were guided, not by the good of the Opposition, but by the desire to keep in with the King. They stiffened in their attitude—a fact which Pitt was much too acute not to notice. It increased his fear of being left to 'play a solo'. Not only was Temple restive, but, as Pitt told Newcastle, he had too much reason for thinking that Devonshire and Rockingham, as well as Temple, would refuse to accept office, if the King recalled him. Newcastle could not but agree, adding that the same was true of Hardwicke, but he hoped 'these Lords would see the necessity of altering their minds'.[2] Hardwicke, at least, did not. 'I have received', Newcastle told Devonshire a few days later, 'a very extraordinary and uncomfortable letter from my Lord Hardwicke, pleased with nobody and nothing, full of jealousies and condemnations of Mr. Pitt'.[3] It boded no good for the cause of Opposition.

Meanwhile, as the remembrance of his failure ceased to rankle, Pitt's interest in politics revived, though not without creaks and groans. Newcastle wooed him assiduously, and at last extracted a promise that he would 'take his part', though he declared that he must live at Hayes for the sake of his health, and could attend the House only on matters of importance—'what he called constitutional points and real Whig principles'.[4] More puzzling was the intertwined problem of Wilkes and Yorke. Pitt was tired of Wilkes: 'he exclaimed against him' said Newcastle, 'and the *North Briton* more than any man I ever heard'.[5] But his dislike of the man did not blind him to the fact that the Opposition's hope of success depended on his point of privilege, and that their prospects were jeopardised by Yorke's defection. It seemed impossible to form a united front, and all because of the ambitions of the Hardwicke family. 'Things go very awkwardly', Newcastle admitted, 'between Mr. Pitt and the Attorney General'.[6] Nevertheless, having, as he believed, softened Pitt, and hoping that Yorke would prove amenable, Newcastle persuaded him to go down to Hayes . Pitt received him with cold civility, and Yorke

---

[1] Newcastle's Notes, 27th September 1763. Add. MSS. 32,951.   [2] *Ibid.*
[3] Newcastle to Devonshire, 6th October 1763. Add. MSS. 32,951.
[4] Newcastle to Hardwicke, 12th October 1763. Add. MSS. 32,951.
[5] *Ibid.*
[6] Newcastle to Legge, 13th October 1763. Add. MSS. 32,951.

responded in kind. It was, he said, a matter of concern to him to hear that he had not given satisfaction to Pitt, towards whom he had a 'constant inclination'; he wished to 'live in good correspondence' with Pratt, and was sorry to differ from him, especially at that moment; but in view of his written opinion, he had no option; if it were necessary to express his difference in the House, he would do so in a respectful manner, as though he were sitting with Pratt on the bench.[1] So Pitt learnt for the first time of the written opinion; he recognised its paralysing power,[2] but that did not reconcile him to it any the more. He bade Yorke good-bye with suppressed fury, and poured out his sense of frustration to Newcastle. If he had known earlier, he would not have 'proceeded in the vain dream that some solid union upon real Revolution Principles and an assertion in earnest of the freedom of the Constitution, in so sacred an article as privilege of Parliament, was indeed practicable'. He ought to have drawn the proper conclusion from the fact that Yorke had lingered on in office 'under a rash and odious Ministry', but now 'this last éclaircissement has given the finishing stroke, as it obliges me to bid adieu to all hope of seeing Mr. Attorney General upon one ground with me and my friends in the notions of liberty and of the great landmarks of the Constitution'.[3] If Pitt was furious, so was Hardwicke: 'My son', he wrote, 'will never submit . . . and if he could possibly incline to it, *I* would be the person to advise him against it. He would lose all character for ever'.[4] Wilkes, in fact, had done what the King had failed to do; he had split the Opposition. The split, once started, rapidly widened. The legal reputation of Hardwicke, Yorke and Mansfield was too overwhelming; one by one the magnates succumbed to it. Newcastle put their point of view succinctly: 'In a point of privilege and in a point of law, Mr. Pitt cannot expect that men of distinction and character will act contrary to their opinion, purely because Mr. Pitt makes a point of it'.[5] More ominously, he told Devonshire that if Pitt persisted 'we must, as was done in the case of the habeas corpus,[6] do our utmost to prevent any ill consequences arising from it'

---

[1] Yorke to Newcastle, 13th October 1763. Add. MSS. 32,951.
[2] 'He saw he was precluded'. Hardwicke to Newcastle, 15th October 1763. Add. MSS. 32,951.
[3] Pitt to Newcastle, 14th October 1763. Add. MSS. 32,951.
[4] Hardwicke to Newcastle, 16th October 1763. Add. MSS. 32,952.
[5] Newcastle to Cumberland, 29th October 1763. Add. MSS. 32,952.
[6] See my *Pitt and the Seven Years' War*, p. 259.

—or in other words, so far from fighting under Pitt's standard they would oppose him openly in the House.[1]

From their own point of view, they had a case. The weight of legal opinion was undoubtedly on their side. Why, as Charles Townshend asked, should they differ from that opinion 'except Mr. Pitt would vouchsafe to give his reasons'.[2] Yet Pitt's reasons were obvious enough, and were of two kinds. On the purely legal side, his position was impregnable. Pratt had given a ruling in open court, and until that ruling was overthrown on appeal or by an act of Parliament, it was the law of the land. True, Yorke had given an opinion in a contrary sense before Pratt had spoken, and that opinion, coming from the Attorney General, had rightly carried great weight at the time. But it was simply an opinion, and no opinion from Law Officers or anyone else either could or should supersede the law. Pitt had no need to go outside Pratt's decision as justification for his attitude; and, *pace* Hardwicke, it would have been no derogation of Yorke's character to have accepted Pratt's decision—under compulsion, if he liked, and only for the time being—and either uphold, or at least not thwart Pitt in Parliament. To insist on his own opinion at that moment was to flatter his own vanity, to flout the law and confound the Opposition.

Politically, Pitt's reasons were almost stronger. The magnates were, or professed to be, convinced of 'the necessity of having Mr. Pitt if any success was to be hoped for';[3] and further, they agreed that 'the whole machine must be directed by him'.[4] In this conviction they asked him to map out the plan which should be followed in the next session.[5] In spite of his doubts of their resolution and constancy, Pitt answered their call; he told them that the only ground of attack which offered any reasonable prospect was the point of parliamentary privilege. But they would have none of it; they rejected his advice out of hand purely in deference to Yorke's opinion, and asked him instead to pursue 'a plan of general opposition'. It may be doubted if they knew what they meant, certainly they could not define it; but whatever it was, such a course did not appeal to Pitt as either desirable in

[1] Newcastle to Devonshire, 2nd November 1763. Add. MSS. 32,952.
[2] Newcastle to Cumberland, 2nd November 1763. Add. MSS. 32,952.
[3] Newcastle to Devonshire, 27th August 1763. Add. MSS. 32,950.
[4] Newcastle's Minute, 11th September 1763. Add. MSS. 32,951.
[5] Newcastle's Minute, 28th September 1763. Add. MSS. 32,951.

itself or likely to succeed. In those days Government was concerned mainly with administration. In Pitt's eyes no one had the
right to obstruct them in the carrying out of their functions, which
is what a plan of general opposition must involve. Opposition
should not be general; it should be precise and particular. The
true function of Opposition should be to convince the King that
his Ministers could not 'carry on his business' because they were
pursuing wrong measures, and that he would be well advised to
change them.[1] That could not be done by obstructive tactics, by
petty pinpricks, or by a *coup de théâtre*. It could only be done by
meeting, and if possible defeating, them on a matter of high
policy. The point of privilege seemed to him just such a matter.
'The liberty of the press', he said, 'was essentially concerned in
this question. . . . When the privileges of the Houses of Parliament should be denied in order to deter people from giving
their opinions, the liberty of the press was taken away'.[2] Pitt's
attitude was statesmanlike, and one may believe that, if it had not
been for the obstacle of Yorke's written opinion, the magnates
would have recognised it as such. But that obstacle remained to
obscure and distort their vision. 'I am convinced', said Rockingham, 'Pitt's only meaning in laying the stress he does upon this
affair, is, from his present inclination, to prefer (in case of opportunity) his friend L. C. J. Pratt to Mr. Yorke'.[3] Against such
prejudice there was no making headway, especially as the magnates offered no feasible alternative. Yet Newcastle still hoped
that all difficulties would be solved if Yorke would resign from
the post of Attorney General, and urged him to do so. After
much havering he did, but with tears in his eyes and a promise to
the King that he would maintain his opinion on privilege against
all comers.[4] Such a resignation could scarcely satisfy Pitt, who saw
that its result must be, not to reconcile Yorke to himself, but to
enhance Yorke's influence with the Opposition. And indeed he
was right. 'Yorke's behaviour', Rockingham declared, 'had been
so great and so meritorious to us, that we were obliged in honour
and gratitude to engage our friends to support him in his point of
privilege'.[5] Twice, at their own request, Pitt had been ready to
lead the Opposition—once on the Preliminaries of peace and now

[1] Newcastle to Devonshire, 2nd November 1763. Add. MSS. 32,952.
[2] Newcastle to Devonshire, 11th August 1763. Add. MSS. 32,950.
[3] Rockingham to Newcastle, 31st October 1763. Add. MSS. 32,952.
[4] Newcastle to Devonshire, 4th November 1763. Add. MSS. 32,952.   [5] *Ibid.*

on the question of privilege—and twice they had melted away from behind him, on the first occasion because of Newcastle's pacifism, and now because of Yorke's ambitions, and in neither case had they offered any alternative which either they or Pitt could pursue. No wonder Pitt withdrew into himself. No wonder the Opposition approached the coming session of Parliament, uncertain, disunited and smouldering.

(ii)

Meanwhile, the Government had not been idle. Directly it was clear that the Pitt episode was over, Grenville took steps to prevent its recurrence. The Ministerial vacancies were promptly filled. Bedford was offered and accepted the post of President, bringing with him the support of his powerful faction; Sandwich succeeded Egremont as Secretary of State and Hillsborough took Shelburne's place at the Board of Trade. More daring, though less entirely successful, was Grenville's effort to become master in his own house. Bute had 'introduced Mr. Pitt to the King', and Bute's influence must be ended. Grenville insisted on his disappearance, and though he failed, if he ever tried, to drive him out of the kingdom, he managed to drive him into the country. Bute retired to Luton Hoo, where for the next three years he played a disturbing, but dwindling, part in political life, as the King's secret adviser.

The confidence induced in the Government by these moves was vastly increased by their success in another direction. At long last Kidgell obtained the copy of Wilkes's *Essay* and handed it to the Ministers. It surpassed their wildest expectations and went to their heads like wine. They became 'very uppish',[1] they indulged in 'monstrous behaviour', particularly Sandwich who 'talked like a madman and with the utmost indecency'.[2] All of them, Grenville included, declared openly that they were 'as sure of their success as they were desirous of it'.[3] They even boasted to foreign ambassadors that 'before the 23rd December l'opposition sera réduite au silence'.[4] Nor was the King less certain: 'the continuation of Wilkes's impudence', he wrote, 'is amazing, when his ruin is

---

[1] Newcastle to Legge, 17th September 1763. Add. MSS. 32,951.
[2] Newcastle to Lincoln, 24th September 1763. Add. MSS. 32,951.
[3] Newcastle to Hardwicke, 3rd October 1763. Add. MSS. 32,951.
[4] Newcastle to Devonshire, 21st October 1763. Add. MSS. 32,952.

so near.[1] With this trump card up their sleeve, the Government planned to begin their game in the upper house, and urged 'fifty-five temporal Lords and eleven Bishops' to attend the first day of the session, telling them that 'business of the greatest importance will probably come on'.[2] Their confidence 'stunned', but did not enlighten, the Whigs, whose apprehensions merely increased their perplexity. Should they support Yorke? Should they follow Pitt? The prospect of reconciling the two seemed further off than ever. Yorke was by now blaming Newcastle for raising Pitt up again when he had been down,[3] while Thomas Walpole, speaking from Pitt's camp, was lamenting 'the melancholy consequences of a second weak, timid, disjointed Opposition particularly upon a plain, popular, and constitutional point'.[4] All was indeed at sixes and sevens with the Opposition.

So the two sides arrayed themselves, the one united, exultant and armed with the poison gas of an obscene poem; the other dispirited, divided, and uncertain what course to adopt. In the welter of the Opposition only Pitt stood firm and settled. 'Your Grace', said Walpole, 'knows how immoveable this man is when his conviction goes with his inclination. He has studied and made himself perfectly master of the subject and is determined to declare his sentiments publickly'.[5] But it looked as if, once more, he was destined, in his own words, to 'play a solo'.

(iii)

Wilkes, meanwhile, had returned to England. His visit to Paris had restored his good humour, and he expressed himself as 'devoted to the service of the Opposition',[6] a devotion for which the Opposition did not feel obliged. They had hoped, with surprising lack of imagination, that his affair might be forgotten, so that if they could not advance against the Government in shining armour, at least the gaps in their seams would not be visible. Their folly was made plain when Parliament met on the 15th November. Wilkes and Grenville both came down to the House determined

---

[1] George III to Grenville, 15th November 1763. *Grenville Papers*, II, 161.
[2] Newcastle to Devonshire, 21st October 1763. Add. MSS. 32,952.   [3] *Ibid.*
[4] T. Walpole to Newcastle, 26th October 1763. Add. MSS. 32,952.   [5] *Ibid.*
[6] Onslow to Newcastle, 29th September 1763. Add. MSS. 32,951.

to raise the same question. Both stood up at the same moment, 'pushing to get the start',[1] Wilkes insistent on his right to complain of breach of privilege and Grenville pertinacious to deliver a message from the King. By all custom the honour belonged to Wilkes, but, after a four-hour debate, the big battalions won and the King's message was read first. It asked the Commons to take the Wilkes affair into consideration, which was no more than Wilkes himself desired. They decided to discuss No. 45 forthwith. Lord North, who was now for the first time and with typical reluctance[2] acting as the mouthpiece of a stronger character, moved that No. 45, besides being false, scandalous and seditious, was insolent to the King and tended to excite the people to traitorous insurrection against the Government. Truly a compendious motion! Wilkes, with bland effrontery and no expectation of success, objected to the word 'false'. When that had been brushed contemptuously aside, Pitt moved to omit the words 'to excite to traitorous insurrection'. His amendment was lost, and North's original motion together with another ordering the paper to be burnt were carried by large majorities. Reporting that same evening to the King, Grenville said that 'both of the divisions were chiefly supported by Mr. Pitt and the latter almost by him alone'.[3] He may well have said so, since it appears from his list of speakers that Pitt rose to his feet no fewer than twenty-one times. Once more he was playing a solo. Of greater interest for the light it throws on the confused thinking of his opponents is a letter written by Barrington two days later. In it he confesses that Pitt's 'present temper' baffles him. 'He speaks', said Barrington, 'as ill of Wilkes and his writing as anybody; he approved the resolution against his Paper No. 45 except one word; but he is very warm on the affair of privilege, which he insists to have been rightly determined by the Court of Common Pleas, and violated by the Secretaries of State. He abused the opinion given by the Crown Lawyers, and treated both the Attorney and Solicitor General very roughly, though the former has resigned, and was supposed to be politically connected with him. I know not what to make of this, in all respects, most extraordinary man'.[4] Pitt was indeed

[1] Walpole to Hertford, 17th November 1763.
[2] See Pemberton's *Lord North*, p. 58.
[3] Fortescue, I, 53.
[4] Barrington to Buckingham, 17th November 1763. H.M.C. Lothian MSS., p. 248

extraordinary, but on this occasion was doing no more than differentiate between a political paper which he disliked and the Government's arbitrary proceedings which he disliked much more. His argument was simple and clear. The paper, for all he knew, might be a libel; he could never learn exactly what a libel was; he was sure, however, that the House was not the proper place for reaching a decision; the question was purely legal and should go to the Courts. But privilege was another matter altogether, and to say, offhand and in the face of Pratt's ruling, that it did not cover libel was the boldest assertion ever made, especially when made for an ulterior purpose. A day must be appointed for hearing Wilkes's complaint and the case of privilege must be taken properly into consideration. Pitt was so far successful that at one o'clock in the morning a weary House agreed to hear Wilkes on the following day.

(iv)

Whilst Pitt was toiling almost single-handed in the Commons, a species of morality play was being enacted in the Lords, with Wilkes as the devil. The House was crowded with the peers and bishops who had been so urgently summoned to attend, and to them Sandwich read Wilkes's *Essay on Woman*. If the Government were relying on the element of surprise, they were abundantly successful. No one attempted to defend the Essay; it was indeed indefensible, and by common consent condemned as 'a most scandalous, obscene and impious libel'. But when the first shock was over, the House had leisure to reflect on the effrontery of the reader, whose life was notoriously profligate and who in fact had been one of Wilkes's boon companions. To see him hold up his hands in horror when he could scarcely smother his enjoyment was intolerable. Before long the disgust at Wilkes's obscenity was swallowed up in disgust at Sandwich's hypocrisy. He never lived it down. But that was to follow. The immediate effect was to abash Wilkes. Obscenity looks so tawdry in the light of day. He was ashamed, and in the ferment of that unaccustomed feeling sought relief in a duel with Martin, Secretary to the Treasury and one of the victims of the *North Briton*. Wilkes was wounded and had to take to his bed.

His wound prevented his appearance in the House on the 16th,

and the Ministry grudgingly agreed to postpone the debate on
privilege so as to give him a chance to be present. In its place they
debated the Address. Pitt made a speech, notable for its moderation. Walpole called it 'obscure'[1] but Barrington hailed it with
enthusiasm, declaring that 'if £50,000 had been given for that
speech, it would have been well expended. It secures a quiet
session; and . . . will give strength and reputation to government
both at home and abroad'.[2] Barrington was not a good prophet;
the session was extremely stormy and the Government almost fell.
Nor was Walpole as perspicacious as usual. The speech was one
of the most diplomatic which Pitt ever made, and in the event
by no means unsuccessful. From his point of view the debates
of the previous day had been remarkable for two facts. On
the one hand the Yorke family had thrown their weight and
their votes uncompromisingly into the Government scale; on the
other hand the Tories and Country Gentlemen had shown an
inclination, definite if slight, to support the Opposition.[3] The
former fact confirmed Pitt's fears that he could place little
reliance on the Whigs, and the latter his hope that he could regain
the Tories. He was sure that in spite of the failure of his audiences,
he had done nothing to alienate the King—a point he maintained
stoutly even against Cumberland[4]—and that his recall to office
was by no means impossible. He must therefore prepare by beginning to collect a party—his own party, the party of which he had
been deprived by the coalition, and which, with the Whigs so
doubtful, was now more necessary than ever. Seen from this angle,
his speech was masterly. He managed to expound his views on all
points, men and parties as well as measures. He began by referring
to his audience with the King. He had not, he said, as was commonly supposed, excommunicated either the peace-makers or
the Tories; his main objection had been to Mansfield; and if he
had recommended the Whigs, it had been as friends of Revolution
Principles rather than as enemies to prerogative. He did not like,
but would not squabble with, the description of the peace, given
in the Address, as safe and honourable; it was neither, but it must
be accepted; and 'it was every man's business to contribute all he

---

[1] Walpole, *George III*, I 253.
[2] Barrington to Mitchell, 17th November 1763. Add. MSS. 6,834.
[3] Cf. 'Many Tories with us,' West to Newcastle, 15th November 1763. Add.
MSS. 32,952.
[4] Newcastle to Devonshire, 2nd November 1763. Add. MSS. 32,952.

could to make it lasting and to improve it, for which purpose he recommended union and abolition of party distinctions as absolutely necessary'.[1] The union which was essential in foreign affairs was desirable in home affairs also: 'He was against reviving party names; but if dissension arose on principles, he must again become a party-man'.[2] The whole tenor of his speech was an appeal to the moderate men of all parties, and a repudiation of faction: it was more particularly addressed to the Tories and Country Gentlemen, and its success was to be seen in the steady trickle of Tories back to their allegiance.

With the Address out of the way, Government returned to the question of privilege. It was brought up on the 23rd November, when the Opposition pressed for a further postponement, owing to Wilkes's continued absence. Government refused, and at the end of an exhausting day carried their point. Yorke on this occasion spoke and voted with the Opposition—there was no danger in voting for mere delay. Pitt was delighted; it seemed as though after all there was to be a united front[3]—strengthened by 'many of the Tory gentlemen';[4] but he would have felt less happy had he known that, directly the division had been lost, Yorke hastened to make his peace with the Government and even began working to win them supporters.[5] He was bitterly opposed to Pitt on the main question. This was debated on the 24th when the Government's object was to overthrow Pratt's verdict and pave the way to Wilkes's prosecution by resolving that libel was not covered by privilege. Though Pitt was suffering severely from gout and could not move without crutches, he struggled up to the House, determined to protest against this surrender of Parliament's rights. His speech is well known because of the attack he made on Wilkes personally. The attack was no doubt exacerbated by moral nausea as well as physical pain, but whatever the excuse, it was unwarrantably savage and not wholly true; it was never forgiven by Wilkes. He said that 'he condemned the whole series of *North Britons*; he called them illiberal, unmanly and detestable. He abhorred all national reflections. The King's

[1] Barrington to Mitchell, 17th November 1763. Add. MSS. 6,834.
[2] Walpole, *George III*, I, 253.
[3] 'Mr. Pitt's look and gesture of joy and approbation was the most remarkable thing in the world'. Onslow to Newcastle, 23rd November 1763. Add. MSS. 32,953.
[4] Grenville to the King, 23rd November 1763. Fortescue, I, 62.   [5] *Ibid.*

subjects were one people. Whoever divided them was guilty of
sedition. His Majesty's complaint was well founded, it was just,
it was necessary. The author did not deserved to be ranked among
the human species—he was the blasphemer of his God and the
libeller of his King. He had no connection with him. He had no
connection with any such writer. He neither associated nor
communicated with any such.'[1] But the savagery enhanced rather
than weakened his main argument. He declared that the surrender
of privilege was highly dangerous to the freedom of Parliament,
since it placed every member at the mercy of the executive. It was
not only dangerous, it was also unnecessary—doubly unnecessary,
first because Wilkes had waived his privilege, and secondly
because Parliament would always hand over offending members
to justice. They had always done so in the past and they would
always do so in the future. In the particular case of Wilkes they had
already condemned his paper as a libel. The motion to surrender
the privilege was useless for present purposes, might not be
binding on future parliaments, and was in any event a betrayal
of the people's liberties by menacing their representatives. Pitt's
efforts were in vain. Parliament gave up their privilege and Pitt
retired to Hayes to remain there broken in health and suffering
agonies for the next two months.

Whilst he was absent the Wilkes affair took several curious turns.
On the 3rd December the hangman's attempt to burn No. 45
resulted in a riot at the Royal Exchange. Harley, the City Sheriff,
had his head broken and his coach damaged; the paper was
rescued, and a jack-boot and petticoat—the old symbols of Bute
and the Dowager Princess—were burnt instead. On the 6th, Wilkes
won his case against Wood, being awarded £1,000 damages, amid
scenes of wild jubilation. On the 24th he escaped over to France,
to the relief of the Ministers, who hoped that his flight would put
an end to him as a political force. And finally, on the 20th January
(1764) he was expelled from the House.

(v)

His disappearance, however, was not the end of the matter.
The House had still to consider his complaint that his arrest and
the seizure of his papers had been illegal because made under a

[1] Almon, I, 497.

general warrant. Pitt had insisted on the debate; he wanted general warrants to be condemned as unconstitutional, repugnant to law and a menace to liberty. But others fought shy of the matter. The Government wished to forget the whole episode; they had had their fill of Wilkes; and the magnates feared that legal arguments might result in a further clash between Pitt and Yorke. They believed that in the union of those two men lay their only hope of success and the continued coolness between them bred a sense of impotence and irritation which tended to break the Opposition into two factions—a Yorke-ist and a Pittite. 'The great point', said Newcastle, 'is not yet settled, whether Charles Yorke and his family will *come into the Opposition at all* on any consideration or reconciliation';[1] and the reason was not far to seek: 'let us flatter ourselves never so much, there can be no solid union with the Yorke family except Charles Yorke has the Great Seal, and my Lord Royston some good employment'.[2] As Newcastle had known Charles from the day of his birth, his opinion must carry weight. Yorke himself went far to justify it by complaining to Grenville —clearly with the hope of being re-employed—that the exigency of the times had '*whirled* him out of so eminent and advantageous a post in the law' [i.e. the post of Attorney General].[3] If Newcastle was a Pittite—by conviction rather than inclination—Rockingham and Devonshire were thoroughgoing Yorke-ists. Neither of them was well disposed towards Pitt; both were at best only reluctant admirers. 'The chief difficulty', said Rockingham, 'will not be with Mr. Yorke'; all would go well if Pitt would only be reasonable.[4] Devonshire agreed, lamenting 'the almost certainty that Mr. Pitt will not do right'.[5]

The trouble, of course, was the old trouble of the Chancellorship. Yorke fancied himself for the reversion, while Pitt favoured Pratt. Pitt has been blamed for making what has been called a cardinal point of obtaining the Great Seal for Pratt; though curiously enough Yorke's insistence on obtaining it for himself has not been similarly censured. But the fact remains that this was not Pitt's original attitude; it was one to which he was driven, perhaps too quickly, perhaps too willingly, but driven all the

[1] Newcastle to Devonshire, 27th December 1763. Add. MSS. 32,954.
[2] Newcastle to Devonshire, 21st December 1763. Add. MSS. 32,954.
[3] Grenville's Diary, 17th December 1763. *Grenville Papers*, II, 239.
[4] Newcastle to Devonshire, 29th December 1763. Add. MSS. 32,954.
[5] Devonshire to Newcastle, 2nd January 1764. Add. MSS. 32,955.

same. Throughout his career he had frequently found his views traversed by lawyers—particularly Mansfield and Hardwicke. If he ever returned to power, he would need a legal champion to set against them, and the two possible candidates were Yorke and Pratt. Pitt had always admired Pratt, and it was neither wrong nor unbecoming that he should wish to see him on the woolsack, especially while Hardwicke was still alive. Yet in spite of his preference, he did not at the outset make a cardinal point of it. On the contrary, anxious to secure a united front on the first great question which arose—the question of privilege—he had, though much the older man and by far the more distinguished, made several approaches to Yorke, with offers that gave him all he desired, so far as it lay in Pitt's power. Yorke had rejected those advances, partly no doubt because he believed his opinion on privilege to be right, but also clearly because he believed his prospects to be better in the Government camp than in the ranks of Opposition; he had been, and still was, running with the hare and hunting with the hounds, which was very obvious to Pitt and did not prepossess him in Yorke's favour. Yet even at this late date, and in spite of rebuffs, Pitt was still prepared to yield to his wishes, provided Pratt was 'first satisfied and made it his own act and desire'—a consummation which Newcastle, after consulting Pratt himself, thought by no means impossible.[1] But Yorke, who was now fishing in Government waters, would have none of it: 'indeed, my Lord', he told Newcastle, 'I do not see my way'.[2] Whether he would 'come into opposition at all' rested upon the view he took of his chances. The fact that his opinion on privilege had been endorsed by so large a majority had gone to his head; he thought he was on the royal road; he declined to discuss the matter with Newcastle, and when Pitt spoke of him with civility, boasted that this was due to 'the impression Mr. Yorke's speech had made upon Mr. Pitt, and which, Mr. Pitt saw, it had made upon the House'.[3] Pitt had done as much as could be expected, and if Yorke would not respond, he was not to blame; nor was it unreasonable of him, having tried and failed with Yorke, to return to his first love, Pratt.

The result, however, was bad. It determined the magnates to

---

[1] Newcastle to Devonshire, 21st December 1763. Add. MSS. 32,954.
[2] Yorke to Newcastle, 26th December 1763. Add. MSS. 32,954.
[3] Newcastle to Devonshire, 19th December 1763. Add. MSS. 32,954.

avoid the great constitutional points which appealed to Pitt, on
the ground that such points 'would infallibly be opposed by Mr.
Yorke and his friends; and therefore should not be attempted at
present'.[1] But what to put in their place they did not know. All
they could suggest was 'personal attacks upon the Ministers and
their measures', particularly Sandwich who had laid himself open
to 'some complaint' by his behaviour over the *Essay*.[2] It was not an
encouraging prospect, for though Newcastle thought such tactics
would be popular and meet with general support, in fact Pitt was
very unlikely to approve, and Yorke almost certain to hold back;
he was not anxious to burn his boats.

Yet in spite of this confusion on the one side and reluctance on
the other, the question of general warrants could not be avoided.
Sir William Meredith and Sir George Savile raised it on the 21st
January, the day after Wilkes had been expelled; and, though
Government did their best to stave it off, a series of hotly-contested
debates began on 13th February (1764) and continued for the best
part of a week. Government tried to confuse the issue by injecting
into the general question, the particular cases of Wood, the Under
Secretary of State, and Carteret Webbe, the Treasury Solicitor,
both members of Parliament, who had played a prominent part
in Wilkes's arrest, and now claimed to be innocent, not because
they had acted rightly, but because they had been acting under
authority. Pitt retorted that their case could not be dealt with at
that stage; if general warrants were shown to be illegal, both of
them must be found guilty, though their conduct might be excused on the plea of precedent. Precedent, however, must not be
overworked. All general warrants were illegal, past as well as
present or future, and their use could be condoned only in
exceptional circumstances. 'The real exigency of the case, of the
time, and the apparent necessity of the thing would always justify
a Secretary of State in every extraordinary act of power',[3] but how
did that apply here? It was notorious that in Wilkes's case
there was no necessity, there was no urgency, there was no danger.
The use of a general warrant had been a wanton exercise of power,
dangerous to liberty. Pitt's attack was so strong that the Government majority sank to ten. With difficulty they were able to white-

---

[1] Newcastle to Devonshire, 19th December 1763. Add. MSS. 32,954.
[2] Newcastle to Devonshire, 21st December 1763. Add. MSS. 32,954.
[3] Almon, II, 13.

wash Wood and Webbe; and thereafter, fearing defeat, they thought it wisest to work for a postponement, and on the 17th February moved that the matter should be adjourned for four months on the plea that it was still *sub judice* in the Courts. Pitt opposed strongly, and on this occasion had the support of Yorke —no doubt in part out of a conviction that general warrants were illegal, but surely also because he had been rebuffed not long before by Grenville, and after the close divisions expected the Government to fall—as indeed was the general expectation. But Pitt and Yorke were both disappointed; the Government carried their point by a majority of fourteen. It might have been different had the Opposition been firmly united from the first, or even genuinely united at the end.

Though Government had saved their skins, they were thoroughly scared. It was the King who put new heart into them. He had followed the whole of the Wilkes proceedings with the deepest interest and the liveliest feelings of affront, and now showed both his growing forcefulness and his obstinacy by dismissing as many members of the minority as he could. 'Firmness and resolution', he told Grenville, 'must now be shown, and no one's friend saved who has dared to fly off; this alone can restore order, and save this country from anarchy. . . . I hope in a fortnight that those who have deserted may feel that I am not to be neglected unpunished'.[1] George had drunk too deeply at Fox's fount! A number of men were dismissed and began to rally round Pitt.

[1] George III to Grenville, 18th February 1764. *Grenville Papers*, II, 267.

X

GRENVILLE LOOKS AT AMERICA

(i)

GEORGE GRENVILLE was intolerably conceited, and to make matters worse, added to his conceit an excessive measure of those faults which often go with it—obstinacy, rancour, resentment, an implacable temper, an inability to forget or forgive. 'All his passions', said Walpole, 'were expressed by one livid smile';[1] and to this day his defects can be seen in the small eyes, the thin lips and the sneering expression of his portraits. Yet he had his gifts, which might have been notable, had he not lacked that great gift of the humble, the capacity to laugh at himself. He was too arid, too obstinate, and even in his better moments too prone to be swayed by bloodless abstractions such as logic and justice, forgetting that the great lever of this world is a forgiving and fructifying love which tempers justice with mercy and sweetens logic with laughter. His abilities were fashioned on the lines of his character—the plodding, persevering, pedestrian abilities, which are always essential but never brilliant. 'He was', said Walpole, 'confessedly, the ablest man of business in the House of Commons', by which he meant the ablest financier. Perhaps it was not very difficult to shine among Chancellors such as Dashwood and Lyttelton, but undoubtedly Grenville had a good grasp of economics as then understood, and possibly a better knowledge of the mechanics of government than most of his contemporaries. Certainly he toiled to make himself perfect; blue books were or should have been his favourite reading.

Now that Wilkes was out of the way, Grenville brought his precise and rigid mind to bear on the country's finances. Pitt's war, as he was never tired of saying, had been expensive and even extravagant; the national debt stood at the appalling figure of £148 millions. Something must be done. He approached the problem with a genuine desire to do his best for his country. In

---

[1] Walpole, *George III*, I, 215.

his own way he was patriotic, but, in keeping with his narrow and almost fanatical character, his patriotism was deep rather than broad, intense rather than inclusive; it was confined strictly to England, and perhaps not even England but only that portion of it which was Whiggish. Unlike Pitt, he took little or no account of the Empire, except from the bleakly statistical angle; and unfortunately in the mechanical marshalling of statistics he was none too accurate.

In 1768 a pamphlet appeared, entitled *The Present State of the Nation*. It was written by one William Knox, under the inspiration, and with the help of, Grenville. Nowadays it is known, if at all, through Burke's more famous answer.[1] Burke tore it to shreds, and assuming that the real author was Grenville, accused him of drawing an exaggerated picture because 'he finds himself out of power; and this condition is intolerable to him'.[2] Yet its inadequacy and the author's motives do not prevent it from being a true representation of Grenville's mind. Even if Burke is right in saying that 'the optics of that politician must be of a strange conformation who beholds everything in this distorted shape',[3] it still remains a fact that Grenville guided himself and, unfortunately, the country by what his optics saw. The pamphlet, therefore, has more than a passing interest for the historian, and a few quotations may not be out of place.

It begins with a highly paradoxical account of the effects of the war on English and French finances, from which it appears that England was hurt by all her successes and France benefited by all her disasters. Except as a forerunner of the modern—erroneous— conviction that no one gains by a war, the account is of course absurd. But the pamphlet comes much nearer truth than Burke is prepared to allow when it describes the pains and problems of inflation after a world-wide war. There is a disagreeably familiar ring for modern ears in such passages as 'the effects of the prodigious revenue drawn from the people since the last peace, already begin to shew themselves in the increased price of labour and the necessaries of life. It cannot be long before they operate upon our manufactures also, and, by raising their price, diminish our exports; and our imports, either open or clandestine, will, from the same cause, be augmented. Both ways the balance in favour of Great

---

[1] *Observations on a Late Publication intituled the Present State of the Nation.*
[2] *Observations*, p. 283.   [3] *Ibid.* p. 244.

Britain will be reduced'.[1] Grenville may have been, as Burke
thought, influenced by personal ends to paint too black a picture,
but it is not unreasonable to suppose that he was worried by the
inflation which he saw on all sides and genuinely pessimistic as to
the future. He would not have been the first or the last to be afflicted
by such feelings. Whatever his motives, he looked round not only
for methods of retrenchment, but also for fresh sources of revenue.
He found the latter in Ireland and America. It was, he wrote, 'a
consolatory reflection to Great Britain, that the members of her
Empire were in much happier circumstances than herself'.[2]
Compared with the £75 millions which England had been forced
to borrow during the war, Ireland had borrowed a mere million,
and America no more than £2,600,000; and, even so, as the
Americans proposed to pay off their debt in five years, Grenville
persuaded himself, by some quirk, that it was not so much a debt
as 'anticipations of their revenue'.[3] America, so Grenville argued,
had benefited enormously by the war and could well afford to
contribute towards the cost of her future defence. In return for her
contributions she should be represented at Westminster. Ireland
was in a slightly different position, and though she also ought to
contribute, deserved to be given some *quid pro quo*. Hitherto she
had been regarded as a colony, but now that the number of the
colonies had been so strikingly augmented, the members were
beginning to outweigh the head;[4] to preserve a proper balance, it
might be as well to incorporate Ireland with Great Britain, at least
to the extent of allowing her a share in the colonial trade.[5] Burke
made great fun of all these proposals, but it is in Grenville's favour
that his suggestions, if mistaken, at least tried to be constructive,
while Burke's observations, if wise, were purely negative. Moreover, they came some four or five years after the event, while
Grenville in 1764 had to look into the future and do the best he
could with his limited knowledge and his unlimited conceit. His
view of the Empire was the normal view of his times—the mercantilist view, in which the colonies were to provide the raw
materials and England the manufactures. It was by no means
entirely selfish, nor, as his proposals show, did Grenville rule out
the prospect of some colonies rising from their inferior status to
full integration with the mother country. Where he failed lament-

[1] *State of the Nation*, p. 61.
[2] *Ibid.*, p. 35   [3] *Ibid.*, p. 35   [4] *Ibid.*, p. 69   [5] *Ibid.*, p. 70

ably was in his knowledge of psychology, of which indeed, in its modern connotation, he had never heard. It was one of Pitt's greatest contributions to the idea of Empire that he regarded the colonists as Englishmen with all the rights and all the claims and all the duties of full citizenship. He had an amazing faculty for putting himself into their shoes, three thousand miles away though they might be. That faculty was denied to Grenville, and, one must regretfully add, to the large majority of his contemporaries.

Having made up his mind to raise a revenue in America, Grenville lost no time. He took the first step in the budget which he opened early in March. What he intended to do was to exact a contribution of £160,000 towards the cost of defending America which he estimated at half a million. His method was threefold; he proposed to lay a tax on sugar, he proposed to suppress smuggling, and he proposed that all deeds should be subject to a stamp duty. As a sort of corollary he proposed to keep up the value of American currency by prohibiting the issue of paper money. Neither the amount, nor the methods were unreasonable in themselves, but it so happened that in almost every respect they hit the colonies in their tenderest spots. A few words of explanation may be desirable.

America was a young country. It required capital for its development, and that capital had been and was being provided by British merchants. Naturally they expected a return for their money. They also expected the Government to operate the Navigation Acts in their favour. The original purpose of those Acts —passed in the seventeenth century—had been to wrest from the Dutch the carrying trade of the world, and admirably they had succeeded. But thereafter, instead of becoming *functus officio*, they had been given a new twist, and throughout the long period of Whig domination, had been used increasingly to secure for British merchants and manufacturers a complete ascendancy in the American market.[1] They provided broadly, that all colonial exports must be carried in English ships; that certain exports 'enumerated' officially—and the enumeration could be varied— must be sent only to England or another colony; and that all imports must be shipped from England alone. The working of these Acts, and the need to pay interest on loans, resulted in the balance of trade being always heavily in England's favour. The

[1] Woodward, p. 125.

consequent drain on America's bullion—in modern parlance the
running down of her gold reserves—would have been intolerable,
and indeed the whole trading system might well have broken
down, but for American ingenuity combined with a convenient
and deliberate blindness on the part of the customs authorities.
The Americans, particularly the turbulent northern colonists,
indulged in wholesale smuggling with the French, Spanish and
Dutch West Indies. The system was beautifully balanced. America
smuggled out fish, flour, horses, and timber in return for molasses,
which she distilled profitably into rum, and specie, which she
used to satisfy her British creditors.[1] For her own internal purposes she relied mainly on paper money. But like all beautifully
balanced systems, it had its drawbacks. The forbidden market in
the French, Spanish, and Dutch Islands was much better than the
free market in the British Islands; it offered molasses more abundantly and more cheaply, and it took vastly more of America's
exports, particularly lumber from the clearings which otherwise must have been left to rot on the ground. It seemed an
admirable system to the Americans, but the British Islands
naturally looked with jaundiced eyes on this foreign undercutting,
and the British merchants in England objected to payments in a
currency depreciated by American paper.

It is now possible to see how Grenville's methods hit the
Americans. The tax on sugar was a piece of tidiness which must
have appealed to him. In 1733 Parliament had imposed a tax of
6d a gallon on foreign molasses entering America. The rate was
prohibitively high, and indeed had been fixed more with a view
to benefiting the British West Indian Islands than to raising a
revenue. But the Americans had no desire to benefit the Islands
at the expense of their own continent; they ignored the Act, with
the help of a benevolent official blindness, and exalted the smug-
ling of foreign molasses into a regular, widespread and lucrative
trade. The Act was now due to expire, and Grenville, well aware
of its practical defects, proposed to substitute a reduced tax of
3d, and at the same time new-model the customs service, so as
to checkmate smuggling. Some revenue would come in and the
British Islands would benefit. It did not, however, work out as
Grenville expected. His reforms and the 3d tax—which was still
prohibitive—certainly drove the Americans to the British Islands;

[1] Miller, p. 74.

but the Islands were unable to provide all the molasses required or to absorb all the goods offered to them in exchange, with the inevitable result that the price of molasses soared because of scarcity, and the price of American exports sagged because of glut. The Americans were hit both ways; they grew resentful and indeed well nigh desperate. Nor was their plight helped by Grenville's Act prohibiting the use of paper money. The issue of such money had long been a troublesome point; the Government had tried to restrain it, partly in the interests of sound finance and still more in the interests of the British merchants; but they had been content with control rather than prohibition. Grenville, with his tidy mind and his fatal love of logic, now insisted on prohibition. The Americans were thus faced with the loss, at one fell swoop, of both their internal currency and their specie from abroad. On top of these disasters, Grenville proposed to raise a revenue from stamp duties to supplement the meagre takings through the Customs, though, in deference to the representations made by American agents, he agreed to delay action for a year in order to give the colonists time to suggest other measures more acceptable to themselves.[1] As they could not, or at least did not, make any counter-suggestions, Grenville introduced his notorious Stamp Act the next year (1765).

(ii)

Meanwhile, what of the Opposition? They had been expected to exploit the moral victories gained during the debates on general warrants, but had shown a surprising lack of enterprise. 'Supineness unparalleled' Walpole called it, arising from 'inability and outward disunion'. He supposed that Pitt was holding himself aloof because he expected to be recalled by the King and wanted to avoid being 'clogged with numerous dependants, odious to the Favourite, and distasteful to himself'.[2] Walpole was right in stigmatising the Opposition's feebleness, but he misjudged Pitt. Undoubtedly Pitt wanted to be recalled and believed that he would be sooner or later; but he did not for that reason hold back, nor did he try to shake off distasteful followers. The fact is that his health was growing steadily worse, and after every great effort in the House he suffered a prolonged and painful reaction. The

[1] See *Mauduit's Account*, Jucker, p. 306.   [2] Walpole, *George III*, I, 304.

marathon debates on general warrants had exhausted him. He returned to Hayes 'in the most acute pain',[1] retired to bed and was still there on the eve of the Budget, when Hester reported that though his pains were abated, the doctor 'does not yet advise his being taken up'.[2] His physical weakness however did not damp his spirits. When visited by the magnates, he discussed their future proceedings with enthusiasm, declaring that he was ready for another battle 'whenever the other gentlemen please'.[3] He deprecated anything that might revive disputes among themselves, and voluntarily but vainly renewed his overtures to Yorke. As Newcastle said, he showed 'a real intention to act with us, in the most perfect concert'.[4] But the Whigs were incurably shallow-minded, and, with Pitt *hors de combat*, forgot all about his great constitutional points and fell back upon their usual farrago of personalities and petty intrigues. With a deplorable want of originality, they tried to embarrass Government by moving that a silly Jacobite pamphlet, entitled *Droit le Roi*, which the Government had so far failed to notice, should be condemned as a seditious libel—a species of *tu quoque* which Rockingham induced Pitt to sanction, though he did so reluctantly and on the under-standing that his name should not be mentioned.[5] They followed up that piece of nonsense, which they gloated over like school-boys cheeking a master, by founding an anti-ministerial club in Albemarle Street; 'but,' commented Barrington, 'I hear no amusements or vice going on there; so I conclude it will soon be abandoned'.[6] Meanwhile they blew up the internal disputes, which Pitt had deprecated, when Yorke introduced a Bill to amend his father's Marriage Act[7]; and at the same time stubbornly main-tained their spirit of listlessness towards the world outside. Newcastle who adored an atmosphere of bustle, was reduced to hoping that when Grenville opened his Budget 'matter enough would arise'.[8]

Matter enough, in all conscience, did arise, but the only man in Parliament who had any inkling of its seriousness was tied by

[1] Hester to Newcastle, 18th February 1764. Add. MSS. 32,956.
[2] Hester to Newcastle, 8th March 1764. Add. MSS. 32,956.
[3] Newcastle to Legge, 23rd February 1764. Add. MSS. 32,956.
[4] Newcastle to C. Townshend, 25th February 1764. Add. MSS. 32,956.
[5] Rockingham to Newcastle, 16th February 1764. Add. MSS. 32,956.
[6] Barrington to Buckingham, 26th February 1764. H.M.C., Lothian MSS.
[7] See Shelley to Newcastle, 21st February 1764. Add. MSS. 32,956.
[8] Newcastle to C. Townshend, 25th February 1764. Add. MSS. 32,956.

the leg. 'When the resolution was taken in this House to tax America', Pitt said at a later date, 'I was ill in bed. If I could have endured to have been carried in my bed, so great was the agitation of my mind for the consequences, I would have solicited some kind hand to have laid me down on this floor, to have borne my testimony against it'.[1] That opportunity was denied him, but he did his best to make his views known. Here was a cause worthy of the Opposition, but the Opposition were not worthy of it. Charles Townshend reported, as though it were a strange phenomenon, that 'Mr. Pitt is against *all* taxation'. Charles, as he showed later on, was not against any taxation, and excused himself from taking an active part in the debate, because, he said, 'I saw the face of the House, the absence of our friends, the opinions impressed upon the former too strong to be shaken, and resistance useless if not imprudent'. Yorke was equally anxious not to be imprudent; he thought 'the questions of expediency and regulation arising out of the Bill now depending too speculative and too nice to be much agitated' and he avoided agitation by staying away.[2] The floor was left for such men as Grenville who if well-meaning, was short-sighted, and Rose Fuller, a West Indian planter, who was very clear-sighted indeed and frankly self-seeking. He found 'the American Bill a very beneficial one to this kingdom and most essentially so to the sugar colonies'—but not, one notices, to the Americans.[3] Fuller's attitude throws a lurid light on Burke's remark: 'Why stop at £300,000 ... America and Ireland are much better able to pay £600,000 than we are to satisfy ourselves with half that sum'.[4]

The Budget was passed with ease, and the Country Gentlemen, who saw a prospect of reduced taxation, returned home 'with the greatest encomiums of the man, who in the terrible situation of this kingdom, can pay debts and raise near eight million for the current service of the year, without any new tax or any new loan'.[5]

Having thus, in anticipation, thrown away the American colonies, Grenville proceeded to throw away our allies on the Continent. He demanded the recall of the Prussian ambassador, mainly because he was in touch with Pitt, and kept on demanding

---

[1] Speech, 14th January 1766.
[2] C. Townshend to Newcastle, 23rd March 1764. Add. MSS. 32,957.
[3] Fuller to Newcastle, 16th March 1764. Add. MSS. 32,957.
[4] *Observations*, p. 296.
[5] Newcastle to Legge, 23rd March 1764. Add. MSS. 32,957.

it until Frederick reluctantly agreed; but in doing so, Frederick told Mitchell, bluntly, 'it was not his Ministers but him we were tired of'.[1] Frederick gave England up and, without attempting to revive the proposal for an alliance between England, Prussia and Russia, which he had frequently suggested during the war, and which was a cardinal point in Pitt's foreign policy, concluded a treaty for himself alone with Catherine of Russia.[2] Concurrently, Grenville was irritating the French Ambassador, and indeed the whole Corps Diplomatique, by curtailing the privileges allowed to foreign Ministers of importing goods free of duty for their personal use.[3] It annoyed the Ministers and affronted their governments, but pleased Grenville, whose idea of foreign policy was that England should never court others, but wait to be courted.[4]

While Grenville was thus bedevilling the problems which Pitt would have to face if he were ever recalled to office, the Opposition, from which he might hope for support, was rapidly disintegrating. Death was taking its toll. Hardwicke died in March, Legge in August and Devonshire in October (1764). All three had been men of weight in the Whig councils; all three had been men of knowledge and experience; all three had held high office. They left no one of comparable stature behind. If Pitt returned, either he would be thrown back on the younger generation, on men such as Shelburne, Townshend, Rockingham, Barré, Conway and Grafton, of whose thoughts and views he knew little, or he must accept men such as Bedford and Sackville, with whom he had nothing in common. If death was carrying off the more experienced, those that remained were showing little interest, or even sense of responsibility. Whilst the Budget was under discussion, the Opposition were absorbed in the election of the High Steward for Cambridge, a post which had become vacant on Hardwicke's death. They wanted to secure it for Hardwicke's eldest son, and were stirred to wrath when Sandwich thought he would like it for himself. Regarding it as much more important to snub Sandwich than to support Pitt's views on American taxation, the Opposition preferred canvassing at Cambridge to voting in the House.   When the debate on the Budget was over,

---

[1] Mitchell to Sandwich, 8th May 1764. Add. MSS. 6,810.
[2] Mitchell to Buckingham, Buckingham's Despatches, II, 187.
[3] Sandwich to Mitchell, 24th July 1764. Add. MSS. 6,821.
[4] Grenville,s Diary, 17th December 1764. *Grenville Papers*, II, 533.

all Newcastle could find to say was that 'if Mr. Pitt's health, Mr. Yorke's circumstances, or Charles Townshend's necessary absence in supporting our cause at Cambridge (where he has done great service and showed himself a most admirable negotiator) had not prevented their attendance, the House would have sat at least till midnight'.[1] That word 'necessary' was symptomatic. Personal ambitions and private feuds were far more essential than public needs.

Parliament rose on the 19th April (1764). The King dismissed a few men notably Conway, who had voted with the minority; and Newcastle hurried down to Claremont to forget politics in entertaining. The numbers of the Opposition, and their hopes, dwindled daily. Townshend, back from Cambridge, noted the general lassitude, and pondering the best means of recovering the position, declared that 'the generous manner in which Mr. Pitt behaved to the whole party last year, his name, his weight, his talents all make his concurrence a necessary part of any union; and I should very much fear any plan would be found ineffectual which had not both the lustre of Mr. Pitt's accession of it, and the declared and active support of Lord Hardwicke's family'.[2]

Pitt's accession, as he had shown not once or twice, was easily to be obtained if the Opposition would follow his lead; but having been now for the third time ignored, it was not surprising that, as Townshend added, 'Mr. Pitt seems withdrawn into himself, and retired to his family and amusements'.[3] Pitt explained his feelings fully to Lyttelton the following June; he admitted that he was full of despair, and complained 'that his measures had been unsupported; that, when the peace and his whole plan had been arraigned the day of the Budget not one single man said one word in his defence or in the defence of his measures, or in condemnation of the peace; that he knew nobody who agreed with him; that he did not know who would join with him, or act upon his plan and principles, if there was to be a change in the administration; that all opposition was to no purpose; that, for one, he would never force himself upon the King; that, however, he would oppose all measures he thought wrong, whoever were ministers'.[4] His complaints were justified, but none the less he

---

[1] Newcastle to Legge, 13th March 1764. Add. MSS. 32,957.
[2] C. Townshend to Newcastle, 30th April 1764. H.M.C. Townshend MSS.
[3] *Ibid.*
[4] Newcastle to White, 19th June 1764. Add. MSS. 32,960.

still showed his willingness to respond to any sign of energy by urging Rockingham to adopt 'more vigorous measures'.[1] Rockingham did nothing of the sort; he merely fostered the suspicions he had always felt of Pitt's motives. 'I do believe' he wrote, 'his plan is that those conversations of his should be repeated and that they should be known in the Closet, that if ever a change comes, he may lay in for standing better there than others'.[2] It is evident that Rockingham, who at this time was thirty-four and had never held any office, was beginning to think himself of more account and more likely to be chosen by the King, than Pitt who was fifty-six and the most successful and experienced Minister of the age. This conceit, and the jealousy of Pitt which it bred, were to bear bitter fruit. But that was in the future. For the present the Opposition stagnated. The only sign of life was an attempt by the cider counties to strike a bargain with Newcastle, under which he would press for the repeal of the Cyder Tax in return for support on some agreed 'national point'.[3] The attempt came to nothing, and would not be worth mentioning, had not Newcastle consulted Pitt before turning the proposal down. Pitt's answer proclaimed his dislike of political bargains and his sense of isolation: 'as for my single self', he wrote, 'I purpose to continue acting through life upon the best convictions I am able to form, and under the obligations of principles, not by force of particular bargains'. He hoped that Newcastle would not attribute this reserve to want of confidence in him; he had always wished to avoid being mixed up in bargains or stipulations; and now that no one was apparently disposed to support him in Parliament, he had 'little thoughts of beginning the world again upon any new centre of unions', nor had he any disposition 'to quit the free condition of a man standing single and daring to appeal to his country at large upon the soundness of his principles and the rectitude of his conduct'.[4] Newcastle took Pitt's letter as a final break with the Opposition, which, he said, he had been expecting. Nor should anyone have been surprised. Pitt had been doing his best to rally the Opposition for two years, and it was, to use his own phrase, a 'strange phenomenon in politics' to find himself so praised in words, so neglected in fact. But if Newcastle was not surprised, Cumberland was.

---

[1] Newcastle to White, 19th June 1764. Add. MSS. 32,960.
[2] Rockingham to Newcastle, 15th September 1764. Add. MSS. 32,962.
[3] Yonge to Newcastle, 17th October 1764. Add. MSS. 32,962.
[4] Pitt to Newcastle, 19th October 1764. Add. MSS. 32,962.

Indeed he was furious, and angrily declared that as Pitt had with-out provocation declined their help, they should no longer think of connecting themselves with him, or supporting him in the House.[1] Pitt might reasonably have retorted that it would be difficult to distinguish between their support and their lack of support; it came to the same thing in the end. But Newcastle, with his experience of Parliamentary storms, saw the danger of doing anything to provoke Pitt. Little as they might wish to believe it, without him the Opposition would be a rudderless boat. The only alternative, and a poor one at that, would be a triumvirate of Conway, Charles Townshend and Yorke. New-castle doubted whether Townshend would 'see daylight enough to engage thoroughly', and as for Yorke, he was more elusive and unpredictable than Pitt himself.[2] What Newcastle feared, and it is a point of some interest, was that Pitt, if driven too far, might coalesce with Bute and form an administration more difficult to dislodge even than Grenville's.[3] In this he was, of course, betraying his essential ignorance of Pitt, who had never said or done anything to warrant such a fear. But did he also, perhaps, unwittingly betray the motives underlying the Whigs' attitude towards Pitt? They had never wanted his policies but only his support. In their relations with him, they were like Sir Antony Absolute, no one more easily led when they had their own way; no one more anxious for a leader, when he led from behind.[4] They had destroyed Pitt's party in 1757, and in doing so had not only sapped the foundations of Pitt's Ministries present and future, but had blighted their own prospects, and indirectly shattered the British Empire.

Whilst the Whigs were solemnly ostracising Pitt, their other and more congenial hero, Yorke, was as solemnly ostracising them. The death of the Master of the Rolls at this moment revived Yorke's ambitions and his love of money. He angled for a return to office, but was so uneasy in his conscience that he wished it to be represented as due to the King's command, not to his own solicitation. When that was refused, he bartered a promise 'to give a cordial and friendly support to His Majesty's measures'

---

[1] Albemarle to Newcastle, 24th October 1764. Add. MSS. 32,963.
[2] Newcastle to Albemarle, 26th October 1764. Add. MSS. 32,963.
[3] Newcastle's Memo., 14th November 1764. Add. MSS. 32,963.
[4] Cf. 'Ever availing ourselves of the idea of his connection with us'. Rocking-ham to Newcastle, 23rd November 1764. Add. MSS. 32,964.

in return for a patent of precedence between the Attorney and Solicitor General.[1] Pitt heard the news with a snort, remarking that he had been racking his brain to find out what degree of inconvenience or consequence to any individual or to the public, it could be, whether Yorke was in or out of employment.[2] But Charles Townshend, seeing both his indispensables apparently lost to the Opposition, thought it wise to renew the private advances toward Grenville which he had actually begun as early as January 1764, and was rewarded in May (1765) with the post of Paymaster vacated by Holland.[3]

Pitt has been charged with refusing to lead the Opposition, though they were ready to follow him. True, they were continually declaring that he was essential, that they wished to put him at their head, that they were ready to support him; but whenever it came to the point, they rejected his advice and went their own way with the result that they had disintegrated as a party. Are we, on the facts, justified in reversing the old adage, and maintaining that words speak louder than deeds?

[1] Grenville to Northington, 26th November 1764. *Grenville Papers*, II, 469.
[2] Onslow to Newcastle, 29th November 1764. Add. MSS. 32,964.
[3] See Jucker, p. 302.

XI

TEMPLE'S DEFECTION

(i)

PITT WAS a statesman in the busy world, not a thinker in his study. It was unlikely that he would deliberately work out a philosophy of life. Yet there can be traced one master idea permeating all his thoughts and actions—the idea of freedom. It was no mere concept in his mind but a passionate and eager belief, moulding his principles and guiding his policies. He pursued freedom everywhere and at all times; but being a statesman rather than a philosopher, he thought of it as a blessing primarily for himself, his family, his friends, his country and the British Empire, and only secondarily, and perhaps more doubtfully, for the outside world. His belief in its virtue seems to have been innate, but was certainly reinforced by the facts of his upbringing and career. Eton began the process of development. He found life there cramping and intimidating; he left without regret, and rebelling at the thought of what he had suffered, gave his own children a private education. In religion he clung to Protestantism because in his view 'the horrors of Rome' and her 'idolatrous superstition' were 'the destruction of all civil and religious liberty'.[1] When he entered politics, the circumstances of his times made it inevitable that he should do so as a Whig. But he soon gave his Whiggism a personal cast. To the great majority of his colleagues Whiggism meant little more than membership of that party which had secured and retained power through adherence to the House of Hanover; it began with George I and was hobbled by his Electorate. To Pitt it meant a great deal more; his Whiggism was essentially English; it went back to the Glorious Revolution, and was based on the liberties, religious and civil, which William III had rescued from Stuart tyranny. He applied his 'Revolution Principles' consciously to his politics both at home and abroad. Any form of oppression, any encroachment on the

[1] Pitt to Warburton, 9th November 1762. Egerton MSS., 1,955.

liberty of the subject, on the freedom of the Press, on the right of free speech, found in him a strenuous opponent. In America he toiled, not so much to acquire fresh territories, as to free the colonists from aggression; and on the Continent his aim was to curb the oppressive power of France rather than to coddle German principalities.

In his own person, the love of freedom showed itself as a tendency towards individualism, a tendency fostered and encouraged by the rebuffs he endured from others. He had entered Parliament as a member of the Cousinhood, and, though consistently loyal himself, had seen the lure of office entice away first one and then another, until he found himself alone, except for Temple, of whose allegiance he was now becoming doubtful. The same fate had overtaken him in his two Ministries; his colleagues had all left him, to follow, not faith, not freedom, not principle, but what they believed to be the rising star. So with the Opposition after his fall; he had led them to the attack, at their own request, but when it came to the point, like a refusing horse, they had thrown him, and had turned away to what seemed to them richer pastures. Whatever he did, whether successfully or not, sooner or later he found himself standing alone. All these experiences led to one conclusion—a distrust of bargains, a dislike of combinations for political ends and a determination to act 'independently of the sentiments of others'.[1] Pitt was an individualist, resolved to be master of his own soul, and the time was now coming when that resolve was to show itself in a reluctance to take office unless sure of a free hand in making and pursuing policies. This insistence on Ministerial freedom was a fresh step in constitutional development. Pitt was no longer content to be merely the King's servant; he must be sure that the King and his Minister saw eye to eye, or at least that the King would not interfere, and especially would avoid importing the ideas of Bute from behind the curtain. As Pitt saw it, power was to pass from the Crown to the Government, subject only to the Crown's right of dismission.

(ii)

The session which opened on the 10th January (1765) and was to prove so momentous in its issue, began and continued quietly.

[1] Pitt to Newcastle, 19th October 1764. Add. MSS. 32,962.

For most of the time Pitt was ill in bed. His advice, when asked, followed the lines he had consistently adopted: battle should be confined to great constitutional points. A general opposition could not be effective, and indeed would serve only to push the Ministry, who possessed the offices, into the arms of Bute, who possessed the power, when all would be lost; if, on the other hand, the Ministers were left to themselves, 'their mutual detestation of each other would infallibly break out',[1] and if that did not complete their downfall, some unexpected event would. His advice influenced some of the Opposition and angered others,[2] but all of them realised that without his backing their efforts were not likely to pay dividends. Consequently in general they remained inactive. But the more impatient and the more weak-kneed were confirmed in their intention of making peace with the Government while they could. Some, like Charles Townshend, ratted openly;[3] others, like Yorke, were more shame-faced and uncertain. But the method mattered very little; the results were the same—the Opposition dwindled in numbers and effectiveness. Sandwich remarked exultantly that 'the Opposition is so low that it scarcely deserves the name of a party';[4] and Newcastle recorded, at Bath where he was taking the waters, the devastating opinion of all the world 'except a very, very narrow clique, that 'we have no head, nobody to lead', apart from a few young men of no experience.[5] The Opposition's lack of capacity was very apparent now that Hardwicke, Devonshire and Legge were dead. It was a point which Pitt could not afford to overlook. The previous November, Lord John Cavendish had asked Walpole who were to be the Ministers, if they succeeded in overthrowing Grenville. Walpole, having no suggestions to make, was forced to admit that 'unless we could form an Administration, we must remain in opposition'.[6] What Cavendish and Walpole knew, Pitt knew better; and it was for that reason that he discouraged actions which could only display the barrenness of the land. When

---

[1] Hamilton to Pery, 7th March 1765. H.M.C. Lord Emly's MSS.
[2] E.g. 'I saw my Lord Rockingham this morning, whose account of Mr. Pitt I think so disagreeable a one that I own for one I shall not be much displeased if he stays away'. Onslow to Newcastle, 19th March, 1765. Add. MSS. 32,966.
[3] Grenville's Diary, 3rd March 1765. *Grenville Papers*, III, 120.
[4] Sandwich to Denbigh, 18th March 1765. H.M.C. Denbigh MSS.
[5] Newcastle to Onslow, 21st March 1765. Add. MSS. 32,966.
[6] Walpole, *George III*, II, 23.

Cavendish came to see him at Hayes, he was kindly but firm; he wished the Opposition well, but did not think they would be wise to bring up the question of Conway's dismissal—that would trench upon prerogative; and was sorry that they had again raised the question of general warrants—that should be left for the time being to the Courts.[1] In short their best policy was to hold their fire and lie low.

Pitt's attitude seemed to them puzzling; but only because he found it difficult to explain his motives. He realised acutely that in the event of a change everything would depend on himself in the Commons, and on Temple in the Lords. With so much resting on his shoulders—for Temple was little real help—he could not hope to keep going if he had at the same time to battle against both his eternal ill-health and the King's disfavour. One or other of those deadweights must be shed. His health was beyond his control, and consequently if he was to return, as undoubtedly he wished to do, the King must assist. The mere defeat of the Government would not be sufficient. Pitt could not form an alternative ministry with the feeble forces at his command; the weakness of his team must be counterbalanced by an assurance of the King's goodwill, or at least of his acquiescence. The idea of forcing himself into the Closet had always been repugnant to Pitt, even when he was able to muster a respectable Cabinet; it was not made the less repugnant now by his conviction of its uselessness. He must come to power, if at all, at the King's request and because the King felt the need of him. To irritate the King, therefore, at this stage, would merely delay, if it did not destroy, his hopes for the future. Hence Pitt's policy of quiescence; hence, too, his regret at the attempts which Newcastle was making to turn Cumberland into a sort of non-playing captain of the Opposition. As Temple remarked, clearly echoing Pitt's views: 'we must not have a Prince of the blood as first Minister; that would entirely alienate the King'.[2] Pitt was not relying on the efforts of the Opposition, nor on Cumberland; he was looking for salvation to the incompetence of the Government and the chapter of accidents, and he was not to look in vain.[3]

---

[1] Walpole, *George III*, II, 48.
[2] *Ibid.*, 21.
[3] See Onslow to Newcastle, 19th March 1765. Add. MSS. 32,966.

(iii)

Meanwhile Parliament had hardly met when Sir William Pynsent, an old gentleman of Somerset, died, leaving a will in the hands of his housekeeper with instructions to give it to nobody but Pitt. On opening it, Pitt found to his unbounded astonishment that Pynsent, who was a complete stranger, had bequeathed to him his whole estate, valued at £40,000—an event which Pitt described, with marked under-statement, as 'so advantageous to Mr. Pitt and his children'.[1] It was indeed: it turned Pitt into a wealthy man, with a fine house and a wide-spreading park at Curry Rivel, high up on the hills overlooking Sedgmoor and the levels of Zoyland, away to the Bristol Channel and the Welsh hills beyond. Though six months were to pass before gout allowed him to set out for Somerset,[2] Pitt took a deep interest in his new estate from the first; it fulfilled one of the dreams of his youth, his desire to be a landed proprietor. He was able to indulge in anticipation his flair for landscape gardening and his itch for 'improvements', and his interest was no doubt enhanced by efforts made—unsuccessfully—to overthrow the will in the courts.

It was while his thoughts were thus happily roaming, and his body was painfully tied to his bed, that Parliament spent 'one slight day on the American taxes'.[3] Here was a matter of high moment, one of the great considerations which in Pitt's view demanded the utmost degree of opposition. And what happened? Charles Townshend supported the Government, for which he was trounced by Barré,[4] and 'two or three gentlemen spoke against the act, but with great reserve and remarkable temper'.[5] No one showed interest. Grenville was supposed to have solved the problem of American defence while sparing English pockets. The colonies might complain, but what tax was not followed by complaint? Such objections were so normal that the House 'refused with scorn even so much as to receive four petitions' which had come from America. Pitt might toss restlessly on his

[1] Pitt to Newcastle, 20th January 1765. Add. MSS. 32,965.
[2] Pitt to Countess Stanhope, 20th July 1765. Mahon, Appendix V.
[3] Walpole to Hertford, 12th February 1765.
[4] *Ibid.*
[5] Burke on American Taxation, Works II, 134.

bed, but he was the one great exception. Elsewhere the indifference was universal. Even so acute an observer as Walpole could tell Mann that 'there has not been an event, from a debate to a wedding, capable of making a paragraph'.[1] He barely saved his reputation by adding the trite, but on this occasion prophetic, remark that 'such calms often forerun storms'. The rights and wrongs, the wisdom or folly of American taxation left him cold, though he might have paused to remember that his father and Pitt—the two great Ministers of the age—had both fought shy of the idea—the former in 1739 and the latter in 1757. What interested him was the sudden illness of the King, which was supposed at the time to be consumption, but was more probably the beginnings of the madness which fell upon him later. Whatever its nature, the illness led straight to the unexpected event for which Pitt was waiting.

Fearful of a recurrence, the King, on his recovery, ordered Grenville to prepare a Regency Bill, reserving power to the King to nominate the Regent and the non-official members of the Council, by instruments in writing. Grenville jumped to the conclusion that the King meant to nominate the Dowager Princess of Wales as Regent, with Bute as a member of the Council —a consummation which Grenville greatly disliked, bearing in mind that he might still be in office when the emergency arose. He was not in the King's confidence, and he was suspicious of Bute. Indeed Grenville had never been *persona grata* to the King and had become less so than ever since the failure of the negotiations with Pitt had thrown the King more completely into his power. Grenville was not the man to soften the King's fall. On the contrary, being a born pedagogue, ridiculously conceited and excessively touchy, he had exploited his victory, taking it upon himself to lecture the King continually, at great length and with that exasperating tone of voice which is the hall-mark of nagging. The King suffered torments, as Grenville observed and even described with smug satisfaction.[2] He would gladly have exchanged Grenville's high-pitched jobations for Bute's cloying devotion, and did in fact consult Bute as far as he was able in a

---

[1] Walpole to Mann, 26th March, 1765.
[2] E.g. 'The King, during the conversation, seemed exceedingly agitated and disturbed, he changed countenance, and flushed so much that the water stood in his eyes from the excessive heat of his face'. *Grenville Papers*, III, 140.

clandestine and furtive manner. Grenville both feared and disliked this hidden traffic, and was consequently anxious to circumvent what he believed to be the King's intentions. With the aid of his cabinet, he prepared a pretty trap into which in due course, and surely to the delight of the high gods, he fell himself. Sandwich was sent to point out to the King that Parliament would certainly want to place some limit on his right of nomination; it would be best to anticipate them, and confine the list to 'the Queen, or any other person of the royal family, usually residing in Great Britain'. The phrase seemed innocuous, and the King accepted it, without noticing that it was vague and capable of different interpretations. It was natural to assume that the words covered the King's mother, but Grenville's private interpretation was that they barred all who were not in the line of succession. The exact meaning was no doubt a matter for legal argument. It might easily have been overlooked, but was in fact raised in the House of Lords by the Duke of Richmond. Though this was unfortunate, Grenville was not at the end of his tether. The King was persuaded, by way of resolving obscurities, to alter the wording to read 'the Queen or any person of the Royal Family descended from the late King', which sounded extremely reasonable and quite certainly excluded the Princess. It is supposed to be a moot point whether or not the King appreciated that fact. Grenville hinted in public that he did, but made it tolerably clear in his Diary that he did not.[1] In any event, the King was greatly distressed when the truth was revealed to him and urged Grenville to have the matter set right while the Bill was still in the Lords. Grenville steadily refused on one pretext or another, but might as well have yielded; for when the Bill was sent to the Commons, they added the Princess's name to the list without further ado. They did in short, what Grenville had told the King was virtually impossible. With that Grenville's cup of iniquity was full. The King decided to get rid of him.

(iv)

The King's decision was reinforced by other events. There were growls from America—about taxation, about the billeting of soldiers in private houses, about French encroachments in

[1] *Grenville Papers,* III, 152.

Newfoundland—growls to which the Ministry did not react either wisely or well.[1] More immediately important, there were labour troubles in England. The silk weavers of Spitalfields— always a storm centre[2]—were suffering from unemployment. By way of helping them the Government proposed to levy a tax on foreign silks, but arranged matters so ineptly that their Bill was rejected in the Lords on Bedford's advice. Up to that point the weavers had behaved with moderation, but they now grew violent and for several days running made such determined attacks on Bedford House that the Duke and Duchess went in fear of their lives and had to summon the guards to their rescue. There was an impression abroad that similar risings were about to take place all over England. In short, the political horizon was threatening, the social atmosphere turbulent and the King resentful. Clearly Grenville must go.

To decide on his dismissal was easy; it was not so easy to arrange for his successor. The obvious, one might say the only, choice was Pitt, and in fact the King asked Cumberland to sound him, with a view to forming a new Ministry. But the approach was not without its difficulties. The King had not yet forgotten his youthful antipathy nor the abortive negotiations of 1763. In his turning to Pitt now, there was an element of compulsion. There was also a dash of hypocrisy; for the King did not really want Pitt; he was still hankering after Bute, and knowing that he could not obtain Bute in person, was hoping to get him by proxy. The proposed new Ministry which he sketched for Cumberland's instruction, was headed by the Earl of Northumberland, and the outstanding fact about Northumberland was that his son had married Bute's daughter. The King, in short, was trying to do what everyone else had tried to do—make a convenience of Pitt; and he was doing it in a moment of anger without pausing to consider the outcome.

Pitt, equally, had his difficulties. He had been bitten more than once, and was correspondingly shy. He recognised that the King was coming to him because he had nowhere else to go. That would not matter in itself. The crucial test was whether he was coming with a changed heart. Unfortunately all the evidence seemed to show that his motive was not a belief in Pitt, but a

---

[1] Newcastle to White, 4th June 1765. Add. MSS. 33,003.
[2] See Mantoux, p. 82–3.

distaste for Grenville, and it was a question how far that would carry him. Pitt could only judge by the past, and the fact was that the King had never pretended to care for him; had treated him shockingly at the beginning of his reign, and in the last negotiations had abruptly rejected all his views after appearing to approve them. Had Pitt been young and in good health, had he been making his way, or even had he felt that the country was in dire straits, he might have been ready to ignore his doubts and run risks; but in fact his health was deplorable, he was surfeited with fame, and the country was in no immediate peril. There was both time and reason for making certain of his footing. On the negative side he wanted reassurance; as he told Cavendish 'he had heard nothing that gave him room to hope the Closet would be *propitious* to him'; on the contrary, Bute's influence still seemed as strong as ever and would no doubt be exerted against him, as it had been against Grenville.[1] What other reason could there be for importing Northumberland? On the positive side, he laid down three conditions, the granting of which would be an earnest of the King's goodwill: first, that all officers and others who had been dismissed for voting with the minority must be reinstated; secondly, that general warrants must be condemned and Pratt's merits recognised; thirdly, that the foreign policy must be altered in the direction of Prussia.

It was the King's misfortune that his relations with Bute and his own ineptitude had alienated from him practically the whole political world. He had no one in whom he could confide, still less employ in matters of delicacy. It was only with much misgiving that he had asked his uncle to approach Pitt on his behalf.[2] The choice was perhaps inevitable, but hardly good. Cumberland was not the best of agents. He was an invalid who had recently suffered an apoplectic fit. Worse still, his relations with both parties were strained. The King had affronted him by omitting his name from the original draft of the Regency Bill, and the two had scarcely been on speaking terms since. On the other side, Pitt's declaration of independence a few months earlier (*see p.* 149) had greatly angered him; he had not only told Newcastle, with every sign of indignation, that 'we should have nothing further to do with Mr. Pitt', but had added that 'neither our cause nor our

---

[1] Cavendish to Rockingham, 21st May 1765. Albemarle, I, 211.
[2] See Cumberland's Statement. Albemarle, I, 186 ff.

friends had any reason to expect favour, support or countenance from Mr. Pitt, if ever he should come to the head of affairs'.[1] Though a reluctant loyalty now led him to obey the King's wishes, it is natural to suppose that he did so with little enthusiasm and perhaps with no great wish for success. It is significant that he found excuses to avoid seeing Pitt personally, sending Albemarle and Temple down to Hayes, while he himself saw Newcastle, Rockingham and Grafton in London. It is perhaps even more significant that before he had had any indication of Pitt's reaction, he asked Grafton whether he thought 'an Administration could be formed (principally out of the Minority) without Mr. Pitt'.[2] Still clearer evidence of his bias was the fact that he failed at first to consult the King on Pitt's three points, saying that he 'did not think it decent to propose them',[3] and instead wanted to wash his hands of the whole affair. In deference however to the King's positive command, he did finally take the step which he should have taken from the first. He made a personal visit to Hayes; but he made it in the guise of an eagle rather than a dove, going there in royal state, accompanied by an escort of guards. At the meeting, he and Pitt were alone together for a time, and were then joined by Temple and Albemarle. Exactly what took place is obscure; it has to be pieced together mainly from a written statement by Cumberland, which provokingly breaks off at the crucial point, and a few revealing remarks which he made to Grafton, eked out by a passage from Grenville's Diary which may perhaps be regarded as Temple's version. Cumberland began by explaining the King's wishes, and then, as he told Grafton, 'had patience to attend to very long discourses which Mr. Pitt held on the subject'[4] —a turn of phrase which suggests inward irritation, if not antagonism. He also told Grafton that he could not always follow Pitt's meaning, which was likely enough, for Pitt stood on an infinitely higher plane—but at least he followed it sufficiently to grasp the trend of his remarks. Pitt pointed out that though he still had 'vigour and strength of mind to undertake business', he could not be expected, in view of his feeble health, to shoulder the burden unless 'he saw a probability of success'.[5] The granting of his three conditions would go some way to reassure

---

[1] Newcastle's Note, 14th November 1764. Add. MSS. 32,963.
[2] Anson, p. 44.   [3] Albemarle, I, 198.
[4] Anson, pp. 45–6.   [5] Albemarle, I, 202.

him, but Cumberland must understand that neither he nor Temple
would take office 'whilst Lord Bute's power existed'.[1] Cumberland
felt able to promise the three conditions, but 'always evaded any
explicit declaration'[2] about Bute's dismissal; on the contrary he
went so far in the opposite direction as to remind Pitt of the King's
wish to have Northumberland at the head of the Treasury.[3] The
consequence was that Pitt refused to commit himself. The door
seems to have been left open, but Cumberland gave the King to
understand that it had been shut, and was perhaps in part justified
by the fact that two days later Temple was reconciled with his
brother, Grenville—a reconciliation in which Pitt was included so
far as social but not political affairs were concerned.[4]

But justified or not, the negotiations had failed. Burke, who at
this point first appears prominently on the political stage, had, in
anticipation, ascribed their failure to Pitt's pride. 'Nothing', he
wrote to Flood, 'but an intractable temper in your friend Pitt, can
prevent a most admirable and lasting system from being put
together; and this crisis will show whether pride or patriotism be
predominant in his character. For you may be assured, he
has it now in his power to come into the service of his country,
upon any plan of politics he may choose to dictate, with great and
honourable terms to himself and to every friend he has in the
world; and with such strength of power, as will be equal to
everything but absolute despotism over the King and kingdom.
A few days will show whether he will take this part, or that of
continuing on his back at Hayes, talking fustian, excluded from
all ministerial, and incapable of all parliamentary service; for his
gout is worse than ever, but his pride may disable him more than
his gout'.[5] Burke was a great orator and a master of magnificent
prose, but as a working politician he was particularly ineffective.
It is a pity therefore that his references to Pitt are so frequently
quoted, as though they were the last word on the subject. This
passage is characteristic; it is beautifully written; it sounds well;
but it has the great demerit of meaning little or nothing. What was
the 'most admirable and lasting system' which, he says, could be
put together, and of what materials was it to be formed? Burke
does not tell us. He could hardly mean Grenville and the Bedfords,

[1] *Grenville Papers*, III, 226.   [2] *Ibid.*   [3] Anson, p. 46.
[4] Newcastle to White, 4th June 1765. Add. MSS. 33,003.
[5] Burke to Flood, 18th May 1765. Prior, I, 121.

L

who were being dismissed with ignominy; and if he thought
of the Newcastle Whigs, how many of them still remained un-
tainted, and what was their particular excellence? The fact is that
there was no statesman of real eminence and very few Ministers of
experience on whom Pitt could call; the burden would rest almost
entirely on his shoulders, and bearing in mind his own ill health
and the King's prejudice, a system dependent on him alone,
though it might well be described as admirable, could only
doubtfully be regarded as lasting. And what was the 'plan of
politics' which he was to dictate? Again Burke does not tell us;
he did not know. Subsequent knowledge however has made it
clear that while Pitt's conditions were to a large extent met by
the King, he was unable to obtain assurance on the fundamental
point of Bute's interference and all that it connoted. What again
were the great and honourable terms which Pitt could command?
Did they by any chance include the earldom which Burke so
strongly reprobated only a year later? Or were they simply a
synonym for the burdens of ministerial office? Pitt's refusal was
not due to pride, nor to an idea that it was more grand to lie on
his back talking fustian than to enjoy almost despotic power. nor
to what modern historians are fond of calling his manic excitement. Temple, who saw Pitt and knew the facts much better than
Burke, found him neither proud, nor mad, nor garrulous, but
'more inclined to come into business again than he expected'.[1]
What prevented him was uncertainty of the King's intentions
combined with great physical prostration.

(v)

The King was obliged to take back his old Ministers. After
such patent humiliation, it might have redounded to their dignity
if they had declined to return; but their conceit, or their love of
power, or both, were impervious to snubs. Grenville satisfied his
outraged feelings by inflicting non-stop lectures on the King. He
pretended to be undecided what he should do, but was in fact
making up his mind what conditions he would impose. His final
list included two—the dismissal of Bute's brother, Stuart Mackenzie, from his post of Privy Seal for Scotland, and the appointment of Granby instead of Cumberland as Commander-in-Chief—

[1] Rockingham to Newcastle, 17th May 1765. Add. MSS. 32,966.

which required the King to go back on promises already given. Though, in the upshot, the King was spared that mortification by Mackenzie's generosity in releasing him from his promise and Granby's willingness to forgo his claim until Cumberland's death, none the less he felt that his honour had been impugned. It was a bitter experience for a young and well-intentioned man with too high a sense of his own dignity and too little an understanding of his own limitations. He reacted by meting out to his Ministers a surfeit of black looks and sullen treatment. By the middle of June relations were so strained that the Ministers were threatening wholesale resignations, and the King was once more making up his mind to dismiss the lot. What gave him pause was uncertainty as to whom he should put in their place. Cumberland suggested Pitt, but the King demurred: 'I shall rather be surprised', he said, 'if Mr. Pitt can be persuaded to accept office on terms not entirely to my dishonour and to that of those worthy men, Lord Rockingham, the Dukes of Grafton, Newcastle and others; for they are men who have principles and therefore cannot approve of seeing the Crown dictated to by low men'.[1] The remark is obscure, but may perhaps refer to Wilkes and Pitt's support of his pleas. Whatever its meaning, it betrays an element of resistance to Pitt's policies in home affairs. The King was equally and more openly opposed to Pitt's foreign policy. 'I am very anxious', he told Cumberland, 'to know what Lord Rockingham and others think of the proposal concerning an alliance with Russia and Prussia, and what they have to propose if Mr. Pitt should decline office without it'.[2] But in spite of the King's reluctance, he had in the end to fall back on Pitt, who was summoned to the Queen's House (Buckingham Palace) on the 19th June (1765). The King awaited the meeting with some apprehension, hoping, to use Albemarle's phrase, that 'the Great Man would not be unreasonable'.[3] But if he was apprehensive, he also knew his own mind. Pitt must appreciate that the King had been abominably used by his present Ministers, and would not put up with similar treatment in the future. At the same time he must not assume that the King would betray such of his servants as had been loyal to him; he would not give them up, nor put others over their heads;

---

[1] George III to Cumberland, 12th June 1765. Fortescue, I, 118.
[2] George III to Cumberland, June 1765. Fortescue, I, 120.
[3] Albemarle to Newcastle, 16th June 1765. Add. MSS. 32,967.

though he would be prepared to take in some of Pitt's nominees. So much for home affairs. In foreign affairs 'the ramming Austria deeper with France and kindling a new war by unnecessary alliances' were things he could 'neither answer to his God nor to his conscience'.[1] In short Pitt was not to have much say in choosing his Cabinet and still less in deciding his foreign policy. The prospect seemed poor. The meeting however lasted three or four hours. Pitt, if we are to believe Albemarle, was 'very pompous'; and the King, if we may use our own judgment, not a little obstinate. There was less difficulty over 'men' than George had feared. Pitt seemed uninterested; he was 'very shy of naming anybody for employments', which to Albemarle seemed 'incomprehensible', but was surely due to Pitt's knowledge that talent was extremely scarce and that there was little to choose between the various mediocrities. When the King agreed to his 'measures' in home affairs and promised to do something for Pratt, Pitt was easily satisfied. Where the break came was over foreign affairs; 'his foreign politics' said Albemarle, 'was not so reasonable, nor did the King give into it'.[2] The suggested triple alliance would, said the King, alarm all Europe, and was something that he 'could not propose to his present Ministers'. By his 'present Ministers' he must have meant those whom he wished to retain in the new administration, with the possible addition of Bute whose influence from behind the curtain was strongly suspected and whose antagonism to Prussia was notorious. There was reason for Pitt to be cautious. He believed with his whole soul that his triple alliance was the only counterpoise to the shortcomings of the Peace of Paris and the only way to avert the war of revenge which he so clearly foresaw, and for which France was already arming. His health forbade him to take office for his own glory, and his patriotism forbade him to acquiesce in foreign policies which seemed to him disastrous. He could endure much in his own person and in the conduct of affairs at home provided he could set the Empire on a firm foundation. But of this there seemed little prospect so long as the King rejected his advice. He did not therefore accept the King's offer, but it was agreed that both should think things over and meet again.

At the second meeting, the King showed signs of yielding. He

---

[1] *Heads of Conversation*. Fortescue, I, 123–5.
[2] Albemarle to Newcastle, 19th June 1765. Add. MSS. 32,967.

was not, he said, averse to the triple alliance 'if found practicable upon further consideration of it'.[1] That was hardly enthusiastic, but Pitt, so far from being 'intractable', was anxious to help, and therefore accepted the sop, throwing his doubts overboard and assuring himself and others that 'the royal dispositions are most propitious to the wishes of the public, with regard to *measures* most likely to spread satisfaction'.[2] The question of 'men' might in the circumstances be left to fortune. In this new atmosphere, Pitt was prepared to accept, subject only to Temple's support, which seemed to him so necessary in his poor state of health and in the 'unconnected' condition to which the coalition had reduced him. Returning from the interview, he wrote to Temple, entreating him to set out at once for Hayes so that they might discuss their plans. He would not have written so urgently, so happily or so trustfully had he known that Temple, now wholly reconciled to his brother and converted to his views, was giving full play to his jealousy, and so far from intending to act with Pitt, was taking advantage of his position to learn Pitt's plans and betray them to Grenville. He came to Hayes, but declined to assist; and when the King made a further effort, wrote cynically 'Portents and prodigies! What new attempt is now to be made'.[3] Pitt and Onslow argued with him far into the night, but without avail; he 'most peremptorily and determinately refused bearing a part in any shape, great or small'.[4] Without Temple's aid, Pitt felt unable to proceed, and so informed the King, returning to Hayes 'completely mortified' and lamenting 'this crisis of my life, the most difficult and painful, on all accounts, which I have yet experienced'.[5] It was a sad moment for Pitt, for England, and for the world.

Temple's manœuvre was undoubtedly aimed at strengthening Grenville's hand; but in that it failed. Nothing would induce the King to recall his old Ministers; rather, he would 'fling himself absolutely into the hands of my Lord Bute and the Tories'.[6] This possibility so frightened Newcastle that he offered to form a new administration without Pitt's help, arguing that 'if those

[1] Albemarle to Newcastle, 22nd June 1765. Add. MSS. 32,967.
[2] Pitt to Grafton, 22nd June 1765. Anson, p. 53.
[3] Temple to Grenville, 25th June 1765. *Grenville Papers,* III, 64.
[4] Cumberland to Albemarle, 25th June 1765. Albemarle, I, 213.
[5] Pitt to Lyttelton, 1st July 1765. Chatham Corr. II, 315.
[6] Newcastle to White, 29th June 1765. Add. MSS. 33,003.

measures were followed at home and abroad which Mr. Pitt had recommended to the King, and His Majesty had consented to, so far from giving any opposition, Mr. Pitt would support them',[1] which was no doubt the next best thing. It was not an easy resolution for Newcastle to take. For some time past the Whigs had regarded an administration without Pitt as a practical impossibility, not so much because of differences of opinion as because of their own lack of metal in Parliament. They were no stronger now; indeed they were weaker; and, in addition, they could not disguise the fact that they were not enamoured of all Pitt's policies. The measures that he advocated seemed to them a mixed bag. Some, such as the condemnation of general warrants and the repeal of the Cyder Tax, they had already supported in the House, and could as easily support again. Others, such as the funding of the national debt and the alliance with Prussia did not present serious difficulties. But the repeal of the Stamp Act and the relaxation of the regulations governing trade in America were of more doubtful aspect, and what was worse would probably prove unpopular; while the restoration of Stuart Mackenzie was positively distasteful. Yet all those were Pitt's measures[2] of which they must now become the champions if they were to propitiate him. Recognising their own want of experience, and being highly nervous of responsibility, they were extremely anxious to have him at their head; and many of them declared that they would take office only on the clear understanding that he might take over the leadership '*whenever* he should see the situation of affairs to be such as to allow him to take that part'.[3] In a word they were to be a caretaker government. The King, desperate to be rescued from Grenville and Bedford, accepted this makeshift administration. Newcastle himself discreetly declined the first place; he took the colourless post of Lord Privy Seal, leaving Rockingham to be Prime Minister, with Dowdeswell as Chancellor of the Exchequer and Grafton and Conway as Secretaries of State. They kissed hands on the 10th July 1765.

[1] Newcastle to White, 29th June 1765. Add. MSS. 33,003.
[2] Grenville's Diary, 25th June 1765. *Grenville Papers*, III, 203.
[3] Anson, p. 54.

XII

ENTER ROCKINGHAM

(i)

NEARLY FOUR years had elapsed since Pitt had resigned. During that time his fortunes had been surprisingly varied and with few exceptions uniformly unfortunate. He had seen his war policy vindicated too late; his victories dissipated by an inadequate peace; his European allies lost through ill-humour and incompetence; and now, as disaster's crown, he saw the splendid fabric of his genius being bartered for the small change of a trifling tax. What was true of his achievements was true of himself. Twice, at the Opposition's own request, he had led them to battle, only to find himself deluded in the end, first by Newcastle and then by Yorke. On the question of general warrants alone had he been supported with any degree of warmth, and his effort on that occasion, unrehearsed and unprepared as it was, had resulted in a near-miss, tantalising as a mirage of the might-have-been. The same mocking spirit had extinguished his hopes in other directions. Three times he had been recalled to office, and three times he had been foiled at the last moment; once by the King's whim; once by the King's ambiguities; and once by Temple's desertion. Through it all he had been buoyed up by the conviction that his country needed the help which he believed he still had the capacity to give. But hope deferred was having its usual effect, and a sick heart was added to a shattered body.[1] It is not surprising in the circumstances that the idea of retirement haunted him, though he never allowed his mind to linger on it too fondly while Grenville remained in office. But Rockingham's appointment altered the situation. Pitt believed the new Ministry to be well-meaning; he hoped it would prove competent. The need for him to remain on the spot was not so pressing; and if the new administration came up to expectations, perhaps he need take no further part in

[1] Cf. 'that my wretched health will ever be [well] I almost despair'. Pitt to Temple, 22nd June 1765. *Grenville Papers*, III, 60.

public affairs, but could enjoy the rest which his work had so
amply earned and his body so sorely needed. The idea was made
the more attractive by Pynsent's timely legacy, though much
would depend upon what his new estate proved to be. The time
had come to explore it. Eleven days after Rockingham had kissed
hands, Pitt set out for Somerset where, he told his cousin, 'I
propose to pass not a little of the rest of my days, if I find the
place tolerable'.[1] He found it more than tolerable, though convinced that it was in great want of his 'improving' skill! Without a moment's loss of time he plunged into the building game,
not only adding to the house and embellishing the grounds
but erecting a graceful column to the memory of his benefactor.
Within three months he was able to assure Temple that 'I advance
apace in brick and mortar'.[2] He was so well satisfied with what
he described as 'the amusing cares of building and gardening with
the whole train of the Arts', that he decided to cut away from the
past, sell Hayes and become a country gentleman in the literal, not
the political sense. He was now no longer a Man of Kent but a
'Somersetshire bystander',[3] and as such proposed to employ the
proceeds of Hayes in 'laying rapacious hands on a considerable
part of the County of Somerset', for, as he declared with a chuckle,
'the passion of dirty acres grows upon a West Saxon of yesterday'.[4] Building, planting, riding and the joys of the family circle
at his own fireside were to be the sum and substance of his life
hereafter.

But Pitt was not a man who could be left in peace. The political
world was perennially interested in him, discussing his probable
reactions, generally with bated breath and always with anxiety.
The new Ministry, in particular, wanted to know what he thought
of them, and how he would treat them. They were very much
divided in their opinions. Some, as for instance Grafton, wished
above all things to bring him again into office; others, like
Newcastle, without going so far, believed his support to be
essential. But there were some, notably Rockingham and his new
secretary Burke, who looked at him with lack-lustre eyes; their
feelings partook of Catullus's '*odi et amo*', they were fascinated by
his brilliance, but preferred to think of it as the iridescence of

---

[1] Pitt to Countess Stanhope, 20th July 1765. Mahon V, App. p. iv.
[2] Pitt to Temple, 29th October 1765. *Grenville Papers*, III, 101.
[3] Pitt to Grafton, 25th August 1765. Anson, p. 58.
[4] Pitt to Temple, 29th October 1765. *Grenville Papers*, III, 101.

decay; they longed for his help, but resented his super-eminence; they were envious of his standing and yet felt a repugnance for a man who was not of their own clay nor yet of their own caste. But whatever their feelings, they dared not let him out of their sight without at least trying to sound him; and so, on hearing that he was off to the country, Newcastle detailed 'my very good friend', General Whitmore, to waylay him 'at Maidenhead Bridge in his way to Somerset' and there put him through a delicate cross-examination. According to Whitmore, Pitt declared 'that from the character and conduct of the new Ministers he was fully persuaded they would do everything necessary to secure the freedom of our constitution at home; the most he feared was with regard to foreign affairs'.[1]

Rockingham acted on the hint. By way of securing freedom at home, he persuaded the King to raise Pratt to the peerage as Lord Camden, and made up his mind to tackle the problem of general warrants: 'Halifax, Sandwich and General Warrants', said Walpole gleefully, 'are sent to the devil'.[2] But, as Pitt had feared, Rockingham was not so forthright or successful in foreign affairs. He played with the idea of renewing the Prussian alliance, and even went so far as to discuss with Mitchell the best way of 'opening an intercourse with the Court of Berlin'.[3] But receiving little encouragement from Frederick, he faltered and let the matter drop.[4] There were reasons in plenty for doubting the quality of the new Administration. The world's comments on it, though less well known, were curiously similar to the description Burke was destined to give of Chatham's Ministry. It was, according to those comments, 'a new political arch almost built, but of materials of so different a nature, and without a keystone, that it does not indicate either strength or duration'; it was 'a lutestring ministry'; it was 'an heterogeneous jumble of youth and caducity, which cannot be efficient';[5] Walpole had 'never heard a more wild proposal, nor one fraught with greater improbability of success'.[6] Nor were the several members remarkable individually for anything but a somewhat speckled honesty. Rockingham, at

[1] Newcastle to Rockingham, 24th July 1765. Add. MSS. 32,968.
[2] To Mann, 12th July 1765.
[3] Fortescue, I, 161.
[4] Fortescue, I, 188.
[5] Chesterfield to his son, 15th July and 17th August 1765. Bradshaw, III, 1322-3.
[6] Walpole, *George III*, II, 135.

thirty-five, was without experience of government; a shy and sickly young man, though very conscious of his marquisate—a silent and tongue-tied politician, capable of winning a measure of support but not of esteem; a well-meaning but indolent leader whose good intentions, if they did not pave the streets of hell, too often trod the road to Newmarket. Perhaps the best summary of his character is his own remark to Cumberland: 'I must say, Sir, that to hesitate is laudable'.[1] Grafton, at twenty-nine, was almost as ingenuous, though not so innocent, as his leader; precariously poised between his duchess and Nancy Parsons, he was living with his inamorata in a cottage at Woodford, very much shut away from the public eye, and waited on only by a maid servant and a boy who came in the morning to clean the ducal shoes.[2] As he was retiring in his private life, so he was diffident on the public stage. He had no desire for high office and regarded 'the lower parts of business' as unbecoming to his rank. It is difficult to see how, in the circumstances, he could ever have gained experience—a disability of which he must have been uncomfortably aware, for it was only with reluctance that he accepted the Seals, and on the distinct understanding that he should stand down in Pitt's favour, whenever Pitt so desired.[3] The other Secretary of State, Conway, was a soldier, honest, brave and upright, but forbidding in manner, touchy over inessentials and, like so many military men, ill-at-ease and irresolute as a Minister. The Chancellor of the Exchequer, Dowdeswell, was a humdrum and hard-working politician, whom Walpole described, a little unkindly but not altogether untruly, as 'heavy, slow, methodical without clearness, a butt for ridicule, unversed in every graceful art, and a stranger to men and courts'.[4] They were not an impressive team, but Pitt gave them full credit for their virtues, and was prepared to support their measures in so far as he found them acceptable. What prevented a closer alliance was not merely Rockingham's coolness or Pitt's ill-health, but something much more fundamental. The new Ministers were admittedly young and ignorant; no one imagined that they could govern in their own right. Pitt therefore looked for the motive force behind, and he found it in two men—Cumberland and

[1] Rockingham to Cumberland, 20th October 1765. Albemarle, I, 242.
[2] Barrington to Buckingham, 24th September 1764. H.M.C. Lothian MSS.
[3] Anson, pp. 44 and 54.
[4] Walpole, *George III*, II, 139.

Newcastle. They were the men of knowledge and experience to whom the new Ministers must turn, and whose voice must carry the greatest weight in their councils. Pitt's relations with both were strained. Cumberland had been instrumental in breaking up his first ministry, and though after the disaster of Closterseven, he had felt a higher regard for Pitt and some touch of gratitude, those kindlier feelings had evaporated in the early days of opposition, and had not been renewed in the course of the recent negotiations. Cumberland was attending all the Cabinet meetings in person,[1] and Pitt had no fancy for sitting in Council with a Prince of the Blood who was not well-disposed towards him nor particularly versed in politics. If Cumberland was unwelcome, Newcastle was anathema. Pitt could hardly have forgotten how Newcastle had played fast and loose with him in his youth, so that the locusts had eaten the years of his prime. Still less could he have forgotten how, when he was battling to save England in her extremity, Newcastle had been a constant thorn in his flesh, thwarting his plans, traducing him at Court, depriving him of his followers, and finally joining with his enemies to oust him on the very eve of victory. Newcastle had been silly and mischievous even when under the restraining influence of Hardwicke. How much worse would he be now that Hardwicke was dead? It is part of the irony of Pitt's life that in this matter he relied on his somewhat debatable logic instead of on his almost infallible instinct. His logic on this occasion was impeccable, but, as logic so often is, at variance with fact. For something like forty five years Newcastle had shown himself incapable of taking a decision —certainly a wise one—without Hardwicke's advice and concurrence. It was only to be supposed that deprived of Hardwicke, his infirmity of purpose, his childishness, his irresolution would have become intensified, and that he would have been a greater stumbling block than ever. Curiously enough, the expectation was false. Newcastle, though still querulous, had grown more mellow, more humble, and more wise. He was one of Pitt's steadiest champions in the Rockingham Ministry, urging his recall or his cultivation in season and out of season, and offering to retire, if his presence in any way hindered Pitt's return. But of this Pitt was not aware. Had he known, his attitude might have been different; but not knowing, he held himself aloof.

[1] Anson, p. 55.

(ii)

Meanwhile the new administration pursued its way precariously. Few people thought it could endure; 'the Ministry', said
Camden, 'is at last upon its legs . . . but I can't yet tell who is
that Prometheus that is to give it animation'.[1] Camden, with his
honours fresh upon him, must be presumed a friend. Those not
so friendly were even more discouraging. 'The second-rate
politicians', said Buckingham, 'who have embarked in the frail
green vessel . . . can never wear those new robes, which hang by
a cobweb to their shoulders, with honour to themselves or
utility to their country'.[2] All the world was convinced that
Rockingham's only chance of survival was Pitt's support. As
Grenville had no desire that Rockingham should survive, he was
busy spreading rumours 'how much Mr. Pitt disapproves of the
present administration'.[3] These rumours reached Grafton, who
in some dismay appealed to Pitt. Pitt's reply, though it has been
misinterpreted, was perfectly clear. Both those who asserted his
partisanship and those who denied it, were equally at fault. He
had had no hand in the selection of the Ministers, but did not
disapprove of them or wish to stop any of them from going into
the King's service. But knowing only too well how profoundly he
and Newcastle had previously differed both in matter and method,
he could not in anticipation feel any degree of confidence
that policies emanating from Claremont would result in 'a
solid system of measures'. Time must tell, and as he assured
Grafton, he hoped very sincerely that affairs might 'turn out so
fortunately and happily, as to make you as full of ardour for
business as I am of disrelish for the political scene'.[4] There
was perhaps some touch of sour grapes in his tone, and no
great enthusiasm for Rockingham, but the outstanding point
was a profound distrust of Newcastle, based on his past
experience.

All this time country air, rural pursuits and the absence of
worry were having their natural effect. Pitt's health improved
steadily until one unlucky day his horse fell with him, bruising

[1] Camden to Temple, 7th August 1765. *Grenville Papers*, III, 77.
[2] Buckingham to Nugent, October 1765. H.M.C. Lothian MSS.
[3] Hopkins to Grafton, 12th August 1765. Anson, p. 56.
[4] Pitt to Grafton, 25th August 1765. Anson, p. 58.

him badly, when his gout returned at once and he was 'reduced back again to the crutches he had got rid of'.[1] To add to his griefs, Hester fell ill of a fever. Still, having a mind at ease, he refused to be downcast. 'I make a shift', he told Nuthall, 'to enjoy the fine weather and a pleasing scene about me, in a one-horse chair'.[2] But though in this same letter he declared that the political scene, far removed from his corporeal eye, was 'too much involved in darkness as yet, for the mental eye to pretend to pry into it', none the less twinges of curiosity were beginning to mingle with the twinges of gout; and possibly the darkness of the mental eye was beginning to be lightened by flashes from America. Pitt let his thoughts wander towards Parliament and began to see himself playing an active part. It had long been his custom to visit Bath as a preliminary; and so now, he told Temple, in a particularly cheerful letter, that 'I propose carrying my legs, since they will not carry me, to Bath, towards the middle of November, if I hold out so long, and try once again to prop up a little a shattered tenement with the help of steel waters'.[3] He had hardly written the letter before he set out and by the 2nd November had reached Wells. There he heard news of import. Cumberland had died suddenly two days earlier. It was a stunning blow for the young Ministry,[4] but might, if handled properly, have had the effect of winning Pitt. Cumberland, if not the most troublesome, was certainly the most powerful of Pitt's quasi-opponents; his disappearance left only Newcastle, who, without support, might possibly, even in Pitt's eyes, be kept in order. Pitt seems to have been softened and almost to have thrown out a feeler. 'Upon public and great things', he wrote to Thomas Walpole, 'what remains for one so strangely circumstanced as I am, to say to a friend? You fully know how I was frustrated in my views for the public good; and the repetition of any part of so unaccountable a story could have neither utility nor entertainment. All I can say is this, that I move in the sphere only of measures. Quarrels at court, or family reconciliations, shall never vary my fixed judgment of things. Those who, with me, have stood by the cause of liberty and the national honour, upon true Revolution

[1] Pitt to Jackson, 13th September 1765. Add. MSS. 9,344.
[2] Pitt to Nuthall, 15th September 1765. Chatham Corr. II, 325.
[3] Pitt to Temple, 29th October 1765. *Grenville Papers*, III, 101.
[4] 'We lost a support in the Closet which we all felt; for on the Duke's most honourable character we placed our hopes and our confidence.' Anson, p. 61.

Principles, will never find me against them, till they fall off and do not act up to those principles'.[1]

The idea that Pitt might fill Cumberland's vacancy had also occurred to Newcastle. He did not pitch his requirements or his expectations very high; he would be quite content if Pitt could be connected with the Ministry in any degree, however small. People said that he wanted to retire. Well then, Newcastle suggested, with a flash of his old bargaining methods, 'he may very probably not dislike to retire with a peerage, the proper reward for his great services to the public.[2] And if he was only called up to the House of Lords and would not accept any employment, . . . that would, in my opinion, do the business; all that is wanted is Mr. Pitt's avowed approbation of and connection with the present Ministers'.[3] He broached the idea to the King, who seemed favourable but was in fact reluctant,[4] and to his colleagues who seemed to be enthusiastic. But, though it was agreed to approach Pitt at once, Rockingham was slow in moving. Just as in 1755 Newcastle, through over-confidence, had postponed his offer to Pitt until too late,[5] so now, in 1765, Rockingham, through hesitation and unwillingness to press the King, dallied too long. When three weeks had passed and nothing had been done, Newcastle complained that 'our Ministers are very *sanguine*; they think themselves sure of the Closet (and *that they certainly are*); they think themselves sure of great majorities in both Houses; and I hope and believe they are; but however I would have put it quite out of question, if I could'.[6] Another week and Newcastle had given up hope: 'I told your lordship', he wrote indignantly, 'my thoughts upon the laying aside the application to Mr. Pitt in my letter of the 26th of last month; your lordship having taken no notice of what I said, I conclude it is all over. I wonder at it'.[7] Rockingham had not, however, laid it aside; he was merely indulging in that hesitation which he found laudable, and in the meantime was making approaches to other persons—to North, to Barré, to Charles Townshend, to Shelburne, and finally to Sackville. If

---

[1] Pitt to T. Walpole, 5th November 1765. Chatham Corr. II, 328.
[2] The idea was not entirely novel—see Bedford to Grenville, 26th June 1765. Bedford Corr. III, 299.
[3] Newcastle to Grafton, 6th November 1765. Add. MSS. 32,971.
[4] George III to Bute, 10th January 1766. Sedgwick, p. 241.
[5] See p. 74, my *Pitt and the Seven Years' War*.
[6] Newcastle to Offley, 23rd November 1765. Add. MSS. 32,972.
[7] Newcastle to Rockingham, 1st December 1765. Add. MSS. 32,972.

they would give their support, Rockingham hoped he might be able to dispense with Pitt whom he knew to be unwelcome to the King. But the first four refused, and Newcastle commented sadly on the fifth that Sackville's accession would have a bad effect on the Whigs and 'what I lament the most, I am afraid it will quite alienate Mr. Pitt'.[1] Newcastle was only too prescient. When at long last Rockingham sent Thomas Townshend down to Bath (5th January 1766), he sent him on a fool's errand. Pitt was not unsusceptible to flattery nor insensitive to antipathies. He had been flattered by the Opposition, who, forestalling Townshend, had come down to Bath in numbers and paid Pitt marked attentions. It was with some inward satisfaction that he confided to Hester: 'It rains civilities upon me here from various quarters; and to my own sense of things, only renders my situation more unaccountable, not to say ridiculous. . . . Many I find are enough disposed to take a view of me; whether from mere curiosity to see a strange new creature, viz. a leader whom nobody follows, or any other reason why, I do not conjecture'.[2] He was obviously pleased when the Duke of Bedford called, and finding him laid up, sat by his bedside 'talking very placidly (and to be serious, very politely) of houses in the Circus, pleasant airings, Somersetshire prospects, etc.'; it all added, said Pitt, to 'my importance in my own eyes'.[3]

It was also in marked contrast with the actions of the Ministry. They were slow to approach him; they came reluctantly; and if they gave a peerage to his friend Pratt, they also chose this moment to give the lucrative post of Vice-Treasurer of Ireland to his *bête noire*, Sackville. Their futilities were heightened by a misunderstanding. Newcastle had invited George Cooke to second the Address, knowing him to be Pitt's friend. Cooke consulted Pitt, and in the course of his letter quoted Newcastle as saying that the Ministry's views on the Stamp Act were exactly conformable to Pitt's ideas. Pitt flared up immediately: 'When his Grace', he replied, 'does me the honour to say that anything is "exactly conformable to my ideas", he is pleased to use the name of a man, who has never communicated his ideas to the Duke of Newcastle upon the present state of affairs, and who is finally resolved never

[1] Newcastle to Rockingham, 1st December 1765. Add. MSS. 32,972.
[2] Pitt to Hester, 18th November 1765. Public Record Office.
[3] Pitt to Hester, 24th November 1765. Public Record Office.

to be in confidence or concert again with his Grace. Whenever my ideas, in their true and exact dimensions, reach the public, I shall lay them before the world myself'. He felt so sore and indignant at the idea of Newcastle speaking for him and so determined to be his own interpreter that he added: 'I shall never depart from the principles, and system of measures, in which I have been so often sacrificed by the Duke of Newcastle, nor accede to his Grace's ministry, because he, occasionally, is pleased to adopt in words, and to mar in effect, any parts of that system, which he has first subverted'.[1] The offending phrase had in fact been Cooke's gloss upon what Newcastle had said and not Newcastle's own words; but before Cooke's explanation could arrive, Pitt had heard of Sackville's appointment, and his breach with the Ministry was complete. 'What', he wrote, 'can I have to do in or near the political world. I was frustrated and disabled from doing any material good last June. The world now is fallen into the Duke of Newcastle's hands; the country is undone; and I am of opinion that no solid system for giving it but a chance for any tolerable degree of safety can be possible under his Grace's auspices, and where his influence colours and warps the whole. . . . When I shall crawl to London, I cannot fix. I would willingly be there for one fortnight, if able; and, after that, wish never to see again a scene of destruction and ruin, laid by faction, before the ashes of the late King were cold (I mean by old servants of the Crown combining with new influences to subvert the then system); and where the same experienced hand now moulds and directs the political machine'.[2] Pitt's antipathies were too inflamed to be easily soothed by explanations, and the meeting of Parliament too near to afford time for them to subside of themselves. Rockingham had had opportunities in plenty between his appointment in July and the meeting of Parliament in December to make a determined and genuine approach to Pitt; but he had dallied too long and was never whole-hearted. The result was that Pitt, if he had ever thought of joining the Ministry, thought so no longer. He must wait now, as he told Shelburne, 'until the King is pleased to signify his pleasure to me, that I should again submit my thoughts upon the formation of such a system, both as to the measures and as to the instruments which are to

[1] Pitt to Cooke, 7th December 1765. Chatham Corr. II, 342.
[2] Pitt to Nuthall, 10th December 1765. Chatham Corr. II, 345.

constitute that system, and that in so ample and full an extent as shall leave nothing to the eyes of men equivocal on the outside of it, nor any dark, creeping factions, scattering doubts and sowing discords within'.[1]

It looked as though Pitt would have to wait for ever.

(iii)

Parliament met on the 17th December (1765), but was almost immediately prorogued till the middle of January. In the interval, the Ministers who had so far failed to make up their minds, did their best to decide how they should deal with American affairs. Probably not one of them was fully aware how vast and important the question was; but even if they had been, they could scarcely have shown greater uncertainty or more irresolution. It is a curious fact that at this moment of crisis not one of the leading figures was able to stand on his own feet, not even Pitt, though his case differed in kind from that of the others. He had been crushed by Temple's desertion, not because he was lacking in firmness, but because he was now without a representative in the Lords, as well as 'naked' and 'unconnected' in the Commons. He would not take office unless he saw some reasonable prospect of success, and deprived of his sole adherent in the Lords, he felt like a craftsman without his tools.

The other leading figures had all become vacillating or obstinate according to their natures, through the loss of some Egeria. The King was yearning after Bute. Without Bute he had no guide other than his native shrewdness and what wisdom he had been able to acquire in five years of kingship. He was still only twenty-seven, and still oppressed with that youthful disease, a sense of his own importance. Being for ever frightened of compromising his dignity, which he misnamed his honour, he had come to be at loggerheads with all his Ministers, one after another and now, having no one else to whom he could turn, was obliged to keep in with the Rockinghams though he did not like them or approve of their policies. He complained that 'their still imbibing those strange ideas in Government that they adopted whilst in Opposition, cannot make me anxious for their continuance'. As, however, he had promised to support them, he must do so, but he

[1] Pitt to Shelburne, December 1765. Chatham Corr. II, 358.

would not be heart-broken if, finding themselves unable to go on, they resigned of their own accord. In that event, how happy he would be if he could form an administration composed of his true friends 'without again entreating Mr. Pitt, which I think would for ever stain my name'. So he hinted wistfully to Bute, though he must have known it was a daydream.[1]

Newcastle was still groping for Hardwicke's lost hand. Deprived of his patient and wise counsellor, he was like a hop stripped from its pole, sprawling helplessly on the ground and scattering bitter fruit. He would gladly have taken Pitt as a substitute but he had an uneasy feeling that he had estranged him beyond recall. Convinced that Pitt was necessary if the Ministry was to survive and seeing no other method, he was even prepared to sacrifice himself and made repeated offers, as genuine as they were unwilling, to resign if such a course would mollify Pitt. But, except as he was distrusted by Pitt, Newcastle now hardly counted in the political world, neither Rockingham nor the King paying him serious attention.

Rockingham himself was feeling the loss of Cumberland, who, if his statecraft was limited, had at least infused into the Ministry a vigour and a sense of purpose which without him were now sadly lacking. As for Grafton, his one aim was to resign the Seals into Pitt's hands.

On these dubious and hesitating men devolved the duty of unravelling the tangle which Grenville's Stamp Act had created. There was no denying the importance and urgency of the matter; it was having repercussions in every direction. America was seething with indignation. There was of course plenty of the froth of popular discontent, with its fantastic suppositions and far-fetched arguments, which did not merit attention; but there was also much solid ground for fear, and actual evidence of hardship. The colonies were not so flourishing as Grenville had supposed. During the war there had been a wave of prosperity, due to the subsidies from England, the profits from victualling the troops, and the trade with the rich West Indian Islands captured from the enemy. All or most of that prosperity had gone. The subsidies had come to an end; large numbers of the troops had been withdrawn and the richest Islands had been restored under the treaty of peace. Beside the loss of legitimate trade, Grenville's Sugar

[1] George III to Bute, 10th January 1766. Sedgwick, p. 245.

Act and his measures against smuggling were doing away with the old illegitimate trade. The colonies in fact were worse off than before and were feeling the post-war depression almost as strongly as England herself.[1] In the circumstances it seemed intolerable that new and hitherto undreamed-of taxes should be heaped on their shoulders. What made the burden worse was a feeling of impotence in face of it. There was no appeal and no escape; the tax was so devilishly ingenious. Unstamped documents being invalid, everyone was interested in seeing that they were stamped. Omission would not bring relief but merely lead to prosecution. The only escape would be to eschew documents altogether, but documents all the world must have, from the merchant in his counting-house to the bride in the vestry. To present troubles were added future fears. This was the first direct tax imposed by the English Parliament. True it was comparatively small, but when American pence began to save English pockets, the appetite would grow by what it fed on. Moreover, it was a serious attack on the rights and privileges of the colonial assemblies. Hitherto they had voted what money was required; if now they were to be stripped of the power of the purse, they would be stripped of all that was worth having. So the colonists argued, and, more ominous, they began to mutter that 'let worse come to the worst we'll call the French to our succour'.[2] Everyone in America was angry or apprehensive; the evidence piled up in the Ministry, warnings pouring in from the Governors and petitions from the governed. If America was seething, the City of London was alarmed. The American trade was being disrupted, and the American debts were not being paid. The Exchequer might net a few thousand pounds, but what was that compared with the millions lost to the merchants?

The Ministers very properly decided that their first task must be to tackle what the King called 'the arduous business of the American colonies',[3] but they found themselves sharply divided in opinion. Should the colonists be coerced or relieved, and what would be the result of either course? Clearly there were two sides to the question, and much could be said on each. Concession however won the day; the colonies were to be given every possible relief in trade and commerce, but it was agreed, with only a

---

[1] Miller, p. 88.　　　　　　　　　　[2] Miller, p. 95.
[3] George III to Egmont, 11th January 1766. Fortescue, I, 220.

mild expostulation from Newcastle, that any concession should 'go hand in hand with resolutions of authority or censures of the riots and tumults'. The real difficulties began when they considered what form the concessions should take. Should they amend or curtail the Stamp Act? Should they suspend it? Should they repeal it? They could come to no decision, and as a last hope agreed, at Grafton's suggestion, to consult Pitt.[1] Yet consultation was not easy. The King's consent had to be obtained, and the King had frequently and emphatically told them that, after his three failures with Pitt, he had no intention of risking a fourth. However, Rockingham seized a chance opportunity of raising the point, and was told that he might consult whom he pleased provided the King's name was not brought into it.[2] Grudging as this permission was, it seemed sufficient; and so on the 5th January, Thomas Townshend was at last despatched to Bath.

When asked his opinion, Pitt refused to give it. His attitude is said to have been unreasonable. But was it? The first duty of any Ministry is to decide on its own policy, and if the Rockingham Ministry, who had all the facts before them, could not come to a decision, it was neither Pitt's nor anyone else's duty to make up their minds for them. It would have been different if Townshend had been coming with an invitation to join the Ministry, but he was doing no such thing; the King had definitely forbidden it and not all the Ministers wanted it. Pitt, therefore, if he had given an opinion, would have been shouldering responsibility without the power or position to guide events. In his view the proper course was for the Ministry to put forward their own proposals in Parliament, when he would support or oppose them as might appear to him best. It was not for him to press his views on the Ministry in advance, or try to force them through Parliament at secondhand. Either he must develop them to the King as the responsible Minister, or he must voice them directly in the House. Townshend accepted Pitt's answer, and then, going beyond his instructions, entered into a general conversation, in the course of which he regretted the failure of the negotiations the previous June, and fished for Pitt's views on his possible return in the future. Pitt's reply was short but clear. He said that he and Temple were no longer connected, but if he ever returned to office, he

---

[1] Rockingham to Newcastle, 2nd January 1766. Add. MSS. 32,973.
[2] George III to Bute, 10th January 1766. Sedgwick, p. 243.

would feel obliged to offer the Treasury to Temple, with Rockingham as the second alternative; the present Ministers seemed to be the only set of men whom he could join, but he would not serve again with Newcastle.

Townshend passed on these scattered thoughts to Rockingham and the King. The former felt affronted at the precedence which Pitt had accorded to Temple over himself,[1] while the latter professed not to be interested in any ideas about government of which Pitt might deliver himself unasked.[2] The effect on Grafton and Conway was to make them eager to resign unless Pitt were brought forthwith into the Ministry; but they agreed reluctantly to stay on when the King told them brusquely that if they did resign, he would not permit them to form his new Ministry for him, but would do it for himself. The Ministry he had in mind, and hoped against hope to achieve, was 'my Dear Friend [Bute] and his friends'.[3] The fate of the Stamp Act and indeed of Rockingham's Ministry depended, not upon Pitt or anything he might do, but upon Bute. If Bute would re-enter politics, everyone else might go. But, to the King's grief, Bute was not responsive.

[1] Newcastle to Page, 7th January 1766. Add. MSS. 32,973.
[2] George III to Bute, 10th January 1766. Sedgwick, p. 243.
[3] *Ibid.*, 244.

XIII

THE ROCKINGHAM MINISTRY

(i)

WHEN PARLIAMENT had met on the 17th December, their attention had been directed to the 'matters of importance' which had occurred in America. Grenville, provoked by that innocuous phrase which seemed to foreshadow the repeal of his act, had moved to substitute the word 'rebellion'. He had been fobbed off for the moment, and the House given a month for deliberation, but the field of battle had been set. There were clearly two camps. On the one side were the partisans of America and the City merchants who had never been enthusiastic for the tax and were now thoroughly alarmed; they spent the month working up their propaganda, promoting petitions from the manufacturing towns and lobbying members. On the other side were the landowners, groaning under heavy taxation and led by an angry and embittered Grenville and the Duke of Bedford, that one-time pacifist who had trembled at France and quailed before Spain but now was breathing fire and slaughter against the colonists. In between stood the Government, uneasy, uncertain, unable to make up their minds. There was also one unknown factor—Pitt, who might or might not be well enough to crawl to the House, and whose views, if he were able to express them, both sides awaited with mingled hopes and fears which must have been very flattering to his vanity.

Parliament reassembled on the 14th January (1766). The Stamp Act at once became the centre of dispute. Some were for enforcing it; some for repealing it, but no guidance was given by the Government. They were waiting on events, and might have waited in vain but for Pitt. He entered the House late, having arrived in town only that morning, but lost not a moment in giving a lead, in words that reverberated through the country and were re-echoed throughout America. His speech was in two parts. In the first, and more measured part, he had made it abundantly clear that he was speaking as in independent man, who regarded every capital measure taken by the Grenville Ministry as entirely wrong, and could feel no more than partial confidence in the present Ministry because he thought he detected traces of an over-ruling influence of which he disapproved. Had he been able, he would have borne his testimony against the resolution to tax America from the first. But he had been ill, and since then the Stamp Act had been passed. He hoped a day would soon be appointed for debating the tax, but as he could not depend on his health, he begged permission to speak now. He would leave to a future day the questions of justice, equity, policy and expediency, and deal only with the question of right. In his opinion England had no right to lay a tax upon the colonies. The Americans were our fellow-subjects, equally entitled with ourselves to all the natural rights of mankind and the peculiar privileges of Englishmen; equally bound by the laws, and equally participating in the Constitution, of this free country; they were the sons, not the bastards of England. With us, taxation was not part of the legislative power. Legislation required the concurrence of Crown, Peers and Commons; but taxation was the voluntary gift and grant of the Commons alone, who made that gift as the representatives of the people, giving and granting their own money. What was true of England, was true of America. The Crown and Parliament were as sovereign and supreme over the colonies as they were over England in every circumstance of government and legislation whatsoever. But for the purpose of taxation they had no right and no power. Nor had the House of Commons any right; for they included no representative from America. It was an absurdity in terms for the Commons of Great Britain to say that they gave and granted to His Majesty the property of His Majesty's Commons of America. It was equally absurd to argue, as some did, that the colonies were virtually represented in the House. On the contrary, the Commons of America were represented in their several Assemblies, and had always possessed and exercised the right of giving and granting their own money. To distinguish between legislation and taxation was essential to liberty. Provided she had first made that distinction, England, as the supreme governing and legislative power, could bind the colonies by her laws, by her regulations and restrictions in trade, in navigation, in manufactures, in everything, except that of taking their money out of their pockets without their consent.[1]

When Pitt sat down there was a perceptible pause. He had given a strong and emphatic opinion, but in terms of the Constitution which seemed novel and unfamiliar; the House needed time to digest them. There were two men, however, to whom his words came home at once—Conway and Grenville. After a moment of reflection Conway rose to accept Pitt's lead with thankfulness; it resolved the doubts and hesitations of both himself and the Government. Grenville, smouldering, indignant and perhaps anxious, rejected Pitt's doctrine *in toto*. The disturbances in America, he said, which began as occurrences, had grown to tumults and riots and were now bordering on open rebellion. If Pitt's doctrines were confirmed, they would end in revolution. Taxation was not separate from legislation; it was a branch of it; and had been, and was still, exercised over persons who were not represented, as could be proved from former acts of parliament, and the present Constitution of the House. The Americans were making his Stamp Act a pretext to throw off their allegiance. Many charges had been levelled against him—charges of issuing orders to prohibit trade, charges of pushing his Act through, huggermugger; but the charges were false. He had discouraged no trade but what was illegal, and the Act had passed through all its stages in full houses with only one division.[2] Anyone who wished to deny that America was bound to yield obedience, must first inform them when America had been emancipated. The seditious spirit in the colonies owed its birth to the factions in the House. When members spoke of expecting disobedience, what were they doing but telling the Americans to stand out, and encouraging their obstinacy with the hope of support from England.

This flat contradiction roused Pitt to a second speech. Strictly speaking, he was out of order; but the House, in awed delight at this battle of the giants, clamoured for him to go on. He was speaking now without premeditation and from a full heart. His words poured from him like a torrent, leaping, sparkling, overflowing, bearing all before it. 'I have been charged', he said, 'with giving birth to sedition in America. They have spoken their

---

[1] Chatham's Speeches, p. 70.
[2] West's *Paper*, No. 2, 14th January 1766. Add. MSS. 32,973.

sentiments with freedom against this unhappy act, and that freedom has become their crime. Sorry I am to hear the liberty of
speech in this House imputed as a crime. . . . The gentleman tells
us, America is obstinate; America is almost in open rebellion. I
rejoice that America has resisted. Three millions of people so
dead to all the feelings of liberty, as voluntarily to submit to be
slaves, would have been fit instruments to make slaves of the rest.
I come not here armed at all points with law cases and acts of
parliament, with the statute-book doubled down in dog's ears to
defend the cause of liberty. . . . I would not debate a particular
point of law with the gentleman. I know his abilities: I have been
obliged to his diligent researches. But for the defence of liberty,
upon a general principle, upon a constitutional principle, it is a
ground on which I stand firm; on which I dare meet any man. . . .
Since the accession of King William, many Ministers, some of
great, others of more moderate abilities, have taken the lead of
Government. None of them thought, or even dreamed, of robbing
the colonies of their Constitutional rights. That was reserved to
mark the era of the late administration. . . . The gentleman boasts
of his bounties to America. Are not those bounties intended finally
for the benefit of this kingdom? If they are not, he has misapplied
the national treasures. I am no courtier of America; I stand up for
this kingdom. . . . When two countries are connected together,
like England and her colonies, without being incorporated, the
one must necessarily govern; the greater must rule the less; but
so rule it, as not to contradict the fundamental principles that
are common to both. . . . The gentleman asks, when were the
colonies emancipated? But I desire to know when they were made
slaves. . . . I will be bold to affirm, that the profits to Great
Britain from the trade of the colonies, through all its branches, is
two millions a year. This is the fund that carried you triumphantly
through the last war. . . . You owe this to America; this is the
price America pays for her protection. And shall a miserable
financier come with a boast that he can bring a peppercorn into
the exchequer to the loss of millions to the nation? I dare not say
how much higher these profits may be augmented. . . . I am convinced the whole commercial system of America may be altered
to advantage. You have prohibited where you ought to have
encouraged, and encouraged where you ought to have prohibited.
Improper restraints have been laid on the continent, in favour of

the islands. . . . Much is wrong; much may be amended for the
general good of the whole. . . . A great deal has been said without
doors of the power, of the strength of America. It is a topic that
ought to be cautiously meddled with. In a good cause, on a sound
bottom, the force of this country can crush America to atoms. . . .
But on this ground, on the Stamp Act, when so many here will
think it a crying injustice, I am one who will lift up my hand
against it. In such a cause, your success would be hazardous.
America if she fell, would fall like the strong man. She would
embrace the pillars of the State, and pull down the Constitution
along with her. Is this your boasted peace? Not to sheathe your
sword in its scabbard, but to sheathe it in the bowels of your
countrymen. . . . The Americans have not acted in all things with
prudence and temper. The Americans have been wronged. They
have been driven to madness by injustice. Will you punish them
for the madness you have occasioned? Rather let prudence and
temper come first from this side. I will undertake for America,
that she will follow the example. . . . Be to her faults a little blind;
be to her virtues very kind. Upon the whole, I will beg leave to
tell the House what is really my opinion. It is, that the Stamp Act
should be repealed absolutely, totally and immediately; that the
reason for the repeal should be assigned, because it was founded
on an erroneous principle. At the same time, let the sovereign
authority of this country over the colonies be asserted in as strong
terms as can be devised, and be made to extend to every point of
legislation whatsoever; that we may bind their trade, confine
their manufactures, and exercise every power whatsoever—except
that of taking their money out of their pockets without their
consent'.

(ii)

Pitt had disclaimed any wish to argue points of law with Grenville; and he was wise, for the relations between England and her
colonies, if they were to prosper and mature, could not be
regulated by parchments or settled in a solicitor's office. They
were the relation of parent and child, to be modified insensibly as
time progressed, and new needs and problems arose for solution.
Yet the fundamental basis of law could not simply be ignored; and
Pitt's argument accordingly began with, and rested upon, two
cardinal points—that taxation was not a part of legislation, and

that there could be no taxation without representation. The latter point was neither new, nor peculiar to Pitt; it was widely held both here and in America, though hitherto no great emphasis had been laid upon it. Grenville and his supporters countered it by arguing, lawyer-like, that it was contrary to fact; and alternatively that if it were not contrary to fact, it failed because the Americans were effectively represented by the merchants trading to America and other interested persons. Whatever either side might say, it was unfortunate that the Stamp Act brought the point into prominence, for brooding over it suggested separatist ideas in other directions, and so heaped fuel on the fire.

Pitt's other point—the divorce between taxation and legislation —was new and unexpected. Though based upon, and supported by, the common form of the King's Speech, it had not been argued before. It was another of Pitt's contributions to constitutional theory, one which made its way very slowly, coming to its full fruition only in the Budget controversy of 1909. But important as this contribution was for the future and helpful as it might have been for the moment, it was transcended by the spirit of tolerance and magnanimity towards the colonies which Pitt exhibited in himself and urged upon the House. He was offering a new conception of Empire which, limited as it was by the mercantilist theories of the age common to England and America alike, yet bore in itself the seeds of a future commonwealth of equal partners, developing gradually as the family grew up and the old economic ideas were exploded. In an Empire such as he envisaged, the good of one became the good of all, and the vehicle of progress was an ordered liberty. Everyman should be as free as was consistent with the well-being of the State. Liberty he loved, 'true real, restorative liberty'.[1] So he declared in the course of that memorable day.

(iii)

Whatever its implications, he had made a wonderful speech. The House fell under its spell, and voted the Address without a division. Conway and Grafton, roused to fresh enthusiasm, were more convinced than ever that Pitt should take over the reins of Government, and Rockingham, struck by 'the amazing powers and

[1] West's *Paper*, No. 2, 14th January 1766. Add. MSS. 32,973.

influence which Mr. Pitt has, whenever he takes part in debate',[1] so far yielded to their pressure as to ask the King for leave to approach Pitt again. But he did so in somewhat halting terms; all he envisaged was more cordiality on Pitt's part. The King, choosing, not without a touch of malice, to regard this as evidence that the Ministry were unable to carry on, refused his permission and made their request an excuse for attempting to recall Bute.[2] But Egmont and Charles Townshend, whom he consulted, dashed his hopes; and three days later a disgruntled and unwilling King was obliged to let Rockingham and Grafton have their way. He made his feelings plain, however, by the type of authorisation he gave. Pitt was to be asked first whether at this time he was disposed to come into the King's service, and secondly, whether, if Temple declined to take a part, that would be a reason for Pitt declining also.[3]

That the King should be cautious was perhaps natural; but it is to be noted that the atmosphere had altered greatly since the previous June. Pitt was no longer invited to meet the King personally, nor was he asked for his advice, nor was he offered a particular post, or indeed any post at all. No two questions could well have been more vague, or more likely to receive guarded answers from a man of Pitt's acute intellect and difficult temperament. The first question was in one sense unnecessary, and almost meaningless. Pitt was always disposed to come into the King's service; that was the aim and object of a political career. The real problem was not Pitt's disposition but the King's. What was he proposing that Pitt should do? Was he merely to prop up a second-rate Ministry under a second-rate premier—much as he had once, for weary years, propped up Pelham's administration—without being given the powers commensurate with the responsibility? That was hardly a task which Pitt could contemplate. Nor would it be enough to suggest that if Pitt were once a member of the Government, in however humble a position, he was bound to exercise immense influence over his colleagues. He had a sufficiently good conceit of himself to know that, but he also knew from bitter experience how greatly he had been thwarted, even when he held a commanding position, not only by his colleagues but by the King himself. He was older now, more physically feeble, less able to undergo tne fatigues of office and

[1] Albemarle, I, 270.   [2] Jucker, p. 404.   [3] Anson, p. 67.

less willing to endure patiently the irritation of constant obstruction. He could hardly be expected to play a subordinate part, and if he was to take a leading part, he must feel confident of royal support, which was not conspicuous as yet, and do his best to select his own colleagues, so far as he was allowed.

The precise nature of his answers has been obscured by the fact that there are three conflicting versions—one given by Grafton, one by Newcastle and one by the King. Grafton's is the only firsthand account; Newcastle's was based on information given by Rockingham; and the King's presumably on the reports he received. Grafton came away from the interview convinced that all was going well. Pitt had replied that he was ready to obey the King's commands and to serve with the existing Ministers, but there must be 'a transposition of offices'—a phrase which he repeated more than once, and which appeared to be ill-received by Rockingham. He also made it clear that Sackville must go. As to Temple, Pitt would be sorry to lose him, but as their views now differed so widely, he must give up all thought of him. Grafton was satisfied that there was clearly a basis for discussion.[1] So apparently was Pitt.[2] The other two versions agree that Pitt was ready to serve and to act with the existing Ministers but they emphasise and expand the reference to the transposition of offices, or as the King calls it 'commutations of employments', and end on a different note. Pitt, according to these accounts, regarded Newcastle, Sackville and Mansfield as 'obstacles', said that Temple must be offered the Treasury, and spoke of the dissolution of the existing Ministry and the formation of a new one under Rockingham, Grafton, Conway and himself, to include 'four openings for his friends in the House of Lords'.[3] Rockingham declared that if the 'commutations of employments' involved the removal of any one of his associates, he would feel obliged to resign in order to show that he was not influenced by self-interest, upon which Pitt said that 'he looked on the negotiations as over, and that he himself was hopeless as to the being able to form such an administration as he could venture to take part with'.[4]

Whichever version is accepted, it is clear that Pitt was disposed to join the Ministry. True, he foreshadowed terms, but that, after

[1] Anson, p. 67.
[2] See Pitt to Shelburne. Chatham Corr. III. 6.
[3] Newcastle's Note, 20th January 1766. Add. MSS. 32,973.
[4] George II's Memo. Fortescue, No. 209, I, 237.

all, was common form in the eighteenth century, and common
sense at any time. It is difficult to see how any of the terms
mentioned in any of the three versions was insuperable. Newcastle
had frequently offered to resign if Pitt so desired; Sackville was a
new importation, not one of Rockingham's old associates; and
Rockingham admitted that, while he valued Mansfield as a
private friend, he disapproved of his politics. One is driven to
the conclusion that the real impediment arose out of Rockingham's attitude, which may have been loyal to his friends
but was evidently cool, if not inimical, to Pitt; as, indeed,
it had been all along. He was 'in earnest' as the King once remarked, 'to keep his ground if possible'.[1] His wishes no doubt
coloured his report to the King, who promptly put an end to the
matter.

To sum up this curious episode, Pitt had provided the Ministry
with the lead they so badly required; and on the first occasion on
which the King had given him an opening, had agreed to co-
operate with them subject to terms. Those terms were barred by
Rockingham without being fully discussed; and the negotiations, to Grafton's sorrow and surprise, were broken off very
abruptly by the King because of what he was pleased to call the
'impracticability' of Pitt's answers. Rockingham was ordered to
be 'extremely civil but firm'[2] in telling Pitt that the discussions
were at an end. Do these facts really support the charge that 'it
was he, more than the King, who destroyed the Rockinghams by
his unreasonable refusal to co-operate with them', or the further
charge that he 'withheld from them the strength they required'?
(*See p.* 10). I find it hard to believe.

Rockingham is not to be blamed for fancying himself more
capable than Pitt—that was mere human vanity; nor for wishing
to keep Pitt at a distance—that was the instinct of self-protection.
But he can be blamed for the shilly-shally of his response to his
Cabinet's insistence that Pitt was essential and to their repeated
demands that he should be invited to join them, let his terms be
what they would. Rockingham neither bowed to their wishes,
nor gave a manly refusal, and by his hesitations and reluctance
created untold difficulties for himself, for his Cabinet, for Pitt and
the King. He himself was continually, as Newcastle once des-

---

[1] George III to Northington, 9th January 1766. Fortescue, I, 216.
[2] George III to Rockingham, 21st January 1766. Fortescue, I, 243.

cribed him, 'in great doubt and uneasiness';[1] Grafton and Conway were for ever undecided whether or not to resign; and the King and Pitt by being time and again half thrust on each other and half fobbed off, were growing heartily tired of a kind of flirtation which was neither pleasant in itself nor fruitful in its outcome, and were far more estranged than was either necessary or desirable. Rockingham and the King were both well-meaning in their respective fashions, but they were opinionated and obstinate; together they played havoc with the political *mise-en-scène*.

[1] Newcastle to White, 9th January 1766. Add. MSS. 32,973.

XIV

THE DECLARATORY ACT

(i)

THOUGH PITT had given the Ministry a lead, they still had to settle their course of action, and had reasons enough for doubting success. Opinions were fluctuating both here and in America, but were beginning to harden in an ominous fashion. So far as the colonies were concerned, Grenville had made two mistakes, first by proposing the tax, and then by delaying the date of its coming into operation. America was in no sense disloyal to the Crown, nor was it anxious for separation from the mother country; but its local assemblies had a tradition of squabbling with the royal governors, and their younger and more venturesome members displayed a normal desire to flout their elders. Hitherto the squabbles had been family bickerings, more heated than malicious, and the oppositions had been based on youthful impatience rather than differences of opinion. Grenville's Acts infused bitterness into the squabbles, and gave the opposition groups something tangible on which to build a policy; while the long pause between the original proposal and its enforcement gave time for both these tendencies to develop. The trouble began with the Sugar Act which, with the prohibition of paper money and the suppression of smuggling, had hit the colonists very severely. They retaliated by a boycott of British goods, and by refusing to pay their debts to British merchants, pleading, not without justification, that Grenville's measures had deprived them of the power. They had relied on the plight of the British merchants to bring Parliament to a better frame of mind, but the Stamp Act shattered their hopes. It did worse than that—it knocked the bottom out of their financial world. The Sugar Act had destroyed their prospects of gain in the future; the Stamp Act threatened to absorb their past savings. There was no hope whichever way they looked. Yet, while they protested with vigour, they did not at first seriously contemplate open resistance. Had Grenville forced the pace, he might conceivably have been successful, partly because the colonists would have had no time to consolidate opposition, partly because they would have found the tax less oppressive than they anticipated. But by deferring enforcement for twelve months, he gave time for fears to be magnified and indignation to come to the boil. He also gave the opposition groups time to conceive revolutionary ideas, and confuse local matters with imperial. It was a bold tilt by the youngsters of Virginia against the older generation that first sounded the tocsin. The Virginian Assembly was dominated by the great landowners, who were proud of their ancestry, regarding themselves as the aristocracy of the New World, and intent on securing to themselves a position in Virginia not unlike that of the Whig magnates in England—a privileged position of power and patronage. Their general attitude towards the Stamp Act was one of resigned, if resentful, acquiescence. There was, however, a younger and more democratic element, which had hitherto envied the position of the great landowners, without much hope of supplanting them. The Stamp Act gave them their chance. If the great landowners were prepared to acquiesce, the youngsters would raise the standard of revolt, and with one and the same stone dislodge their elders and smash the tax.

The natural leader of this young group was Patrick Henry, to whom Bancroft attributes 'benignity of temper, pure life and simplicity of habits'.[1] But Bancroft's geese are notoriously swans. Henry seems to have been a lively young spark in a hurry. He was endowed with the gift of the gab, to which he added an itch for popularity, a large dose of impudence and an unfailing eye for the main chance. Coming from the west with little to recommend him beyond a reputation for wit and a taste for dancing, he first failed in business and then took to the law, bouncing the authorities into giving him a licence after only six weeks' training. Luck offered him a chance to display his undoubted forensic gifts in a *cause célèbre* known as the Parsons' Cause, in which he questioned the long-standing right of the British Government to disallow Acts passed by colonial assemblies. Working himself into a state of simulated indignation, he declared that a King who acted in this way, 'from being a father of his people, degenerated into a tyrant, and forfeited all rights to his subjects' obedience'. That was in 1763, when Henry was twenty-four years of age. His

[1] Bancroft, *American Revolution*, II, 312.

speech shocked his hearers, but won him sufficient popularity to ensure his election to the Assembly two years later. He had barely taken his seat when the controversy over the Stamp Act arose. Henry saw his chance, and took it with great skill. Waiting until the older and more responsible members had gone home and the House was one of the thinnest ever known, Henry suddenly produced a series of resolutions which, in a flaming speech bordering on high treason, he exhorted the Assembly to adopt. The first five, though they sounded revolutionary and greatly perturbed his hearers, contained little to which Pitt would not have subscribed. They declared that Americans possessed all the rights of Englishmen; that the principle of no taxation without representation was an essential part of the British Constitution; and that Virginians could be taxed only by their own Assembly. The sixth and seventh resolutions went further, denying the validity of the Stamp Act or any similar Acts, and denouncing anyone who upheld them as enemies to the colony. The first five, after a stormy debate, were carried by tiny majorities. The last two were never put. They were, however, published and in due course accepted as part of the American faith.

That was in May 1765. The next month, James Otis of Boston, who had been particularly shocked by Henry's resolutions, advised the calling of a Congress to which all thirteen colonies should be invited, and at which the question of 'a united representation to implore relief' should be considered.[1] Not all the colonies responded, but a congress at which the majority were represented met at New York in October. Grenville's Act, it was clear, had supplied the colonies with a cause transcending the petty jealousies which divided them and induced an aspiration towards 'liberty' which hitherto had been non-existent, or at most latent. Whither it would lead, who could tell?

Side by side with orderly and constitutional movements, there was blowing up a violent popular reaction. The explosion came in August with the arrival of the stamps. Riots broke out; houses were wrecked, the stamp-masters were terrorised and their stamps burnt. 'I did not know', George Meserve the New Hampshire stamp-master reported at a later period, 'whether I should have escaped from this mob with my life, as some were for cutting off my head, others for cutting off my ears and sending them home

[1] Bancroft. *American Revolution*, II, 318.

with my commission'.[1] Such and the like were the stories which came flooding into England at the end of October, to agitate the newly-appointed and inexperienced Rockingham Ministry.

(ii)

If the news from America was frightening, it was at least clear; everything pointed in one direction. In England the position was much more confused. There were many conflicting interests, both within Parliament and without. In the country at large, there were two strongly opposed views. On the one side were all who felt the weight of taxation to be oppressive, and wanted to be relieved of part of their burden. They argued, with much justification, that America ought to share in the cost of her protection, whether against the French or against the Indians. The actual method of raising funds in the colonies interested them not at all; but they felt angry and exasperated at what seemed to them the lawlessness and violence, not to mention the ingratitude and selfishness, of the colonists. They were solid for coercion. On the other side were the merchants and manufacturers who had originally regarded the idea of taxing the colonies as a matter of politics which hardly concerned them, but had recently been changing their tune. What alarmed them was not the constitutional issue, nor any theory of taxation, nor were they particularly squeamish over violence and lawlessness. Their feet were firmly planted in their own counting-houses, whence they noted with growing concern that the export trade to America had 'lately suffered a great and sudden diminution and stagnation'. They believed the trouble to have arisen from Grenville's anti-smuggling activities, but wherever the cause lay, they wanted it removed. They said so in a series of petitions to the Treasury.[2] The longer the troubles lasted, and the more hectic the reports from America, the more vehement the merchants became. They were solid for repeal. Grenville in fact, had split England as successfully as he had united the colonies.

The split was accurately reflected in Parliament. Grenville in the Commons and Bedford in the Lords were loud in their condemnation of the Americans and fierce in their demands for

---

[1] Meserve to Conway, 31st July 1766. Quoted Miller, p. 100.
[2] Treasury Minute, 15th November 1765. Add. MSS. 32,971.

severity. They believed—and it must be counted to them for righteousness—that any concession would be taken as a sign of weakness and would lead to disaster. This fear not only sharpened their tongues, but shaped their intrigues. When Bute was supposed to be making overtures to them—though in fact he was not—their first thought was to take no action which might throw 'Lord Bute, with all the weight he can carry, into the scale of Administration upon the present important question of exerting the sovereignty of Great Britain over America, which once gone is irretrievable'.[1] It was a thought which troubled many of the members: 'The only thing I am clear in', Edward Sedgwick wrote to his friend, Weston, 'is that the right of the British Legislation to tax the colonies is clear and incontestable, and that it must not, cannot be given up, without annihilating the British Constitution in British America'.[2] So far as Grenville was concerned, however laudable his intentions, his judgment was warped by a conviction that the repeal, or even the modification, of the Stamp Act would be a personal affront placed on him by Parliament. As Beckford impatiently remarked on one occasion, 'he was mad on the Stamp Act, and could think of nothing else'[3]—an attitude of mind which made for intolerance.

On the other side, Rockingham and his adherents were disposed towards conciliation, but as they were moved mainly by the desire to improve trading conditions, they differed greatly on the question of degree. The Yorke family, as one might imagine, were harsh and legalistic. Hardwicke concurred in the idea of repeal only 'from the necessity of the times and the universal clamour which the merchants and manufacturers had raised', and disapproved of the 'tame despatches' which were sent to America;[4] while Charles Yorke insisted on a declaration of England's rights, clamping down on his own legal thunderbolts with regret. Egmont and Conway, in contradistinction, were for mildness and reason.[5] Rockingham, apparently with some idea of compromise, wanted to combine 'relief in trade and commerce' with 'resolutions of authority',[6] an idea in which Newcastle saw little virtue,

[1] Diary: *Grenville Papers*, III, 356.
[2] Sedgwick to Weston, 24th December 1765. H.M.C. 10th Report, Weston *Papers*.
[3] Walpole, *George III*, II, 293.
[4] Albemarle, I, 284.
[5] Newcastle to Rockingham, 1st January 1766. Add. MSS. 32,973.
[6] Rockingham to Newcastle, 2nd January 1766. Add. MSS. 32,973.

maintaining that he would 'incline rather to be deficient in that which is only a declaration in words than in the other on which depends the most material interests of this country'.[1] But as 'resolutions of authority' chimed in with the Ministry's idea of their own importance, besides being a sop for the Opposition, they were accepted without much difficulty. Less easy to decide was whether the Stamp Act should be repealed or modified. It was Pitt's speech on the 14th January, which finally weighted the scale for repeal.

Amid these cross-currents, there were two further points of view which should not be ignored, each approximating towards one of the main lines of thought, yet differing from it in emphasis and to some extent in kind—the points of view of Pitt and the King. Pitt was hot for conciliation, not only on behalf of trade and commerce—highly as he rated them—but even more on the grounds of justice. It might be—it was—folly to lose the benefits of American trade for the shadow of American taxes, but it was morally wrong to oppress our own kindred, denying them the rights we claimed for ourselves and imposing on them burdens we had rejected for ourselves. If they were bound with extraneous cords, they would rightly resist; but if they were bound by a mutual pride in the Empire, they would play their proper part and the whole body politic would gain. Pitt's moral convictions expanded as the Ministry's views contracted. He had at first been willing to proclaim in the strongest terms England's sovereign authority in all but taxation; but the more Rockingham harped on a declaratory act which threatened to include, and would certainly not exclude, the right to tax America, the more he swung away from what seemed to him on second thoughts unnecessary and dangerous. He was oppressed, as he told Shelburne, by the thought that 'the ruinous side of the dilemma to which we are brought is the making good by force there, preposterous and infatuated errors here'. Force would be fatal one way or the other, and as insistence in 'upholding the legislative and executive authority over America'[2] showed every sign of leading to force, he fought shy of it. As early as the 21st January, Rockingham found him 'strongly for the repeal of the Stamp Act, but as to the other parts of the question, the asserting the right of Parliament, Mr.

---

[1] Newcastle to Rockingham, 3rd January 1766. Add. MSS. 32,973.
[2] Pitt to Shelburne, December 1765. Chatham Corr. II, 358.

Pitt did not seem so strong as he was the other day in his speech'.[1]
His weakening on that point continued, until it led him in the
end to oppose the Declaratory Act, an attitude which, in Burke's
words, provoked Rockingham to look 'in the face a person he had
long respected and regarded, and whose aid was then particularly
wanting; I mean Lord Chatham'.[2] Burke chalked up that look to
Rockingham's credit, but it was to prove a key to the undoing of
the Empire.

The King's point of view was a curious amalgam of constitutional correctness and personal desires. He had promised the
Rockinghams, when they first took office, to give them his
support, and was disposed to pride himself on keeping his word,
though he had the meanest opinion of their talents and would
have broken his promise without compunction if he could have
found a decent excuse. But the fact is that he had no option.
Thanks to Bute and his own past follies, there was no one else to
whom he could turn. The stock of political leaders was exhausted;
Bute dared not come back; Fox would not; and the King could
hardly recall Grenville or Bedford. True, there remained Pitt;
but the King had persuaded himself, perhaps not unwillingly,
that Pitt was impracticable. Rockingham, in short, was his only
hope, and there was always the possibility, so dear to the King's
heart, that if Rockingham felt, or could be made to feel, the need
for further support, he might make advances to Bute, who might
in the circumstances return.[3] The King's policy was thus clear;
he must accept Rockingham's advice, but need not be too scrupulous in letting others know that he had views of his own.
Accordingly on the question of the Stamp Act, he told Rockingham that he preferred repeal to coercion; but he told others that
he preferred modification to repeal. Having thrown this apple of
discord into the arena, he sat back hopefully to await events.

(iii)

In this strained and expectant atmosphere, the Ministry, timid
by nature, felt the need for caution. They were wise, for problems
were knocking insistently at the door. The first came in the shape
of a petition passed by the New York Congress. It frightened

---

[1] Rockingham's account, etc., 23rd January 1766. Add. MSS. 32,973.
[2] Speech on American Taxation. Works II, 128.
[3] George III to Bute, 10th January 1766. Sedgwick, p. 244.

them. A continental congress was a new and alarming portent, and its petition only too likely to rasp tempers. Conway worked hard to suppress it, and was consequently the more dismayed when, on the 27th January (1766), Cooke, who was Pitt's friend and the member for Middlesex, moved for its presentation. The storm which Conway had feared duly followed. Someone denounced the Congress as a dangerous federal union and called for the rejection of its petition out of hand. Pitt's reaction to such a perverse view was as vehement as might be expected. The Congress, he declared, was no more dangerous than the familiar gatherings of politicians in their clubs and coffee-houses, or for that matter at Newmarket. The petition ought to be accepted because it was innocent, dutiful and respectful; it ought to be accepted because the right of the colonists to be heard was incontestable. Representation and taxation were indissolubly linked; and the Stamp Act, by the manner in which it had been passed, had broken the original compact between this country and America.

His advocacy carried away a number of Rockingham's followers who urged Conway to fall in with his views. But Sir Fletcher Norton, an ex-Attorney General and an old enemy who had clashed with Pitt more than once and, in his blustering, loud-mouthed fashion, was no mean opponent, attacked Pitt's doctrines in the manner of a bullying advocate, declaring that Pitt was sounding the trumpet to rebellion and ought to be called to the Bar of the House, or even sent to the Tower. He was obviously voicing the opinion of a large section, for according to Sackville, 'the House immediately joined in the idea and gave such shouts of applause as I never heard, so much that Mr. Pitt seemed greatly disconcerted and got off awkwardly enough when he was permitted to speak in his justification, but I cannot say he retracted his opinion'.[1] When Conway bowed before the storm and a little apprehensively 'declared against the Petition',[2] Cooke was, with difficulty, persuaded to withdraw his motion.

The omens for the Repeal Act seemed unpropitious; but a week later the Ministry salted the ground in a series of preliminary resolutions. There were five of them, and it was symptomatic that they were all, in varying degrees, adverse to the colonies. The

---

[1] Sackville to Irwin, 31st January 1766. H.M.C. Stopford-Sackville MSS.
[2] Conway to George III, 28th January 1766. Fortescue, I, 246.

first laid down that Parliament 'had, hath and of right ought to have full power and authority to make laws and statutes of sufficient force and validity to bind the colonies and people of America, subjects of the Crown of Great Britain, in all cases whatsoever'. It was an immensely popular resolution. It enabled members to eulogise themselves by commending the dignity of the British Constitution and affirming the omnipotence of Parliament; it enabled Grenville to expatiate on the wickedness of the Americans who resisted his Stamp Act; and it enabled the Ministers to claim that in repealing that Act they were moved by magnanimity alone. In short everyone could pay homage to the excellence of English institutions and their own wisdom and virtue. There were only three men disinterested enough to think of the colonies—Pitt, Beckford and Barré. They disliked the whole resolution and disagreed with the last four words; but though they kept the debate going until the small hours, their efforts were in vain. Pitt reported ruefully to Hester the next morning: 'the resolution passed, for England's right to do what the Treasury pleases with three millions of free men'.[1] It was a sad day for Pitt, but a happy one for Grenville, whose Stamp Act had now been vindicated.

The four remaining resolutions were debated two days later. They were of less moment, being concerned mostly with matters of fact; they affirmed that there had been tumults in America; that the tumults had been encouraged and inflamed by the votes of the Assemblies; and that the sufferers by the tumults should be compensated. The resolution that the authors of the tumults should be brought to condign punishment was dropped as being unnecessarily emphatic, and perhaps because it was incapable of fulfilment.

These resolutions, like Henry's, were mere gestures of defiance. They did no good; on the contrary, they created an unyielding atmosphere, in no sense favourable to conciliation or repeal. The immediate result was to encourage the advocates of coercion. The very next day (6th February 1766) the Lords carried by a majority of three, and against the Government's advice, a motion 'to enforce the Stamp Act in the colonies *vi et armis*'.[2] It was

---

[1] Pitt to Hester, 4th February 1766. Chatham Corr. II, 363—where the letter is misdated.

[2] Chesterfield to his son, 11th February 1766. Bradshaw, III, 1,335.

particularly observed that Bute voted in the majority, giving as was supposed a clear indication of the King's preference. Encouraged by this example, Grenville proposed a similar motion in the Commons. In a narrow view his motion was not unreasonable. Indeed it seemed the natural corollary of Conway's five resolutions, for, as Nugent pointed out, if they were not enforced, they would be nothing but a harlequin's sword held over the heads of the colonists.[1] But the Commons were more responsible than the Lords; they recognised that the acceptance of Grenville's motion 'would have amounted to an immediate declaration of war';[2] and when Pitt drove the point home by emphasising the absurdity of passing a resolution to enforce an act which might be repealed in a few days time, they gave a decisive negative to the motion. The size of their majority 'staggered all the politicians',[3] and so affected the House that when America was next debated all went smoothly. 'The whole of things' Pitt commented, 'is inexplicable. Tuesday last, in the Lords, the Ministry lost by *three* votes the question we debated yesterday; which was by us completely retaliated; for we overturned and beat, *à platte couture*, the triumphant factions, and brought them to agree, in words and substance, to somewhat more moderate even than the Ministry themselves meant'.[4] Rockingham was sufficiently heartened to remonstrate with the King for blowing hot and cold over the question of repeal. But by the same token Grenville and Bedford were roused to greater efforts, the latter clamouring for the King's authority to demand modification instead of repeal, and even offering to set up a new Government if the King would get rid of Rockingham.[5] The King administered a very proper snub; it was not, he replied, constitutional for the Crown to interfere personally in matters which had been referred to Parliament.[6] Feelings were running high, and the issue was regarded as doubtful by all except Pitt. He remained sanguine, encouraging the Ministry 'to put the best construction on all the King's words and actions'[7] and to go forward with high hopes.

[1] Walpole, *George III*, II, 204.
[3] Sackville to Irwin, 10th February 1766. H.M.C. Stopford-Sackville MSS.
[2] *Ibid.*   [4] Pitt to Hester, 11th February 1766. Chatham Corr. II, 376.
[5] Memo. by the King, and Duke of York to the King, 18th February 1766. Fortescue, I, 272-3.
[6] George III to Duke of York, 18th February. Fortescue, I, 273.
[7] Onslow to Newcastle, 12th February 1766. Add. MSS. 32,973.

On the 21st February (1766), matters came to a head. Conway asked for leave to introduce a Bill for the repeal of the Stamp Act. He drew a harrowing picture of the chaos which the Act had created—at home a disastrous drop in exports, a great increase in bad debts, and wholesale unemployment; while in America there were hardships and riots on the continent, and famine in the islands. The outlook was even more terrifying, it offered nothing but a total loss of trade and the prospect of war, while France and Spain stood on the sidewalks eagerly awaiting their chance. Grenville and his followers presented the opposite picture. They emphasised how dangerous it was to drop a tax merely because it was unpopular; the precedent would spread and if the Stamp Act went today, the Navigation Acts would go tomorrow. Nor would a declaratory act help, if the Government dare not exert the right they claimed. In giving up the right of taxation, they were giving up the brightest jewel in the Crown. How could they justify themselves to the King, to the House, to the country?[1]

Grenville omitted to point out that the difficulties he painted should have been envisaged before the Stamp Act was passed, and in any event did not do away with the evils which had followed. Yet neither the evils nor the difficulties could be ignored, if a solution was to be found. Pitt recognised the fact. He had come down to the House on crutches, but full of fight. 'Thank God', he wrote to Hester before setting out, 'I am able to send a good account of myself, legs excepted; more properly, one leg only excepted. I must get up to the House as I can; when in my place, I feel I am tolerably able to remain through the debate, and cry Aye! to the repeal, with no sickly voice'.[2] He did better than that; he spoke for an hour and a quarter, and by way of meeting the dilemma which Grenville had posed, declared that he would be an Englishman first and then an American. It was the miserable state of this country, the distresses of the manufacturer, the unhappy wife and starving child, the universal bankruptcies that would ensue which had brought him to the House. All these afflictions were united in a focus which would burn up and destroy everything unless the cause were rooted out. Parliament by adopting Conway's resolutions had determined their authority *de jure*; they should now be ready to show mercy *de facto*. He did

[1] Walpole, *George III*, II, 210.
[2] Pitt to Hester, 21st February 1766. Chatham Corr. II, 390.

not himself admit that Americans could be taxed, but if after being relieved, they still remained contumacious, he would be for as strong measures to enforce and compel obedience to the laws as anyone. Until that time arrived, he was for absolute, total and unconditional repeal.[1]

At two o'clock in the morning the House authorised the introduction of the Bill, and as the Members trooped home, the crowds which had waited anxiously at the doors gave vent to their feelings of joy. Conway was cheered heartily, Grenville was met 'with scorn and hisses'. But the hero of the day was Pitt. When he appeared, lame, gaunt and tired, 'the whole crowd pulled off their hats, huzzaed, and many followed his chair home with shouts and benedictions'.[2]

Perhaps more interesting, as evidence of character, were the respective reactions of Rockingham and Pitt. Rockingham demanded an audience of the King and proceeded to crow over him lustily. 'I remarked to His Majesty', he recounted to Newcastle, 'how strong the torrent of opinion in favour of repeal was and is, when notwithstanding the checks of seeing so many persons in His Majesty's service voting against it, and notwithstanding the great combinations that were in the House of Commons against it, and ultimately the knowledge that had lately been given of His Majesty's own sentiments being for modification, yet nevertheless 275 were for the total repeal and 167 only for modification. I also told him of the immoderate joy in the lobby and of what sorts of persons it was composed, and then ended with lamenting that His Majesty had not adhered to the repeal'.[3] Pitt's reaction was very different. His first wish was to share his joy with others; his second to offer thanks to God. 'Happy indeed', he wrote to Hester, 'was the scene of this glorious morning, when the sun of liberty shone once more benignly upon a country too long benighted. My dear love, not all the applauding joy which the hearts of animated gratitude, saved from despair and bankruptcy, uttered in the lobby, could touch me, in any degree, like the tender and lively delight, which breathes in your warm and affectionate note. . . . Wonder not if I should find myself in a placid and sober fever, for tumultuous exultation, you know, I think not permitted to feeble

[1] West's note, 21st February 1766. Add. MSS. 32,974.
[2] Walpole, *George III*, II, 212.
[3] Rockingham to Newcastle, 22nd February 1766. Add. MSS. 32,974.

mortal successes; but my delight, heartfelt and solid as it is, must want its sweetest ingredient (if not its very essence) till I rejoice with my angel, and with her join in thanksgivings to protecting Heaven, for all our happy deliverances'.[1]

(iv)

Rockingham's interview with the King, in spite of his boasting, does not seem to have been entirely reassuring. No doubt the King was not submissive; and Rockingham may have felt much as Lord Frederick Cavendish who remarked about this time, 'we are in a very droll situation. Here is [an] administration supported by Mr. Pitt and the whole voice of the nation carrying on triumphantly this very important measure, the repeal, against the combined forces of Bedford, Bute and Grenville, assisted I doubt by the King's declared opinion'.[2] In such a droll situation Pitt's help seemed very essential, not so much for immediate purposes, as for future security. Rockingham began to regret his *non possumus* attitude of the previous month; perhaps he had been too stiff; perhaps it would have been wiser to study Pitt's conditions, in the hopes of being able to meet them. Would it be possible, even at this late date, to reopen the negotiations?

It was no doubt a pity that Rockingham was at once so irresolute and so tongue-tied. Instead of approaching either Pitt or the King with concrete proposals, he sought out Shelburne and delivered himself of a number of obscure hints, which on reflection Shelburne supposed were intended for Pitt and consequently passed on to him. Rockingham, it seemed, wanted to form a central party, unconnected with either Bedford or Bute, but was 'under the greatest apprehensions it would hitch'. There were some individuals—members of his own party—who, in Rockingham's opinion, must be included in any 'new-cast system', and though he felt pretty certain that Pitt would not treat them harshly, he must, for his own satisfaction, be sure. There were others, Newcastle and Yorke for instance, who, he believed, 'might be brought into everything that was desired', i.e. would resign—but must be let down gently. All must be cut and dried before the King was approached, or the scheme would fail and very possibly Grenville be recalled. And the arrangements must

[1] Pitt to Hester, 22nd February 1766. Chatham Corr. II, 393.
[2] Cavendish to Lennox, 23rd February 1766. H.M.C. Bathurst MSS.

be made quickly as Grafton and Conway clearly intended to bring things to a crisis.[1] These *obiter dicta* left Pitt cold. His former interviews with Rockingham had not prepossessed him in his favour, and the course of events since had widened the gulf between them. Rockingham's emphasis on the declaratory act and especially his insistence on the right of taxation, were serious stumbling-blocks, because they disclosed differences of principle, and were hurtful to the colonial cause. No less important in Pitt's eyes was the method of approach. Rockingham was hinting at a sort of intrigue, an alliance to storm the Closet, without any consideration of the King's wishes or his probable attitude and without any guarantee of success. Pitt heartily disapproved of such a procedure, as, indeed, he had done all his life. His answer therefore was decisive. Rockingham's plan could not bring things to a satisfactory conclusion; he was posing as master of King and public, claiming to make openings in his own right for 'seekers of offices and candidates for Ministry'. Pitt was neither. 'I shall never', he said, 'set my foot in the Closet, but in the hope of rendering the King's personal situation not unhappy, as well as his business not unprosperous; nor will I owe my coming thither to any court cabal or Ministerial connexion. The King's pleasure and gracious commands alone shall be a call to me, I am deaf to every other thing'.[2]

Whether Shelburne passed on Pitt's reply is not clear; but in any event Rockingham made a further indirect approach two days later, this time through Nuthall. But in doing so, he made it quite evident that his real object was simply to avoid 'breaking to pieces the present administration'. Pitt was to be a prop for the existing Ministry, not to form one of his own. Pitt's reply was that he must await the King's commands. To act otherwise would be the highest presumption in a private individual.[3] When considering whether Pitt is to be blamed for 'his unreasonable refusal to co-operate' it is to be noted that, in fact, he was ready to negotiate in January when Rockingham came to him armed with the King's authority; and in fact held back in February only because Rockingham put forward vague proposals with evident hesitation and without either details or authority. The significant point was

[1] Shelburne to Pitt, 24th February 1766. Fitzmaurice, I, 377.
[2] Pitt to Shelburne, 24th February 1766. Fitzmaurice, I, 382.
[3] Pitt to Nuthall, 28th February 1766. Chatham Corr. II, 400.

Rockingham's reluctance. Whenever he moved, it was because
he had been pushed by his colleagues. He made it sufficiently clear
that he was acting against his will, and he avoided by every means
bringing the King into the picture. His approaches, in short, were
unwilling, half-hearted and unofficial. Bearing in mind their
character, Pitt received them with greater encouragement than
they deserved. What he was not prepared to do was to lend his
name to Rockingham without any guarantee of the use which
Rockingham would make of it. If Rockingham was sincere, he
would press for Pitt first in the Closet, not at Hayes. Pitt was under
no delusions about the reluctance of the King to restore him to
power, and until that reluctance had been overcome, he was
bound to regard Rockingham's half-hints as either delusions or
self-interested. As he told Mitchell who had expressed his disappointment at not finding Pitt in office, 'it was all along evident
to me that all expectations of the kind you allude to, never had a
real foundation'.[1] Pitt left Rockingham in no doubt as to where
the key lay; and if Rockingham ignored his suggestions, there
was clearly nothing to be done.

Rockingham did ignore the suggestions, and four days after the
Nuthall interlude proclaimed his wide divergence from Pitt by
introducing the Declaratory Bill. Although at a later date Burke
maintained that Rockingham had 'preserved the authority of
Great Britain' by that Bill,[2] there can be little doubt that its only
justification was expediency, and its immediate effects were a
partial triumph for the Opposition, and a final end to all possibility
of a coalition with Pitt. He would have nothing to do with
the Bill or the Government which introduced it; and, in his
speech, for the first time alluded to the desirability of Rockingham's fall. The Bill, he asserted, was wrong in theory and in fact;
the only result of passing it would be to confirm the world in
their view that we were exceeding our rights, and to reopen the
wounds in America which were now healing over. He registered
his total dissent. He never opposed any Bill so entirely from
principle and conviction; and his wish now was that a good
administration could be set up, formed to the liking of the
King and the approbation of the people.[3] His remarks about a

[1] Pitt to Mitchell, 13th April 1766. Add. MSS. 6,833.
[2] Speech on American Taxation. Works II, 131.
[3] West's *Paper*, 4th March 1766. Add. MSS. 32,974.

new Ministry led to a little banter, which, as so often, degenerated into acrimony, with some show of temper on Grenville's part and of heat on Pitt's.[1] In the course of the altercation, Pitt praised Bute in his private capacity, and went out of his way to speak well of the Tories, two facts which according to Sackville 'convinced everybody that Mr. Pitt wished to be in office, and that he was resolved to declare to every denomination of men in that House that he had not the smallest objection to act with either of them'.[2] Sackville was pleased to exaggerate; but there can be little doubt that the Bill had destroyed Pitt's belief in Rockingham, and disposed him in consequence to look elsewhere.

(v)

Pitt's estrangement was a serious blow to the Ministry. Rockingham had owed far more to Pitt's benevolence than he had realised. It had been his main prop, and from the moment it was withdrawn his fall became certain; for in spite of his good conceit of himself, no one had accepted him for his own sake. The more important members of his Cabinet regarded him as a stop-gap, pending Pitt's arrival; and the King had welcomed him simply as an antidote to the oppressive Grenville. But, elated with his recent successes, he meandered happily on, imagining that he was rising in favour with the King, and indifferent to Pitt's growing restiveness.[3] Not that Pitt acted hastily or unreasonably. On the contrary, where he agreed with the Government's policy he was still ready to help, as he showed by seconding Dowdeswell's motion for the repeal of the Cyder Tax (7th March). But Rockingham, who was jealous, took a perverse pleasure in irritating him, and as though to drive the goad home, next proposed a reduction in the vote for the militia (17th April). The Cabinet can hardly have given the matter careful consideration, or seriously meant it, for they promptly gave way when Pitt, coming down to the House in a fine frenzy, threatened that 'he would go to the farthest corner of the island to overturn any Ministers that were enemies to the militia'.[4] A few days later there was a brush over the old question of general

---

[1] Walpole. *George III*, II, 216.
[2] Sackville to Irwin 11th March 1766. H.M.C. Stopford-Sackville MSS.
[3] Cf. 'it was my Lord Rockingham's opinion that . . . everything might go on with ease and success. Newcastle to White, 11th July 1766. Add. MSS. 33,003.
[4] Walpole. *George III*, II, 224.

warrants. The Government wished to declare such warrants illegal in cases of libel alone; Pitt was determined to declare them illegal in all cases whatsoever and, somewhat surprisingly, was supported by Grenville. The Rockinghams jumped to the conclusion that Pitt had made up his quarrel with the Cousinhood, and were correspondingly angry and dismayed. But they were wrong. Pitt had always made it clear that he stood apart from every faction. It was, in one sense, a sore point with him. He would much have preferred to have had his own party, but having been foiled in 1756 he had ever since made a rueful virtue of necessity, proclaiming his 'naked' condition more often than was either necessary or desirable. Having taken his stance, he lived up to it, always professing himself more interested in 'measures' than 'men', and always affirming his willingness to work with anyone, Whig or Tory, who stood by 'Revolution Principles'. Nor in adopting this attitude was he acting very differently from others. Enmities among the factions had a curious habit of disappearing at the dictates of interest; and even Rockingham, who so prided himself on loyalty to his party, knocked, however half-heartedly, at a number of doors which on grounds of consistency he should have avoided.[1] Walpole assumed that on this occasion Pitt acted as he did because he was 'in his hostile mood',[2] but in fact Pitt's motive was a burning desire to carry a point which he believed to be essential to liberty.

On the 24th April, there was another debate on American affairs, when it was suggested that Dominica should be made a free port for French goods. The proposal appeared to offer greater advantages to the Islands than to the continent, and for that reason struck Pitt as unseasonable. Subsequently he came to believe that it would be sacrificing the Islands to 'a speculative project' and opposed it strongly.[3] At the moment however he had not fully made up his mind, and to avoid being merely obstructive, agreed that it was an important question which should be 'thoroughly weighed and considered' after both parties had been consulted.[4] The debate had a further and a different interest. Pitt couched his remarks in what Rigby, with prophetic insight,

---

[1] Cf. his willingness to treat with Bute's friends as individuals, though not as a party. Newcastle to White, 3rd May 1766. Add. MSS. 33,003.
[2] *George III*, II, 225.
[3] Pitt to Nuthall, 11th May 1766. Chatham Corr., II, 419.
[4] Newcastle to White, 3rd May 1766. Add. MSS. 33,003.

described as 'a kind of farewell speech'; it proved in fact to be one of the last which he made in the Commons. In the course of it he said that, on account of his health, he was going first to Bath and then to Burton Pynsent, and did not know when he should return to the House. He hoped, however, for the sake of the country, that all factions might cease, and that a Ministry might be appointed acceptable to the King and public alike, and composed of men whose qualifications were so outstanding and so well known that they would enhance the Government's reputation both at home and abroad.[1]

This desire for a change chimed in with the popular view. By common consent the Ministry would and should disintegrate unless Pitt joined their ranks. Grafton was anxious to resign and vacancies remained unfilled because no one would accept them. Pitt had been well disposed at the start though a trifle hesitant, confidence being, as he said, 'a plant of slow growth in an aged bosom'.[2] But Rockingham had squandered his stock of good will; he had shown no eagerness; he had been elusive and shy; his approaches to Pitt had been half-hearted and quickly dropped. Pitt had been neither consulted not kept informed, so that he had been obliged at times to oppose Government motions openly in the House. He complained that the treatment meted out to him was inconsistent with the Ministers' professions, and he especially disliked Rockingham's persistence in asking him to 'explain himself to the King's Ministers', i.e. state his conditions for accepting office, in spite of his reiterated declaration that he had no right to discuss such matters without the King's prior command.[3] Rockingham's action, whether Pitt knew it or not, was deliberate, and was intended to keep Pitt out. He told Thomas Walpole that 'he did not approve of saying anything to Mr. Pitt by order of the King',[4] and informed Grafton, still more emphatically, that 'he would never advise His Majesty to call Mr. Pitt to his Closet, that this was a fixed resolution to which he would adhere'.[5] Rockingham, with amazing blindness, saw no reason why his administration 'should not carry on very well and with honour to themselves' without Pitt's help. Grafton scouted

---

[1] Rigby to Bedford, 24th April 1766. Bedford Corr. III, 333.
[2] Speech, 14th January 1766. Almon, II, 32.
[3] Thomas Walpole, Conversation, etc., 18th April 1766. Add. MSS. 32,974.
[4] *Ibid.*
[5] Grafton to Conway, 22nd April 1766. Anson, p. 71.

o

the idea and seeing no hope in Rockingham, finally told the King that he could not, as a man of honour, continue to form part of a Ministry 'that set Mr. Pitt at defiance'.[1]

Grafton's resignation was not the only one. But Rockingham was impervious to losses. 'I do not imagine', he said, 'resignations will go far; if they do, I do not think much will happen from them'.[2] So convinced was he that he was essential to the King. It is a tribute to the King's constitutional correctness that he kept his temper when Rockingham forced him, much against his will, to accept the youthful Duke of Richmond as Grafton's successor, and avoided the obvious retort when Rockingham blandly remarked that although his friends advised him to resign and he himself wished to retire, he thought he owed it to the King to go on.[3] Rockingham had at least this justification—that the King did wish him to remain, but only in the belief that by remaining he would be forced to coalesce with Bute.[4]

There were, however, limits to the King's patience, and Rockingham filled up the cup of his iniquities by mortifying the King in that very tender spot, his honour. When the Duke of Cumberland died, Rockingham agreed to obtain parliamentary sanction forthwith to divide Cumberland's parliamentary grant between the King's three brothers. But he failed to bring the matter before the House, and the King, who had promised his brothers, was obliged to eat his words. It infuriated him. 'My prudence', he told Egmont, 'is now exhausted. I am inclined to take any step that will preserve my honour'.[5] Blindly rushing on his fate, Rockingham chose this moment to urge the King to dismiss some of Bute's friends who had voted against Government measures, and to create a number of peers. The King not only refused, but appealed for help to Northington, who precipitated the crisis by informing his colleagues that he intended to resign. It was the end. Pitt was invited to come up to town and advise 'how an able and dignified Ministry may be formed'.[6]

[1] George III to Northington, 28th April 1766. Fortescue, I, 295.
[2] Rockingham to Newcastle, 25th May 1766. Add. MSS. 32,975.
[3] George III to Egmont, 16th May 1766. Fortescue, I, 307.
[4] See Egmont to George III, 1st May 1766. Fortescue, I, 298.
[5] George III to Egmont, 28th May 1766. Fortescue, I, 347.
[6] George III to Pitt, 7th July 1766. Chatham Corr. II, 436.

XV

THAT PEERAGE

(i)

TIME HAD been modifying the King's opinion of Pitt. On his accession he had spoken of him as the 'most dishonourable of men', and 'a true snake in the grass',[1] and had wanted to show him 'that aversion which will force him to resign'.[2] But by now the personal dislike had moderated, and some inkling of his abilities had supervened. What George principally feared was that, if Pitt were recalled, he might insist on bringing Grenville and Temple with him, which the King declared would make him 'a slave for life'.[3] On the other hand he knew that Pitt was not so virulent against Bute as the other leaders had been, and though he would certainly refuse to accept Bute as a colleague, would not object to the King seeing him as a private friend.[4] On the whole the pros outweighed the cons, but there was one further and formidable obstacle—the memory of the abortive negotiations of the previous year. The King could not bear the thought of a further rebuff, and would probably have stumbled on as best he could, if Rockingham had not outraged his feelings. Rockingham, in short, could have remained in office, if he had shown either ability or tact. But he had shown neither. Burke, on Rockingham's dismissal, published *A short Account of a late Short Administration*, which he evidently regarded as a glorious record and a complete justification. But what stands out most prominently is its negative character. Rockingham had repealed this and condemned that and abolished the other; but of positive achievements there was little sign. It was perhaps early days for a forward move; but nothing in the record suggests that Rockingham was conscious of any requirement beyond sweeping and garnishing the house. If his abilities were small, his tact was smaller and

---

[1] Sedgwick, pp. 45 and 47.　　　　　　　　　[2] *Ibid.*, p. 50.
[3] George III to Bute, 10th January 1766. Sedgwick, p. 244.
[4] George III to Bute, 12th July 1766. Sedgwick, p. 253.

had recently broken down altogether. The King's sudden resolve
to recall Pitt was not the fruit of political wisdom, but, like all the
changes he had made, an effort to escape from a Ministry which
he had set up for himself and of which he had since become
disillusioned. His hopes now were centred in Pitt's sketch of what
a Ministry should be—one composed of able men regardless of
the factions to which they nominally belonged. It appealed to the
vague idealism which the King had imbibed in his youth, and not
the less because it did not rule out the purveyor of that idealism—
Bute.

Pitt was at Burton Pynsent when the King's letter reached him.
He had left London in poor health and much inclined to retire.
Indeed he was in process of burning his boats by selling Hayes to
Thomas Walpole. But with the natural perversity of the human
heart, he had scarcely reached Bath before he began to regret
Hayes; it was so full of memories for him.[1] Then with the return
of health—'the air of this hill and my horse have quite set me up
again'[2]—he began to recall, wistfully, the fascinations and excite-
ments of the House. His friends would not let him alone. They
supplied him with news; they passed on the compliments paid to
him. It was all exceedingly delightful. Pitt was but human; he was
pleased in spite of himself to hear that Grafton had praised him as
the only man who could give weight and dignity to the Government, and glowed with satisfaction at Grafton's readiness to step
down from his high estate and wield a mattock or a spade under
'that able and great Minister, Pitt'.[3] The King's letter arrived at a
psychologically favourable moment. Pitt had just admitted that
'the old surly English leaven works still in a retired breast. Farming, grazing, haymaking, and all the *Lethe* of Somersetshire cannot
obliterate the memory of days of activity'.[4] The King's letter
offered a prospect of more such days, and Pitt responded gladly:
'I shall hasten to London as fast as I possibly can; happy could I
change infirmity into wings of expedition'.[5]

There was another reason which lent not only wings to Pitt's
feet, but a song to his heart. From his earliest days he had hankered after a peerage; he had longed for the time when he could

[1] Pitt to Hester, 5th May 1766. Chatham Corr. II, 416.
[2] Pitt to Nuthall, 1st June 1766. Chatham Corr. II, 423.
[3] Bishop of Carlisle to Grenville, 29th May 1766. *Grenville Papers*, III, 243.
[4] Pitt to Countess Stanhope, 20th June 1766. Mahon, V. Appendix, p. vi.
[5] Pitt to George III, 8th July 1766.   Chatham Corr. II, 438.

stand on an equality with the great men whose trappings he envied as truly as he despised their abilities; he had yearned to meet them face to face without the heartburn of jealousy or the enforced humility of subordination. There had been a time when the Duchess of Marlborough's will had raised his hopes with its glimpse of vast reversionary wealth; and he had told Grenville, with coy optimism, that if those prospects matured, he intended to live as a gentleman should, with 'a town house of some expense' and a pocket borough of his own.[1] Twelve years had passed since then, and those particular prospects had vanished. But Burton Pynsent had fallen into his lap instead, and if he was not quite the rich man of his dreams, he was rich enough to carry off a peerage with *éclat*. He had been pondering the possibility ever since he had come into his new estate.[2] It was a mirage which to some extent moulded his policy, making him anxious to deal with that fount of honour, the King, directly rather than through the Ministers. But nothing seemed to come of it all; he was getting older and more infirm; his friends were dying off and the King was showing himself less well-disposed. Pitt had grown weary and had forced his mind to accept the idea of retirement, when suddenly, like manna from heaven, this passport to honour had fallen at his feet. It was his last chance and he must seize it.

(ii)

Pitt arrived in London on the 11th July (1766), and at once made his way to the Chancellor, through whom he had received the King's letter. To him he professed a desire of proceeding in a temperate and prudent fashion, but carefully avoided entering into details; those were reserved for the King. Equally carefully, he stressed the fact that his state of health made it impossible for him to take an active office, so, indirectly, staking out a claim to a retreat in the House of Lords.

On the 12th he went down to Richmond to see the King. The two approached each other warily; both had much to gain and much to lose. The King wanted a stable Government; he wanted a defence against Grenville and the Bedfords; he wanted to have

[1] Pitt to Grenville, 2nd November 1754. *Grenville Papers*, I, 131.

[2] Cf. 'Lord G. Sackville thinks, from some obscure expressions of Lord Temple, that Pitt would take a peerage and leave the House of Commons to George Grenville'. Walpole to Holland, 28th May 1765.

Bute and Bute's friends around him. But he knew he was running
a risk. If the negotiations with Pitt failed once more, his plight
would be pitiable; he would have no one to whom he could turn.
Pitt on his side wanted his peerage; he wanted also a free hand to
deal with the many problems which the changing Ministries of
the past few years had ignored or never noticed. If the King
refused him his peerage, or tried to tie his hands too tightly, it
might be better to shrug off ambition and bury himself again in
Somerset—once and for all.

Pitt began on the lines which the King had once commended
—'he wished as far as it was possible to dissolve all factions and
to see the best of all parties in employment'; but as that could not
be achieved in a moment, he proposed to take the Rockinghams
as a basis and introduce new blood by degrees. One wish he had
—that Temple should be his First Lord of the Treasury; but in
view of their estrangement, the offer must come from the King
himself; if Temple refused, Pitt would go on without him. The
King agreed to sound Temple, and then broached the subject of
Bute and his friends. He found Pitt accommodating. Provided
Bute kept clear of politics, Pitt could see no reason why the King
should not 'frequently have the comfort of his conversation', for
Ministers should not presume to meddle with the King's private
acquaintances. As for Bute's friends—Mackenzie should be
restored to the Privy Seal in Scotland; Norton, in spite of a bad
reputation, should be given something; and Northumberland,
Despencer and Ellis would be kept in mind for employment as
opportunities offered, 'but as they brought no share of abilities
with them, they must wait a little'. So the preliminaries were
sketched, with some degree of mutual satisfaction.[1]

(iii)

True to his promise, the King sent for Temple, who arrived
in no very good humour. He thought he should have been
summoned before Pitt, and being angry had called on Grenville
by the way, in order to stoke up his fires of resentment. With the
King he was 'very guarded', inclining, as the King told Pitt, 'to
quarters very heterogeneous to my and your ideas'.[2] Then he

---

[1] George III's *Memorandum*, Fortescue, I, 176, where the wrong date is assigned.
[2] George III to Pitt, 15th September 1766. Fortescue, I, 375.

went to see Pitt, and, on his own showing, behaved in a most peremptory and provocative manner. He claimed 'at least' equality with Pitt, and on that basis demanded a series of appointments obviously intended to get rid of the Rockinghams and substitute the Bedfords.[1] When he found Pitt unwilling to agree, he flew into a temper, accused Pitt of wishing to be 'sole and absolute dictator',[2] and flung himself off, declaring that he would not be 'a capital cypher, surrounded by cyphers of quite a different complexion, the whole under the guidance of that great Luminary, the great Commoner, with the Privy Seal in his hand'.[3] Going back to the King, he told him that 'he would not come in as a child to go out as a fool'—a phrase of which apparently he was not a little proud, as he repeated it on several occasions. What exactly he understood by it may be open to doubt, but it is certain that by refusing to come into Pitt's Ministry he went out of ministerial life for good and all. Having quarrelled with Pitt, it was typical of him to suppose that he had impressed the King. It was also typical of him to broadcast spiteful letters in order to harm Pitt, telling Gower, for instance, quite gratuitously, that he had recommended him for the post of Secretary of State, but Pitt had not approved.[4] An offensive, hurtful man, with scarcely one redeeming quality! By contrast Pitt's version of the disagreement was 'very different'.[5] He softened the asperities in his report to the King and, with loving thoughtfulness, wrote to Hester of 'our dear Lord Temple', and spoke of 'the kind and affectionate behaviour which he held throughout the whole of our long talk'.[6] Perhaps he was foolish, for even white lies find us out. Hester, glad to think that the estrangement between her husband and her brother had ended, even though they still disagreed on 'public situations', wrote happily to suggest an interchange of visits.[7] Temple not only refused the invitation but found it 'indispensably necessary' to inform his sister of his indignation at Pitt's proposals and to repeat his fustian about 'great cyphers', and 'going in like a child to come out like a fool'.[8] Hester's answer was dignified

[1] See W. G. Hamilton to Temple, 30th July 1766. *Grenville Papers*, III, 286.
[2] Cotes, *An enquiry into the Conduct, etc.*
[3] Temple to Grenville, 18th July 1766. *Grenville Papers*, III, 267.
[4] Temple to Gower, 19th July 1766. *Grenville Papers*, III, 272.
[5] George III's *Memorandum*. Fortescue, I, 177.
[6] Pitt to Hester, 17th July 1766. Chatham Corr. II, 448.
[7] Hester to Temple, 22nd July 1766. *Grenville Papers*, III, 279.
[8] Temple to Hester, 27th July 1766. Chatham Corr. II, 467.

and sad: she had believed too easily what she had hoped so strongly; but 'you know my faith and I hold it fast, that the blessing of Heaven will still be given to upright and virtuous intentions'.[1]

(iv)

Hester's first letter, which had been so scurvily answered, had been particularly, if undesignedly, forgiving; for Temple's arrogance had greatly agitated Pitt. His health had been wretched for months, and the hurry and excitement of travelling up to London had resulted in feverish exhaustion. 'Three hot nights in town' had laid him low, and he had gratefully accepted an invitation to Charles Dingley's house at Hampstead—'this bower of refreshment', as he called it, 'which indeed I began to want extremely'.[2] The pure air and the quiet surroundings were having a soothing effect when Temple's violence undid all the good. Pitt's nerves were thoroughly out of order; the quarrel prostrated him and the fashionable remedy of bleeding still further sapped his strength. He could not hide his condition from Hester, who hurried up to town to lavish on him her store of loving comfort and support. It was, however, several days before he was sufficiently recovered to see the King.

When he could get about, the business of Cabinet making was soon completed. Grafton became First Lord, Conway remained as one Secretary and Shelburne came in as the other. Northington exchanged the Chancellorship for the post of Lord President, and was succeeded in his old office by Camden. Pitt took up a strategic position as Lord Privy Seal, a sinecure office which gave him leisure from departmental duties and time for ministerial leadership. These six men formed the Cabinet, with the task of policy making. Of the remaining Ministers, the most important was the Chancellor of the Exchequer. Pitt, with great hesitation and only at Grafton's urgent entreaty, offered the post to Charles Townshend, who finally and unfortunately accepted it, though he declared that he was relinquishing the Paymastership with regret and going 'from a lazy to a laborious employment, from cheerfulness to anxiety and from indifference to some degree of

---

[1] Hester to Temple, 2nd August 1766. *Grenville Papers*, III, 289.
[2] Pitt to Hester, 15th July 1766. Chatham Corr. II, 444.

responsibility'.[1] By the 1st August, Walpole could tell Mann that 'everything is settled but a few lower places; and as but few have resigned, and some full as important are acquired, I see nothing at present to prevent the new establishment from lasting.'[2]

The Ministry of which this was the beginning is best known in Burke's description of it: 'he made an administration, so checkered and speckled; he put together a piece of joinery, so crossly indented and whimsically dove-tailed; a cabinet so variously inlaid; such a piece of diversified mosaic; such a tessellated pavement without cement; here a bit of black stone, and there a bit of white; patriots and courtiers, King's Friends and republicans; Whigs and Tories; treacherous friends and open enemies;—that it was, indeed, a very curious show; but utterly unsafe to touch, and unsure to stand on'.[3] As this is so commonly quoted in condemnation, it may not be out of place to remark that Pitt's Cabinet, as Pitt first set it up, consisted solely of men who had either held, or been invited to hold, office by Burke's hero, Rockingham; that the majority of the other Ministers had been Rockingham's appointees; and that the 'treacherous friends', to whom Burke referred and whose actions must shortly be recorded, were almost without exception Rockingham's followers.

Not many of Rockingham's old Ministry were dismissed. There was Rockingham himself, who might have been Pitt's partner had he not deliberately thrown away his chances. His subsequent behaviour, therefore, with its mixture of peevish resentment and sheer bad manners, was the less excusable. Pitt, though irritated by an attempt on Rockingham's part to interfere in the appointment of the Chancellor of the Exchequer,[4] paid him 'a visit of respect', intending, as a matter of courtesy, to give him prior information of the changes.[5] Rockingham, with incredible bad manners, allowed Pitt to be ushered into the hall, and then deliberately refused to see him.[6] 'It was', said Onslow, 'as personal as possible. The opinions on the propriety of this are various. He himself is very happy with what he has done'.[7] Pitt was said to have remarked that he was 'resolved never to be angry again, but

[1] Townshend to Sackville, 1st August 1766. H.M.C. Stopford–Sackville MSS.
[2] To Mann, 1st August 1766.
[3] Speech on American Taxation. Works II, 138.
[4] See Pitt to George III, 25th July 1766. Fortescue, I, 381.
[5] Pitt to Grafton, 27th July 1766. Anson, p. 95.
[6] Rockingham to Newcastle, 27th July 1766. Add. MSS. 32,976.
[7] Onslow to Newcastle, 28th July 1766. Add. MSS. 32,976.

that if this had happened twenty years ago, Lord Rockingham should have heard of it, for he would have taken no such usage from the first Duke in the land'.[1] The incident, babyish in itself, is worth recording for the light it throws on Rockingham's past sentiments and future behaviour.

Besides Rockingham, Newcastle was dropped. Pitt softened the blow by the offer of a pension of £4,000 p.a., which Newcastle refused, with a quiet dignity as becoming to him as it was unusual. Sackville was dismissed without comment, as he probably expected. In general, those who were displaced were angry; those who failed to obtain promotion, indignant. Yorke, in particular, declared unblushingly that honour forbade him to continue as Attorney General now that Camden had become Chancellor;[2] he resigned—a self-sacrifice to thwarted ambition. But one way or another, the posts were filled without too much trouble or more than the normal amount of heartburning, and Walpole was able to comment that 'there seems no doubt of the strength of the new Administration'.[3]

Pitt had built, as he had told the King he would, on the foundation of the Rockingham Whigs. On the 28th July he added the coping, and the new Ministers arriving at the Queen's House to kiss hands, learnt for the first time that he had become the Earl of Chatham. They were appalled; it seemed the end of the Ministry before it had begun. The Commons had lost their virtue. 'There was', wrote Grafton, 'but one voice among us'. Yet, however natural, however justified their dismay, one must needs recognise, on looking back, that Pitt's peerage was the inevitable offspring of his genius and his inferiority complex, the one deserving and the other desiring the honour. Pitt's whole life had led up to it. It was conceived in the miseries of his schooldays when he was driven to explore the paths of snobbishness; it was cradled in the injustice he suffered at Walpole's hands and the indignity of his forced subservience to Pelham and Newcastle; it was fostered by the frustrations of his great Ministry and the mocking impotence of his dismissal; it grew in allurement as such men as Murray and Fox passed him in the race for honours; it flamed into dazzling possibility with the possession of Burton Pynsent; and it justified

[1] Lloyd to Grenville, 29th July 1766. *Grenville Papers*, III, 283.
[2] Yorke to Newcastle, 29th July 1766. Add. MSS. 32,976.
[3] Walpole to Holland, 2nd August 1766.

itself by the need of his shattered body for a sinecure office. Undoubtedly it fulfilled a deep desire of his heart, the desire to overcome the nagging sense of inferiority before the great ones of the land, the desire that led him to flaunt himself in public, to demand ceremonious attention from his underlings in office, to surround himself in private with a retinue of servants, and to lay out vast sums and expend vast energy on fine houses and spacious parks. He wanted the world not only to recognise but to acclaim the genius which he knew to be his; for however assured he might be of his power, his certitude was clouded over and dimmed for him unless it was confirmed from without—by the plaudits of the crowd, if by nothing else; but best of all by the glamour and glory, by the scarlet and ermine, of a peer's robes.

If the Ministers were dismayed, the people at large were infuriated. Lampoons abounded. Yet, through the flood of abuse there ran a current of deep sadness, the sorrow of a people mourning a lost leader. 'Strange! that Ambition should itself defeat, And bid a man grow little to grow great'.[1] 'It is difficult', says the historian of eighteenth-century caricature, 'to account for the extraordinary odium which was attached to Pitt's elevation to the peerage'.[2] Yet not perhaps impossible. The people had little faith in the Whig oligarchy, and no sympathy with its innumerable factions. They expected nothing from their rulers, believing them to be corrupt and concerned only with their own interests. Offices, in their eyes, were sources of ill-gotten wealth, and peerages so many marks of successful jobbery. But Pitt was different; he had refused the perquisites of office, he had despised the badge of honours, and he had toiled with singleness of heart for England's glory, in which all alike shared. The people regarded him as someone apart—not of the Whig aristocracy, not of themselves. He stood as the embodiment of England's genius, the England that was made by all the generations of all her sons—their wisdom, their follies, their victories and defeats—the England that deep in their patriotic souls they knew to be the leaven of the world, by which mankind must rise and prosper, or for ever sink into disrepute. And by accepting a peerage, Pitt had betrayed their trust, he had shattered their ideal, and brought back the pall of night over their drab lives. Their wrath was the fury of

[1] *Whitehall Evening Post*, 7th August 1766. Quoted add. MSS. 5,823.
[2] Wright. *England under the House of Hanover*, I, 432.

disillusionment. It was, of course, unreasoning and unreasonable; and yet to some extent justified; for Pitt's appetite for outward magnificence was a flaw in the true brilliance of his genius.

It was also a profound mistake. Possibly, though not probably, he might have remained in the Commons, if Temple had agreed to become First Lord. Pitt knew that he was poorly represented in the Lords; and with Temple against him in policy, with Rockingham spiteful and angry, and with Newcastle at best apathetic, he may have felt that his presence was more necessary in the upper than in the lower House. If so, he allowed his ambitions to cloud his judgment. His place was in the Commons, look at it how one would. That was the scene of his past triumphs, that was his spiritual home. It was there that his most virulent enemies were to be found; it was there that dangers were most likely to arise, not only from opponents, but from weak leaders like Conway or wayward followers like Townshend. They needed his strong hand as well as his guidance. Nor was his physical weakness an excuse. Everyone knew that if he took office, he must remain in Olympian isolation, guiding policy from a remote sickroom, and appearing in person only on great occasions. He could have done what he liked, provided he remained the Great Commoner. But he allowed ambition to bemuse him. He went to the Lords and was lost —'Pitt was adored—but Chatham's quite unknown'.[1] His patent of nobility became his epitaph, and a mocking fate led him forthwith through what may surely be called the valley of the shadow of death, to emerge two years later, a stranger in a new and unfamiliar world.

(v)

Chatham was to be allowed little more than a matter of weeks. It may therefore be convenient, before dealing with his policies, to finish off the story of his Cabinet. It is the story of some part of the 'treacherous friends' to whom Burke referred.

Chatham took office with clear-cut ideas of what his Ministry should be. The King defined those ideas as 'destroying all party distinctions and restoring that subordination to government which alone can preserve that inestimable blessing liberty from degenerating into licentiousness'.[2] Chatham himself was less flamboyant, speaking simply of 'a great comprehensive and

---

[1] *Whitehall Evening Post*, 7th August 1766.
[2] George III to Pitt, 29th July 1766. Fortescue, I, 385.

conciliating plan'[1] He was stricken down before he had brought his ideas to fruition; and as chaos followed, with disaster hard upon its heels, it is not surprising that his aims should have been distorted, and his progress towards success overlooked. What *is* surprising is the tendency to brush him contemptuously aside as a manic-depressive, and to exalt Rockingham—the inarticulate, the ineffectual Rockingham—into a species of political Bayard—the statesman *sans peur and sans reproche.*

As he looked at the great Whig party which had set the Hanoverians on the throne, and, crushing all opposition, had governed England for the last fifty years, Chatham saw that it was no longer a party in any true sense of the word, and equally that that portion of it which went by the name of Opposition was not a true opposition. The Whigs, who had started so well, had fallen from grace, splitting into a thousand warring factions, each intent on its own advancement, each concerned with the spoils of office rather than the toils of administration. Feuds were bitter and personal, because profiteering was at a premium and patriotism at a discount. The whole system was corrupt spiritually whatever it may have been in terms of cash. Chatham had long pondered over the problem which it presented, and now believed, or at least hoped, that in his second Ministry he might rescue politics from their degradation, just as in his first Ministry he had rescued England from her enemies. His ambition was to restore the Whig party to its pristine virtue, and purge it from faction, so that it might once again become the repository of true 'revolution principles'. Every individual who stood by those principles was eligible to be a member, whether he now called himself a Whig, a Tory, a King's Friend, or a follower of one or other of the innumerable factions. Those who did not subscribe to true revolution principles would automatically become members of the Opposition, and might combine with each other as and how they liked. It was no part of Chatham's duty to mould or lead the Opposition; but he recognised the possibility of its emergence, and viewed the prospect with unconcern: 'unions, with whomsoever it be, give me no terrors: I know my ground, and I leave them to indulge their own *Dreams.* If they can conquer, I am ready to fall'.[2]

The broad outline was clear; the method was more

---

[1] Grenville to Temple, 20th August 1766. *Grenville Papers*, III, 303.
[2] Chatham to Grafton, 26th November 1766. Anson, p. 107.

uncertain. It has been said that 'everyone had surrendered' to
Chatham,[1] but Chatham knew better. He had the support of
the King and a small group of devoted followers, but the
faction leaders were against him to a man, their attitudes running
through the whole gamut from cold aloofness to embittered
venom. What Temple thought has already been recorded. Grenville was as malicious. In his own words 'I never engaged myself
in any shape either in or out of office, to support Mr. Pitt's
Measures or Administration. This I desire you will tell everybody
whom you see'.[2] Mansfield was 'not at all pleased with the present
times', being firmly of opinion that the Government could not
last,[3] and Bedford wanted to 'wash his hands of the business'.[4]
Rockingham, wishing, as Walpole remarked, 'to figure as leader
of a party even out of place'[5] was angry and resentful and his
actions followed suit. Chatham was 'very sensible of the run there
was against him';[6] and Sir Joseph Yorke, looking on from the
calm atmosphere of the Embassy at the Hague, explained the
reasons for it: 'the great struggle', he said, 'which will determine
future power in the issue will be probably at the next general
election, and all that is doing just now seems calculated for that
period, all sides striving to destroy the others' popularity before
the dissolution of this Parliament'.[7] The bitterness with which the
factions were imbued is almost incredible. When, for instance,
Jenkinson, a civil servant, who had been on the most intimate
terms with Grenville for ten years or more, wrote to say that he
had accepted a post in Chatham's Ministry, 'Mr. Grenville', as
he tells us himself in his Diary, 'returned no answer, and forbid
his porter ever to let him into his house again'.[8] Chatham himself
was not without his share of partisan enmity, though he tried
hard to curb it, refusing to speak ill of his opponents when he
could say no good of them.[9] Perhaps for that very reason he

---

[1] See p. 10, *ante*.
[2] Grenville to Lloyd, 8th August 1766. *Grenville Papers*, III, 298.
[3] Winchilsea to Rockingham, 3rd August 1766. Albemarle, II, 6.
[4] Bedford to Gower, 17th August 1766. Bedford Corr. III, 342.
[5] Walpole. *George III*, II, 265.
[6] Substance of a Conversation, etc., 7th September 1766. Add. MSS. 32,977.
[7] Joseph Yorke to Mitchell, 29th August 1766. Add. MSS. 6,836.
[8] Diary, 3rd December 1766. *Grenville Papers*, III, 393.
[9] Cf. 'The gentleman with whom he held this conversation, said some favourable
things of the Duke of Newcastle and the Marquis of Rockingham, their integrity,
their perseverance in support of the true interest of their country, etc. Lord
Chatham seemed civil, but did not enter at all in what had been said upon their
subject'. Conversation, etc., 7th September 1766. Add. MSS. 32,977.

realised how difficult a task it would be to reconcile all the conflicting elements, and very wisely determined to hasten slowly. The method he proposed was not unlike the one he had adopted so successfully in his previous Ministry. At the outset he would rely on the Rockingham Whigs; they had clamoured for his help, and so were presumably well-disposed. They would form his nucleus. As far as possible he would turn none of them out, though 'there must be some removals to make way for his friends'. Generally speaking, the normal wastage would provide him with sufficient openings, and if he had to create some artificially, he would either offer compensation, or strip pluralists of part of their holdings.[1] Future vacancies would be offered to the best men regardless of the factions to which they belonged, and though at first the offers might be rejected, sooner or later the prestige and emoluments of office would prove irresistible, especially if Chatham were as successful as he hoped to be in his policies at home and abroad. Each recruit thus won would be a further step in the process which Chatham's enemies denounced as the sacrifice of party to the King's prerogative, but which Chatham regarded as the revival of the 'revolution Whigs' in the interest of good government.

His plan worked well. Very few of the Rockinghams were dismissed, still fewer resigned, and the rest, including Rockingham himself, were quiescent. The first jolt to the system was easily survived. In the middle of August, Egmont, First Lord of the Admiralty, resigned, ostensibly because he was out of sympathy with Chatham's policy. Chatham at once offered the post to Bedford's relation, Gower, apparently in order 'to withdraw all opposition from the Bedfords';[2] and when Gower refused, told the King, with a sigh of relief, that the way was now open for appointing a Board of Admiralty 'with a sea-man at the head'.[3] Saunders, who was one of Pitt's admirals and incidentally a Rockingham Whig, was offered and accepted the post.

Yet, though Rockingham was quiescent, he was not a happy man; he resented his loss of office; he resented Chatham's elevation, and not the less because his own followers seemed to accept it with satisfaction. His object—and one may sympathise with it—

---

[1] Newcastle to Rockingham, 18th September 1766. Add. MSS. 32,977.
[2] Gilmour to Mitchell, 26th August 1766. Add. MSS. 6,860.
[3] Chatham to George III, 23rd August 1766. Fortescue, I, 389.

was to return to power, and he guided himself accordingly. Like Hardwicke, he believed that Ministers who wanted to return should 'leave as many of their friends in Court, or place, as they could', any other conduct being tantamount to 'lying down and dying without any hope of a resurrection'.[1] Rockingham had no intention of lying down and dying, and therefore at the outset allowed, and even encouraged, his followers to remain in office. He thought they would be useful as spies; and that, in any event, to grow angry and quarrel with them would merely be playing into Chatham's hands.[2] But his followers took his advice too completely and too cheerfully; they remained in office in too great numbers, and Rockingham began to wonder if his own services would much longer be required. It irked him to hear that Chatham was in high spirits, boasting of his influence at Court and his expectation of being able to maintain his position;[3] it was grievous to think that Chatham was consolidating his position, while Rockingham was making no progress at all. He began to revise his opinion about leaving his friends in office. Perhaps he should try a different tack.

The opportunity came in November. Chatham, wanting to benefit a youthful admirer, John Shelley, often known as the Little Commoner, proposed to appoint him Treasurer of the Household, and in order to create the vacancy, asked Lord Edgcumbe, the then holder of the post, to accept instead a Lordship of the Bedchamber. Edgcumbe, who 'at all times professed himself too solicitous to keep or obtain a place',[4] refused the simple exchange, and demanding too high a price for compliance, was dismissed. The affair was trifling in itself. As Walpole had once pointed out to Richmond, 'no man of half the importance of Mr. Pitt had ever brought so few dependants'.[5] He was amply entitled to bring another, and no one could really claim that a shuffle of minor offices, however distasteful to the holders, was a matter on which the rise or fall of ministries should depend. But, as it happened, Edgcumbe had the disposal of four seats in Parliament, and had recently given one gratis to Conway's nephew—a fact which placed Conway under an obligation he could not decently deny. Feeling uncomfortable, he remonstrated

---

[1] Hardwicke to Newcastle, 7th December 1760. Add. MSS. 32,915.
[2] Rockingham to Newcastle, 29th August 1766. Add. MSS. 32,976.
[3] Conversation, etc., 7th September 1766. Add. MSS. 32,977.
[4] Walpole. *George III*, IV, 81.   [5] Walpole. *George III*, II, 249.

with Chatham, but without avail. Edgcumbe had to go. Conway's annoyance seemed to Rockingham a heaven-sent chance. He promptly summoned a meeting of his principal followers and harangued them, as he himself admitted, 'in rashness and warmth'. They must not allow their friends to be dismissed one by one; they must show their resentment by mass resignations, carrying Conway with them if possible; that would bring Chatham to his knees and enable them to mould a new administration nearer to their hearts' desire.[1] He had his way. Portland, Scarborough, Monson, Bessborough, Saunders, Keppel and Meredith all resigned. But to their chagrin Conway held back, and Chatham, though put to some trouble, was able to fill their places with men from other factions. The resignations, as Barrington remarked, were 'very factious and ill-judged' and had merely resulted in the restoration of 'most of those who have been driven out of the King's Service by different Administrations'.[2] Rockingham had to confess that he had 'no idea what was to be done',[3] and six weeks later was writing sadly that 'the state of us and our friends, viewed through political glasses, would appear a forlorn hope, and that no immediate success could be expected'.[4] Though he looked wistfully to the future, all he had in fact accomplished was to drive a number of his own followers out of office, against their wishes and indeed against the wishes of the whole party.[5] When some years later Burke described Chatham's Ministry as a tessellated pavement, he forgot that the main artificer of that tessellation was Rockingham himself.

[1] Rockingham to Scarborough, 20th November 1766. Albemarle, II, 19.
[2] Barrington to Mitchell, 14th December 1766. Add. MSS. 6,834.
[3] Hardwicke to Charles Yorke, 28th November 1766. Albemarle, II, 28.
[4] Rockingham to Dowdeswell, 8th January 1766. Albemarle, II, 32.
[5] See 'I have great reason to fear and indeed to know that the resignations will not be received by the party in the manner it was imagined; nor be generally, or at all, followed by those in employment in the House of Commons'. Newcastle to Portland, 24th November 1766. Add. MSS. 32,978.

XVI

THE CHATHAM MINISTRY

(i)

CHATHAM'S ADVENT had the same effect in 1766 as it had had ten years earlier—a sudden quickening in the tempo of government, a new sense of urgency. There was a tautness and thrust about his handling of affairs which was in marked contrast with Newcastle's dilatory tactics and Bute's formlessness and fumbling. His pushful energy, coming, as it did, immediately after Rockingham's diffident methods, flustered his younger and more inexperienced colleagues; they were a little frightened. Many years later, the recollection of those times and the feelings they had engendered, prompted Grafton to remark that Chatham 'was admired, but was rarely liked';[1] and in much the same way, Walpole, out of loyalty to a friend, recorded in his memoirs that Conway dropped all intercourse with Chatham because of his exasperation over the Edgcumbe episode.[2] One may agree that masterful men are rarely popular and often tread upon tender corns, but the plaints of their more timid colleagues should not be taken too easily as evidence of megalomania. Nor should *obiter dicta*, without at least some testing. Let us take a few instances from the first three weeks of Chatham's Ministry. On the 1st August, Charles Townshend wrote that 'everything proceeds from Lord Chatham to the King and from thence without any intermediate consultation to the public';[3] on the 7th August the Prussian Ambassador was astonished to see Chatham, as he was coming out of the Closet, give written notes—presumably orders, to the Ministers waiting in the ante-chamber;[4] and on the 20th August, Sackville let drop that Chatham had 'the sole confidence and consequently the absolute direction of the whole'.[5] All of which seems ample justification for the common charge that

[1] Anson, p. 103.   [2] Walpole. *George III*, II, 273.
[3] Townshend to Sackville, 1st August 1766. H.M.C. Stopford-Sackville MSS.
[4] Tunstall, p. 376.
[5] Sackville to Irwin, 20th August 1766. H.M.C. Stopford-Sackville MSS.

Chatham, in a fit of manic excitement, was behaving arrogantly, haughtily, and like a dictator—until one realises that at the very moment when Townshend was writing, Chatham was attending a Cabinet meeting which went on so long and so late that Chatham was unable to report its decisions to the King in person and had to do so by letter;[1] that the Prussian Ambassador had no more idea than we have what was in the notes which he observed; and that Sackville, not being a member of the Government, was speaking simply from hearsay. Chatham no doubt put forward his views strongly and forcefully—he felt them strongly and forcefully; he may even have put them forward occasionally in notes—he was very conscious of the importance of the *mot juste*; but he put them forward to his Cabinet and was always ready to listen to criticism, and to bow to it if it was convincing. For the most part, however, as Grafton records, Chatham took the lead 'in so masterly a manner, as to raise the admiration and desire of us all to co-operate with him'.[2]

Chatham towered over his contemporaries not only in the forcefulness of his methods but in the breadth of his vision. It was as well; for there were many great questions depending which his predecessors had never noticed, or had ignored, or worse still mishandled. There were four in particular. There was the problem of Europe, which had been shelved temporarily by the Treaty of Paris but was not for that reason the less menacing; there was the problem of America, which Grenville had bedevilled and Rockingham had merely plastered over; there was the problem of India, now rising in acute form for the first time; and there was the constitutional problem, posed by Bute and complicated by the King, which demanded solution if a stable government was to be evolved. Chatham gathered them all to his bosom without loss of time.

(ii)

The problem of Europe came first, because on it hung the safety of the country. Chatham had not disapproved the terms of the peace merely because they fell short of his victories. In a sense, the way in which the skin was divided was of secondary importance.

[1] Chatham to George III, 1st August 1766. Fortescue, I, 386.
[2] Anson, p. 105.

What roused Chatham to lasting fury was that the framers of the peace had at once burked the immediate issue and ruined the hope of future amelioration. In every direction they had failed. The issue of peace was two-fold—to give the colonies protection, and to assure England that France would never again be able to molest her. Neither object had been secured, for France had been left the means to recuperate both by sea and by land. There was nothing to stop her from becoming again a rival in the race for colonies; there was nothing to stop her even from threatening the cliffs of Dover. At sea, the peace had given her the right to fish in the Gulf of St. Lawrence, which in Chatham's eyes offered her an inducement to rebuild her marine and the best of training for her young sailors. The advantage was one which England, as mistress of the seas and winner of the war, could have denied her, but instead had yielded up, weakly and criminally. On land, we were ourselves powerless against her. We needed the help of allies, and Bute had alienated both Germany and Russia. There was no one left on our side to keep her in check on the Continent, while on her side the Family Compact remained unbroken and full of promise. France, in short, had a clear field; and Chatham noticed with growing dismay how eagerly and how successfully, under Choiseul's able guidance, she was taking advantage of it. The signs were multiplying. 'I see more reason every day', wrote Jenkinson from Paris, 'to apprehend that France will extricate herself sooner from the difficulties which the war has brought upon her than we shall'.[1] And when she had recovered, all the world knew that she intended to have her revenge. It must be Chatham's task to set matters right—so obviously that Choiseul half expected him to plunge into war at once, if only to retrieve his lost popularity: 'ce que nous avons à craindre c'est que cet homme altier et ambitieux, ayant perdu sa considération populaire, ne veuille se relever de sa perte par des exploits guerriers et des projets de conquêtes qui puissent lui procurer de la réputation'.[2] Not that Choiseul was right. Chatham had no desire to renew the war. What he was anxious to do was to recover the lead we had lost by the peace, and so make a war of revenge too dangerous a gamble for France. To accomplish this, he set two objects before himself—first, to strengthen the navy, in order to retain the

---

[1] Jenkinson to Grenville, 10th August 1766. *Grenville Papers*, III, 302.
[2] Choiseul to Guerchy, 11th August 1766. H.M.C. Lansdowne MSS.

mastery of the seas; and secondly, to secure allies on the Continent, in order to put a restraint upon France.

The first object was the easier, in that it was under his own control, but otherwise it was uphill and dispiriting work. At the end of the war the navy had stood supreme; there was nothing to touch it. But the glory had departed. Chatham found it in a state of decay, the numbers down, the discipline bad and the administration unenlightened and corrupt. France and Spain had stolen a march upon us and now had over one hundred ships ready or on the stocks to England's sixty-two. The disparity seemed likely to increase. Choiseul had realised the source of England's strength, grasping, however dimly, the tremendous influence of sea power. He had also appreciated, as Chatham had done, that France had nothing to fear, or for that matter to gain, on the Continent: the Family Compact gave her all the security she needed; no one was likely to attack her. It should consequently be her policy to look beyond the seas. There was still plenty of room in the world for French expansion if only she had the ships, and ships were what Choiseul intended to give her. He had in fact begun to do five years earlier, what Chatham was only just setting out to do. More than that; he had searched round for means of distracting and worrying the English fleets. It was now that France seriously contemplated the conquest of Corsica; in her hands it would give the Mediterranean fleet plenty of occupation by threatening Minorca and English trade to the Levant. So, too, he encouraged Spain to make trouble in the Falkland Islands and obstruct ships sailing in the southern seas. Anything which hampered England, anything which kept her on tenterhooks, was so much gain. Chatham determined to checkmate him. His first need was a strong and vigorous Admiralty. Perhaps for that reason he felt no dismay when Egmont resigned from the post of First Lord. Egmont was an eccentric man, mainly remarkable for his ambition to revive the feudal system.[1] In 1763, he had been preferred by Grenville to the Admiralty, where he had found the Navy in a poor state,[2] but had done little to amend it. Ultimately, under Rockingham, he had become 'the most desponding part of a very desponding Administration'.[3] Certainly he was not the man for the job. His

---

[1] Walpole. *George III*, I, 308.
[2] See Egmont to Grenville, 16th April 1764. *Grenville Papers*, II, 290.
[3] Hamilton to Temple, 1st July 1766. *Grenville Papers*, III, 255.

disappearance enabled Chatham to appoint a seaman in his place
—first Saunders, and then Hawke, and it was Hawke who, no
doubt under Chatham's inspiration, laid it down as a maxim that
the British navy must be equal to the navies of France and Spain
combined.[1] Having set the administration going on right lines,
Chatham turned to more detailed matters. He despatched Byron
to the Falkland Islands, to make good our possessions there; he
gave orders for the fortification of Pensacola in the Gulf of Mexico
as a check on French encroachment in Central America; and he
contemplated strengthening the Mediterranean fleet to keep an
eye on Corsica. At the same time he promoted contentment in the
Navy by increasing the half-pay of lieutenants and captains. A
reasonable harvest for six months of office.

His second object—the quest for allies—was far more difficult.
Not only had Bute alienated our previous friends, but the whole
atmosphere on the Continent had altered. Chatham wanted to
create a northern bloc—England, Prussia and Russia—in a defensive alliance against the united House of Bourbon, but the
inducements which he could offer were neither immediate nor
obvious. They needed a more long-sighted vision than was
vouchsafed to either Catherine of Russia or Frederick of Prussia.
Still, the attempt had to be made, and had to be pressed home.
It was a task which would need exceptional skill, and for that
reason Chatham thought it best to appoint his old and experienced
friend, Hans Stanley, as Ambassador Extraordinary to Russia.
The emphasis was laid on Russia, because she seemed the most
likely to agree. She had recently signed a treaty of commerce with
us, and had shown a disposition to enter into a still closer alliance,
provided we would support her against the Turks. The proviso
was of moment to Russia, whose relations with Turkey were
strained, but was unacceptable to England, who had no ambition
to be embroiled in warfare at the other end of Europe for
objects in which she had no concern. It is possible that Stanley
might have overcome this impediment, if he had ever reached
St. Petersburg; but he never had the chance. The scheme broke
down.

Frederick was the stumbling-block. Ever since the peace, he had
been absorbed in putting Prussia on her feet again—building
houses, reviving agriculture, restoring trade and commerce—and

[1] Burrows, pp. 280-1.

had not been too successful.[1] He was therefore reluctant to plunge, even at a distance, into fresh adventures. If he were to be tempted, he would undoubtedly look in another direction—one suggested to him, all unknowingly, by the pretty Princess Electoral of Saxony, whose plight at Dresden in 1759 had roused Pitt's chivalry but had left Frederick cold.[2] She had since then become Electress and as such had appealed to Frederick for support against Russia in her claim to the crown of Poland. Unfortunately for her, Frederick was at the moment negotiating a treaty with Russia for himself and in no mood to introduce irrelevancies. He put the lady's appeal aside deftly, but not unkindly, for she had recalled to his mind his long-standing ambition to acquire Polish Prussia,[3] conjuring up visions which ultimately led to the partition of Poland. With such aspirations straining towards the east, it was unlikely that he would think twice of France. She meant nothing to him. Indeed, it was, as Carlyle says, curious how, in spite of his watchful speculations, he 'saw nothing to dread in France, nothing to remark there, except carelessly, from time to time, its beggarly decaying condition, so strangely sunk in arts, in arms, in finance'.[4] When, therefore, Mitchell approached him, he was elusive and shy, holding aloof for reasons at once personal and political. Chatham he trusted, but there was no assurance that Chatham would remain in office or even retain his popularity. On the contrary, he had done himself irreparable harm by his peerage.[5] Other administrations might easily spring up at a moment's notice, in which Frederick could feel no confidence—only a memory of ill-usage and injustice.[6] Until he saw the English Government settled on a more stable foundation, he preferred to stand apart. So much for the personal side. On the political, the argument reached the same end by another route. War, said Frederick, was unlikely at the moment, and it was a mistake to enter into alliances too far in advance—they were more apt to create jealousies than to promote peace. It would be wiser to wait until the storm was seen to be rising.[7] Moreover, any new war

---

[1] Cf. 'the disappointments he has met with in the execution of divers projects relative to the internal government of his dominions'. Mitchell to Conway, 4th December 1766. Add. MSS. 6,810.

[2] See my *Pitt and the Seven Years' War*, p. 312.   [3] *Cambridge History*, VI, 729.

[4] Carlyle, Fred. IX, 247.

[5] Mitchell to Chatham, 17th September 1766. Add. MSS. 6,810.

[6] Mitchell to Chatham, 6th December 1766. Add. MSS. 6,810.

[7] Mitchell to Conway, 4th December 1766. Add. MSS. 6,810.

between England and France was likely to be one 'in which the natural interest of his country might not lead him to take any part'[1] and very probably would flare up in a quarter of the world where he could be of little use.

Though Mitchell renewed the attack more than once, Frederick was not to be shaken. Chatham had to postpone his scheme and 'wait for a more favourable opportunity'.[2] Had his health remained good, that opportunity might have arisen within a year, for in October 1767 Mitchell reported that Frederick was growing discontented with Russia as an ally, and was inclined to look elsewhere.[3] But Chatham was by then too ill even to be told. No further opportunity came in his lifetime. Chatham might have said of Prussia, as he once said of Britain, 'it is too much the temper of this country to be insensible of the approach of danger, until it comes with accumulated terrors'.[4] Fifty years later, the northern alliance for which he pleaded became necessary, not to prevent but to end the Napoleonic wars. Had Chatham been successful in 1766, the course of history would surely have been altered and much suffering avoided, not only in America but in Europe, not only for England but for Germany.

(iii)

The problem of America appeared for the moment to be quiescent but the appearance was deceptive. It was no less pressing than the problem of Europe. As Chatham told the Lords at a later date: 'the situation of our foreign affairs was undoubtedly a matter of moment . . . but there were other matters still more important and more urgently demanding attention—the distractions and divisions which prevailed in every part of the Empire'.[5] The urgency, curiously enough, sprang out of Rockingham's attempts at conciliation. The repeal of the Stamp Act had merely applied a salve to raw feelings; it had not touched the core; while the Declaratory Act had injected a slow poison, which, though unnoticed at first, quickly began to itch and rankle.

America presented two broad problems—the one, how to

---

[1] Mitchell to Conway, 17th September 1766. Add. MSS. 6,810.
[2] Anson, p. 98.
[3] Mitchell to Conway, 31st October 1767. Add. MSS. 6,810.
[4] Speech, 22nd January 1770.
[5] Speech, 9th January 1770.

finance the colonies; the other, how to deal with the vast un-
settled lands peopled by Indians.[1] The two were interconnected,
since the largest element of expense was the cost of protection,
and the need for protection sprang out of the clash with the
native inhabitants. There had always been trouble, but with the
disappearance of the French, that trouble was intensified. The
Indians were now free to concentrate against the English all
their baffled fury, all their sense of oppression, all their indignation at wrongs endured, all their helpless grief at the slow
extinction of their way of life. 'Brother', they cried out, 'we and
our dependants have been for some time like giddy people not
knowing what to do; wherever we turned we saw our blood, and
when our young men wanted to go hunting the wild beasts in
our country, they found it covered with fences, so that they were
weary crossing them, neither could they get venison to eat or bark
to make huts'.[2] The conspiracy of Pontiac (1763–6) showed how
strong were their feelings and how dangerous their resentment.

It is in Grenville's favour that he recognised the existence of
both problems and set himself to find a solution; it was England's
misfortune that he found it too easily. He settled the boundaries
of the newly-acquired possessions, and at the same time strictly
forbade the colonists to buy lands belonging to, or reserved for,
Indians, whether within or without the colonial boundaries. Nor
would it be enough to plead that the Indians wished to dispose of
their lands; they had been too often beguiled, complaining, with
bitter recollection, that 'the rum bottles hung at every door to
steal our lands'.[3] Purchases, if any, were to be made for the King
and in his name, at specially convened public meetings.[4] Having
thus guaranteed the Indian lands and settled the size of the colonies, Grenville settled the forces required for their protection,
accepting Newcastle's estimate of 10,000 men, though this number was much in excess of the pre-war garrisons. The annual cost
of the troops Grenville put at £500,000 and on that basis assessed
the contribution which the colonists should make.

His scheme was no doubt foolproof on paper; but it took no
account of human feelings or human failings. It was impossible to
curb the expansion of the colonies or restrain the ebullient energy

[1] Morison, p. xvii.
[2] Proceedings at a General Congress. Morison, p. 57.
[3] *Ibid.*, p. 60.
[4] Proclamation, 8th October 1763. Morison, p. 1.

of the westerners by mere proclamation; and it was asking too
much to expect the colonists to pay for a protection which they
believed to be as unnecessary as they were sure it was undesirable.
Grenville's solution, imposed in a rough and overbearing manner,
did nothing but create turmoil.

Rockingham proposed to set all to rights by repealing the
Stamp Act, and certainly the Repeal produced a revulsion of
feelings; the colonists turned to fireworks and junketing, and
the City merchants to self-congratulations. Burke, in his *Short
Account*, declared roundly that 'the distractions of the British
Empire were composed'. But indeed they were not. The Repeal
did nothing positive except revive the problems. The expansion
of the colonies was still curbed; dealings with the Indians were
still forbidden; the garrisons still remained in America; the
method of their payment was still unresolved; and the relations
with the mother country had still to be settled. Moreover, if the
Repeal soothed the surface rash, the Declaratory Act encouraged
the development of secondary symptoms. The colonists had begun
to ask awkward questions and give disturbing answers. They
had got into the way of discussing the theory of government, and
the Declaratory Act kept their interest alive. They pored over
their Charters; they debated the virtues of Pym and of Hampden;
they analysed the works of Locke; they discussed the laws of
nature and the rights of man; and they applied the wisdom of the
past, without qualification, to new and different circumstances.[1]
It was a heady pastime, at which they grew extremely agile,
arguing for instance, that the Mutiny Act, which required them to
quarter soldiers in America, was 'virtually as much an act for
laying taxes on the inhabitants as the Stamp Act',[2] and as such
rightly to be resisted, or at least shaped to their liking. The
colonies, so far from being composed, were restlessly enquiring
and examining, testing all things and holding fast whatever seemed
to their advantage. This was the legacy handed down by Grenville
and Rockingham. Clearly something more was necessary.

As in the case of the European problem, Chatham began his
reconstruction from the bottom. Hitherto the responsibility for
America had been divided between the Secretary for the Southern
Department and the First Lord of Trade. The arrangement was

[1] See Miller, chap. 8.
[2] Governor Franklin to Shelburne, 18th December 1766. Mumby, p. 163.

amorphous and unsatisfactory, and from time to time abortive efforts had been made to improve it, usually by ambitious First Lords of Trade, hoping to become a third Secretary. Chatham swept this system away. His Secretary for the Southern Department was Shelburne, a young politician of considerable promise, able and willing to carry out his views, and in whom he had great confidence. He decided that Shelburne should be given the full responsibility and that the Board of Trade, under Hillsborough, should become 'a Board of Report upon reference to it for advice or information on the part of the Secretary of State'.[1] It was an arrangement in which he took a strong personal interest, and he was correspondingly irritated when a few weeks later, while he was at Bath for his health, he received two letters on the same day envisaging its overthrow. One was from Shelburne reporting that Conway had offered the Embassy at Madrid to Hillsborough, and the other from Grafton suggesting Burke for the Board of Trade. He replied forcefully to both, telling Shelburne that he could not imagine the motive for 'this desultory step, unfixing the most critical office in the kingdom, so happily fixed through and by my channel';[2] and informing Grafton that Burke might be a man of parts and an ingenious speaker but held 'notions and maxims of trade' which Chatham could never endorse.[3] His vehemence quashed the proposals.

With the administration, as he hoped, firmly established, Chatham proceeded to develop his new policy; but he had no intention of rushing into it precipitately. His method was always deliberate. As he once told the Lords: 'It was a maxim he had observed through life, when he had lost his way, to stop short lest by proceeding without knowledge, and advancing from one false step to another, he should wind himself into an inextricable labyrinth and never be able to recover the right road'.[4] It was not enough to know that his predecessors had gone astray, nor was it sufficient merely to repeal their Acts.[5] Two things were necessary

---

[1] Fitzmaurice, II, 2.

[2] Chatham to Shelburne, 19th October 1766. Chatham Corr. III, 115.

[3] 'Nothing can be more unsound and more repugnant to every true principle of manufacture and commerce than rendering so noble a branch as the cottons, dependent for the first material upon the produce of French and Danish Islands, instead of British'. Chatham to Grafton, 19th October 1766. Anson, p. 108.

[4] Speech, 9th January 1770.

[5] Cf. 'It is not repealing this or that Act of Parliament, it is not repealing a piece of parchment, that can restore America to our bosom: you must repeal her fines and her resentments'. Speech, 20th January 1775.

—first, to enforce compliance with the laws so long as they remained on the Statute Book, or, as Chatham put it, 'to support the superiority of Great Britain over her colonies';[1] and secondly, to be ready and willing to consider amendments 'upon a respectful and well-grounded representation of the hardship or inconvenience'.[2]

The first essential was not easy at the moment. Besides the Stamp Act, now repealed, the colonists had two positive sources of irritation. They objected to the quartering of soldiers under the provisions of Grenville's Mutiny Act, and they disliked having to pay compensation to the victims of riots as recommended by Rockingham's Resolutions. The former trouble was manifested mainly in New York, where the greatest number of soldiers was concentrated; and the latter in Massachusetts, where the Governor had 'required' payment instead of 'recommending' it. In both places there had been opposition. Chatham's aim was conciliation, but not appeasement.[3] He could not, therefore, ignore the resistance; compensation was clearly desirable, whether or not the Governor had been tactless; and until there had been time to go into the question of the forces in America, the quartering must continue. But if he must roar, it should be as much as possible like a dove. He would do nothing to exacerbate feelings, nor would he approach the colonists in the old hectoring fashion. His new methods had an immediate result, not in abolishing acrimony all at once—that was too much to expect—but in reducing the turbulent waves to a diminishing swell. Though the effect was less exuberant than that which had followed the repeal of the Stamp Act, it was perhaps for that very reason the more likely to endure. The outlook for the future was not unhopeful. Nevertheless, as might be expected, reports of trouble continued to arrive from time to time, especially from New York. They greatly agitated Chatham, who was far from well, and became increasingly oppressive as his health declined.[4]

[1] Bedford's *Journal*, 19th October 1766. Bedford Corr. III, 348.

[2] Shelburne to Governor Moore, 9th August 1766. Mumby, p. 160.

[3] Cf. 'Measures for the proper subordination of America must be taken', but he 'hoped he was not understood to intend any violent measures towards the Americans at this time, unless absolutely necessary'. Bedford's *Journal*, 24th and 31st October 1766. Bedford Corr. III, 349.

[4] Cf. 'Lord Chatham desires to submit his opinion, that the disobedience of the assembly of that province to the Mutiny Act is a matter so weighty and big with consequences, which may strike so deep and spread so wide, that it ought, on no account, to rest on the advice of meetings of the Cabinet, and the course of office, but go before Parliament'. Chatham to Grafton and Shelburne, 17th February 1767. Chatham Corr. III, 214.

The second essential was a matter of investigation. Chatham was not prepared to introduce reforms until he was sure of his ground. Shelburne was accordingly given the task of collecting information. Before he had completed his work, Chatham had broken down, but the lines of his enquiries were significant, opening up a new and hopeful vista. Grenville had ridden the colonies on a tight rein, clamping his own theories upon them without any qualms. The new aim, as outlined by Shelburne, was more modest, more wise and more liberal, tending towards a measure of devolution, and basing itself on facts. Local questions —as for instance the terms of trade with the Indians, which varied from colony to colony, or the conflict between French and English law in the newly conquered lands—should as far as possible be left for local decisions, subject only to the general guidance of the mother country. The Judges should be given an enhanced dignity by security of tenure. Religion, too, should be free; episcopacy should not be enforced, nor should Roman Catholics be penalised. There should be stability, but not stagnation, and new settlements should be encouraged. In such a movement lay a possible solution of the financial problem. Grants of land carried quit-rents. Payment had not been very regular in the past, but could no doubt be tightened up; and with an improved collection from all grants, both old and new, it might be possible to raise sufficient funds to meet the Government's reasonable demands, or at least 'to lighten the burden which lies upon the mother country'. It would help, if the cost of the army could be reduced, and surely, now that the war was over, there must be room for retrenchment. To test these possibilities, the Governors were instructed to return detailed accounts of their revenues and expenditure, with estimates of their future requirements; while General Gage was ordered to examine the distribution of the troops with a view to cutting down the numbers.[1] In short a fresh approach was adopted, which at least held out the hope of breaking the impasse created by Chatham's predecessors.

(iv)

Grafton was convalescing at Wakefield when on Saturday, 23rd August (1766), Chatham wrote to him 'I trust to heaven we

[1] Fitzmaurice, II, pp. 30–37.

shall have your Grace confirmed safe and well by Sunday. The
next week we all hope to fill with important objects. Meetings
upon E. India affairs (the greatest of all objects, according to my
sense of great), as well as the whole outline of the ensuing
Session'.[1] India had always been familiar to Chatham as the scene
of his grandfather's labours, and the East India Company as the
source of his wealth. But in the last half-century—that is, during
Chatham's own lifetime—both country and company had under-
gone spectacular changes. In 1707, the year before Chatham's
birth, the Emperor Aurungzebe died. From that moment the
Mogul Empire began to disintegrate, but from the European
point of view the change was not at first very apparent. The
English and French Companies, confined to a few widely-scattered
settlements on the coast, were interested only in commerce; they
took little note of the conspiracies and assassinations which
abounded in what today might be called the succession states,
looking on them as little more than a background to their own
local rivalries. The situation changed, however, with the appointment in 1735 of Benoît Dumas as Governor of Pondicherry. It
occurred to that far-seeing man that there were advantages to be
gained by entering into alliances with native potentates and
taking a part in their dynastic quarrels. He acted accordingly, and
before long the French were exercising a powerful influence, not
only in that coastal stretch of south-east India which included
both Madras and Pondicherry and was known as the Carnatic,
but also throughout the whole of that southern portion of India
known as the Deccan. His successor, Dupleix, continued and
developed this policy, until at last his ideas were enlarged 'not
only to the conquest of the Carnatic, but to the extirpation of all
other European nations, and even to the reduction of the whole
Mogul empire, and to make it a dependent state on the Crown of
France'.[2] The result was that the French Company were much
more favourably placed than the English during the Franco-
British wars in the middle of the century, and at one time had
only been prevented from driving the English completely out of
the Carnatic by the sudden emergence of Clive as a 'heaven-born'
general, who by a series of brilliant actions had restored the
position by 1753. But India was still in a ferment. It was not

---

[1] Chatham to Grafton, Anson, p. 102.
[2] Clive. A Letter to the Proprietors of the East India Stock, p. 4.

therefore surprising that a little before the outbreak of the Seven Years' War, Surajah Dowlah, the vicious, untrustworthy, incompetent young man who had just succeeded to the throne of Bengal, should at the instigation of the French pick a quarrel with the English, storm Calcutta and enact the tragedy of the Black Hole (20th June 1756). The news spread quickly to Madras where Admiral Watson, with a small squadron was keeping an eye on Pondicherry. Although in poor health and anxious to take advantage of Admiralty instructions, just received, to bring his ship home, Watson brushed his orders aside and at once set out for Calcutta, though he had to sail in the teeth of the monsoon, which that year was 'uncommonly tempestuous'.[1] He arrived in the Hoogly on the 14th December (1756), bringing Clive with him. There followed that astounding campaign in which, after recovering Calcutta, Clive went on to defeat Surajah Dowlah at Plassey (23rd June 1757), and then in the course of a few months to conquer the three provinces of Bengal, Bihar and Orissa.

The position in which Clive found himself at the end of 1758 was not a little bewildering. He and the Company were 'astonished at the completeness and rapidity of the success';[2] but he alone seems to have realised something of its implications. Though the immediate problem of what to do with these vast new possessions was solved by the appointment of native rulers, it was obvious to Clive that this solution was at best a temporary expedient. The rulers were dependent on English support and sooner or later full responsibility must be taken over by the English. The question was how that responsibility was to be handled. Clive himself had little doubt. The East India Company was a trading concern; its Directors were business men, subject to yearly reappointment, and residing 10,000 miles away; its Proprietors were a number of scattered shareholders, utterly ignorant of the East and unversed in the art of government. In India its servants were traders and accountants; its army a few men employed to guard its warehouses, its navy a fleet of merchant vessels. It had neither the knowledge, the experience, nor the men to rule an empire larger than Great Britain. Nor was it right that it should confuse the collection of revenues with the amassing of profits. Clive wrote to Pitt. Conditions in the East, he explained, were always changing; and the opportunity, if not the necessity, for the Company to

[1] Ives, p. 96.   [2] Grant, p. 162.

take the sovereignty upon themselves would certainly arise before long. Nor would it be difficult: two thousand Europeans would be sufficient. But 'so large a sovereignty may possibly be an object too extensive for a mercantile company'. A more appropriate body would, surely, be the nation. The acquisition would prove a source of immense wealth—an income of over two millions a year—and make England paramount in India. It was worth consideration.[1] The letter reached Pitt in October 1759, the year of victories. It stirred him to admiration, but did not blind him to difficulties which Clive had failed to notice. Certainly Clive and the Company must be supported against the French, and one of the very few references to East Indian affairs which can be found in Newcastle's papers, describes how, on receipt of Clive's letter, 'Mr. Pitt was mightily for sending them two battalions' in the hope of being able 'entirely to defeat and disappoint the French there'.[2] But the assumption of sovereignty over the Indians, though very practicable and from one point of view very tempting was another matter altogether. Pitt had not overlooked the developments in India. He had already been making enquiries and had found that the Company's Charter had another twenty years to run; and that the legal authorities were inclined to regard the recent conquests and acquisitions as lawful possessions of the Company. Pitt himself went more deeply into the matter. In his view, neither the Company nor the Crown had any right to the vast revenues of which Clive spoke; they belonged to India and should be used for the benefit of the Indians.[3] Pitt's views were clear and uncompromising. He would be glad enough to drive the French out of India; he would be glad enough to acquire a monopoly of the trade for England; but he had no ambition to exercise suzerainty over a foreign country, nor did he think it right to exact tribute from a conquered people. Equally, he was not prepared to 'nationalise' or forcibly dispossess a private undertaking merely because it was successful. He was not to be tempted by the prospect of easy, but ill-gotten, gains.

Throughout the remainder of the Seven Years' War Pitt kept an eye on India, dispatching from time to time such troops and ships and funds as might be required, until at last with the fall

[1] Clive to Pitt, 2nd January 1759. Chatham Corr. I, 387.
[2] Newcastle to Hardwicke, 15th October 1759. Add. MSS. 32,897.
[3] Walsh's account, 26th November 1759. Chatham Corr. I, 392 (*n.* 2).

of Pondicherry (15th June 1761) 'the power of France was extinguished'.[1] He was accordingly roused to intense indignation when Bute agreed in the Preliminaries of Peace to the mutual restitution of conquests.[2] What conquests, he asked, had France to restore? 'All the conquests which France had made had been retaken and were in our possession, as were likewise all the French settlements and factories'.[3] Clive added his voice to the protest, and in the definitive treaty the terms were a little softened in England's favour. France regained the various factories which she had possessed at the beginning of 1749, in return for which she renounced all pretensions to any British possession and agreed not to erect fortifications or keep troops in Bengal.[4]

Meanwhile, events had been taking their course in India. After Clive's successes, the influence of the English was unbounded, and in a country torn by revolutions the temptation to abuse it was correspondingly great. It was too easy to amass wealth by promoting changes of rulers and exacting 'presents', or by demanding monopolies in trade and exemptions from taxation. Clive himself, still a comparatively young man, was fond of money and not very scrupulous in its acquisition. He left India in February 1760 possessed of an immense fortune, of which it may at least be said that he had deserved it by his genius and earned it by his services. But the example was infectious, and after his departure, a host of others, without his excuse, rushed in to make their fortunes in a hurry and by means that did not always bear examination. The depredations became too widespread and notorious; there was friction; there was retaliation; there were massacres; and finally war broke out again, which in the end led to the military occupation, not only of Bengal, Bihar and Orissa, but of Oudh as well.

The quarrels among the members of Council at Calcutta, the stories of corruption, the endless revolutions in the provinces and the extraordinary extensions of the conquests roused uneasy feelings in England, and in 1764 the Directors, at the urgent request of the Proprietors, sent Clive to enquire into these strange happenings and restore order. He arrived at Calcutta in May 1765 and by the following August had carried out a complete reorganisation, the effect of which was to confer on the Company

[1] Lecky, II, 503.
[2] Jenkinson, III, 171.
[3] Speech, 9th December 1762.
[4] Jenkinson, III, 185.

Q

the virtual sovereignty over Bengal, Bihar and Orissa together
with certain territories in the Deccan, subject only to the payment
of annual tributes to the Emperor and the Nabob. Clive, in short,
had followed the lines he had sketched for Pitt in 1759, merely
substituting the Company for the Crown. But while the Company
obtained a yearly income which Clive computed at £1,650,000,
it was under no obligation, nor was it much better qualified than
before, to govern the country well. Its suzerainty was perhaps an
inevitable development; certainly it paved the way ultimately for
an era of great peace and prosperity; but in itself it could only be
a passing phase. Clive had 'laid the foundation of the future
system, and prepared the instruments with which it was to be
built up',[1] but the actual building remained to be done. His work,
though full of promise for the future, was full of problems for the
present. Amongst the most pressing was the point which he
himself had put to Pitt in 1759—Was so large a sovereignty an
object too extensive for a mercantile company?—a point which
was no longer a hypothetical question capable of being ignored,
but a *fait accompli* demanding to be considered.

The news reached England in May 1766, shortly before Chatham
took office. It 'excited no inconsiderable sensation in the minds of
the English public',[2] as well as a large diversity of opinions. So
far as the Company was concerned, the Proprietors imagined their
fortunes were made and clamoured for inflated dividends; the
Directors, on the other hand, were anxious to hold back, being
not a little apprehensive about the costs of their new duties. In
the City the fluctuations of the stock raised fears—or hopes, as
the case might be—of another South Sea Bubble. In the country
at large the vast wealth amassed by individuals shocked the
conscience of some and roused the envy of others; and both alike
were inclined to search for scapegoats. Ironically, they hit upon
Clive—the one man who had served India best and more than any
other earned his fortune.[3]

But the most important reaction was Chatham's. He saw from
the first that Clive's solution was not final. It was impossible that
a trading company, acting under a temporary charter, could be the
owners of a great empire. Their charter was now due to expire in

---

[1] Dodwell, *Dupleix and Clive*, p. 272.   [2] Grant, p. 276.
[3] 'The popular opinion is not at present in his [Clive's] favour'. Wedderburn to
Grenville, 25th September 1766. *Grenville Papers*, III, 323.

fifteen years' time and could be cancelled, by notice, at an earlier date. What right would the Company have to their new possessions when their charter lapsed? What right had they now? The legal pundits might give what interpretation of the law they liked, but it was certain that 'the King's Bench could have no judicature over the East Indies';[1] it could neither endorse nor annul the Company's act of conquest. Now, or in fifteen years' time, the problem must be faced; and better now than later. But if a solution were necessary, who was to give it? Most of the authorities were interested parties. Clearly the Company could not be allowed to decide for itself. Nor could the King; for though the charter derived from him, public opinion would never allow the Crown to arrogate to itself vast revenues which might make it independent of Parliament. Nor could government pronounce finally on a matter which involved elements of law, private property and the royal prerogative; at most it 'could only interfere in preventing unreasonableness and oppressions'.[2] Nor did Chatham feel disposed to lay down the law himself; his part, so he said, was that of an 'unbiased judge' rather than a 'proposer of plans'.[3] The issues were too great for any person or body less than the nation as a whole to decide: 'the consideration must of necessity come into Parliament'[4] 'where the question of right can alone be decided';[5] and to enable Parliament to reach a considered opinion, there must first be a full investigation into the facts—the terms of the charter, the details of the Company's trading, the extent of their new possessions, the conditions under which they had been acquired, the amount of the revenues, and the proposals for their administration. Chatham explained his views to the Cabinet who agreed to warn the Company that their affairs would be discussed in Parliament when it met in November.[6]

The notification came as a bombshell. It sobered the Directors who at their next quarterly meeting (24th September 1766) 'threw out a great many terrors of the interposition of Parliament'; and it provoked the Proprietors into snatching their profits, while the going was good, by insisting on a substantial increase in the rate

[1] Walpole. *George III*, II, 315.
[2] Walsh to Clive, October 1766. Chatham Corr. III, 95 (*n.*).
[3] Chatham to Grafton, 23rd February 1767. Chatham Corr. III, 218.
[4] Walsh to Clive, October 1766. Chatham Corr. III, 95 (*n.*).
[5] Chatham to Grafton, 10th January. Anson, p. 112.
[6] Grafton to Chatham, 27th August 1766. Chatham Corr. III, 59.

of dividend.[1] They were strongly backed by all Chatham's enemies in the House and by all the champions of private property outside.[2] Worse still, the two most important Ministers in the Commons, Conway and Charles Townshend, veered toward the Opposition —Conway at the instigation of Rockingham, and Townshend because, as Chancellor of the Exchequer, he wanted to strike a bargain with the Company.[3] The effect of this domestic revolt was that Chatham, beginning to reap the dead-sea fruit of his earldom, was forced to entrust the conduct of the business in the Commons to a private member, Beckford, with the uncomfortable suspicion that he might not be properly supported.

Beckford, however, managed the preliminary moves with striking success, in spite of virulent opposition not only from Grenville but from the whole Rockingham clique—Burke, at their head, mouthing his own peculiar abuse of Chatham, which would have been profane if it had not been so blatantly vulgar. The Company were sufficiently alarmed to pass a resolution empowering the Directors to treat with the Government (31st December 1766); and the Directors, in true counting-house style, sent Grafton a list of the benefits they expected to receive. Chatham dismissed it as 'captious and preposterous'.[4] They then hinted through Shelburne at their ideas for an agreement: 'I think', Chatham commented, 'the project very liberal to the Company and to the Proprietors, and also take notice that there is no restriction upon the application and use of the portion of the revenue supposed to be indulged to the Company, an omission of the utmost consequence and danger'.[5] The comment is interesting for the light it throws on Chatham's ideas. He had from the first revolted at the notion of striking a bargain with the Company. They had their rights, for which, if necessary, they should receive compensation; but the first step must be to settle what those rights were. It was undeniable that they were sovereigns *de facto* over a large empire in India, but were they sovereigns *de jure*? Parliament must decide. If the verdict went against the Company,

---

[1] Shelburne to Chatham, 5th October 1766, Chatham Corr. III, 93.
[2] 'The people can hardly believe . . . they will break through the charter of the East Indies which was purchased by the Company, and which has been repeatedly confirmed by many solemn Acts of Parliament'. Grenville to Temple, 21st September 1766. *Grenville Papers*, III, 322.
[3] See Anson, p. 109.
[4] Chatham to Grafton, 10th January 1767. Anson, p. 112.
[5] Chatham to Shelburne, 3rd February 1767. Chatham Corr. III, 188.

as Chatham was disposed to assume, the sovereignty, willy-nilly, would have to be taken over by the State, and the Company compensated—probably by the grant of trading privileges and an extension of their charter. If, unexpectedly, the verdict were in the Company's favour, the Government, on the principle of 'preventing unreasonableness and oppression', would have to ensure that the Company carried out their duties properly and spent at least the greater part of the revenue on their Indian subjects. It was altogether a tricky business, and Chatham was doubly anxious to keep the negotiations in his own hands.

He had, however, by this time retired to Bath, worn out and ill, hoping by a course of the waters to return invigorated when Parliament reassembled in January (1767). Indeed, he made a great effort to come up on the appointed date, but 'was compelled through excess of pain to return to his bed'.[1] It was not until the 2nd March that he finally managed to arrive in town. Meanwhile Townshend had taken advantage of his absence to begin a private negotiation of his own with the Company—at first tentatively but with growing confidence until towards the end of January (1767) he was openly expressing his disagreement with Chatham's policy[2] and setting his colleagues by the ears. Cabinet meetings, as Grafton lamented, acquired 'a *peevish* cast'.[3] Chatham should have been used to obstruction; he had suffered from it throughout the whole of his previous Ministry—but at least in those days his health had been comparatively good and he had been able to defend himself. Now, shackled to his bed by pain and weakness, he wrote bitterly to Grafton: 'Allow me, my dear Lord, to say that it is not my absence which affects this business, but an unfortunate original difference of opinion among the King's servants, which, totally contrary to my notions, by enervating at the outset the principle of Parliamentary enquiry, shook the whole foundation of this great transaction, and has, in my opinion, thrown it into confusion inextricable'.[4] While he lay helpless, Townshend rushed blithely on, and at the end of February found another reason for his plan. Through his own carelessness, his Budget proposals were defeated,

---

[1] Anson, p. 112.
[2] 'Mr. Townshend has ventured to express his difference of opinion with Lord Chatham and his deputy Alderman Beckford'. Grenville to Buckingham, 27th January 1767. H.M.C. Lothian MSS.
[3] Grafton to Chatham, 21st January 1767. Chatham Corr. III, 168.
[4] Chatham to Grafton, 23rd January 1767. Anson, p. 113.

the Land Tax being reduced by one shilling. During the debate, he
had spoken of employing the money he expected from the Company in the reduction of the national debt; now he would have to
use it for balancing his Budget. Such was the state of affairs when
Chatham returned. As soon as he realised the situation, he decided
to get rid of Townshend; but to England's lasting misfortune,
before he could find a suitable successor, he had suffered that fatal
breakdown which kept him for two years in the darkness of
despair. Townshend, so unexpectedly reprieved, was free to
cobble up a temporary arrangement with the Company under
which, in return for the payment of £400,000 p.a., they were
confirmed in their sovereignty for a further two years and allowed
to raise their dividends to twelve per cent. It could not be said of
Townshend at the conclusion of the affair as it had been said of
Chatham at the beginning, that he was 'certainly not only the most
vigorous, but the most comprehensive and judicious Minister this
country ever had'.[1] It is true that Townshend had managed to
reach a decision, but he had failed to reach a solution and had
missed all the deeper issues, doing no particular good to England
and much positive harm to India. 'Hitherto', as the historian of
the Company notes, 'the wars waged by the Company had been in
their essential nature and principle, *defensive*. The Company, or
rather their servants, now entered on what may be designated
wars of alliance . . . and to these succeeded, in one or two instances,
wars for dominion'.[2] Townshend had done nothing to stop, and
much to encourage, them. So, in sad fashion, Chatham's policy
was frustrated, and his fears confirmed.

(v)

Chatham's ideas on the constitutional problem are best exemplified by his actions. As already recorded, he had told the King
that 'he wished as far as possible to dissolve all factions and to see the
best of all parties in employment'. He had been led to that desire
by his distaste for the political methods of the time, and his doubts
of their efficiency. The fact is that the long Whig supremacy had
turned politics, which should be the art of statesmanship, into a
species of gang warfare. Cabinet-making had degenerated into

[1] Walsh to Clive. October 1766. Chatham Corr. III, 95 (*n*).
[2] Grant, pp. 282–3.

hard bargaining between petty chieftains, whose aim was not the good of the country, nor, as a rule, the promotion of any particular policy, nor necessarily their own inclusion in the Ministry, but simply the attainment of peerages, pensions and places for themselves, their friends and relations. It is true that from time to time there appeared to be a cleavage of principle, as, for instance, between Grenville's Stamp Act and Rockingham's Repeal; but even in such cases the difference was rarely fundamental; usually it was a matter of procedure, or perhaps of timing. Rockingham did not deny the right to tax the colonies but only the expediency. It was Chatham who denied the right. Indeed Chatham was the one statesman of the age who invariably emphasised principles, and it was the novelty of his proposals, combined with his impatience over the customary bargaining, that made him so unpopular with the politicians and so popular with the people.

The King re-echoed Chatham's wish, but while at bottom the dissolution of factions meant, for Chatham, the substitution of policies for bargains as the basis of party, it meant, for the King, freedom from what he was pleased to call slavery. Though the King was fond of the phrase, he might have found it hard to explain. All he knew was that however often he changed his Ministers, he always ended by feeling himself cribbed, cabined and confined. He kicked very heartily against the pricks, not knowing that his *malaise* sprang from faded recollections of Bute's idealism, and was unlikely to vanish until the limits of constitutional monarchy had been much more clearly marked out, and politics had taken on something much nearer the shape which Chatham envisaged. In the meantime he must make do with his prerogative —ill-defined as it was and much suspected. It came on the stage very early in Chatham's Ministry.

The harvest had been poor, and the resultant scarcity was made the more oppressive by the export of corn to Europe, where famine conditions provided an excellent market. Worse still, the greater the scarcity the higher the price. Hunger was driving the people to desperation, and everywhere riots were breaking out which had to be forcibly suppressed. All the troops that could be spared were engaged upon the job, and Barrington computed that there was need 'for 30,000 more at least to keep the mob of this country in order'.[1] The obvious course for Government was to

[1] Barrington to Buckingham, 30th September 1766. H.M.C. Lothian MSS.

prohibit the export of corn, but they had no authority under existing Acts and Parliament was not sitting, nor could it be recalled in time, to increase their powers. Chatham, however, was not the man to be daunted by parchment difficulties. There were, in his view, necessities which were above the law, and hunger was one of them. Steps must be taken at once to remedy the shortage; if powers did not exist, they must be created. But if the law must appear to be flouted in order to deal with a crisis, it was the more necessary to vindicate it elsewhere—the riots must therefore be put down with a high hand. He told the Cabinet that an embargo must be placed on the export of corn by the use of the royal prerogative—it existed for just such a purpose—and advised Shelburne to set up a special commission to try rioters who were guilty of felony and make an example of one such man in every county.[1] Being too ill to attend the Cabinet meeting in person, he made a point of writing 'to give his opinion *publicly* for the embargo upon corn which he had strenuously advised in *private*'.[2] And so, on the 24th September, as Walpole noted, 'the King by the unanimous advice of his Council, took upon him to lay an embargo, which was never done before in time of peace'. Walpole anticipated 'much clamour among the interested', though he thought that in general the move would be popular.[3]

Very possibly Chatham also anticipated clamour. His enemies were active—Temple and Grenville openly, Rockingham more discreetly. There were signs too of defection among some of the Ministers. Townshend was the main source of trouble; he was discontented because Chatham did not make enough fuss of him and so he disclaimed all share in administration and abused the Cabinet.[4] He was so clearly hostile that Chatham even at that early date was seriously contemplating his dismissal.[5] But Townshend was not alone; Conway was inclined to be sulky, and North was very conscious of 'the uneasiness of his situation'.[6] These underground rumblings did not perturb Chatham unduly, but he had them well in mind when, early in October, he went to Bath for his customary course of waters prior to the meeting of Par-

---

[1] Chatham to Shelburne, 9th October 1766. Chatham Corr. III, 98.
[2] Chatham to Townshend, 24th September 1766. Chatham Corr. III, 73.
[3] Walpole to Mann, 25th September 1766.
[4] Whately to Grenville, 20th October 1766. *Grenville Papers*, III, 332.
[5] Onslow to Newcastle, 24th October 1766. Add. MSS. 32,977.
[6] Whately to Grenville, 20th October 1766.

liament. The conclusion to which he came was that it would strengthen his administration as well as promote his constitutional views if he could win over 'people of property and credit to give it weight and permanency'.[1] Bedford's presence in Bath provided an opportunity. Chatham approached him and found the response not unfavourable; Bedford said that he had no factious views and did not desire to oppose or weaken the hands of government. After consulting his friends he presented his terms—Gower, Weymouth and Rigby to be reinstated in 'employments of magnitude'; Marlborough to be given the Garter; Lorne to be made a peer; and the rest of his followers to be provided for as occasion should offer.[2] Clearly he knew how to open his mouth. Political manœuvring in the eighteenth century was not unlike bargaining in an Eastern bazaar—one started with the sky. Chatham quietly put Bedford's terms aside. He was not, he said, proposing to get rid of Ministers wholesale, but to fill vacancies with the most suitable men. At the moment, he had one vacancy—the Postmaster's office—which he thought might suit Weymouth; and two prospective vacancies which might be appropriate, if and when they arose, for Gower and Rigby. Bedford and his friends declined the offer; one bird in the hand was not enough, nor was its value much enhanced by two more in the bush; they would prefer to wait 'till the bottom should be enlarged'. A few weeks later, the resignations over the Edgcumbe affair altered the situation. Chatham was now able to make a firm offer of posts for Gower and Rigby as well as Weymouth; he also gave an assurance that Marlborough should have his Garter before long and a *douceur* in the meantime. Bedford was disposed to accept. 'Lord Gower and I', he wrote, 'agree in opinion, that, if ever our friends mean to come into court, this is the properest opening we are likely to have'.[3] But Bedford's friends, if not great statesmen, were at least keen men of business; they had an eye for the main chance; and weighing the probable effect of so many resignations, decided that Chatham's necessity was their opportunity. What had satisfied them before, satisfied them no longer. Bedford, at their bidding, opened his mouth wider. He produced a list as long as his arm, including a seat in the House of Lords for his son,

---

[1] Bedford's *Journal*, 19th October 1766. Bedford Corr. III, 348.
[2] Bedford's *Journal*, 31st October 1766. Bedford Corr. III, 351.
[3] Bedford to Marlborough, 29th November 1766. Bedford Corr. III, 355.

Tavistock, which, as Chatham remarked, 'seems entirely distinct from the reasonings which may affect the other'.[1] The King rejected Bedford's 'extravagant proposal' out of hand, and inveighed against 'the rapaciousness of his friends'—descriptions with which Chatham agreed, though, with his usual perspicacity, he exonerated Bedford: 'the source of this strange error', he said, 'lies somewhere else'.[2] The transaction, however, in its wearisome details, exemplifies very clearly the political methods which Chatham wanted to destroy, and perhaps helps to explain why the King thought of himself as a slave.

Though the negotiations led to nothing, they were indirectly useful. Grenville was determined to raise in the House the clamour which Walpole anticipated; and as the meeting of Parliament drew nearer, thought it as well to secure Bedford's backing. They had once been allies, and now, in conjunction, might surely be able to exploit Chatham's daring use of the King's prerogative. But Bedford and his followers were not interested, being in the middle of their negotiations with Chatham. Though he had refused their terms for the moment, the negotiations had not yet broken down, and would no doubt be renewed before long. For the rest, Chatham was in office and seemed likely to remain there; decidedly he was a better proposition than Grenville. And so when Grenville threw out feelers, he made little progress. Bedford was profuse in compliments, but opined that in its present 'melancholy and disordered state' the kingdom needed to be helped rather than hampered, and therefore he 'doubted whether he and his friends should disturb the Government'.[3]

Grenville, however, was not destined to stand alone; incongruously he was supported by Rockingham. Though arch-enemies in everything else, they were at one in their hatred of Chatham. When Parliament met on the 11th November (1766), Suffolk in the Lords and Grenville and Burke in the Commons dilated on the illegality of the Order in Council prohibiting the export of corn and the failure of Government to recall the House, castigating what they called the Ministry's ignorance and blunders. Chatham had no difficulty in refuting the charges; Parliament could not

---

[1] Chatham to George III, 1st December 1766. Fortescue, I, 419.
[2] Chatham to George III, 2nd December 1766. Fortescue, I, 421.
[3] Grenville's Diary, 9th November 1766. *Grenville Papers*, III, 381.

have been recalled in time, and the summons would merely have encouraged the merchants to push on faster with their exports while they could; as to the Order in Council, of course it was not strictly legal, but it was justified on the ground of necessity and would be whitewashed by a Bill of Indemnity. In the Upper House Bedford made a temperate speech and in the Lower his followers stayed away. In neither House did Chatham's opponents dare to challenge a division.

The Bill of Indemnity offered more scope. Grenville made great play with some blundering expressions of Beckford, insisting, with a bully's desire to intimidate, that the words should be taken down; he also demanded that the Bill should be extended to cover persons who had advised the Order as well as those who had acted under it—so, by implication, giving Chatham a rap over the knuckles. But no one was really interested in the former point, and Chatham disposed of the lattter by agreeing that the Bill should be made as strong and as wide as possible.[1] Grenville was reduced to wishing that he could find some point on which he could differ from the Ministry and so 'be able to gall them with the repetition of this odious subject'.[2] He could find none, and, even after the Rockinghams had been stirred to anger by the Edgcumbe affair, the combined Opposition could muster no more than 48 votes to 166 in the only division there was—'a signal victory', Walpole commented, 'in Lord Chatham's circumstances'[3]

In the Lords, the Bill of Indemnity passed without a division; but not without a malevolent stab at Chatham. Richmond demanded an explanation of the doctrine that necessity authorised government to dispense with the law. The legal pundits—Northington, Camden and Mansfield—indulged in sterile argument about the King's prerogative and the Constitution. Chatham, by contrast, seized the essential point; the law had been over-ridden, not as a mere exercise in prerogative, but because of the people's need; the people must be judges whether they had benefited or not; his own aim was simply to restore order and good government, and his desire was to conciliate parties.[4] Richmond, who had never forgiven Chatham for putting Shelburne over his head, here saw a chance of venting his wrath. Did Chatham, he asked,

[1] Chatham. Corr. III, 128 (n).
[2] Grenville to Temple, 21st November 1766. *Grenville Papers*, III, 344.
[3] Walpole. *George III*, II, 286.
[4] Grantham to Newcastle, 10th December 1766. Add. MSS. 32,978.

imagine he could restore order and conciliate parties by affronting people of the first quality? He hoped the nobility would refuse to be browbeaten by an insolent Minister. Chatham retorted that when the people condemned him, he would tremble; but until that time, he was ready to face the proudest connexion in the country; he challenged Richmond to produce a single example of his insolence. Tempers were hot, and the House had to intervene.[1] But though, as the French Ambassador reported, Chatham had kept his temper the better of the two,[2] he felt deeply wounded at this unprovoked attack by a man barely half his age;[3] and the wound went the deeper because it shattered his illusion that an earl's robes would automatically give him that sense of equality with the great which he so passionately desired.

When Parliament rose for the Christmas holidays, Chatham went down to Bath. He was desperately ill and desperately tired —but not despairing. In his great Ministry it had taken him two years to break through the tangled thickets of obstruction and come within sight of victory. It might take him as long again, but at least he had set his policies in motion and could hope for the best. Indeed, he had better grounds for hope than he knew, for the factions which opposed him and which he was set on destroying, were dying of inanition. The Bedfords were quiescent and half disposed to join him; Bute was well inclined;[4] and Rockingham, trying to hold his faction together while he searched for allies, and ruining his chances by being 'pretty peremptory' with anyone who did not at once bow to his wishes,[5] was coming to the reluctant conclusion that 'the strength of administration will at present increase'.[6] But, good as his prospects were, Chatham had overlooked one thing, one important difference from his previous Ministry—he was ten years older; his strength was decaying, his nerves were overstrained, his mind was near snapping. When the time came for Parliament to reassemble, he was unable to bear the pain and fatigue of the journey to town—a fact which 'afflicted him beyond expression'[7] because he recognised that unless he were present,

[1] Grenville's Diary, 10th December 1766. *Grenville Papers*, III, 396.
[2] Williams, II, 229.   [3] Walpole. *George III*, II, 291.
[4] Barrington to Mitchell, 14th December 1766. Add. MSS. 6,834.
[5] Newcastle's Short Account, etc., 18th December 1766. Add. MSS. 32,978.
[6] Rockingham to Newcastle, 10th December 1766, Add. MSS. 32,978.
[7] Chatham to Shelburne, 31st January 1767. Chatham Corr. III, 181.

the East Indian affair, 'this transcendent object' as he called it,[1] was likely to be mishandled by Townshend and Conway from whom he had 'the misfortune to differ *toto coelo*'.[2] The rest of the Cabinet seemed unable to control them. Grafton, in his *Apologia* written many years later, suggested that this was because 'Lord Chatham did never open to us, or to the Cabinet in general, what was his real and fixed plan',[3] and Walpole adds in his most categorical style that 'it was plain he [Chatham] had determined to give no directions, for he sent none. He corresponded with none of the Ministers'.[4] Yet his many letters, some of which Grafton printed, and which give the lie to Walpole, seem real enough and plain enough, and certainly their message never varied. Walpole adds that 'Grafton was charmed to be idle'; but Walpole does him less than justice; Grafton's trouble was youthful indecision; Townshend could too easily overawe and override him.

Townshend, whose chief characteristics, besides vanity, were a scintillating oratory and a gay insouciance, had matters all his own way. He expressed his difference of opinion with Chatham openly, traversing his wishes for India and ridiculing his views on America. Carelessly and boastfully, he played with fire; it singed his fingers and might have seared his heart, but for his death before the conflagration had spread over continents. By the end of December (1766) he had successfully blocked Chatham's plans for India; by the end of January (1767) he had taken his first step toward the quicksands of American taxation. On the 26th of that month the House debated America. Grenville, riding his hobby horse, moved that the colonists should bear the expenses of the troops there, and Townshend, airily brushing the proposal aside, pledged himself, in a thoughtless moment, to find a revenue nearly, if not quite, sufficient for the purpose. 'What he means', said Shelburne, 'I do not conceive'. Perhaps Townshend himself was not very sure, but the pledge had been given and there were hearers in plenty to remind him of it.[5]

Townshend's vagaries, added to the known friction in the Cabinet and Chatham's continued absence, came as a tonic and refreshment to the Rockinghams. They began to pluck up courage for the first time since the fiasco of their resignations; they toyed

[1] Chatham to Townshend, 2nd January 1767. Chatham Corr., III, 153.
[2] Chatham to Grafton, 10th January 1767. Anson, p. 111.
[3] Anson, p. 110.   [4] Walpole. *George III*, II, 293.
[5] Shelburne to Chatham, 1st February 1767. Chatham Corr. III, 185.

with the idea of uniting with the Bedfords; they contemplated mollifying Grenville with some non-ministerial post, and some were even daring enough to whisper of 'getting rid of my Lord Chatham and risk the consequences' even if that meant restoring Grenville to power.[1] Between them they hatched a plot to upset the Budget. It should not be difficult; a snap division would surely secure a reduction of the Land Tax. Grenville had half pledged himself to it when he was Premier; the Country Gentlemen would welcome it; and the near approach of an election would be an inducement to others. Rockingham's more responsible followers such as Savile and Burke doubted the propriety, but the Yorke family pressed eagerly forward with the scheme and Rockingham gave it his blessing.

On the 27th February, Townshend, blissfully ignorant of the danger, introduced his Budget. He proposed the usual Land Tax of four shillings, and gaily promised to reduce the national debt with the money which he expected to get from the East India Company. Dowdeswell, who as an ex-Chancellor of the Exchequer ought to have know better, moved for a reduction of the tax by one shilling. The Country Gentlemen gave him their support, and Dr. Hay reminded Townshend of his pledge to tax America. Townshend, beginning to see the red light, explained that 'it was to be done by degrees and on mature consideration';[2] but too late; the expected windfall from India and the revenue from America seemed justification enough and the House voted for the reduction. It was a resounding victory for the Opposition, but politically it did them no good. They had, as Walpole remarked 'no other satisfaction than in the perpetration of the mischief. No popularity ensued; the City, where the national interest was best understood, condemned such public disservice, and spread the cry of disapprobation'.[3] But financially Townshend was now committed both to making a bargain with the East India Company and to taxing the colonies.

Three days later, Chatham, who had been creeping painfully and by short stages up from Bath, arrived in town. He was utterly exhausted, but the news of what Townshend had been doing roused him to a final effort. If the reports, he wrote to Grafton, which he had received were true, 'the writer hereof and the Chancellor of

[1] Newcastle to Rockingham, 22nd February 1767. Add. MSS. 32,980.
[2] Walpole. *George III*, II, 299.   [3] *Ibid.*, 302.

the Exchequer aforesaid cannot remain in office together; or Mr. C. Townshend must amend his proceeding. Duty to the King and zeal for the salvation of the whole will not allow of any departure from this resolution'.[1] He instructed Grafton to offer the post to North, who refused it. Before he could nominate anyone else, he had suffered a complete breakdown, physical and mental.

[1] Chatham to Grafton, 4th March 1767. Mahon, V. App. XVI

XVII

CHARLES TOWNSHEND

(i)

FOR THE next two years, as history tends to emphasise, England's Prime Minister was mad. His symptoms are matter for medicine, not biography; the doctors must give them appropriate names; and if the past is any criterion, the names will change. But to one layman at least, the symptoms seem to be as much those of utter exhaustion as of mental derangement. Chatham displayed a strong repugnance to any form of mental effort, and when the King coerced him, much against his will, into seeing Grafton, the strain of turning his mind to public affairs was not only pathetically unrewarding, but seems to have given him almost physical pain. At times he indulged in some whim or fancy, as for instance a wish to enlarge the house he was occupying at Hampstead, or a longing to repurchase Hayes, or again, as historians are fond of recording, a taste for roast chicken at inconvenient times. These fancies do not appear to have been unreasonable in themselves, but became extravagant because he failed, or perhaps was unable, to appreciate their cost and the trouble they involved. Though even this may not be true; for in August 1767, finding 'the transacting of any business so uneasy to him', he gave Hester a general power of attorney,[1] possibly to avoid excess as well as effort. As time went on, he sank deeper into melancholy and developed a craving for solitude, until finally, for practical purposes, he was lost to sight and almost to memory. Grafton, the one member of his Ministry who saw him in his illness, has said all that a biographer needs to say on this subject: 'though I expected to find Lord Chatham very ill indeed, his situation was different from what I had imagined; his nerves and spirits were affected to a dreadful degree; and the sight of his great mind bowed down, and thus weakened by disorder, would have filled me with grief and concern, even if I had not long borne a sincere attachment to his person and

[1] Hester to Nuthall, 17th August 1767. Chatham Corr. III, 282.

character. The confidence he reposed in me, demanded every return on my part; and it appeared like cruelty in me to have been urged by any necessity to put a man I valued, to so great suffering as it was evident that my commission excited. The interview was truly painful'.[1] For the biographer, this period of darkness has only two points of interest: first, the unshakable conviction of Chatham's doctor, Anthony Addington, that he would recover, which must have been a solace to the sad Hester, and perhaps —who knows?—to the afflicted Titan; and secondly, those movements in the outside world which set the stage on which Chatham was to reappear.

(ii)

Chatham had so often been away ill for long periods, that at the outset his absence seemed in no way abnormal. It took the world time to realise that this attack, whatever its nature, was more severe and enduring than others. At first, there were the usual sneers that his gout was 'political',[2] or that he was indulging in mystery to enhance his prestige; then it began to be whispered that he was mad,[3] and, finally, people shrugged their shoulders and forgot him. But what may be called the two transitional periods have their uses for the biographer. In the first, when his absence was thought to be temporary, it was apparent, in spite of divisions in the Cabinet, how commanding a position he held, and how easily, had he been well, he could have put down incipient dissensions. In the second, the King and Grafton, alarmed at the possibility that he might never return and worried by the growing strength of the Opposition, wished, in the jargon of the day, to widen the bottom of administration, while still retaining the magic of Chatham's name. Their endeavours, which were quite unsuccessful, made it very clear, at least for posterity, that the Opposition was more deeply divided and more completely riddled with jealousies than Chatham's Cabinet had ever been. It is that fact which justified the determination of both the King and Chatham to crush the hydra of faction, which was entirely out of hand and rapidly making decent government impossible. In the end, the death of Townshend and the emergence of North as the

[1] Anson, p. 137.
[2] See Rockingham to Newcastle, 24th January 1767. Add. MSS. 32,979.
[3] 'Report says that he is mad.' Sackville to Irwin, 7th April 1767. H.M.C. Stopford-Sackville MSS.

King's strong man, created what was in essence a new Ministry, and one which became new also in name when Chatham shortly afterwards resigned.

The broad facts of the first period have already been recorded. Chatham had sketched his plans for dealing with the great questions of the day, and had gone to Bath to recuperate. He had hardly turned his back when dissension arose in the Cabinet. The authors of that dissension were Conway and Townshend. Conway was an unhappy man, mainly because he was not allowed to be happy. He was well-meaning and conscientious, and he admired Chatham; he was also poor and needed his salary as Secretary of State. Left to himself, he could have settled down quietly and carried out his job with a measure of efficiency, if without *éclat*. But Rockingham's jealousy of Chatham, not the less virulent because it was tongue-tied and sneaking, thought that in Conway it had found the perfect weapon. Conway might fancy himself Secretary of State, but Rockingham knew that he was the sword of Damocles hanging over Chatham's head. At the appropriate moment, to be settled by Rockingham, Conway was to resign and bring Chatham and his Ministry toppling down. Conway did not see matters in quite the same light. He would have liked to help his old leader, Rockingham, but he disliked the idea of resignation, which meant poverty for himself, and he had no particular wish to hurt his new leader, Chatham. Whatever pangs there are in divided loyalty, Conway suffered. He half-accepted Townshend's views on the East Indian question for Rockingham's sake, and half-struggled against them for Chatham's sake; and being half disloyal to both was wholly uncomfortable himself.

Charles Townshend was another story altogether. By common consent he was not merely one of the bright boys of Parliament; he was the brightest boy. Lady Hervey said of him, when he died, that he was 'a shining, sparkling star';[1] and Burke some years later, borrowing her imagery, spoke of him as a 'luminary' rising over the horizon as Chatham sank in the west. If he must be compared to a heavenly body, perhaps he had best be called a meteorite, for his course, however brilliant, was unpredictable and erratic; and when he came at last to earth, he made a sizable dent in the British Empire. Originally, some small degree of conviction, inflated with a good deal of vanity, had made him anxious to strike a bargain

[1] *Letters*, p. 325.

with the East India Company before Parliament debated the Indian problem. In Chatham's absence he had worked for that end, and by getting the promise of an offer from the Company had been able, not only to delay Beckford's motions in the House, but to some extent to force Chatham's hand. It was hopeless, said Chatham, on hearing what he had done, to expect the House to discuss the Company's affairs when they had been assured that 'a proposal from the Company was upon the point of being made'. In the circumstances, the proposal must be awaited; it would almost certainly prove to be 'very inadequate'; and when it was found to be so, matters could no doubt be wheeled back again on to the right lines.[1] Chatham had clearly been annoyed. He had never approved of Townshend, and would indeed have left him in the rich obscurity of the Pay Office, if it had not been for Grafton. The charm which Townshend was always able to exert over his fellow men, until they had dealings with him, had dazzled Grafton, who was ten years his junior and much given to hero-worship; he had pleaded for Townshend to be appointed his Chancellor of the Exchequer. Chatham, out of his greater knowledge, had demurred, warning Grafton that his wish might lead to 'many unexpected disappointments';[2] but Grafton, in his infatuation, had pressed hard, and Chatham had reluctantly given way. He was not, therefore, altogether unprepared for Townshend's insubordination, but he was not the less exasperated. Foreseeing that Townshend might have to go, he warned Grafton early in December (1766), that if Townshend's ideas on India were to prevail, 'the whole becomes a *farce* and the *Ministry a ridiculous phantom*', adding that 'Mr. C. Townshend's fluctuations and incurable weaknesses cannot comport with his remaining in that critical office'.[3] Early in January, he wrote two letters of advice and caution to Townshend himself;[4] and, as they seemed to bear no fruit, on the 23rd January, gave Grafton a still more emphatic warning; the source of their troubles, he said, was not the factions from without but 'a certain infelicity, (I think incurable) which ferments and sours (as your Grace has observed) the councils of his Majesty's servants'.[5] It was becoming abundantly

[1] Chatham to Shelburne, 31st January 1767. Chatham Corr. III, 181.
[2] Anson, p. 92.
[3] Chatham to Grafton, 7th December 1766. Anson, p. 110.
[4] Chatham to Townshend, 2nd and 6th January 1767. Chatham Corr. III, 153 and 158.
[5] Chatham to Grafton, 23rd January 1767. Anson, p. 114.

clear that Chatham's patience was nearly exhausted, and that Townshend's licence was soon to be shortened. When, at the end of February, Townshend was defeated on the Land Tax, he himself recognised that his days were numbered, and openly 'spoke of himself as turned out'.[1] On Chatham's arrival in London a few days later, no one doubted what he intended to do or his ability to do it. Conway and Townshend were both in a chastened mood and in Parliament were careful to keep silence 'on the difference of opinion in the Cabinet',[2] The King, putting their changed attitude down to the right cause, wrote jubilantly to Chatham: 'now you are arrived in town every difficulty will daily decrease'.[3] Chatham acted at once; he offered Townshend's office to North, and on North's refusal, would certainly have looked elsewhere and gone on looking till he had succeeded, but for his sudden collapse. Townshend was saved, and the Empire lost, by a matter of hours.

The second phase followed quickly. As soon as Townshend realised that he had been reprieved, there was no holding him. The sense of power went to his head; and necessity, after his defeat on the Budget, together with the recollection of his own boasts in the House and a malicious desire to flout the now impotent Chatham, drove him irresistibly onwards towards his proposals for America. His swashbuckling extravagancies were such that Grafton, with bitter memories of Chatham's warnings, would fain have dismissed him, but in view of North's refusal to accept office, and in the absence of further light from Chatham, was afraid to move. Yet inaction itself brought no relief. The work of the Session had still to be carried on, and with dissensions in the Cabinet and a tendency among the opposing factions to coalesce, the Government's majority dwindled daily. The fact is that India and America were issues far too great for a young and inexperienced leader, who, in his own rather pathetic words, had been deprived by Chatham's illness of 'an assistance which I never expected to have been without'.[4] He came to the mortifying if humble conclusion that unless Chatham could return to keep Townshend in order, some one must be introduced into the Cabinet who could. To whom he should turn was a question on which he longed for Chatham's advice; and at last, after several ineffectual efforts of his

---

[1] Walpole. *George III*, II, 307.
[2] Conway to George III, 6th March 1767. Fortescue, I, 460.
[3] George III to Chatham, 7th March 1767. Fortescue, I, 462.
[4] Grafton to Chatham, 29th May 1767. Anson, p. 134.

own, managed through the King's intervention, to get that sad interview with Chatham (31st May 1767), to which reference has been made. In the course of it Grafton poured out his troubles —Conway's opposition on the East India business; Townshend's 'unaccountable conduct', his 'flippant boasting' that he could raise a revenue in America, and the 'blind and greedy approbation' which the House displayed for his proposals. It was a melancholy story to be told by a young man whose ideals were high for all the errors of his way, and was made no less melancholy by the need to admit that, unless reinforcements could be obtained from outside, the Ministry must fall. When Chatham by a painful effort had concentrated his mind on Grafton's story, he entreated Grafton to remain at his post, adding that if allies were necessary, it would be better to negotiate with Bedford rather than Rockingham.[1]

It is ironical but true that after such pains had been taken to obtain Chatham's views, not a soul paid any attention to them. Grafton, Camden and Northington advised the King to regard Chatham's Ministry as dissolved, and to invite whichever of the opposition parties he thought best to form a new administration. The King demurred; he was anxious to keep Chatham; he had no desire to recall Rockingham, and he dreaded the thought of falling again into the hands of either Grenville or Bedford. Grafton accordingly struggled on to the end of the session (2nd July 1767), and then asked leave to resign. The King made one more despairing appeal to Chatham, and when that failed agreed that the time had come to set up a new Ministry; 'nothing', he assured Grafton, 'can now divert me from doing what I think is necessary for the welfare of my dominions'.[2] It is significant, however, that what he thought necessary was to enter into negotiations with Rockingham rather than with Bedford.

(iii)

Before entering into the details of those negotiations, it may be as well to trace the development of Rockingham's ideas since he had lost office. His first reaction had been one of sullen acquiescence, which rapidly gave way to what he called 'warmth' and a desire for revenge. His childish rudeness in refusing to see

[1] Anson, p. 138.
[2] George III to Grafton, 3rd July 1767. Fortescue, I, 496.

Chatham, when he called, can be excused as mere petulance, but the explanation which he gave was deliberate self-deception: 'if', he told Conway, 'at any time I appear or am warm, I desire it may be attributed to the strong persuasion that I am in, that Mr. Pitt's intentions and conduct are and will be the most hostile to our friends'.[1] He had, and knew he had, no grounds whatever for such a persuasion. It would have been far more true to say that Rockingham's intentions and conduct were most hostile to Chatham. He showed the way his mind was working by instigating the resignations[2] in connection with the Edgcumbe affair, not out of genuine indignation, but in the hope of putting administration 'upon the foot which has always been my desire. I mean that it should be composed inclusive of some of our friends who have lately been removed'.[3] In conformity with his wishes, his friends had resigned, but they did so with reluctance, and soon realised that they had made a tactical error of the first magnitude; they had alienated Chatham, driving him towards the Bute and Bedford factions, without doing themselves or their party any good. 'I doubt', Newcastle admitted sadly, 'we took a hasty step in the resignations which has by no means answered the ends proposed.'[4] But while Newcastle continued, however diffidently, to urge that Chatham should be cultivated, Rockingham maintained his hostile attitude. Anything was better than truckling to Chatham. The great object was to get rid of him, and for that purpose it might even be as well, in spite of wide differences of policy, for Rockingham to respond to the tentative approaches which Grenville and Temple made to him at the end of the year. Rockingham discussed terms with them, but broke away on learning that their intention was to make either Temple or Grenville First Lord of the Treasury. That, said Rockingham, was tantamount to 'making both of them the Minister', and Rockingham had a better candidate—himself.[5] Nor did he imagine that he would have long to wait. It was clear to him that Chatham had got into a 'scrape' over Indian affairs,[6] that he was at his wits' end, had no plan and was suffering from 'political' gout which kept him conveniently

[1] Rockingham to Conway, 26th July 1766. Albemarle, II, 6.
[2] 'Lord Rockingham is much for *resignations*.' Hardwicke to C. Yorke, 22nd November 1766. Albemarle, II, 25.
[3] Rockingham to Scarborough, 20th November 1766. Albemarle, II, 24.
[4] Newcastle to Albemarle, 7th January 1767. Add. MSS. 32,979.
[5] Rockingham to Dowdeswell, 8th January 1767. Albemarle, II, 31.
[6] Rockingham to Newcastle, 9th January 1767. Add. MSS. 32,979.

out of the way.[1] It was in the same spirit of unreasoning enmity that Rockingham promoted the plot to reduce the Land Tax, though his wiser and more experienced followers warned him that he would simply be creating difficulties for the country which he would have no power to remedy.[2] Ill-temper however prevailed; Rockingham had his way and reduced the tax, but his action so far from destroying the Ministry merely damaged his own reputation. The victory, said Savile, was 'only a fine prospect over a ha-ha, which one can't get to'.[3] Rockingham's own comment betrays his utter want of statesmanship. All he had to say after disrupting the country's finances was that 'though in truth it is not quite a serious defeat, it is a very unpleasant event [for the Government]'.[4] Yet, even if not quite serious, he hoped it would prove mortal, and on that supposition began to angle for Charles Townshend and Conway as the most likely rats to desert the ship; 'if they should come to us', he said, 'I think a good administration with prudence and temper may be formed'.[5] Finding the Ministry tougher than he expected,[6] and Townshend and Conway more coy than he had hoped, this volatile weathercock turned in a new direction; he had glanced towards Temple and Grenville; he had beckoned to Conway and Townshend; now he sighed for Bedford. By the end of March 'our great object', it appeared, was 'to have the most perfect and cordial union with the Duke of Bedford's friends and to establish a perfect confidence amongst us and *them*'. Inconsequently, but not uncharacteristically, his letter describing this new *volte face*, ended with a declaration that 'the weight we have only arises from the firmness of our conduct and our consistency'.[7] But alas! fresh difficulties arose. Bedford —and Newcastle for that matter—was sure that Chatham was too strong to be overborne by anything less than a union of all the factions in opposition. It would therefore be necessary to bring Grenville into the picture. Grenville was willing to help, but he 'would not take an employment under my Lord Rockingham';

---

[1] Rockingham to Newcastle, 24th January 1767. Add. MSS. 32,979.

[2] 'If . . . *no more equitable tax be found*, and £450,000 must be had for *necessary* purposes, why, it must be had. There is an end. . . . Never let us drive a wrong or a dubious point.' Savile to Rockingham. Albemarle, II, 34.

[3] Savile to Rockingham. Albemarle, II, 41.

[4] Rockingham to Newcastle, 1st March 1767. Add. MSS. 32,980.

[5] Rockingham to Newcastle, 5th March 1767. Add. MSS. 32,980.

[6] 'We were beat—147 to 180.' Rockingham to Newcastle, 10th March 1767. Add. MSS. 32,980.

[7] Rockingham to Newcastle, 26th March 1767. Add. MSS. 32,980.

nor, he imagined, would Rockingham take an employment under him. There was only one solution—both must stand down, and 'some third impartial person be appointed'.[1] It is hardly necessary to add that Rockingham was no more disposed to accept a third person than he had been to accept Grenville or Temple. There was only one God-given leader in England, and Rockingham was the man. Sackville, by way of stressing the obvious, remarked that 'they are not likely to agree any further than in the demolishing the present Minister'.[2] Nor did their disagreement much matter; in the absence of any invitation to Court they were merely shadow-fighting. But the position altered when, early in July (1767), the King instructed Grafton to negotiate a reconstruction of the Ministry. That gave all the factions a footing, and a chance. The King inclined towards the Rockinghams and Grafton concurred after he had sounded the Bedfords privately and without success.

(iv)

Grafton lost no time in beginning the tedious, slow-motion palavers that were characteristic of eighteenth-century negotiations. He saw Rockingham on the 3rd July, and hinted that changes were in contemplation. Rockingham, in a high state of excitement, babbled about it to his cronies till four o'clock in the morning.[3] What did Grafton mean? Had he only minor changes in view, or did he aim at a 'solid plan'? And if the latter, would he try to play off the Rockinghams and Bedfords against each other? Did he know his own mind or, 'being at a loss how to turn himself', was he just floundering?[4] Four days later Grafton shed a little more light. There was another interview at which, rightly or wrongly, Rockingham got the impression that he was being invited not simply to join the Government, but to take the Treasury. His inordinate vanity was tickled and his fear of rivals allayed; he asked for, and obtained, permission to impart the news to Bedford.[5] When he had done so, the factions fell into a

---

[1] Substance of a conversation, etc., 28th March 1767; and Newcastle to White 30th March 1767. Add. MSS. 32,980.
[2] Sackville to Irwin, 7th April 1767. H.M.C. Stopford-Sackville MSS.
[3] Albemarle to Newcastle, 4th July 1767. *A Narrative*, etc., p. 108.
[4] Rockingham to Newcastle, 4th July 1767. Add. MSS. 32,983.
[5] Rockingham to Newcastle, 7th July 1767. Add. MSS. 32,983.

whirlpool of manœuvring which is not without its interest. As Rockingham had been offered the Treasury, none of the other faction-leaders—Bedford, Grenville and Temple—would take office themselves—they were far too proud—but they were anxious and willing to secure places for their followers, in the conviction that if they could only secure enough they would soon oust Rockingham and edge themselves into power. Rockingham on the other hand knew that he could not stand alone. It was therefore to the interest of all to have what they called a comprehensive plan—the factions now in opposition must unite. So they all said and indeed kept on saying. It is ironical to note that in their eagerness to overthrow Chatham and outwit each other, they hit on the very device—the destruction of 'parties'—which Chatham had advocated as the basis of good government. Had they succeeded, Burke would no doubt have echoed his leader's words and called the result a 'solid plan'; but in fact it would have resembled Burke's 'tessellated pavement without cement' far more truly than Chatham's Ministry ever did. Chatham was the only leader capable of fusing all the parties into one because he was the only leader whom all admitted, however reluctantly, to be pre-eminent. Without Chatham, it was exceedingly difficult, if not impossible, to get a true coalition. The only real bond between the faction-leaders was envy of Chatham and their dilemma was to find a policy which they could all adopt and at the same time present with decency to the world. Bedford did his best; they were uniting, he said, 'to rescue his Majesty and this country out of the hands of the Earl of Bute, and to restore strength and energy to the King's government, upon a constitutional footing, free from *favouritism* [i.e. Bute] and the *guidance* of a Minister, not in a responsible employment' [i.e. Chatham].[1] For popular consumption that was good enough, since the belief in Bute's influence was very widespread and there was a growing restiveness at Chatham's absence; but as a basis for government it was fantastically brittle. Bute was no longer interfering, and the idea that a Prime Minister could only function if he were in a 'responsible employment' was a mode of thinking already obsolescent. Not only the cement but the foundations and the superstructure of the proposed coalition were all plentifully lacking.

The opening of official negotiations was delayed by a genuine

[1] Bedford to Rockingham, 16th July 1767. Bedford Corr. III, 373.

misunderstanding. Rockingham, believing that he was premier-elect, and as such was required to set up what for all practical purposes would be a new Ministry, wanted—precisely as Chatham always did—to see the King, in order to obtain direct authorisation. But the King certainly, and Grafton more doubtfully, did not recognise Rockingham as premier-elect; he was to come in as a prop for the existing Ministry, and might very easily find himself dismissed if and when Chatham returned. The King therefore was not prepared to see him; all he wanted was Rockingham's proposals, which he would consider at his leisure and change at his will. Rockingham felt obliged to give way. But it mattered very little in what guise he set about Cabinet-making. Directly the faction-leaders got down to details of policy and personnel, the seams of the coalition promptly split. Rockingham, according to his own account, became 'warm',[1] and according to Bedford, 'flew into a violent passion'.[2] Bedford, though more restrained was by no means calm, and the meeting broke up at two o'clock in the morning 'with mutual declarations that all which had passed during the whole transaction should be considered as if it had never been.'[3] The Opposition had shown itself to be a mass of incompatible elements, not to be feared. Grafton and Conway took heart of grace and decided to carry on as caretakers for Chatham.

(v)

Though the Opposition bubble had burst, there still remained the Townshend problem. His vagaries were not to last long, but they were to do untold damage, putting the coping-stone on the folly of Grenville's Stamp Act. Yet greatly as he is to be blamed for his lack of wisdom, his actions were perhaps less the outcome of reckless flippancy than of failure to act on Chatham's plan of stopping short when he had lost his way, 'lest by advancing from one false step to another, he should wind himself into an inextricable labyrinth'. Townshend wound himself very thoroughly as the result of one thoughtless speech. He had long taken an intelligent, if wayward, interest in American affairs. As early as 1763, when he had been at the Board of Trade, he had observed

---

[1] Rockingham to Hardwicke, dated 2nd, but should probably be 22nd July 1767. Albemarle, II, 50.
[2] Bedford's *Journal*, 20th July 1767. Bedford Corr. III, 382.
[3] Whately to Sackville, 21st July 1767. *Grenville Papers*, IV, 71.

with no favourable eye the tumults and commotions in the colonies, and had inclined towards stricter financial measures and firmer control. In 1764 he had given his vote for Grenville's Stamp Act, and though the next year he had voted for its repeal, he had expressed the view that 'America should be regulated', and a new system introduced, to do away with anomalies in the various charters and to make the executive and judiciary independent of the Assemblies.[1] In a word, he recognised that Government should tackle the problem of America. Now, in 1767, like the majority of his contemporaries, he felt that the colonists were reacting too slowly to the gesture of Rockingham's repeal. Indeed, the colonists were making things very difficult for their friends in England. They were touchy and truculent, with much of the sea-lawyer in their attitude, especially towards the provisions of the Mutiny Act. Even Chatham had been constrained to speak of them as 'those irritable and umbrageous people quite out of their senses'.[2] Their quibbles over the billeting of soldiers and their patent reluctance to recompense the sufferers from riots, gave Grenville some excuse for reviving his harsh policy when the question of troops for America came up in January (1767). He proposed that the estimate should be cut by a half, and then 'defrayed by America and the West Indies'.[3] The proposal was so impracticable that there was no prospect of its being adopted. Perhaps for that very reason Townshend felt justified in treating the whole subject flippantly. He rejected Grenville's motion out of hand, but more as untimely than improper. He was, he said, in spite of appearances, still a supporter of the Stamp Act. It was obviously right that the colonists should pay for their own protection; nor was there any legal difficulty. Chatham's distinction between internal and external taxes was 'absurd, nonsensical and ridiculous',[4] but even so, Townshend could, if he wished, keep the distinction and yet find a revenue in America which would substantially cover the cost. He was being needlessly impertinent to his leader, whose policy he ignored or failed to understand, and wantonly defiant on the subject of taxes. The whole speech was mere exhibitionism; it did not represent Townshend's immediate intentions. But the Opposition at once seized

[1] Bancroft, III, 8–9.
[2] Chatham to Shelburne, 7th February 1767. Chatham Corr. III, 193.
[3] Grenville to Buckingham, 27th January 1767. H.M.C. Lothian MSS.
[4] *Ibid.*

on his assertion that the cost could be met in America, and in spite of his attempt—too late—to water it down, they held him to it.[1] Townshend had taken the first false step. It provided Parliament with an excuse for that cutting down of the Land Tax which drove him to take a further and a longer step along the labyrinthine path. He now thought himself obliged to make good his idle boast, in order to help in balancing his budget.

Although Bancroft declares that Townshend meant 'to lay the foundation of a vast American revenue',[2] it is reasonably clear that his ambitions were much more modest, and that he set about his task with some misgivings. The loss of the Land Tax, unfortunate as it was, did not seem to him a proper basis for American taxation. America could not be asked merely to make good an English deficit; and if she was to be asked to pay for herself, the demand must be shown to be reasonable. When, therefore, the matter came before the Cabinet (12th March), he insisted that taxation must go hand in hand with reform; the whole system of adminis-tration must be overhauled 'with a view to a general reduction of expense', and the revenue at which they should aim must be 'a particular sum' related to that expense. Unless this were done, he could not make good his promise and must think up some way of excusing himself to the House.[3] In making these proposals he was obviously trespassing on Shelburne's department, and he knew it,[4] but thought he had no option. There was a further difficulty; the time was much too short; the reorganisation of America could not be conjured like a rabbit out of a hat. But again Townshend had no option, and he forced his colleagues to agree by threatening to resign.[5] Shelburne, on this, lost heart and ceased to attend Cabinet meetings,[6] so leaving the field clear for Townshend.

Having thus half forced himself, and half been forced, to accept responsibility for all American affairs, Townshend opened his so-called American budget (13th May), in an unusually serious frame of mind.[7] His speech had little enough to do with taxation.

---

[1] Shelburne to Chatham, 1st February 1767. Chatham Corr. III, 184.
[2] Bancroft. *American Revolution*, III, 83.
[3] Shelburne to Chatham, 13th March 1767. Chatham Corr. III, 232.
[4] Bradshaw to Grafton, 14th May 1767. Anson, p. 176.
[5] Grafton to Chatham, 13th March 1767, and Bristol to Chatham, 5th April 1767. Chatham Corr. III, 231 and 240.
[6] Fitzmaurice, II, 58.
[7] 'So consonant to the character of a man of business and so unlike the wanton sallies of the man of parts and pleasure.' Walpole. *George III*, III, 24.

He dealt at length and in generous mood with the disturbances in America. Parliament must not, and he hoped would not, regard all North America as equally culpable; some of the colonies had complied fully with all demands of both billeting and compensation, others had complied in part; only New York had 'treated the whole legislative power of this country obstinately, wickedly, and almost traitorously in an absolute denial of its authority'.[1] It was neither becoming nor wise for Parliament to engage in controversy with the colonies; nor was it prudent by punishing all to induce them to unite among themselves. It would be better to assert the sovereignty of Parliament by a single act, which, he advised, should be aimed at New York alone. As a punishment for disobeying Parliament, her Governor should be ordered to give no assent to any acts of her Assembly until she had submitted.[2] At the end of his speech he dealt shortly with his financial proposals. He repeated his opinion that Parliament had 'a power of taxation of every sort and in every case', internal as well as external; but added that taxation should be 'moderate and prudent'. He did not intend to propose any taxes as Chancellor of the Exchequer, but would as a private man mention 'for the future opinion of the House in a Committee of Ways and Means', some articles on which port duties might be imposed. The revenue to be expected might amount to between thirty and forty thousand pounds, and could, if thought right, be increased later. He ended by moving three resolutions, dealing solely with the punishment of New York. The debate revolved almost exclusively round these resolutions; the taxes were hardly mentioned. So the plan which was to have such startling results was, as Walpole said, 'too lightly adopted'.[3]

From Walpole's day to the present time men have wondered at the smallness of the prize for which Townshend gambled and lost the colonies. Yet perhaps they do him injustice. On that first fatal day in January he had been wayward and boastful; but thereafter he was caught up in the web of circumstance. Everything suggests that he moved forward with an uneasy mind, and it is quite certain that his figure of £40,000 was not the last word. He told Parliament that the tax could be increased. He did not tell

[1] West's *Paper*, 13th May 1767. Add. MSS. 32,981.
[2] Walpole. *George III*, III, 23.
[3] Walpole. *George III*, III 21.

Parliament that it could be abolished; but he reminded them very significantly that he himself 'had been for repealing the Stamp Act to prevent mischief'.[1] If his new taxes led to trouble, would he have been against repeal? The smallness of the prize suggests that he was as yet only flying a kite, and that what he would do in the future must depend on results. The pity is that he died (4th September), before he had heard them. He never had the chance to recover his step, and so bequeathed his folly to the time when Chatham should return.

[1] Walpole. *George III*, III, 23.

XVIII

CHATHAM RESIGNS

(i)

AS TOWNSHEND had lived too long, so he died too soon, for England's comfort. Whatever his faults, he had dominated the Cabinet and dazzled the House. His death left a gaping void, which North's promotion was inadequate to fill. Grafton, it is true, was at first content; the House was up; America's reaction to the new duties was as yet unknown; the Opposition was at loggerheads with itself; and he and his Ministers were happily engaged in schemes for the better government of Ireland and Canada. Yet there were troubles in the offing which grew steadily more threatening. The country was still suffering from the economic results of the war, aggravated by bad harvests and ice-bound winters. Prices were soaring, no one knew why; rations were short; the standard of living was falling; the poorer classes were becoming both ravenous and riotous. Circumstances seemed to demand a statesman of the calibre of Townshend rather than of Grafton, who was sufficiently uncertain of himself and the future to welcome an approach which the Bedfords made to him in December (1767). They were tired of the wilderness and he was weary of responsibility. With both sides willing, the resultant negotiations ran smoothly. Bedford found Grafton more accommodating, and Grafton was under the delusion that he was less so, than Chatham had been.[1] The upshot was that Bedford obtained posts in the Government for four instead of three adherents, and posts of far greater importance than Chatham had offered. Gower became Lord President instead of Master of the Horse, Weymouth Secretary of State instead of Postmaster, and Rigby Vice-Treasurer of Ireland instead of some minor appointment. To these there was added Sandwich in a secondary office. Except for Gower, the Bedfords were not a savoury crew, but they were older, more experienced, and far more forceful

[1] Anson, p. 173.

than Grafton. There could be little doubt that, unless Chatham returned at an early date, this new tail would soon wag the dog; and when it did, even the pale ghost of Chatham's Ministry would be at an end. The new Ministers began to entrench themselves at once. Indeed, before sealing the bargain they had assumed without contradiction that Chatham was dead to politics, and that his friend Camden was now devoted to Grafton 'without any reserve of fidelity to his former master'.[1] By way of reducing Chatham's influence still further they demanded that Shelburne should be shorn of half his powers, surrendering the colonial business to a new third secretary of state. Their triumph was obvious when Grafton, bowing to their wishes and making what excuse he could to Shelburne, handed American affairs over to Hillsborough, from whom Chatham had deliberately taken them not eighteen months before. The King was reluctant to accept the Bedfords especially in such force; he observed, as Grafton records, 'a shyness towards our new allies' and cautioned Grafton against yielding too easily to their advice.[2] But Grafton was as urgent for his new allies as he had once been for Townshend; and he was equally unfortunate in his choice, for Sandwich had scarcely taken office when his one-time boon companion whom he had so shamelessly hit below the belt, the almost forgotten Wilkes, returned to England for a second and more tempestuous round.

(ii)

When first he had fled to France, Wilkes had hoped to negotiate a compromise and so be able to return, but after his expulsion from the House (20th January 1764), after his conviction for republishing No. 45 and the *Essay on Woman* (21st February 1764), and particularly after his outlawry (1st November 1764)—all in his absence—he gave up hope. 'I think myself', he wrote, 'an exile for life, with no foolish hopes, not even on the restoration of Mr. Pitt and the Whigs'.[3] He was perhaps the less perturbed because he imagined that what remained of his fortune would enable him to live comfortably on the Continent; but the mismanagement of his agent, who went bankrupt, and his own expensive pleasures

---

[1] Lyttelton to Temple, 1st January 1768. *Grenville Papers*, IV, 249.
[2] Anson, p. 183.
[3] Wilkes to Cotes, 17th February 1764. Add. MSS. 32,868.

soon reduced him to something like penury. Straitened circumstances made him keep a watchful eye on the English political
scene, and his hopes rose on Grenville's fall. So did his prospects,
for Rockingham, under the impression that he was a deserving
case, made him an allowance out of his own and his colleagues'
pockets and hinted vaguely at the possibility of a pardon. Wilkes
was sufficiently encouraged to pay a flying, but infructuous, visit
to England in May (1766) in order to sound Rockingham. He
made another, equally unsuccessful, in the following October to
see Grafton, who fobbed him off with a suggestion that he should
approach Chatham—a suggestion that Wilkes took very much
amiss. This last failure to soften the heart of authority roused him
to a pitch of wrath which expressed itself, first, in his well-known
philippic against Chatham, entitled *A letter to the Duke of Grafton*,
and then in a determination to owe his salvation to no Minister,
but to work it out for himself. He made up his mind to stand for
Parliament at the General Election which was due to be held in
March 1768. When the time came, he returned to England, and
with characteristic effrontery stood for the City of London.
Failing there, he promptly offered himself to the County of
Middlesex, for which he was elected on the 29th March, amid
scenes of uproarious jubilation. Indeed, the ferment was so
exuberant that it embarrassed Wilkes himself, and since it continued on and off for years, it demands some explanation.

Riots were common throughout the eighteenth century, particularly during the second half. Some of them were due to the prejudices and curious waywardness of crowds, but in general there
were two main causes—politics and economics. In Wilkes's case the
two were fortuitously interwoven. The burst of enthusiasm which
carried him into Parliament was a revival of the popularity he
had won in 1763 by opposing Bute, that bugbear of the people.
It was purely political. But there were other currents as well. His
reappearance coincided with a time of great economic stress,
when the effects of that change in the life of the country, known
as the Industrial Revolution, were beginning to make themselves
felt. Their first impact was especially severe on the poorer members
of society. In the rural areas, the system of enclosures adopted
by the great landowners, though good for agriculture, was
driving out the small-holders and depopulating the countryside.
The process 'lay at the root of all the evils of the period—the high

s

cost of necessaries, the demoralisation of the lower classes and
the aggravation of poverty'.[1] The same results were observable
in the towns, but from different causes. There had been an amazing
outburst of inventiveness which in a few years had substituted
machinery and the factory system for the old methods of manufacture by piecework at home. The workers, believing that machinery would deprive them of their livelihood and regarding factories
as little better than prisons, were distracted by fears and given
to bursts of destructive violence. They had no trade unions to
voice their grievances, which were many and real, and no method
for securing decent conditions or adequate wages. Their only
resource was petitions, which were sometimes presented in an
orderly fashion, but too often were accompanied by rioting. At
the time of Wilkes's return there were a number of such riots.
Though they had nothing to do with the election, some of them
became entangled with the political crowds and no one was much
disposed to differentiate between the various tumults. Nor were
the Government altogether wrong in placing both to Wilkes's
account; for there was a definite link. Pitt's popularity had to a
large extent sprung out of a belief that he was the people's champion; he did not belong to the class of great landowners intent on
enclosing the commons; nor was he imbued with that ruthless
love of money which seemed to be the hall-mark of manufacturers.
It was to him that the people looked for the cure of their ills, and
it was his apparent desertion to the enemy which caused the out-
cry of rage and despair when he took his peerage. But Chatham's
loss was Wilkes's gain. Wilkes stepped into the vacancy left by
Chatham, and the people, mourning their lost leader, gave him a
double share of loyalty.

The fact that he had been elected as the people's new champion
did not endear him to the Ministers, who were at their wits' end
to know how to deal with him. There were two possible courses;
they could ignore him or they could crush him. Chatham had
suggested the former course when Wilkes had visited England
two years earlier,[2] and Walpole now thought it would be the
wisest, as Wilkes could do no harm in the House and would
'sink to contempt'.[3] But the King, smouldering at the recollection
of past insults, insisted on stern measures: 'I think it highly

---

[1] Mantoux, p. 180.   [2] Anson, p. 193.
[3] Walpole to Mann, 31st March 1768.

proper to apprize you', he wrote to North, 'that the expulsion of
Mr. Wilkes appears to be very essential and must be effected'.[1] It
was a view which had little appeal for Grafton, who had counten-
anced Wilkes, albeit timidly, in 1763, and since then, as a member
of the Rockingham Ministry, had no doubt contributed towards
his allowance.[2] But it was entirely to the taste of the Bedfords,
who, in the person of Sandwich, owed him the lasting grudge
that comes from a knowledge of injury done. It was no less to the
taste of Mansfield who hoped by Wilkes's downfall to revenge
himself on Camden. The Bedfords and Mansfield were too strong;
they overbore Grafton, silenced Camden and brushed Shelburne
aside. But even when the Cabinet had agreed to crush Wilkes,
they found the task exceptionally involved. There were legal
problems which might be manipulated but could not be burked,
and Mansfield and the Government plunged from one dilemma
to another. Nothing could be done in the Courts so long as Wilkes
remained an outlaw, but the reversal of the outlawry would revive
Wilkes's claims for damages against Ministers as well as the
Government's actions against him, and it was by no means clear
what the upshot would be. It took the Government the remainder
of the year to straighten out the tangle. There was much chicanery,
besides several ugly incidents, involving loss of life, and the
resultant trials were occasions of embarrassing popular excitement. Eventually, however, Wilkes's outlawry was declared
invalid, he was sentenced to two years' imprisonment and heavy
fines for his past sins, and on the 3rd February 1769, was expelled
from the House. But if the Bedfords and the King rejoiced,
imagining that Wilkes was now finished, the people became the
more determined. Wilkes was re-elected, not once nor twice, but
three times—in February, March and April. On the first two
occasions the House contented itself with expelling him again,
but in April they went farther and, asserting that he was incapable
of sitting, they declared his unsuccessful opponent, Colonel Luttrell, the duly elected member. No doubt they did not fully
appreciate what they were doing; they were angry and annoyed
and anxious to put an end to what seemed to them an intolerable
position. But, in fact, they had thrown down a challenge which

[1] George III to North, 25th April 1768. Mumby. p. 231.
[2] Cf. 'I don't think that the Duke of Grafton will be forward to come to a final
resolution upon Wilkes's affairs'. Newcastle to Rockingham, 13th April 1768.
Add. MSS. 32,989.

could not be ignored without leaving the whole Constitution in jeopardy. In effect they were claiming the power to nominate the members of their own House, and so to by-pass the electorate. One may suppose that in practice no harm would have followed; but the people were more perceptive of the danger than the Commons, and they reacted to Luttrell's election in much the same way as the colonists reacted to Rockingham's Declaratory Act. They were full of vague alarms, and their apprehension created a strained and threatening atmosphere throughout the country.

(iii)

Wilkes was not the only disturbing element, nor the only victim of government harshness. The Bedfords had their eye on Shelburne; they wanted to get rid of him, as the one true exponent of Chatham's views still left in the Cabinet. If he were ousted, they had no doubt of being able to control the others; Grafton being lazy and Camden weak, they would have matters all their own way. But Shelburne hung on, with a tenacity which had something of the heroic in it. He was young; he was unpopular; he was disregarded; but he knew that he alone was following the path which Chatham had marked out. The Cabinet had long since thrown his policies overboard, and if Shelburne went, there would be no one left to bear witness to the faith, and Chatham, when he returned, would find all in confusion. Shelburne therefore stuck to his post doggedly, doing his best by executive action to forward the policies which Chatham had approved. But by now he was too dejected to attend Cabinet meetings, which was perhaps an error in tactics. He kept himself aloof and was looked at askance by his colleagues,[1] who pressed the King to get rid of him, alleging that he was continually thwarting their measures.[2] From their own point of view they were right, and the fact lent force to their argument. But they had no need to push hard, for the King was anxious to be convinced. His preliminary shyness of the Bedfords had worn off; he had become reconciled to them,

---

[1] Cf. 'The Bedfords declare everywhere that they have the whole in their hands. They abuse the Duke of Grafton and continue to persecute Shelburne'. Hamilton to Calcraft, 20th July 1768. Chatham Corr. III, 333 (*n*).

[2] 'That has induced most of the members of my administration separately to mention to me the impossibility of his longer continuing in office'. George III to Grafton, 5th October 1768. Fortescue, II, 49.

and had found, to his delight, that on all the great questions of the day, their views coincided with his own. It was a relief to his immature brain to be freed from the effort of following the far-sighted ideas of 'that great man'[1] Chatham, and to turn instead to the one absorbing consideration which made all decisions easy —the requirements of his own honour. Obviously his honour demanded the coercion of the colonies, the destruction of Wilkes and the appeasement of France—all points in which the Bedfords concurred.

It is indeed curious how completely Shelburne was at variance with his colleagues, and still more curious how uniformly disastrous his supercession proved to be. So long as he had been in charge of American affairs and following Chatham's plan, the ferment provoked by Grenville's taxes and Rockingham's Declaratory Act had been steadily abating. On the two sources of friction—the billeting of soldiers and the imposition of stamp duties—Chatham had decreed that while the general attitude should be lenient and the idea of taxation dropped, resistance to the Mutiny Act must be met with firmness. Shelburne followed this course precisely. In accordance with Parliament's decision New York was punished for refusing billets by the suspension of her legislative powers, but Shelburne seized on the first sign of repentance as an excuse to remove this disability.[2] His handling of the matter was eminently successful; the disturbances were dying down, and might well have vanished altogether, if Townshend's duties had not fanned the flames of resistance anew. The colonists argued that Townshend, by wresting to his own purpose the accepted distinction between internal and external taxation, had found a way—apparently legal—of taxing them to any extent he pleased, and had made sure of payment by holding over their heads this new threat to deprive the Assemblies of their powers.[3] The vice in which he held them was intolerable and must be broken. By the time that their reaction was known, Shelburne had gone; but there is no doubt that he would have dealt with this new situation much more sympathetically and with much better results than his successor, Hillsborough. Chatham's policy, so far as Shelburne was allowed to carry it out, had proved itself

---

[1] George III to Grafton, 5th October 1768. Fortescue, II, 49.
[2] Shelburne to Sir H. More, 18th July 1767. Fitzmaurice, II, 61.
[3] Miller, p. 183.

to be˜ right. Chatham, in short, had once more been saving the Empire as surely as Grenville, Townshend and the Bedfords were losing it.

As with America, so with Europe. Shelburne was imbued with Chatham's distrust of France and Spain and kept a watchful eye on them. Both were pursuing aggressive policies, neither was carrying out the terms of the Treaty of Paris, nor were they willing to settle outstanding differences. They preferred, it seemed, to have a *casus belli* up their sleeves. Indeed, Choiseul was openly preparing for a war of revenge and had settled the approximate date: 'Nous aurons', he wrote, 'certainement en 1770 la plus belle armée, une marine respectable, et d'argent en caisse. Les ministres du roi travaillent avec le plus grand zèle et la meillure intelligence à ces trois objets'.[1] Spain was equally intractable; she failed to pay the Manila ransom, and made trouble in the Falklands. It was with a clear perception of the inherent dangers that Chatham had set on foot his abortive negotiations for a northern alliance, and he had bequeathed to Shelburne the task of securing a just settlement of outstanding claims. Shelburne maintained so firm an attitude that France and Spain, though yielding nothing, felt obliged to remain quiescent. But the whole atmosphere changed with the arrival of the Bedfords. Choiseul soon became aware of Shelburne's diminishing credit. It was obvious to him that Chatham's policy was likely to be reversed, and that henceforth the Government would elect for peace with France and Spain and coercion in the colonies. He was certain that the colonies would resist and believed that while they were making trouble for England, France could recover her influence in the Gulf of Mexico and absorb much of the American trade.

There were further possibilities. It occurred to Choiseul that while England was otherwise engaged, France might safely snap up Corsica and so strengthen her position in the Mediterranean. Shelburne, alive to his intentions, protested that what Choiseul was doing was a violation of the Treaty of Aix and as such could not be tolerated. His firmness had a sobering effect, but was soon discounted by the patent reluctance of the Bedfords to support him and still more by the indiscretion of Mansfield, who, in Paris of all places, declared openly that 'the English Ministry were too weak, and the nation too wise to support them in entering on a

[1] Choiseul to Merci, 22nd December 1766. Fitzmaurice, II, 4.

war for the sake of Corsica'.[1] Shelburne was pushed aside, and Grafton, taking the responsibility upon himself, made a feeble gesture which had no effect whatever. France acquired Corsica and England suffered a rebuff which was wholly unnecessary, as her navy was still paramount and could easily have protected the island. 'British policy', said Burke, not unjustly, 'is brought into derision'.[2]

By September (1768) the King had persuaded himself that Shelburne's cup of iniquity was full and that he must go. He so informed both Camden and Grafton. They were not altogether surprised but were none the less uneasy. Shelburne had been Chatham's own choice, and though they 'entirely despaired' of ever seeing Chatham back again in the saddle, they felt some hesitation at so blatantly overriding his wishes. Camden, with the faint-heartedness which was becoming habitual, told the King that he agreed with him as a private man, but in his public capacity 'thought it best for himself to take a neuter part'.[3] To Grafton he was more revealing but no more decisive; 'I understand', he wrote, 'your Grace's plan is fixt; and I saw plainly, the last time I was in town, that Lord Shelburne's removal was determined. What can I say to it, my dear Lord? It is unlucky. The Administration, since Lord Chatham's illness, is almost entirely altered, without being changed. . . . Lord Chatham is at Hayes, brooding over his own suspicions and discontents. His return to business almost desperate; inaccessible to everybody, but under a persuasion (as I have some reason to conjecture) that he is given up and abandoned. This measure, for aught I know, may fix his opinion, and bring him to a resolution of resigning. If that should happen, I should be under the greatest difficulty'.[4] Camden clearly had little in mind beyond the effect which Shelburne's removal might have upon himself. Of the rights and wrongs of the case, of the benefit or disservice to the country, he seems to have been oblivious. Perhaps the King was justified in remarking that his letter did not 'convey the idea of his being a great statesman'.[5]

Grafton was as weak-kneed as Camden. He too feared Chatham's possible reaction; he too thought for a moment of resigning.

[1] Anson, p. 204.　　[2] *Present Discontents*. Burke's Works II, 41.
[3] George III to Grafton, 15th September 1768. Fortescue, II, 42.
[4] Camden to Grafton, 29th September 1768. Anson, p. 214.
[5] George III to Grafton, 5th October 1768. Fortescue, II, 49.

But, like Camden, he was concerned mainly with himself and his own convenience. He offered no real objection to the dismissal of Shelburne and even allowed the King to send him down to Hayes in order to break the news to Chatham. The King sketched out the whole plan of action. As Chatham was invisible, Grafton would of course approach him through Hester. She must be instructed to remind Chatham of his promise 'to defend whatever steps you [Grafton] might find necessary to take during his confinement'; she must also recall Grafton's previous hint that Shelburne might have to be removed, if he did not mend his ways, and then explain that as he had not mended his ways, his dismissal could no longer be delayed. Finally, Hester must pass on, as a message from the King himself, that the King 'cannot see any reason to fear Lord Chatham will act improperly'.[1]

Grafton did as he was told. He saw Hester, who carried off a difficult conversation with admirable tact, but was at the disadvantage of having to deal with a man whose mind was already made up. She wanted to avoid giving her own opinions and to impress upon him Chatham's views, of which she was well aware. But it was precisely her opinions which he had come to gather; he was not interested in Chatham's views; all he wanted to know was what prospect there was of Chatham's return, and whether he was likely to resign if Shelburne were dismissed. On the question of resignation, Hester was rightly cautious: 'my Lord's health', she said, 'is very bad', and left it at that. When pressed on the question of his return, she was forced to admit that there was 'but small prospect of his ever being able to enter much again into business'. With that admission, she had in fact, though she did not realise it, sealed Shelburne's fate. If Chatham was unlikely to return, Grafton had made up his mind to fall in with the King's wishes. Only if Chatham's return were imminent, or if his resignation were certain would he contemplate a different course. But this Hester could not be expected to know, nor that the remainder of the conversation, though from her point of view the most important part, was so much waste of time. There was no need, she said, to worry Chatham, in order to discover his views on Shelburne. She had already mentioned the report of his intended removal, and Chatham's comment had been clear and unmistakable. He had declared that it was 'quite contrary to the King's

[1] George III to Grafton, 5th October 1768. Fortescue, II, 49.

service', and would 'never have his consent nor concurrence'. Nor
was he any better reconciled to the proposal of which he had heard
for dismissing Amherst from his position as Governor of Virginia.
Either event would be 'most unhappy and very unfortunate'.[1]

Grafton's report to the King was a striking, though perhaps
unconscious, example of *suppressio veri*. He had left Hester, he
said, after a very long conversation, without knowing any better
than before how Chatham would react to Shelburne's dismissal.
Chatham's very emphatic protest, as recorded by Hester, he
watered down to a bald remark that 'he [Chatham] saw that his
Majesty's affairs would be most truly prejudiced by the loss of the
Earl of Shelburne's abilities', and left the King to infer that
Hester had acquiesced in his retort that when Chatham knew the
facts better, he would judge differently.[2] In the King's opinion
the way was now paved for what he called 'the greatest strengthening of Administration', and he told Grafton, that 'on Wednesday (12th October 1768) we will fix on the most eligible means
of putting it into execution'.[3]

But on the Wednesday a snag suddenly appeared in the shape of
a letter from Chatham, asking the King's permission to resign, and
adding that he could not 'enough lament the removal of Sir Jeffrey
Amherst and that of Lord Shelburne.'[4] It was a shock, but not
without its silver lining. As Grafton pointed out to the King,
Chatham had written under the impression that Shelburne had
already gone. Luckily that was not the fact, and the King would
appreciate, as vividly as Grafton himself, that there was all the
difference in the world between Chatham resigning on the dismissal of Shelburne and Shelburne's quitting on Chatham's resignation.[5] The King applauded Grafton's distinction—it was
'judicious'—and dubbed Chatham's letter 'improper'; but both
were sufficiently alive to the advantages of Chatham's name to do
their best to keep him. Both wrote imploring him to remain.
Their efforts had one comforting result. Chatham's reply pleaded
ill-health: 'all chance of recovery', he wrote, 'will be entirely
precluded by my continuing longer to hold the Privy Seal'.[6]

[1] Memo., 9th October 1768. Chatham Corr. III, 337 (*n*).
[2] Grafton to George III, 10th October 1768. Fortescue, II, 51.
[3] George III to Grafton, 10th October 1768. Fortescue, II, 52.
[4] Chatham to Grafton, 12th October 1768. Chatham Corr. III, 338.
[5] Grafton to George III, 13th October 1768. Fortescue, II, 58.
[6] Chatham to George III, 14th October 1767. Chatham Corr. III, 343.

The King was jubilant: he had brought off a coup. 'I think myself' he said, 'amply repaid the having wrote to him, as it [his reply] contains an open avowal that his illness is alone the cause of his retiring.'[1] The King, it seems, was easily repaid, and as skilful as Nelson in failing to observe what he had no mind to see. He accepted Chatham's resignation on the grounds of ill-health, and, a few days later, had the pleasure of accepting Shelburne's, on no stated ground whatever. Bristol became Privy Seal and Roch-ford succeeded Shelburne. With those appointments, the last trace of Chatham's influence had gone. One or two persons, it is true—Camden for instance, and Bristol and, strangely enough, Hillsborough—made half-hearted gestures of a willingness to resign, and were glad when Chatham did not encourage them. Meanwhile the Bedfords rejoiced; their road was now clear, and they had not, as yet, any inkling that its end was ruin.

(iv)

The King had been wrong in fearing Chatham's resignation. Mansfield, with characteristic spite, tried to make out that it was 'meant to be so timed as to do mischief at home and abroad',[2] but if so, it was a total failure. As Walpole said, the sensation it caused was 'imperceptible almost'.[3] One might have thought that Shelburne's resignation carried more weight, for his example was followed promptly by Barré who with greater knowledge of Chatham had completely changed his previous opinion, and not long after by Dunning, the Solicitor General. Barré had been confessedly influenced by friendship alone, but Dunning had the further reason of a difference of opinion with North on the sub-ject of Wilkes. At the moment, Wilkes was a far more potent factor in politics than Chatham. His treatment by Government had provided all the excitement of the election. Indeed, months before his actual appearance in England, the pamphleteers had been busy canvassing the questions with which he was associated —general warrants and the seizure of papers—and urging electors to throw out any member whose attitude towards those matters was suspect.[4] His daring return to England, his unexpected election

---

1 George III to Grafton, 14th October 1768. Fortescue, II, 58.
2 Mansfield to Rockingham, 16th October 1768. Albemarle, II, 83.
3 Walpole. *George III*, III, 169.
4 See *The Contest, passim.*

for Middlesex and his subsequent misfortunes, added substance
to the battle of words, and when Parliament met (8th November)
he dominated the scene, for all that he was in prison. But the
dexterity with which he kept the ferment alive, by blackening the
characters of Barrington and Weymouth, or making fools of
Sandwich and March, or embroiling the Lords with the Commons,
was outclassed by the folly of Government in proclaiming Luttrell
elected. That was the last straw, and the popular fever became
universal. Indeed the times were ripe for some such upsurge in
the political world. Chatham with his genius and Wilkes with his
cleverness were both true children of their age. In their own
sphere they were manifestations of that new spirit that was
blowing through the whole country, demanding the suppression
of ancient evils, demanding redress for present ills, demanding
reform and enlightenment for the future, and showing itself in a
dazzling outburst of activity in art, literature, commerce and
invention. But this stirring of the spirit, if it was to find an outlet,
had inevitably to overthrow the inertia of convention and that
fear of novelty which is inherent in mankind. There was bound
to be a clash. 'This', said a Grub Street pamphleteer, 'is a time
when disquiet rages at home, dissatisfaction abroad, when distractions are in our councils, division amongst our nobles, and all
public business at a stand.'[1] In like manner Grafton at the other
end of the social scale, was lamenting that 'the internal state of
the country was really alarming'.[2] Everywhere public meetings
were being held at which petitions were passed calling for the
dissolution of Parliament. Hopes were stirring, passions rising
and expectancy was in the air. So matters stood in England when
the House was prorogued on the 9th May 1769.

Nor were matters more hopeful abroad. Walpole had told Mann
the previous December that 'the times wear a very tempestuous
aspect, and while there is a singular want both of abilities and
prudence, there is no want of mischievous intentions' and had
added with less than his usual perspicacity, 'luckily, America is
quiet; France poor, foiled and disgraced'.[3] Alas! for his foresight.
Corsica, after a desperate resistance, fell to the French the following May (1769). And in America the Townshend duties were
running their destined course. As yet the colonies had no strong

---

[1] *The Contest*, p. 7. [2] Anson, p. 229.
[3] To Mann, 20th December 1768.

wish to break away from the mother country. Restlessness there was and much anxiety, but the underlying desire was to reach a compromise between Parliament's claim of unlimited sovereignty and the extremists' ambition for complete independence. Chatham had suggested as a basis the distinction between external and internal taxation. It was one which, whether logical or not—and the historians declare it was not—had the supreme political merit of being pragmatically sound; the colonies were prepared to accept it. But Rockingham had cut the ground from under it by his Declaratory Act, and Townshend had made a mock of it openly. Between them they had put the loyalty of the colonies to an impossible test. Townshend's duties were received in stunned silence; they had smashed Chatham's compromise and thrown into high relief the implications of Rockingham's Declaratory Act. The colonies now found it to be 'a clear, concise and comprehensive definition and sentence of *slavery*'.[1] The stunned feeling was slow in passing, but it was succeeded by a resolution the more determined because the less vocal; the colonies would neither break the law, nor pay the taxes; they would boycott English goods, convinced that 'England had greater cause to fear the loss of their trade, than they the withholding of her protection'.[2]

Boston was the centre of disaffection; it was she who decided 'to set on foot manufactures and to cease importations'.[3] but she realised that her actions would be far more effective if she were supported by her sister colonies. The prospect of support was not good; the colonies had always squabbled among themselves, and the centrifugal tendencies were still strong. When New York had taken the lead in resisting the Mutiny Act, she had stood alone; and her sense of isolation had contributed largely to her surrender. Was there much more hope of concerted action now? Boston was doubtful; but ventured to circulate copies of a proposed petition to Parliament, and hint at the advantages of a united effort (11th February 1768). She was justified in both her fears and hopes. The idea of resistance was frightening, but it was recognised that there was a fundamental distinction between resisting the Mutiny Act and resisting Townshend's duties. Although, in their suspicious frame of mind, the colonists had argued that billeting was a form of taxation, they knew perfectly

---

[1] *Principles and Acts of the Revolution in America.* Quoted by Miller, p. 182.
[2] Bancroft, III, 162.   [3] *Ibid.*, 124.

well that it was different both in kind and degree. There was nothing unusual or despotic in the demand; it was limited in extent and varied from colony to colony. Moreover, most of the colonies had accepted the burden in whole or in part, and were not disposed to play on what must be considered a bad wicket. The Townshend duties were different; they were taxation open and unabashed; they were new, universal and in American eyes unlawful; worse still, they could be increased until they became unendurable. The resistance to them was something in which all the colonies could join. Yet mutual jealousies, innate conservatism, and perhaps loyalty to the mother country, acted as a brake; it was only with slow and hesitating steps that the other colonies gave their adherence. They were pushed on by Hillsborough's handling of the matter. He was determined to isolate Boston on the question of taxation, as New York had been isolated on the question of billeting, and crush her before she had time to do further harm. As soon, therefore, as he heard of the Boston circular, he issued a counterblast—crude, harsh and psychologically inept—ordering Boston to rescind her letter, and the other colonies to ignore it, on pain of having their Assemblies dissolved. Inevitably, the colonies fell into line behind Boston.

Boston thus fortified and deprived of the safety-valve of her Assembly, adopted a more truculent attitude towards her unpopular and cowardly Governor, and looked so threateningly on the newly-appointed Board of Customs, that the faint-hearted Commissioners retreated to the castle and clamoured for troops to protect them. Troops and ships were sent; but while the King, at the opening of Parliament (8th November 1768), spoke stoutly of defeating 'the mischievous designs of those turbulent and seditious persons, who, under false pretences, have but too successfully deluded numbers of my subjects in America',[1] the Ministers were clearly becoming nervous. Hillsborough went so far as to tell the American agents at what, today, would be called a press conference (6th December 1768) that the Cabinet had no fondness for the acts of which the colonists complained, and that he personally regarded Townshend's Budget as so anti-commercial that he wished it had never existed; the colonists, however, must understand that Parliament would never do away with the taxes

---

[1] 'This, of course, must be the language of the Speech'. Camden to Grafton, 4th October 1768. Anson, p. 216.

on the grounds of principle, but only of expediency; the form of complaint must therefore be changed.[1] The trouble, in short, however Hillsborough might seek to disguise it, lay in the *amour-propre* of King and Parliament and in the implications of Rockingham's Declaratory Act; it did not lie in Grenville's Stamp Act, which was now dead, nor in the Townshend duties, which could as easily be killed.

America loomed large at Cabinet meetings. Amongst other steps, it was decided that governors should be required to reside in America. Unfortunately this policy, wise in itself, involved the removal of Amherst from his sinecure post as Governor of Virginia, in favour of Bottetort, a semi-fraudulent and bankrupt peer of winning manners, who was only too anxious to leave the country. Chatham could not approve the dismissal of Amherst. It meant the disappearance from the public stage of another of his followers.

But more important than any appointments was the problem of the Townshend duties, which were bringing in no money and were fomenting rebellion. The Cabinet would have been glad to get rid of them. Most of the Ministers now agreed that it was 'inexpedient to tax the colonies',[2] but did not see how to draw back. The Bedfords and Grenville could not forget their belief in the justice of making the colonies 'contribute to the public burthens for their own defence';[3] and the Rockinghams were obsessed with the need to uphold the Declaratory Act which '*we* brought in to fix and ascertain the rights of this country over its colonies'.[4] Only Chatham's followers could vote for repeal with a clear conscience, and they were few and disregarded. Yet the problem had to be faced. The crucial discussion took place on the 1st May 1769, when, by five votes to four, it was decided to take off all the duties except that on tea. The reason for the exception was neither clear nor convincing. Taxes should be imposed to produce revenue, or to control trade; but no such reason was pretended here. The Cabinet Minute authorising Hillsborough to inform the colonies of their decision, contented itself with the broad, unnecessary and on the whole provocative statement that 'no measure should be taken which can any way derogate from the

[1] Bancroft, III, 263.
[2] Camden to Grafton, 4th October 1768. Anson, p. 216.
[3] Grenville to Pownall, 17th July 1768. *Grenville Papers*, IV, 318.
[4] Rockingham to Harrison, 2nd October 1768. Albemarle, II, 80.

legislative authority of Great Britain over the colonies', and went on to say that the Government did not think it 'expedient or for the interest of Great Britain or America to propose or consent to the laying any further taxes upon America for the purpose of raising a revenue', a remark which could have been applied with equal or greater truth to the tax on tea. The fact is that the exception was a sop to their *amour-propre*. In an effort to be 'kind and lenient' to the colonies, the opponents of the tax persuaded the Cabinet to soften the first draft of the minute, but Hillsborough, probably through sheer lack of perception, lost the whole effect by using a paraphrase in his official despatch in which 'the parts of the minute which might be soothing to the colonies were wholly omitted'.[1] It was not the first time he had altered a draft approved by the Cabinet.[2] An unreliable and conceited man!

Grafton, many years later, declared that Hillsborough's despatch 'was calculated to do all mischief, when our real minute might have paved the way to some good'.[3] But he deceived himself. It was the retention of the tax, not the exact wording of the despatch which did the mischief and did it thoroughly. By the middle of 1769 there was as much ferment in America over tea as there was in England over Wilkes. Truly the state of the country, both within and without, was really alarming.

[1] Anson, p. 230.
[2] See George III to Hillsborough, 27th March 1768. Fortescue, II, 13.
[3] Anson, p. 283.

XIX

CHATHAM RETURNS

(i)

CHATHAM'S BREAKDOWN had not been a sudden affair. It was the culmination of months, if not years, of ill-health; and he was to need months, if not years, in which to recover. For some time after his first collapse he grew steadily worse, losing not only mental grip but physical strength, and becoming in every respect a mere shadow of himself. The lowest point seems to have been reached in the summer or autumn of 1767, about the time in fact, of Grafton's interview (31st May), and his own relinquishment of personal affairs (17th August). It was now that those in closest touch gave up writing to him direct and instead addressed their letters to Hester.[1] She exercised discretion freely in withholding messages, assuming, as she told Grafton, that she would be forgiven if she waited 'till some little degree of amendment in Lord Chatham's health may render it less anxious to communicate anything of business to him'.[2] Her authority was not questioned; nor did she, in her turn, question the authority of the doctors. The medical profession was in high repute in eighteenth century England, and had its own peculiar methods and pharmacopoeia. Chatham's cure, according to the doctors, was dependent on his ability to have a fit of gout, and until that happy time, they laid him 'under the prohibition of meddling with all business whatever'.[3] Hester with the utmost strength of her deep and abiding love, saw to it that the prohibition was obeyed.

Progress was painfully slow, but by the end of the year Chatham had apparently turned the corner. At all events Hester now felt able to pass on messages sometimes without delay, and not least a long letter from Shelburne on the proposal to remove

---

[1] Cf. Bristol to Hester, 30th July 1767, informing her of his resignation from the Lord Lieutenancy of Ireland. Chatham Corr. III, 27).
[2] Hester to Grafton, 31st July 1767. Anson, p. 155.
[3] Hester to Shelburne, October 1767. Chatham Corr. III, 288.

American affairs from his control. Chatham was still shrinking from responsibility, but was quite capable of grasping the salient facts, and told Shelburne that he could not possibly object to any arrangement which had Shelburne's 'cheerful acquiescence'.[1] The early months of next year (1768) showed a further marked improvement. Lord Bottetort wanted Chatham, in his official capacity, to seal a charter to which objections had been lodged. Chatham refused to do so, until the objectors had been heard, and feeling himself unable to conduct the necessary enquiry, offered to resign. On being pressed, however, by the King, to remain, he agreed to the seal being put temporarily into commission so that others might hold the enquiry, and he discussed the procedure at length with Camden before handing over the seals in person.[2] As 1768 progressed, he was able to attend to an increasing number of small matters, in which, if no great thought was required, yet some degree of judgment was necessary. He also seems to have begun turning his mind once more to matters political, for in September Camden said he had reason to believe that he was brooding over his own suspicions and discontents, under a persuasion that he had been given up and abandoned.[3] Camden did not state his authority, but if his belief was founded on fact, it showed that Chatham was awakening from the lethargic insensibility in which Grafton had found him. Certainly he had grounds for discontent; his policies had been jettisoned, his advice ignored and his friends disgraced. When, therefore, in October, Amherst and Shelburne were dismissed, he could come to no other conclusion than that he would gain nothing by continuing to hold office. Even if his health were restored, he would find himself a mere cipher in an alien Ministry which apparently had the King's confidence and had entrenched itself in policies entirely repugnant to him. He would have to start afresh, and perhaps it would be better to start as a free man rather than as a member of a jangling Ministry divided against itself. The indifference of his erstwhile followers must have confirmed him in his views, for there was a touch of something like contempt in the letters which he wrote acknowledging their excuses for remaining in office. Yet, looking back on the course of history, it is

[1] Hester to Shelburne, December 1767. Chatham Corr. III, 299.
[2] See Camden to Chatham, 18th February and 20th March 1768. Chatham Corr. III, 320 and 323.
[3] Camden to Grafton, 29th September 1768. Anson, p. 214.

T

but too possible to regret his resignation. Had he held on for a few months, he would have returned to active life as a Minister, and as such would have been able to press his views on the King, who might have found it more difficult to dismiss him than to ignore him. The dice in short would have been loaded slightly in his favour instead of heavily against him.

Hester hoped that freedom from office would benefit his health;[1] and no doubt the doctors looked for great things when he suffered a fit of gout in November.[2] Whether either was conducive to recovery is a matter of opinion, but certainly his improvement continued, possibly at a faster pace. Temple who visited Hayes about this time found him 'in bed, rather weak, though less so than he had often seen him with the gout, but his mind and apprehension perfectly clear'.[3] By the next January (1769), Chatham had resumed the management of his own affairs, and was happily arranging for the purchase of an estate adjoining his fields at Hayes.[4] By April he was taking a lively interest in Wilkes's reiterated elections.[5] That same month Chatham 'ventured, for the first time, to take the air in a carriage';[6] and by July he regarded himself as normal: 'I have recovered', he wrote, 'so much strength and general health in the course of the last month, as to be much the same I used to be for ten years past'.[7] He signalised his recovery by attending the King's levee, where George received him most graciously, asked him into the Closet, and expressed the regret he had felt when Chatham had resigned. But what the King said was less significant than what he failed to say; he did not invite Chatham to take office again.

(ii)

The King's backwardness was not unintentional. He might possibly, though not probably, have been more forthcoming, if Hester had not recently patched up Temple's quarrel with Chatham, thus ending a family feud which had always distressed her

---

[1] Hester to Ann Pitt, 24th October 1768. Chatham MSS. G.D. 8–10. Public Record Office.
[2] Hester to Grafton, 17th November 1768. Chatham MSS. G.D. 8–10.
[3] Grenville's Diary, 25th November 1768. *Grenville Papers*, IV, 404.
[4] Chatham to Jackson, 28th January 1769. Add. MSS. 9,344.
[5] Hester to Dingley, 2nd April 1769. Chatham MSS. G.D. 8–10 Public Record Office.
[6] Chatham to Granby, 27th April 1769. Chatham Corr. III, 355.
[7] Chatham to Temple, 7th July 1769. Grenville Corr. IV. 426.

but had not been unwelcome to the King. Chatham might now so easily demand a place for Temple, and Temple was not *persona grata*. Nor was that the only reason for backwardness, far from it. The King had been brought up to regard Chatham with loathing as the most dishonourable of men, and though he had damped down his antipathy when obliged to recall him to office, he had done so out of necessity, not from any change of heart. The old dislike was lurking close beneath the surface, and Chatham's behaviour in the Closet was calculated to bring it to the top. He did what had not been done for years; he laid down the law to the King and found fault with his policies. It did not so much matter that he disapproved of the arrangements made for India, speaking of the East India Company's Board as a set of dictators—the King himself disliked the 'nabobs'; but it was monstrous that he should belittle the Wilkes affair, declaring that if it had been brushed aside contemptuously from the first, none of the subsequent troubles would have happened.[1] Wilkes was an obsession with the King; Wilkes had called him a liar and slandered his mother; Wilkes had made fools of them all, and Wilkes was not to be forgiven. His expulsion from the House was, in the King's eyes, 'a measure whereon almost my Crown depends'.[2] How could Chatham talk of treating the matter with contempt!

The fact is that the King had a natural aversion to Chatham, and the personal feelings were not offset by any identity of aims. On almost every point the King's policy was the exact reverse of Chatham's. Though he had swallowed Chatham in order to get rid of Rockingham, there can be little doubt that differences of opinion would have come to light shortly, if Chatham's health had not broken down so soon. In strong contrast to this uneasy alliance, the King had found himself, from the moment of Chatham's collapse, in a position that was almost ideal; in the Closet he had to deal only with the lazy and weak Grafton who rarely attempted to argue; while in the outside world he had the protection of Chatham's name.[3] What more could he want? There had been a moment of alarm when the Bedfords had been introduced, but it had vanished when he found that their views coincided with his inmost wishes. On all the main questions of the day

[1] Anson, p. 237
[2] George III to Hertford, 27th January 1769. Fortescue, II, 75.
[3] Cf. 'Your name has been sufficient to enable my administration to proceed.' George III to Chatham, 23rd January 1768. Fortescue, II, 7.

they were ready to abandon Chatham and support the King; they believed in coercing the colonies, in persecuting Wilkes, in appeasing France. Perhaps from the country's point of view their most unhappy step had been to slight Frederick. He had rebuffed Chatham in 1766, but was now having second thoughts. There was trouble in Poland, where France and Russia were supporting rival factions. Choiseul, to further his own ends, had persuaded Turkey to declare war on Russia, and Frederick, alarmed at this new turn, had suggested that England and Prussia should jointly offer to mediate. One can imagine how eagerly Chatham would have jumped at the chance; but he was still *hors de combat*, which enabled the King to put another spoke in his policy and isolate England still further, by a curt refusal.[1] Frederick retired again to his half contemptuous, half puzzled watch on English politics, and the hope of Chatham's northern alliance was irretrievably gone.

When Chatham reappeared, Frederick had withdrawn; France had acquired Corsica; Wilkes was in prison; the Colonies seemed to be quiet; and the world of fashion had put politics aside to revel in the latest nine-days' wonder—the bigamous marriage of Elizabeth Chudleigh to the Duke of Kingston.[2] Only the tiresome petitions from the country demanding a new parliament ruffled the calm. There seemed to be no need for Chatham. As the King remarked, he was 'a charlatan, who in difficult times affected ill-health to render himself the more sought after'.[3] Now that easy times had returned, let him go.

(iii)

If the King was not anxious to recall Chatham, Chatham at his first appearing was not anxious to be recalled. Though he had recovered his health and had grown fat,[4] he was still haunted by the memory of his breakdown. Nor was he any longer spurred on by ambition, which had either died or been sated.[5] Yet, as he took stock, he could not fail to note that the world to which he had awakened was in a worse condition than the world he had left.

---

[1] Mitchell to Cathcart, 28th February 1769. Add. MSS. 6,810.
[2] Lady Temple to Temple, 21st March 1769. *Grenville Papers*, IV, 414.
[3] Durand to Choiseul, 1st February 1768—quoted Bancroft, III, 121.
[4] Walpole. *George III*, III, 248.
[5] Anson, p. 237.

Not one of the points, which had then seemed pressing, had been settled; and to them had been added the Wilkes-Luttrell affair which, from mishandling, had grown into a problem of high constitutional import. The country, too, was in a ferment, demanding redress of grievances by the novel method of a flood of petitions. Chatham would have been less than himself, if his blood had not been stirred. Though his age and infirmities might, as he told the Lords, have justified him in retiring, he soon began like an old war-horse, to champ at the bit: 'the alarming state of the nation', he declared, 'called upon him, forced him, to come forward once more, and to execute that duty which he owed to God, to his Sovereign, and to his country'.[1]

Being no longer a member of the Government, he could only execute that duty as a member of the Opposition. But where was the Opposition; and in what sort of fettle? It needed a large infusion of his own energy and strength if it was to do any good at all. Not that it should be difficult to stir it into life, for Chatham's appearance always lent vigour and urgency to the political world. Long before his return, the mere fact that Temple had visited Hayes gave rise to all manner of gossip; and what was simply a family reunion was supposed to presage the Government's fall. Since then Chatham had dined and wined with Temple and Grenville; the three were united again, and might form the basis of a new Opposition. Many people hoped they would. But they were units only, and Chatham needed battalions. Where was he to find them? Of his old Cabinet, Grafton was a renegade and Camden a very shaky reed; of his contemporaries Newcastle had recently died (17th November 1768), Holland had gone abroad for his health, and Mansfield was as much an enemy as ever. His obvious allies were the Rockinghams. They had been the backbone of his late Ministry until Rockingham had forced them to resign, and his only quarrel with them had been over the Declaratory Act. There seemed no point in reviving the memory of that dispute at a time when Chatham, as he said, was 'entirely ignorant of the present state' of America and for that reason unable and unwilling to discuss its problems.[2] The country was faced at the moment by a constitutional point of greater importance and more

[1] Speech, 9th January 1770.
[2] Speech, 9th January 1700.

immediate urgency, and as he and the Rockinghams were at one
on that point 'former little differences must be forgotten'.[1]

Chatham was in earnest: Parliament, he said, 'must, it shall be
dissolved'.[2] Many of the Rockinghams were also in earnest; but
not Rockingham himself, nor his principal adviser, Burke. They
were jealous of Chatham, the former of his capacity for leadership,
the latter of his oratory. Chatham had hardly left the palace after
seeing the King, before Burke was whispering in Rockingham's
ear that if Chatham was to be the architect of a new Ministry, 'the
building will not, I suspect, be executed in a very workmanlike
manner, and can hardly be such as your lordship will chose to
be lodged in', Chatham, he went on, unless he had been specially
summoned by the King, had gone simply 'to talk some significant, pompous, creeping, explanatory, ambiguous matter, in the
true Chathamic style'.[3] That was, no doubt, a tribute to Chatham's
oratory, for no one but a skilled orator could make his matter at
once pompous and creeping, or be explanatory and ambiguous at
the same time; but the remark conveys clearly enough Burke's
opinion of Chatham. It was not a high one. The two were poles
apart in character and method, though close enough in thought,
and if they had been less antagonistic might have done more good.

Both were anxious to serve their country and as the times
were alarming and action desirable, each made use of his own
particular talent. Burke sat down to write a political pamphlet,
his *Thoughts on the Cause of the Present Discontents*. In it he developed
his theory of the 'double cabinet', the one being the ostensible,
the other the real seat of government. It was apparently the habit,
if not the function, of the latter, to which Burke gave the anony-
mous title of 'the cabal', to traverse the former, while showering
rewards and honours on its own adherents. By following this
course, it had overthrown the balanced controls of the Constitution, thus giving rise to the 'present discontents'. The remedy,
according to Burke, lay in the determination of honest and resolute men 'never to accept administration unless this garrison of
king's men . . . be entirely broken and disbanded, and every work
they have thrown up be levelled with the ground'.[4] Burke did not
say who was to do this preliminary demolition, but he called the

[1] Portland to Rockingham, 3rd December 1769. Albemarle, II, 143.
[2] *Ibid.*
[3] Burke to Rockingham, 9th July 1769. Corr. I, 87.
[4] Burke, Works II, 77.

band of honest and resolute men a 'connexion', connexions being,
as he said, 'essentially necessary for the full performance of our
public duty, accidentally liable to degenerate into faction'.[1] The
reader was left to infer that Rockingham's faction was essentially
a connexion, and all other connexions accidentally factions. The
pamphlet was too far removed from fact to be good history, too
long to be good propaganda, and too negative to be good politics.
It had one further drawback; it appeared too late, being published
(23rd April 1770) a bare fortnight before Parliament rose. Whatever its merits, it was, as Walpole complained, 'at once too diffuse
and too refined; it tired the informed and was unintelligible to the
ignorant'.[2] But it was Burke's contribution to the problems of
the day, a contribution in which most of the Rockinghams had a
finger,[3] and beyond which they seemed unable to progress.

Chatham's contribution was different. He also wished to deal
with the present discontents, but in Parliament instead of in pamphlets, and by action rather than theory. Before the House met he
did his best to rally the Opposition, talking vigorously to Camden, trying hard to influence Granby,[4] and summoning his old
admirals, Saunders, Keppell and Brett to the fight.[5] More particularly he invited Rockingham to a personal interview in order
'to remove former misunderstandings and to cement a common
union between the friends of the public'.[6] But Rockingham sent a
frigid reply which was in effect a refusal. No meeting took place;
no plan was concerted.[7]

(iv)

Parliament met on the 9th January (1770). Chatham was in his
place and rose to speak immediately the Address had been moved.
He was fully aware that his task would be difficult, and that
part of that difficulty was of his own making. Had he been
still in the Commons, he would have known how best to approach

---

[1] Burke, Works II, 80.
[2] Walpole. *George III*, IV, 86.
[3] Cf. 'The pamphlet underwent the criticisms and scrutiny of the leaders of the
party before it went to press.' Albemarle, II, 144.
[4] Chatham to Calcraft, probably 5th November 1769. Add. MSS. 43,771.
[5] Hood to Chatham, 3rd December 1769.
[6] Walpole. *George III*, IV, 22.
[7] Chatham to Calcraft, 8th January 1770. Chatham Corr. III, 388.

his audience, but in the Lords he had to face an alien and pre-
dominantly hostile House. The last time he had appeared there, he
had been grossly insulted, and he was well aware that there was an
undercurrent of distaste and resentment, if not disdain. Worse still,
his belief that the Wilkes affair was at the root of the discontents
would be highly displeasing to the King, and also to all those who
looked to the Court for advancement, since the King, though
Chatham did not know it, had already issued what might be called a
three-line whip, expressing the hope that 'every man in my service'
would take an active part in the debate'.[1] Nor was Chatham's
remedy likely to appeal to the peers. In the old days he had often
lectured the Commons on their dignity and importance, encouraging them to throw off Newcastle's yoke and resist the encroachments of the Lords. They had responded, and their stature had
risen to new heights. Now Chatham would have to reverse that
process and invoke the Lords to withstand the Commons on behalf
of Wilkes—a man of no morals and less character, who had insulted
the King and made a mock of their Lordships, but who in his
unworthy self represented the outraged rights of the people.
Chatham could justify this reversal only by enlarging the argument, to include both Lords and Commons in the greater sphere
of the Law, where everyone, peers and commons and even Wilkes,
stood on the same footing. But to enter the realm of Law would
expose him to the attack of Mansfield, that master of legal subtlety.
To counter him he needed the support of Camden and he was by
no means sure how far he could rely on a man to whom the Court
had recently been extremely gracious in the hope of preventing
'the Great Seal appearing in opposition'.[2] Chatham was uneasily
aware that unless stiffened from without, Camden might easily
waver into 'exceptions' and bemuse both himself and his subject.[3]
Hence, for all his hopes that Camden was 'firm and in the rightest
resolutions',[4] he must have felt how solitary he was and how
difficult his position. Perhaps for that very reason his speech was
on a high plane. At the outset he stumbled and was hesitating,
but soon gathering confidence, he spoke with deep feeling and
the eloquence which such feeling engenders, urging the Lords
as 'the grand hereditary counsellors of the Crown', to tell the

---

[1] George III to North, 7th January 1770. Fortescue, II, 125.
[2] Anson, p. 245–6.
[3] Chatham to Temple, 8th November 1769. *Grenville Papers*, IV, 477.
[4] Chatham to Calcraft, 8th January 1770. Chatham Corr. III, 388.

King plainly that Wilkes's wrongs were the cause of the nation's 'notorious dissatisfaction', and to warn him that their intention was to enquire into the proceedings which had deprived Wilkes of his common right and the electors of Middlesex of their free choice of a representative. Mansfield, as Chatham had supposed, denounced the motion as an attack on the Commons; they alone were judges of their own rights and privileges, and if on any occasion their decisions were wrong, there was no redress. Such a theory was one which Chatham could never accept and he answered in a second speech of rising fervour. The Commons were certainly subject to law—the law enshrined in Magna Carta and the Bill of Rights which proclaimed freedom and denounced tyranny. He had never expected to hear a divine right, which had been exploded in the case of kings, 'attributed to any other branch of the legislature'. Such a doctrine was not only bad for Parliament; it was fatal for the people. It would restore to the Commons that usurped power which in Cromwell's time 'abolished the House of Lords and overturned the monarchy'; they would, though only one branch of the legislature, become all-powerful. He summed up this argument in a phrase which forestalled the famous saying of a future historian: 'unlimited power', he said, 'is apt to corrupt the minds of those who possess it; and this I know, my Lords, that where law ends, there tyranny begins'.[1]

His motion was lost, but the gage had been thrown down. He had shaken the Government to its foundations, and the Opposition to its senses. Camden rose, not to indulge in 'exceptions', but to admit his past weakness, confessing that he had hung his head in Council and disapproved by looks what he had feared to denounce in words; but now he would regard himself as a traitor and enemy to his country, if he paid any regard to the illegal and unconstitutional action of the Commons. In the Lower House there were similar scenes; Granby regretted the vote he had given for Wilkes's expulsion; Dunning supported the petitions demanding the dissolution of the House; and Savile declared that they were sitting illegally and had betrayed their trust.

Camden recognised that he would have to go, and his knowledge of the fact is the measure of his sincerity; for Camden was a poor man with a large family, and the loss of his salary as Chancellor would mean a sharp drop from affluence to comparative

[1] Speech, 9th January 1770.

poverty. No doubt that daunting prospect had tied his tongue in Council, and now to Chatham's regret[1] it decided him not to resign of his own accord, but to await dismissal. It was not long in coming. The King, implacable as ever, was for immediate execution; but Grafton with greater caution advised delay till arrangements had been made for a successor. His caution was to be more speedily and more tragically justified than he imagined. Charles Yorke was the chosen candidate—-Yorke who had so often and so persistently been the jest of whatever irony sits above the Courts and plays its tricks on aspiring lawyers. He was forty-seven now, and for forty-seven years he had been destined, first by his father and then by himself, to ascend the Woolsack. Now after so many false starts his time had come. But in what horrid guise! Between him and his ambition stood the loyalty which bound him to Rockingham, and no less the tacit disapproval of his profession which deplored the dismissal of a Chancellor for the mere giving of a legal opinion, even if it was distasteful to Government. Yorke havered; he would and he would not; but at last not altogether unwillingly he was bullied by the King into acceptance. He had fulfilled his ambition and three days later (20th January 1770), he had fulfilled his destiny; he was dead —by his own hand, it was generally supposed. But no one knew, and no one knows, the real facts. His family was decently reticent, and of the outside world some said he died of remorse at betraying his friends, while others declared that mental agitation and over-indulgence had burst a blood vessel. Explain it as they might, Yorke was dead. The Woolsack, empty again, had lost its savour, and the Great Seal was perforce put into commission. It was a shrewd blow at the Government, and was made no more endurable by the resignations of Granby, Dunning and James Grenville as well as three or four Court officials. All the world supposed that the Ministry was falling, and behind the scenes a distracted Grafton was making up his mind to retire.

Chatham did his best to speed the good work by urging any Minister he could influence to resign. He also induced Rockingham, willy-nilly, to enter into a close alliance which was proclaimed openly a few days later (22nd January), when Chatham supported a motion made by Rockingham for the Lords to consider the state of the nation—a critical motion of censure.

---

[1] See Chatham to Calcraft, 17th January 1770. Chatham Corr. III, 397.

Yet this first joint action made it plain, for all who had eyes to see, that there was a fundamental difference between the two which must ultimately drive them apart. It was not a question of policy, still less of theory, but of outlook, temperament and method. In his first moment of enthusiasm Chatham had called the Rockinghams 'spotless', but if they were so, it was only because they held aloof from the rough and tumble of life; they neither went down to the market place to chaffer nor soiled their hands with digging; they were negative, inert and static, they were tepid and finicky, while it was impossible for Chatham to be other than positive and dynamic. Rockingham was wet tinder to Chatham's fiery flint; sparks might be showered upon him but could never kindle a flame in the mute ineffectiveness of his soul.

Their speeches were typical. Rockingham took his stand on Burke's theories, affirming that the discontents at home and the troubles abroad were all due to an increase of the royal prerogative. He meandered over the whole field of recent legislation, doling out censure with a lavish hand, but resting on no particular point and passing over the Wilkes affair with a marked and uncandid restraint—it was a 'single breach'; to repair it was no doubt good but not sufficient in itself; we must look back to ultimate causes. At this pregnant point Rockingham did look back and saw—nothing. With nothing to offer he could only hope that the Lords might somehow discover for themselves 'how to establish a system of Government more wise, more permanent, better suited to the genius of the people and at least consistent with the spirit of the Constitution'—a hope highly correct and proper which Grafton could and did accept, but void of any suggestion on which the new system could be based.

Not so Chatham's speech. He indulged in no meandering but concentrated on three main points—Corsica, the army in Ireland, and the Wilkes affair—going in each case directly to the core, and offering advice which, being based on eternal truths, has a meaning for this generation no less than for his own. Corsica had fallen to the French and we had done nothing to save it. 'My Lords', said Chatham, giving voice to the proud tradition of all that is best in British history, 'I cannot agree that nothing less than an immediate attack upon the honour or interest of this nation can authorise us to interpose in defence of weaker states, and in stopping the enterprises of an ambitious neighbour. Whenever that narrow, selfish policy has prevailed in our councils, we have constantly experienced the fatal effects of it. By suffering our natural enemies to oppress the powers less able than we are to make a resistance, we have permitted them to increase their strength; we have lost the most favourable opportunities of opposing them with success; and found ourselves at last obliged to run every hazard, in making that cause our own, in which we were not wise enough to take part, while the expense and danger might have been supported by others. . . . I fear, my Lords, it is too much the temper of this country to be insensible to the approach of danger, until it comes with accumulated terror upon us'. Chatham was speaking of an aggression which gave the Corsican Bonaparte to France and in due course fastened the Napoleonic wars ineluctably on our shoulders. If his words had been written in letters of gold on the doors of the Cabinet and in the House of Commons, what sufferings later ages might have been spared!

The army in Ireland was a different story. While Chatham had been ill, the Government, rightly supposing that an enlarged Empire needed an enlarged military force, had decided to increase the army in Ireland from twelve to fifteen thousand men. But the Irish parliament had seen no reason why the cost of policing the Empire should fall on them alone, and in the bargaining which had followed, the Government had promised that they would always leave twelve thousand men in Ireland unless their hands were forced by invasion or rebellion. Chatham deplored this promise, and indeed it made nonsense of the augmentation. When he had been in control, the whole Irish army had been at his disposal to use as he thought best; in future only the extra three thousand men would be available for service overseas. 'The army', said Chatham, 'is the thunder of the Crown. The Ministry have tied up the hand which should direct the bolt'. He was expounding a basic truth of strategy, and particularly the strategy of an aggregate of nations. There must be a central authority to decide how and when the troops from every part can be used to the best advantage.

But the main point of his speech, to which he turned both first and last, was the violence done to the Constitution by Luttrell's adoption as member for Middlesex. Chatham did not look upon that as a 'single breach', but as an undermining of all the rights of all the electors. It was possible to believe, as Junius once said, that 'the majority of the House of Commons, when they passed this dangerous vote, neither understood the question, nor knew the consequence of what they were doing',[1] but the people at large understood and knew that a Constitution which had been ravaged once, might be ravaged again. They were in revolt and would not become tranquil until the violation had been effectually repaired. If it were not, 'may discord', said Chatham, 'prevail for ever', for 'when the liberty of the subject is invaded, and all redress denied him, resistance is justifiable'. Here was a threat to which the King reacted with misplaced spirit. He was no coward and he was very obstinate; the idea that he might be wrong never crossed his mind; instead, he metamorphosed Chatham back again from 'that great man' to 'the blackest of hearts'; and later added by way of good measure that he was 'a trumpet of sedition'. But whatever effect Chatham might have upon the King, he was not content merely to preach resistance; the Government must be offered a reasonable alternative and a way of escape; they must be shown not only the malady but the cure. What was the ultimate cause of all the discontents? It was not really an increase of the royal prerogative; it was not a lack of 'connexions', it was not even the presence of factions. Those troubles were symptoms, not causes. The true cause was the divorce between the people and their representatives, and that divorce could be traced ultimately to some form of corruption, whether it were the largesse of the Crown, or the influx of wealth from the Indies, or the purchase of votes by designing men. It was not so much the waste of public money which was to be deplored, as the pernicious purposes to which that money was applied: 'the corruption of the people is the great original cause of the discontents of the people themselves, of the enterprises of the Crown, and the notorious decay of the internal vigour of the Constitution'. The cure must be found in electoral reform, aimed at setting up a system which would do away with the possibility of corruption and at the same time create 'a permanent relation between the constituent and representative body of the people'. The necessary change must be made with caution. Others might think it wise to start by cutting away the boroughs, those 'rotten parts of the Constitution', but not so Chatham. Amputation was wholly negative, and if the knife went too deep might prove fatal. Perhaps it would be better to regard those boroughs, as he regarded his gout, as 'the natural infirmity of the

---

[1] Junius, I, 203.

Constitution', to be carried about with us and borne with patience. It would be better to concentrate on building up the sound parts, the counties and the great trading cities, which were too large to be debauched and had still preserved their independence. Their representation might be enlarged, and as a beginning Chatham suggested the addition of a third member for every county. But all these matters were for fuller consideration at the enquiry for which Rockingham's motion had called.[1] So Chatham introduced, for the first time, the great subject of reform. Walpole dubbed his advice 'wild and indigested'[2] which was perhaps a measure of its novelty and of the difficulties it was likely to encounter. Certainly, it was no more than a seed, but like the grain of mustard, it was destined to grow from that time to this and wax a great tree.

The Speech decided Grafton. He had long been restive, finding the Bedfords uneasy partners on whom he could place no reliance, and now he threw up the sponge. On the 22nd he told the King for the last time that he must resign. The King tried hard to dissuade him, but finding his efforts in vain, summoned North to the palace that same evening and offered him the post. North hesitated, and for five days Chatham's fate and England's destiny hung in the balance. 'You must easily see', wrote the King, 'that if you do not accept, I have no Peer at present in my service that I could consent to place in the Duke of Grafton's employment'.[3] The King—and it is to his credit—had gauged to a nicety the worth and morals of the Bedfords. But he had overlooked those Peers, and among them Chatham, who were not at present in his service, and because of that oversight it became ironically true that '*faute de mieux*' was the one and only expressed reason for the appointment of England's most disastrous Prime Minister. Grafton's resignation took effect on the 27th January, and North's promotion was announced three days later.

---

[1] Speech, 22nd January 1770.
[2] Walpole. *George III*, IV, 39.
[3] George III to North, 23rd January 1770. Fortescue, II, 126.

XX

THE INEFFECTIVE OPPOSITION

(i)

GRAFTON HAS come down to us in the acid etchings of Junius. We have all read, with the tingling pleasure which springs from unsurpassed invective, the story of Grafton's mistresses, his lack of propriety, his indolence, his inordinate love of Newmarket, his fumblings in the political world. Junius was unsparing: 'I do not', he wrote, 'give you to posterity as a pattern to imitate, but as an example to deter'.[1] Yet in spite of Junius, it is possible to forget the shortcomings in pity for a man who was essentially the plaything of fortune. Grafton took office against his will, in the reluctant belief that duty called him. Had Chatham, who was his sponsor, retained his health and been able to guide events, Grafton might have served his country in decent obscurity and with some degree of credit. But with Chatham's disappearance he found himself in a false position. The bow of Odysseus had been thrust, unsought, into his hands, and though he did his best to bend it, the strength was not there. Realising his weakness, he invited the Bedfords to come to his aid. They did come; but instead of helping, they came, like the crowd of hungry suitors, to ravage and destroy the Ministry and debauch Grafton himself. In the consciousness that he had meant well, he never recognised the completeness of his failure. Had he done so, he might have understood why Chatham, at his reappearance, looked coldly on him; but not recognising it, he felt chagrined and hurt.[2] The consequences were unfortunate. Not only did he cling to office for a further seven months, but when at last he did resign, he made no effort to pull down the Ministry with him or to join the Opposition. On the contrary, he made a point of supporting North and encouraging his friends to do the same, thus lending an element of stability to North's administration in its first uncertain days when it was most obnoxious to attack, and when Chatham was

[1] Junius, I, 161. [2] Anson, pp. 237–8.

opposing it with a vehemence unusual even for himself. Politically, it was not wise of Chatham to show his resentment so openly; but wrath at betrayal by those we have trusted is apt to warp judgment. Moreover Chatham was puzzled; Grafton's resignation seemed to him 'an incomprehensible mystery, on any other supposition than that of the Ministry breaking up; and even in that case, it is equally without a solution';[1] how much more so when in fact the Ministry did not break up and Grafton continued to give it his support. Chatham's surprise was not peculiar to himself.[2] But, surprised or not, his onslaught on the Government, for all its success in persuading individuals to resign, was unsuccessful in the one point that mattered. The King had determined to have no dealings with either Chatham or Rockingham. Both of them had demanded the dissolution of Parliament solely because it had obeyed the King's orders to make an end of Wilkes, and sooner than grant a dissolution on such grounds, the King declared he would have recourse to the sword.[3] By his own energy he kept Parliament going, and with obstinate courage cobbled up the vacancies. It was in this fashion and with this setback that Chatham began his second Seven Years' War—a war against the King and indeed the Whigs on behalf of democracy, on behalf of electoral reform and an end of corruption, on behalf of sweet reasonableness in the conduct of the Empire, and above all on behalf of liberty and justice for the individual. Chatham fought hard and was defeated. It was a tragedy—but a tragedy which had a happier ending after the curtain had fallen. Chatham did not live to see it, but he was in part revenged by posterity. Though the Empire was torn in half, the good work of reform which he had begun rose again from its ashes, revived and grew strong, and has flourished exceedingly ever since.

(ii)

Chatham's effort on the 22nd January, was followed, as so often, by a fit of the gout. It was a thousand pities, for the Lords had agreed to consider the state of the nation on the 24th. As Chatham was too ill to be present, the debate, at Rockingham's request, was deferred for a week, and as it happened that week

---

[1] Hester to Calcraft, 30th January 1770. Chatham Corr. III, 413.
[2] See Mitchell to Cathcart, 10th February 1770. Add. MSS. 6,810.
[3] Walpole. *George III*, IV, 41.

proved to be of decisive importance, for in the course of it Grafton resigned and North took office, so transferring the weight and authority of government from the Lords to the Commons. More than that, in the same week the Commons themselves considered the state of the nation (31st January), and upheld North by a majority of forty. The debate in the Lords two days later was thus bound to be something of an anti-climax. Much of the time was taken up in recrimination between individuals, still more in a concerted attack on Camden, but Chatham, though telling a twice-told tale, yet managed to raise the debate to a higher level. The basis of his argument was that the Commons had violated the English Constitution by invading the rights of election; 'the laws had been despised, trampled upon, and destroyed'. Their action could only be regarded as 'part of that unhappy system which had been formed in the present reign, with a view to new-model the Constitution as well as the Government'. Chatham was advancing steadily to a conviction that the King himself was at the bottom of all the discontents, by interfering too directly in the working of Parliament and by choosing his Ministers, not in accordance with the wishes of the people, but with a view to promoting his own policies and gratifying his personal resentments. But Chatham had not yet reached his final conclusion; he was still prepared to regard the Ministers as primarily responsible. 'Ministers,' he said, 'held a corrupt influence in Parliament'. And so he came to his moral: it was particularly necessary for the Lords 'to stand forward and oppose themselves, on the one hand, to the justly incensed, and perhaps speedy, intemperate rage of the people; and on the other, to the criminal and malignant conduct of his Majesty's Ministers: that they might prevent licentiousness on the one side, and depred-ation on the other'.[1] The debate continued till past midnight when Rockingham's motion was lost. But the end had not yet come. Marchmont, suddenly and without warning, but clearly in order to muzzle Chatham, moved 'that any resolution of this House, directly or indirectly impeaching a judgment of the House of Commons in a matter where their jurisdiction is competent, final and conclusive, would be a violation of the constitutional right of the Commons'. In itself the motion was unexceptionable, but in its particular context it simply begged the question. The grava-men of Chatham's indictment as he pointed out was that the

[1] Speech, 2nd February 1770.

Commons had passed judgment in a matter in which their jurisdiction was *not* competent, final and conclusive. That was the crucial point. He went further, arguing, from the particular to the general, that the Commons, by themselves and without the concurrence of the other two branches of the legislature, could never have a jurisdiction that was competent, final and conclusive, in any case where the liberties of the people were invaded or the determination of the Commons was itself unconstitutional. No one answered him, nor his complaint that the motion had been introduced without notice at the fag end of a long day. 'If', he said with that sudden eloquence which never failed him when he was moved, 'the Constitution must be wounded, let it not receive its mortal stab at this dark and midnight hour, when honest men are asleep in their beds, and when only felons and assassins are seeking for prey'.[1] But the Lords were not interested in eloquence; Chatham's plea was unheeded.

His failure did not damp his ardour or his determination. Victory had never come to him easily, and experience had made him believe that if the enemy was to be routed, the attack must be pressed without intermission by every means and from all sides; and so ten days later he moved a fresh motion—that the capacity of a person to be elected did not depend finally on a determination of the House of Commons. It met the usual fate, and his effort was followed by the usual fit of gout. Chatham's ill-health was a sore handicap in itself, but it was something more and something worse. It afforded the Rockinghams an excuse for weakening in their allegiance to a union which they had never sincerely embraced and which was becoming daily more distasteful to them. Burke had never forgiven Chatham for an early snub and Rockingham was still mutely outraged at the thought of playing second fiddle to anyone, even to the most famous statesman in Europe. The cloven hoof soon began to show itself. When Chatham had fallen ill in January, Rockingham had agreed to postpone his motion, ostensibly in compliance with Chatham's request, but, as he naïvely admitted, also and perhaps more, because he was indisposed himself and had not prepared his speech.[2] When next Chatham fell ill, Rockingham was not so

---

[1] Almon, II, 233.
[2] Rockingham to Hester, 24th January 1770, two letters. Chatham Corr. III, 401-410.

ready to put off a motion—for an increase in the strength of the Navy—which he and his followers had decided to spring on the Lords without notice. It was a matter in which Chatham was deeply interested, and on which he could speak with far greater authority than Lord Craven who was to move the motion, or the Rockinghams who were to support it. He asked that it should be deferred. Rockingham could not very well refuse for indeed there was no immediate urgency; but he agreed ungraciously and with sufficient signs of irritation to make Temple comment that 'our friends give themselves too many airs of taking the lead'.[1] From some points of view it might have been better if the debate had not been deferred, for Chatham's contribution though intensely interesting as a mirror of his thoughts, had little or nothing to do with the motion. In his speech he developed the theory of Bute's over-riding influence. That influence, he declared was still existing and throughout the reign had prevented the formation of any independent ministry. It was the cause of all the unhappiness, all the disturbances, of the nation; it had duped Chatham himself. When he had been recalled to office, he had found the King all that was amiable and condescending but he had soon found also that there was 'something behind the throne greater than the King himself'. That something had thwarted all his efforts and the result was only too obvious. Before he had fallen ill 'he had formed, with great pains, attention and deliberation, schemes highly interesting and of the utmost importance to this country; schemes which had been approved in Council, and to which the King himself had given his consent. But when he returned, he found his plans were all vanished into thin air'. Whether Chatham really believed that Bute was still exerting an influence or whether he was referring indirectly to the Princess Dowager, or George III, is matter for debate, but there can be no doubt that this speech marked a further stage in the development of his war against the King. As a by-product, it roused Grafton to fury. He looked upon it as an attack on himself and retorted that Chatham's words were 'only the effects of a distempered mind, brooding over its own discontent'—a thought, incidentally, which he had borrowed from Camden. Chatham replied with devastating truth that from the time of his illness, Grafton's conduct had shown 'a gradual

[1] Temple to Hester, 19th February 1770. *Chatham Papers*. Public Record Office.

deviation from everything that had been settled and solemnly agreed to by his Grace, both as to measures and men, till at last there were not left two planks together of the ship which had been originally launched'. As for his distempered mind, it had always been sufficiently vigorous to support his principles, from which he had never departed—an illuminating sidelight on the nature and extent of his illness.[1]

To find fresh points by which the interest in Parliament might be maintained was not easy, and was made no easier by the growing listlessness of the Rockinghams, not to mention North's mounting majorities in the Commons.[2] Yet Chatham strove by indirect as well as direct means. No debate which he attended was allowed to pass without some reference to the burning question of constitutional reforms, and at times a chance word led to an uproar, which at least served the purpose of publicity. A case in point was a debate on the Civil List (15th March 1770), in the course of which Chatham remarked that Camden had been dismissed 'for the vote he gave in favour of the right of election in the people'. It was true enough, but pandemonium followed; some Lords demanding that he should be sent to the Bar and others, egged on by Mansfield, moving that his words should be taken down. Several Ministers, no doubt with uneasy consciences, were anxious to smooth things over, but Chatham disconcerted them all by seconding the motion himself. 'My words,' he declared, 'remain unretracted, unexplained and re-affirmed. I desire to know whether I am condemned or acquitted'.[3] No direct answer was given, but a sullen, discontented and mainly perverse House resolved that nothing had appeared to them to justify Chatham's assertion. Having so resolved it made haste to shuffle the matter out of sight.

Meanwhile Chatham was busy mobilising other forces. It seemed to him that there was much virtue in petitions, and that one from the City of London would lend particular weight to the demand for a new Parliament. The City had the previous June, (1769), presented to the King an uncommonly forceful petition setting out the misdeeds of the Government and beseeching redress, but had received no answer. Since then Chatham's friend

---

[1] Speech, 2nd March 1770. Almon, II, 234.
[2] Cf. 'The seeing that the majority constantly increases gives me great pleasure'. George III to North, 28th February 1770. Fortescue, II, 132.
[3] Speech, 15th March 1770.

Beckford, had become Lord Mayor and Chatham now instigated him to renew the attack. Under his guidance the City presented (14th March), a formidable remonstrance in which they referred to their previous petition and told the King that 'their complaints remain unanswered; their injuries are confirmed; and the only judge removable at the pleasure of the Crown has been dismissed from his high office for defending, in Parliament, the Law and the Constitution'. They demanded, with something approaching threats, that the existing Parliament should be dissolved and the Ministers responsible for the ills removed for ever from the King's Councils.[1] Though the King brushed the remonstrance aside as 'disrespectful to me, injurious to my Parliament, and irreconcilable to the principles of the Constitution',[2] the Court party was undoubtedly shaken.[3] Nor could there be any doubt about the popular ferment, 'this foaming ebullition', 'this tempest of outrage' as Dr. Johnson called it.[4] 'Every blank wall at this end of the town', wrote Walpole, 'is scribbled with the words Impeach the King's Mother.'[5] Junius from his hidden lair, Wilkes newly released from prison (17th April), and the City of Westminster in a by-election all contributed fuel to the fire. Chatham himself carried on the work by introducing a Bill on the 1st May, to rescind the resolutions of the Commons on the Middlesex election. As the Bill required the assent of the Commons and King as well as the Lords, he could hardly have hoped that it would pass. He had of course designed it as propaganda, but he was much hampered by Rockingham who was lukewarm, and Richmond who thought it 'best to give over opposition for this year'.[6] Chatham modified the Bill to meet their wishes but at the same time expressed with some pungency a hope that 'the end of the hunting season' would ensure a full House when it came to be debated.[7] More interesting than the numbers attending or the inevitable defeat, was the opening which the Bill gave Chatham for a more direct attack on the King than he had yet made. 'I am afraid', he told the Lords, 'this measure has sprung too near the throne—I am sorry for it; but I hope his Majesty will soon open his eyes'.[8] Three days later (4th May), he edged still nearer the

[1] Addresses, etc., p. 17.   [2] *Ibid*, p. 19.
[3] See Calcraft to Chatham, 17th March 1770. Chatham Corr. III, 429.
[4] Johnson. *False Alarm*.   [5] To Mann, 15th March 1770.
[6] Richmond to Rockingham, 18th April 1770. Albemarle, II, 178.
[7] Chatham to Rockingham, 29th April 1770. Albemarle, II, 177.
[8] Almon, II, 261.

throne by a motion of censure on the answer which the King had
been advised to make to the City's remonstrance. The session was
now drawing to an end, and Chatham thought it highly expedient
before the House rose, to move directly for a dissolution of
Parliament as a proof of the Opposition's unalterable determination. But Rockingham's reluctance was growing; he objected
on the curiously unrealistic ground that 'it is neither for your
Lordship's honour nor for ours, to suffer ourselves to be sworn
every day to keep our word'.[1] Such an argument was a haughty
gesture rather than a fighting attitude, and did not appeal to
Chatham, who introduced his motion on the 14th May, and in the
course of his speech reiterated the need for electoral reform.[2] The
details of his speech are not known, as it was made in a House
from which the Government had excluded strangers—a tribute to
Chatham's persuasiveness as well as evidence of their own shut
minds. It should have encouraged the Opposition, but could not
stir up the apathetic and faint-hearted Whigs.

Parliament rose and Chatham retired first to Hayes and then
to Burton Pynsent. He had hoped much and he had been disappointed. Yet his efforts had not been entirely vain. Throughout
the session he had concentrated on the Middlesex election out of
conviction and also perhaps because it was the only issue on which
all elements of the Opposition were united. But he had a further
and a more compelling reason, based on the circumstances of the
times. Today no one doubts that his views were correct; the
Commons had no right to declare Wilkes ineligible or Luttrell
elected;[3] today anyone may argue at ease how far the Government's lawlessness would have had serious repercussions. But
conditions were different then; the rights were uncertain and the
dangers obvious. Chatham was entering into a contest with the
King for the possession of Parliament, a contest in which passions
had risen and were continuing to rise. When passions run high,
dangers look large and it is the part of a wise man to forestall
them. Chatham failed in his immediate object, but he helped to
keep the issue alive; and when passions had cooled the justice of
his views prevailed. In 1782 the Commons admitted their wrong-
doing, and vindicated Chatham as well as Wilkes by expunging

[1] Rockingham to Chatham, 11th May 1770. Chatham Corr. III, 455.
[2] See Rigby to Bedford, 14th May 1770. Bedford Corr. III, 412
[3] Taswell-Langmead, p. 580.

the obnoxious resolutions from their Journals. In addition to that particular struggle, Chatham had broadcast the seeds of reform. They were never to die, and in fact had already born minor fruit in the shape of Grenville's Act on contested elections—the first and a famous step in the reform of Parliament itself.[1] The real disappointment of the session was not Chatham's apparent failure, but the attitude of the Rockinghams. They had not been willing or forceful allies, and had made it clear that there was a wide gulf—was it psychological or temperamental? a matter of up-bringing or heredity?—between themselves and Chatham. They disliked petitions; they despised the City; they detested the least appearance of 'mob-rule'. Their assumption of superiority gave offence to Chatham's humbler followers; their lukewarmness roused suspicions in the City; and their negative gentility exasperated Chatham. He had kept himself well in hand, ignoring slights, compromising differences of opinion and offering patient encouragement.[2] But the return was small, and the future could not be regarded as hopeful.

(iii)

'Lord Chatham', said Walpole when the Session had ended, 'has met with nothing but miscarriages and derision. Disunion has appeared between all parts of the Opposition'.[3] Walpole was right, and there were two reasons—Rockingham's inertia and North's parliamentary skill. The Opposition could never surmount Rockingham's stubborn belief in his own divine rights, and as those rights produced nothing but touchiness, there was little hope of united or vigorous action. The lack of it made North's task the easier. For all his physical disabilities—his slobbery mouth, his starting eyes, his 'coarse figure and rude untempered style'[4]— North had in large measure the qualities required for a leader of the Commons. He was imperturbable, and naturally good-humoured, an excellent debater, a master of witty repartee, an indefatigable worker, and, what was perhaps more useful still, the possessor of a thick skin and an obstinate temper. Rebuffs and even defeats meant nothing to him. All he lacked was statesmanship which is a rare quality. To make up for its absence, he had

---

[1] Maitland, p. 370.
[2] Winstanley-Chatham and the Whig Opposition, p. 353.
[3] To Mann, 24th May 1770.   [4] Walpole. *George III*, I, 257.

the solid backing of the King and no rival in the House. Chatham
was safely in the Lords and Grenville, the only man in the Commons who could vie with him, was old and ill. North had nothing
to fear from the Opposition unless, in Walpole's words, 'experience teaches them to unite more heartily during the summer,
or the Court commits any extravagance, or Ireland or America
furnishes new troubles'.[1] The Opposition was to have the benefit
of all those aids, but could make nothing of them. On each
occasion fate intervened at the crucial moment.

Whilst Parliament was up, pressure on the Government could
be maintained only through petitions, which Chatham encouraged,
especially in the City and in Rockingham's county of Yorkshire.
But in June Beckford's death deprived the City of their strong
man and knowledgeable guide, and as a consequence their
councils were distracted by quarrels between the partisans of
Wilkes and Horne, and their petition marred by inexperience.
'*Fortiter in re* I recommend but less invective in words'[2] was
Chatham's comment on the first draft. The petition as finally
presented (21st November) was not without punch,[3] but the
City's influence had diminished and the King felt able to dismiss it
with a reply as brusque as it was short. The Yorkshire petition
was even more unfortunate; it never materialised, because on the
day appointed for its formal adoption Rockingham was in town
discussing an offer which the Government had made to him
through Mansfield. The offer came to nothing, not because of
Rockingham's loyalty to his own party, but because he found he
was not to be First Lord, and no other place was good enough.
But the abortive negotiation had successfully thwarted the Yorkshire petition.[4]

Mansfield, who had promoted the offer, no doubt had quite
other objects in view. In the first place during the summer he had
fallen foul of the populace in the matter of the rights of juries,
thus offering a ready target to the Opposition. In the second place
he was suffering from an uneasy conscience. Ever since Camden's
dismissal in January, the Great Seal had been held in commission,
and Mansfield had been drawing £5,000 a year as temporary
Speaker of the House of Lords. He had taken no steps to have

---

[1] To Mann, 24th May 1770.
[2] Chatham to Shelburne, 4th October 1770. Chatham Corr. III, 472.
[3] Addresses, etc., p. 23.   [4] Walpole. *George III*, IV, 117.

this interim arrangement ended; nor did he wish to take any. The fact was notorious; it gave rise to comment and was shortly to be underlined by Junius.[1] Mansfield always shrank from criticism, but here his timidity was at war with his avarice; he was loath to give up this handsome emolument. It would ease his fears on both these points to have Rockingham muzzled by being made a member of the Government.

Rockingham himself was innocent of any other guile than a groundless conceit, but his willingness to talk to Mansfield was symptomatic. He was tired of opposition; he was out of phase with Chatham; the split was coming. 'I was in town on Wednesday last,' wrote Chatham, 'saw Lord Rockingham, and learnt nothing more than what I knew before; namely that the Marquis is an honest and honourable man, but that "moderation, moderation" is the burden of the song among the body'.[2] As though to confirm Chatham's estimate, Burke was, at almost the same moment, writing 'all that wise men even aim at is to keep things from coming to the worst'.[3] Chatham could never have endured such a defeatist doctrine. 'For myself,' he wrote, 'I am resolved to be in earnest for the public, and shall be a *scarecrow of violence* to the gentle warblers of the grove, the moderate Whigs and temperate statesmen'.[4]

(iv)

It was abnormal for Chatham to be half-hearted; it was impossible for him to be faint-hearted, but, old and crippled as he was, it was a superhuman task to carry an Opposition, both half-hearted and faint-hearted, on his back. It was made no easier by the knowledge which he had imparted to the King when he had last entered the Closet[5] that he could no longer sustain the burden of office. His function now, like that of Moses, was to lead others to the promised land which he was not to enter himself. The 'moderation' of his colleagues wearied him, and by way of a tonic, he decided to throw off dull care and even the delights of home and pay a visit with his eldest son to Burton and the West. He was away for some five or six weeks, and during that time renewed

---

[1] *Letter to Lord Mansfield.* Junius, I, 315.
[2] Chatham to Calcraft, 28th July 1770. Chatham Corr. III, 469.
[3] Burke to Shackleton, 15th August 1770.
[4] To Calcraft, 28th July 1770.   [5] Anson, p. 237.

the correspondence with Hester which, for all its stilted language, so clearly irradiates their mutual love and confidence. There is a gay and almost playful strain running through his letters. Gone is the great Minister, gone the stately earl, gone, too, the over-powering dignity, the rolling periods, the flashing eye. In their place Hester found a 'facetious journalist' with a happy genius for recording wonderful occurrences and spinning strange yarns. His tales, so he was assured, sent the family in to breakfast in high glee. Hester, on her side, retailed in her more practical style those small events which give the flavour to life: 'we drive out in the little chaise and the two boys squire us . . . we saunter in the high fields . . . the oak is fallen, the scrubby elm is down and the lawn looks much better, as you knew before it would'.[1] Chatham revelled in these details of home, and tried, with awkward and unaccustomed gambols, to answer in kind, sending Hester a staccato catalogue of Burton's delights: 'Dairy enchanting, Pillar [erected by Chatham in memory of Sir William Pynsent] superb, Terrass ravishing, and Moretown, Wooly Park etc replete with rural delights . . . I had almost omitted the Portico, by day and night; such a silver mantle thrown last night over Troy Hill was never seen by youthful poet'.[2] The weather was hot and fine; there were crops to be carted; there were friends to be visited; and there was much spoiling of the young Pitt to be done. The days flowed tranquilly by and brought serenity on their wings. 'I am now at peace', Chatham wrote,[3] and one may hope that the words were true and that his fiery, storm-tossed soul had its moment of rest. But the culmination of his happiness went far deeper than golden days and pastoral pleasures, to find its perfect content in the hope, so frequently expressed, 'that we may go over the same scenes perhaps together next year'.[4]

(v)

Whilst Chatham was away, events were stirring in the great world, even as far away as the Falkland Islands. For a hundred and fifty years after their discovery the Falklands had lain unclaimed and disregarded, but in 1765, Egmont had established a small and

---

[1] Hester to Chatham, 31st July 1770. P.R.O., G.D. 8-9.
[2] Chatham to Hester, 6th August 1770. P.R.O.
[3] To Hester, 11th August 1770. P.R.O.
[4] To Hester, 15th August 1770. P.R.O.

struggling settlement on one of the western islands which Chatham, with an eye to its strategic possibilities, had reinforced the next year. In one of the eastern islands Spain had recently acquired a little harbour. These two settlements kept their distance until January 1770 when the Spaniards suddenly sailed into Port Egmont and ordered the English out. High words passed, and Captain Hunt, the English Governor, returning to England early in June, reported the probability of a clash. The Government paid no attention, assuming it to be a local squabble which would soon blow over. In August James Harris, a young and budding diplomat of four-and-twenty, who in the interval between two Ambassadors was in charge of our embassy at Madrid, reported that according to his information, Don Francisco Buccarelli, the Governor of Buenos Aires, had the previous May been fitting out an expedition in order to expel the English.[1] The Government even then did not take the news very seriously, though Weymouth instructed Harris to demand restitution. In spite of hopeful despatches from Harris, matters went from bad to worse, and when France was found to be implicated[2] war appeared to be inevitable. The alarm was general; the dockyards became busy; press-gangs were sent out. It was obvious that the matter would be raised in Parliament when it met on the thirteenth of November (1770).

War is always a testing time for the Opposition which must somehow temper its policies with patriotism. Its actions are often enlightening. They were so here. The Opposition was not a united body; it was composed of four loosely connected groups. Grenville's followers, who formed one of them, were thrown into confusion by Grenville's death on the day that Parliament met; they were like sheep astray and soon wandered off to the Court party; they hardly counted. Wilkes, on the other hand, the leader of the popular section, was very much alive to the occasion. He saw a chance of refurbishing his own popularity, which seemed to be on the wane, by refusing, as a magistrate, to back press warrants, thus stopping the activities of the press-gang in the City. His action was not wholly selfish, nor was it intended to be unpatriotic. Press-warrants were of doubtful legality and the

[1] Harris to Weymouth, 23rd August 1770. Malmesbury Diaries, I, 51.
[2] 'The very great military preparations they are making, and particularly the marching of such a considerable body of troops towards the coast', etc. Rochford to Harcourt, 21st December 1770. British Diplomatic Instructions, XLIX, 117.

press-gang was not the most desirable method of conscription. Wilkes would have liked to reform the system, and did in fact persuade the City to minimise the ill-effects of his action by offering higher bounties for volunteers.[1] But inevitably his action widened the breach with Chatham who, though himself no admirer of the press-gang, could not admit that a crisis was the proper time for attempting reform. In his eyes Wilkes and his fellow magistrates were 'labouring to cut off the right hand of the community' and for that reason ought to be summoned to the bar of the House.[2] The third group, Rockingham and his friends, presented yet another facet. As ever, they were negative in their outlook. Their contribution was to remind Government that in March they had moved for an increase in the strength of the navy; and remarked what a pity it was that Government had paid no heed to them! The taunt was no doubt justified, and would have been more so if the motion on which it was based had not been simply a snap division; but to harp on it now was as helpful as crying over spilt milk.

Chatham was unable to be present on Parliament's opening day, because he was paying a last tribute to his brother-in-law, Grenville. On this occasion the Rockinghams waited for him unasked. When trouble was about Chatham was essential. They held their hand till he could be present, and then, on the 22nd November, Richmond opened the way for him by moving that the papers on the Falklands should be laid before Parliament. Weymouth refused the request, but spoke with marked reticence. He was followed by Hillsborough who was not only indiscreet, but saw fit to dwell at some length on the need to pay 'infinite regard and tenderness' to Spanish susceptibilities. It was too much for Chatham who began his speech by demanding indignantly that Ministers should think more of English rights than of Spanish *punctilio*. He knew all about Spanish Ministers; he had often negotiated with them himself, and had experienced nothing but want of candour and good faith, until at last he had been 'compelled to talk to them in a peremptory decisive tone'. The idea of protracting negotiations in order to salve Spanish *punctilio* was absurd and insupportable. When his indignation had exhausted itself, he warned the House that they were debating matters of 'the most extensive national

[1] See the author's *Life of Wilkes*, p. 238.
[2] Speech, 22nd November 1770.

importance', and therefore he must pass beyond the strict limits of the motion.

If the speech which followed, magnificent in its sweep and profoundly wise in its provisions, is to be fully savoured, the background as it appeared to Chatham must be borne in mind. For him, the Bourbon powers in general and France in particular had always been the rival most to be dreaded in the struggle for colonies and trade. If England was to prosper and hold that high position which Chatham believed to be hers by right, the challenge of the Bourbons must not only be withstood at the moment, but destroyed for all future time. His whole life had been devoted to that end, and when at long last his hand seemed to be grasping the prize, it had been suddenly and wantonly snatched from him. Hence his bitterness over the Peace of Paris and those who had taken part in it. They had made a mock of all his toil and sweat and in his eyes were traitors to England, to her destiny, to her glory. He knew that as the war had not been brought to its final conclusion, it must sooner or later be renewed, and it added to his bitterness to have to watch helplessly the rearming of France under the skilful guidance of Choiseul, and parallel with it, the decay of England's military resources under the shifting and incompetent ministries of the last ten years. The war was coming, and the date would be settled by France! How did the Falkland Islands fit into this picture? Surely if it were a local dispute, if the officials on the spot had acted without authority, they would be disowned at once and reparation made. The mere fact that the Spanish Ministers wished to argue was the worst of signs. Even if their immediate object was limited, at the very least they were, as the diplomats suggested, 'taking advantage of our divisions and frenzy at home with the colonies, to force us from those seas';[1] and when France began moving troops towards the coast, it was time to believe that their objects were not limited. The country must be prepared to face, not a trifling affair at the other end of the world, but the possibility of full-scale war, at a time when our navy was at its lowest ebb, when we had no allies, and when we were hampered by unrest at home and discontent in the colonies. It was against this background that Chatham made his speech.

He had, he said, no wish to impede negotiations or to see papers

[1] Robert Walpole to Harris, 1st December 1770. Malmesbury Diaries, I, 59.

which the Government were anxious to keep dark. Whatever people might think he was not a warmonger. He would far prefer peace, but it must be a solid peace, not one of those 'disgraceful expedients by which a war may be deferred but cannot be avoided'. He had, indeed, a better reason than most for desiring peace, since he knew the preparations which had been making abroad and our own defenceless condition. His charge against the Government was that they had destroyed 'all content and unanimity at home' while leaving us exposed to foreign enemies. As for the present trouble, the Government had taken no steps until they had heard that the first blow had actually been struck. They had not been remiss through lack of intelligence, for they had received plenty. But even if they had received none, the true source of intelligence was not information but sagacity—'sagacity to compare causes and effects; to judge of the present state of things, and discern the future by a careful review of the past'. What they had done since was wholly inadequate, as he knew from his own experience of naval requirements. Out of that experience he would tell them what they should have done, comparing the services which must be provided with those actually available. It was prudent to make proper provision in times of peace; in war it was a necessity. National defence had three main objectives: first to maintain a naval force in home waters superior to the combined fleets of France and Spain; secondly to maintain a powerful squadron in the west to protect our colonies and commerce; and thirdly to keep a force at Gibraltar commensurate with our interests in the Mediterranean. None of those objectives had been secured. We had barely eleven ships for the Channel, two in the West Indies and one at Gibraltar. Five ships which had been under orders for Gibraltar two months ago were still in English ports, and the garrison at Gibraltar was barely half the safe number. Great Britain herself was not secure; Spain had at that moment a fully equipped fleet at Ferrol superior to anything we could send against it. As with the navy, so with the army—the regiments were all under strength and no orders had been given to increase them to their full establishments. Nor was our position any better abroad than at home. Bearing in mind the relative populations of Great Britain and of France and Spain combined, it was obvious that we needed allies. We should not enter into engagements which would tend to involve us in a

Continental war, but alliances with some of the German princes would be useful and perhaps necessary, not to defend England, but Ireland. Finally there was England herself: 'we may look abroad for wealth, or triumphs, or luxury; but England is the mainstay, the last resort of the whole Empire. To this point every scheme of policy, whether foreign or domestic, should ultimately refer'. What had the Government done to satisfy or unite the people? 'Something substantial, something effectual must be done'. The public credit too must be kept up; he was not himself competent to speak on Treasury matters, but the Government must keep a sharp eye on all who advance money to the State and too often take special care of their own emoluments—'the whole race of commissaries, jobbers, contractors, clothiers and remitters'. The crisis demanded a wise, a firm, a popular administration; the dishonourable traffic of places must cease and the favours of the Crown must not flow 'invariably in one channel'. The need of the times was for a national government: 'it must be popular that it may begin with reputation. It must be strong within itself, that it may proceed with vigour and decision'.

The speech had a tremendous effect, as Chatham had intended. 'I mean,' he had said, 'to alarm the whole nation—to rouse the Ministry, if possible . . . to awaken the King'. Certainly he jolted them into action. The Government, fearful of his influence, decided to gag him by closing the House to strangers, and did so amid scenes of wild disorder on the 10th December. They also engaged Dr. Johnson to write a counterblast, in which, when the crisis was safely over, he allotted one of his more capricious definitions to Chatham's speech, calling it 'feudal gabble'.[1] But the Government paid heed to it none the less. Rochford hastily consulted 'the most intelligent persons in navy matters',[2] the King copied out in his own handwriting a memorandum on the present state of the navy,[3] while Barrington struggled as best he could with the insoluble problem of finding officers for the army.[4] All, in fact, was energy, even if misplaced; and all at the same time was fear and fright. Weymouth in the Cabinet urged strong

---

[1] Johnson. *Thoughts on the Falkland Islands.*
[2] Rochford to George III, 6th December 1770. Fortescue, II, 174.
[3] Memorandum, 6th December 1770. Fortescue, II, 177.
[4] 'All the vacancies of Ensign are not filled, because I am got to the end of my list of applications'. Barrington to George III, 18th December 1770. Fortescue, II, 187.

measures and the recall of Harris, and failing to carry his colleagues with him, resigned on the 16th December. But the threat
of war did not recede with his disappearance. Five days later
(21st December) the Cabinet was driven to order Harris's return.
and war seemed certain, when Louis XV dispersed the cloud
as rapidly as it had gathered by dismissing Choiseul (24th December) and writing to his brother of Spain: 'my Ministet would
have war, but I will not'.[1] Is it fanciful to see in the French King's
action the last and greatest effect of Chatham's speech? Choiseul
had many enemies, not forgetting that 'wonderfully dizened
Scarlet-woman', the Dubarry.[2] They had long been working for
his downfall, but he had gaily and gallantly held them at bay.
The only change in the situation this late December was the emergence of Chatham with a flaming speech that to the Spanish
Ambassador at least betokened war.[3] Chatham was a name of
dread on the Continent, and war with England lost its allure if
Chatham was to be the enemy. It may well be that his speech,
and its implications, were the final straws which weighted the
scales against Choiseul. But be that as it may, Choiseul went, and
on the 22nd January 1771 the Spanish Ambassador signed the
Declaration which restored Port Egmont to England.[4]

(vi)

As the issue of the Falklands affair did not rest solely with
England, Chatham might well have thought it enough to make
his protest and offer his suggestions, especially as they were
proving effective.[5] But Rockingham could not let well alone; in
his eyes there was a chance of making party capital out of the
threat of war, and he was determined to seize it. Having no constructive thoughts to offer, he urged Chatham to keep 'attacking
the administration for their neglect in not arming earlier'.[6] How
far Chatham thought this wise or patriotic is not clear; but being
anxious to keep the dwindling Opposition together, he did as he

---

[1] Quoted Pemberton. Lord North, p. 130.
[2] Carlyle. *French Revolution*.
[3] Cf. 'Prince Masserano said he saw we meant war'. George III to North,
23rd November 1770. Fortescue, II, 172.
[4] Jenkinson, III, 234.
[5] Cf. 'The intelligence was not quite slighted'—Chatham to Countess Stanhope,
16th December 1770. Chatham Corr. IV, 54.
[6] Rockingham to Chatham, 26th November 1770. Chatham Corr. IV, 26.

was asked.[1] It is noticeable, however, that so long as the threat of war continued, he mingled with his censures on the Government a measure of reassurance for doubting hearts. He had been blamed, he said, for revealing the nakedness of the land, but indeed he had divulged nothing that was not known to 'every coffee-house boy in Portsmouth'; his object had been almost parental, to warn the Ministers and open the King's eyes. Most of the Ministry were 'ignorant, futile and incapable', but he approved of Weymouth's endeavours and frowned on the City's attempt to obstruct pressing.[2] Though Chatham completely outshone his adversaries— 'they were babes to him'[3]—the policy thrust on him by Rockingham was not successful; it strained the loyalty of some, like Camden, who felt the times too dangerous for party politics, and served to weary others who preferred hunting in the shires to suffering *ennui* in the House.[4] 'Matters,' said Chatham with some bitterness, 'are hastening to a crisis in the interior of the thing called Opposition'.[5] It was a pity, because, as the echoes of the Falklands affair died away, Chatham was anxious to press ahead with those constitutional reforms, which seemed to him far more important and more abiding than the exploded embroilment with Spain. England was passing through a crisis, which in fact was the birth pangs of democracy. It showed itself at the time in popular ferment, though perhaps no one had any clear idea of its meaning or of its likely upshot. But, though Chatham saw at best through a glass darkly, he managed with his infallible instinct to grasp the essentials; the struggle was on behalf of 'liberty', which was claiming its own in many directions and on many subjects. The struggle however was one and indivisible, and a struggle in which the part he had to play could never be in doubt. The two most prominent, and perhaps most fundamental aspects were what he called the 'electors' rights',[6] with which he combined the need for parliamentary reform, and the 'juries' right to judge',[7] which was bound up with the freedom of the press. To him these were matters of vital importance, and in fighting for them he found

[1] Cf. 'Lord Rockingham still pressing, I acquit myself of a promise to execute his desires'. Chatham to Camden, 8th December 1770. Chatham Corr. IV, 46.
[2] Walpole. *George III*, IV, 139.
[3] *Ibid.*
[4] Cf. Richmond to Chatham, 20th February 1771. Chatham Corr. IV, 97.
[5] Chatham to Calcraft, 28th November 1770. Add. MSS. 43,771.
[6] See Chatham to Shelburne, 26th November 1770. Chatham Corr. IV, 23.
[7] See Chatham to Calcraft, 7th December 1770. Add. MSS. 43,771.

himself opposed by the King with his injured feelings, by North with his boast that he had never voted on the popular side, by a Government of arrogant nonentities, and by a majority of notorious time-servers. As allies he had, in effect, only a small group of personal adherents, whose ranks had recently been much thinned by death. There were other supporters, but they were more apparent than real. There was the doubtful backing of the City, much divided in its loyalties, and there were the Rockingham Whigs whose help was fitful not only by reason of irregular attendance in the House, but even more by reason of their half-hearted, unwilling and jealous acquiescence in his leadership. These combined drawbacks were now to prove fatal.

In the early months of the year, Chatham had come within an ace of overthrowing the Government and forcing himself on the King. In the middle of the year, when North had consolidated his position, the King and Government hit back. Their method was to promote actions for libel, and their agent was Mansfield. His doctrine that the duty of juries was confined to determining the fact of printing and publishing and that it was for the judge to decide whether or not the paper was a criminal libel, gave him complete *carte blanche* for finding the defendants guilty. The Government's destined prey was Junius; but, failing to discover his identity, they brought his printers and publishers to trial. The people at large were quick to recognise that the war had been transferred from the Houses of Parliament to the Law Courts, and they lost little time in countering this new attack by flouting Mansfield's doctrine, or alternatively giving verdicts flagrantly opposed to the 'facts' which alone they were allowed to judge. There could be only one end to such a conflict—the breakdown of justice. The need for a solution was obvious, and as the Government did not apparently intend to move, the duty clearly fell to the Opposition.

None of them doubted the true remedy; it was, to overthrow Mansfield's doctrine and give the juries full powers. The trouble arose over the method. Chatham wanted to proceed by stages, and as a first move to secure the appointment of a parliamentary committee who should enquire into the whole question of the administration of justice, and the constitutional powers of juries. Rockingham, on the other hand, wished to introduce a bill at once, specifically giving juries the rights which Mansfield denied them. Rockingham's method has been called 'the common-sense view',[1] but Chatham had plenty of grounds for doubting if common sense was sufficient. A bill such as Rockingham contemplated might well have been adequate if Rockingham had been in power and sure that his bill would be passed. But Rockingham was not in power, and the prospects of his bill were of the slightest. If, as he emphasised, he did not mean to challenge Mansfield's doctrine but 'to leave the past just where it is',[2] the only argument left to him for changing the law was the popular unrest, and the Government might not unreasonably represent it as a pandering to lawlessness. The weight of opposition would be tremendous: the judges would cling to their vested interests, the Government to a potent weapon against their opponents, and the King to so satisfactory a means of gratifying his personal resentments. Who would support it? The mob, maybe, clamouring at the doors, but few within. The bill in fact would be dead before it had been conceived; and when its carcass had been thrown out, what would the position be? Mansfield's doctrine would have been confirmed as the law of the land; the juries would have lost all semblance of right to flout his instructions and the Opposition would have shot the final bolt in their locker. The last state would have been worse than the first. Better to leave the juries to conduct their own battle in their own way.

Chatham's method was more subtle and more hopeful. Mansfield's doctrine was neither unchallengeable nor unchallenged. There was a rival doctrine, propounded by Camden, which maintained that juries already possessed the full rights demanded. If this doctrine could be established, no bill would be required. A dogfight on the subject between the lawyers was not likely to produce much good, but it was possible that a parliamentary committee, with its quota of laymen, might come down on Camden's side, if only to quell the disorders in the courts. In any event, the two contrasting doctrines would have been published to the world and thereafter the Opposition would have had some ground for introducing a bill, and could have done so without compromising their position. They could have fought first for the confirmation of Camden's view, and failing in that, for a change in the law. In a word, Rockingham's method invited

---

[1] Winstanley. *Chatham*, p. 420.
[2] Richmond to Chatham, 20th February 1771. Chatham Corr. IV, 97.

immediate and crushing failure, while Chatham's offered two, if not three chances.

The proof of the pudding was in the eating. Early in December (1770), renouncing the help of 'the lukewarm, the wavering and the treacherous',[1] Chatham raised the point himself in the House of Lords (5th December), declaring that the directions lately given to juries were 'dangerous and unconstitutional', and asking for a debate.[2] The next day, at his instigation, Sergeant Glynn moved in the Commons for the appointment of the committee which Chatham desired. In both cases the motions were lost, but they were not without immediate effect. Mansfield felt obliged to lay on the table of the House a copy of his charge to the jury, which Camden declared to be unintelligible and on which he put a series of questions. Mansfield refused to reply on the ground that he had been taken by surprise, whereupon Chatham agreed to postpone the debate to a more convenient time. If Walpole is to be believed, 'the dismay and confusion of Lord Mansfield was obvious to the whole audience; nor did one peer interpose a syllable on his behalf'. In short, an admirable beginning had been made, and it greatly puzzled Walpole that 'not a word more was said on the subject, either when the Parliament reassembled after the holidays, or during the whole remainder of the session'.[3] The reason was simple; the Rockinghams, who had offered only tepid support for Glynn's motion, made its rejection the excuse for drafting a bill of their own to be presented by Dowdeswell. When they approached Chatham for his support, he reluctantly agreed to give up his own method, but urged that the bill should be made declaratory, not enacting, and that it should be entrusted to Camden. One would have supposed that the first request, wise and reasonable in itself, would have appealed to politicians who had sponsored the Declaratory Act of 1765. But it did not. Nor did the second request, though based on the obvious fact that legal matters are best dealt with by lawyers. Dowdeswell suggested some compromise, but Rockingham brushed it aside,[4] and looking deep into Chatham's Machiavellian mind discovered in it nothing but a fear that the Rockinghams 'might get credit', and a determination to 'accommodate' only 'if he and his friends were to

---

[1] Chatham to Shelburne, 26th November 1770. Chatham Corr. IV, 23.
[2] Almon, II, 343-4.   [3] Walpole. *George III*, IV, 147-8.
[4] See Rockingham to Dowdeswell, 14th February 1771. Albemarle, II, 203.

appear in public as the leaders of the business'[1]—innuendoes which would have carried more weight, if he had not added that 'everything which has passed confirms me more and more that it is essential that we should pursue [our plan] both for the sake of the public and our own credit'. What was bad in Chatham, was it appears, good in Rockingham! Chatham, who was innocent of the charges, was left for the moment to fulminate at the tyranny which 'connexions' seemed to breed; but at the last moment, Rockingham tried to win him over by a personal interview. Chatham remained 'perfectly unconvinced' by his arguments, but, unlike Rockingham, was anxious to go as far as he could. He foresaw, and warned Rockingham, that if the Government, as they well might, simply gave a silent negative, it would be disastrous 'to any assertion of the jurors' rights'; the best he could do in the circumstances would be to support the introduction of the 'wrong bill' on the understanding that he would press for its amendment in committee.[2] So it was agreed. But Chatham's fears proved only too true. The Opposition united in pressing for a bill, but differed on the shape it should take, while, as North reported to the King, 'the friends of Government sat still', and left the Opposition to fight amongst themselves.[3] The silent vote was sufficient; it gave the *coup de grâce* to any further assertion of the jurors' rights and also ended Chatham's painful alliance with the Rockinghams. As Chatham is usually blamed for this breakdown, it may not be inappropriate to observe that all efforts at compromise came from him, none from Rockingham; and that while he was content to ascribe Rockingham's attitude to the tyranny of party shibboleths, Rockingham and Burke persistently—and revealingly—ascribed Chatham's attitude to a mean desire for undeserved credit. Nor is it out of place to remark that when, twenty-one years later, Fox settled the rights of juries, he did so on the lines marked out by Chatham—by means of a declaratory act.

(vii)

Chatham's fight for constitutional freedom had been based on two points—the Middlesex Election and the Rights of Juries. The one was now stale and the other dead. They were both to

[1] Rockingham to Dowdeswell, 11th February 1771. Albemarle, II, 200.
[2] Chatham to Shelburne, 2nd March 1771. Chatham Corr. IV, 108.
[3] North to George III, 7th March 1771. Fortescue, II, 226.

revive and in both he was to be justified, but for the moment they
were extinct volcanoes. Interest had passed to another phase—the
freedom to report parliamentary debates, which had been engin-
eered by Wilkes and was essentially concentrated in the Commons.
Chatham's usefulness was at an end; he had lost his fight. There
were many apparent reasons. He had been outmanœuvred by
North and the King; he had lost many staunch followers by
death; he had been weakened by the squabbles in the City; he
had suffered from the ineffectiveness and the jealousies of the
Whigs; he had been hampered by ill-health. Yet none of these
need have been fatal. There was a more profound cause—he had
been the architect of his own defeat. Once he had been known as
the Great Commoner, and whatever that title implied, it certainly
meant that his sway over the Commons was immense. By them
and through them he was as nearly omnipotent as any Minister
could hope to be. He had gained his influence largely by appealing
to their pride and raising their status. When subsequently he
became a peer, he lost more in virtue than he gained in rank. By
entering the portals of the House of Lords, he did not automatically acquire any influence over them, nor could he hope to raise
their status. He did indeed remind the peers in season and out of
season that they were the 'grand hereditary counsellors of the
Crown', the descendants of those iron barons who had wrested
Magna Carta from a reluctant King, the protectors of the people
against the arbitrary power of the House of Commons, and the
saviours of the State; but the peers were not so much impressed
with their own importance as Chatham was; they were more used
to their trappings and their position; and they were far from
relishing this constant harping on their duties. They did not
respond as Chatham expected, for indeed the House of Lords was
not his proper sphere, nor could he hope to succeed in a battle
waged from within its walls. He had lost contact with the people,
and had never made contact with the peers. He was essentially
'single and unconnected', and as such too weak to face the King
and the King's friends, and the whole army of placemen. His
defeat was inevitable, and the Lords made it more so by shutting
their House to strangers. Even the echo of his voice was to be
withheld from the people. The wonder is not that he was defeated,
but that he came so near success.

XXI

BURTON PYNSENT

(i)

CHATHAM HAD fought his battle against every sort of odds and had failed. One by one his supporters had dropped from him, some wrapping themselves up in the mantle of their good intentions, others hunting for fleshpots at Court or foxes in the country. At last he stood practically alone, a solitary figure wasting eloquence and wisdom on the 'Tapestry' in the House of Lords.[1] He recognised his failure; indeed he had seen it coming. By the time Parliament rose (9th May 1771), he had made up his mind to retire and he hastened down to Burton Pynsent to begin a new life. Except for one brief reappearance, in response to an urgent request, he remained aloof from politics for the next three years, and might have remained so until his death, had not American affairs in the end compelled him to don his armour again for his last fight. Until that time there was little enough in Parliament to attract his attention, still less his interest. Great matters certainly were stirring in the depths, but they had not yet broken surface where all was deceptive calm. "The Court', said Walpole, 'was predominant',[2] and Junius agreed.[3] He might have added that nothing was being done. In this sterile lull before the storm the Ministry contented themselves with executive functions—keeping the weavers in order, or trying to peg the price of corn.[4] No great questions were agitating, or rather none was recognised, and such matters as ruffled the surface were not likely to appeal to Chatham. The first half of 1772 was almost wholly occupied with the misfortunes of the royal family—too banal to command either

---

[1] Cf. 'Just returned from the Tapestry'. Chatham to Hester, 25th January 1771. Chatham Corr. IV, 86.

[2] Walpole. *George III*, IV, 235.

[3] 'I think no reasonable man will expect that, as human nature is constituted, the enormous influence of the crown should cease to prevail over the virtue of individuals'. Junius, I, 333.

[4] 'The monthly magazines become suddenly tamer in style ... the caricatures give place to views of towns and gentlemen's seats'. Wright, II, 19.

pity or respect. The King's two brothers, Cumberland and Gloucester, had contracted secret marriages which now came to light.
In both cases they were blatant misalliances. Cumberland had
chosen a widow, Mrs. Horton by name, the daughter of the
disreputable Lord Irnham, the sister of the notorious Colonel
Luttrell, and a designing minx in her own right, with few, if any,
of the traditional attributes of a princess. Gloucester was more
discerning though hardly more discreet; he had married Lord
Waldegrave's widow—a recognised beauty of spotless reputation,
but the illegitimate daughter of Sir Edward Walpole. The King,
pained and indignant, forbade his brothers the Court and demanded a Royal Marriage Act to give the sovereign powers over the
matrimonial affairs of his family; its passage occupied most of the
session. Hard on the heels of his brothers' disgrace came the disaster of his youngest sister, Caroline Matilda, who had been
married at the age of fifteen to the King of Denmark, an incipient
madman, and now—poor girl—at the age of twenty-one was
found guilty of adultery, divorced from her husband, and only
saved from life-long imprisonment by the firmness of the British
Ambassador and the efforts of the King.[1] These sordid matters
would have been highly distasteful to Chatham, nor were they
lightened for anyone by the sudden death of the Princess Dowager.

   If the first half of the year proved grievous for the Royal family,
the second half bade fair to be calamitous for high finance. When
the war had ended, there had been an insistent demand for capital
to promote the many-sided developments which marked the
dawn of the industrial revolution. The vast amount of paper
credit which had resulted was generally regarded as dangerous.
Hence the failure of a London banking house in June too easily
gave rise to a panic. 'It is beyond the power of words', said the
Evening Post, 'to describe the general consternation of the met-
ropolis yesterday. No event for these thirty years past has been
remembered to have given so fatal a blow to both our trade and
credit as a nation'.[2] The *Evening Post* exaggerated, but it was a fact
that the first failure was followed by others both at home and
abroad. An explosive situation was developing and was made the
more perilous by the difficulties into which the East India Company had fallen through Townshend's mishandling of their affairs.

---

[1] *Cambridge Modern History*, VI, 750.
[2] Quoted, Fulford, p. 27.

They found themselves unable to pay the agreed tribute to Government, and North felt obliged, towards the end of the year, to set on foot an enquiry into their whole position, and to spend the first half of 1773 passing an India Act, of which it has been said that 'it was obviously open to the gravest objections from many sides'.[1] Its details do not concern Chatham's story, but one factor does. There were seventeen million pounds of tea lying in the company's warehouses, which North gave them leave to export to the colonies direct instead of through England. His object was the blameless one of benefiting both the Company and the colonies. But good intentions are not enough without either wisdom or luck. What he was actually doing was to provide the ingredients of the Boston Tea Party, and so incidentally to pave the way for Chatham's return.

(ii)

Meanwhile Chatham, like a weary Titan, was resting from his labours. The younger men must take up the burden, if they could and would, though, in fact, the younger men were far to seek. Chatham had been the mainspring of opposition, and when he had gone 'the spirit of opposition was at an end'.[2] There was no political life for him had he wished for it, and he could therefore turn with the greater zest to the new life at Burton. But changed skies could not change his nature. He took down to Burton the same characteristics that he had always displayed, and as their effect was to be very marked, it may be worth while giving them a moment's consideration. Macaulay concluded that Chatham was extremely affected and without simplicity of character. But was that more than a superficial judgment? Of course, he had mannerisms in plenty, but from what did they take their rise? Were they mere empty gestures deliberately adopted to acquire an undeserved reputation, or did they not rather spring up, like weeds in a garden, from some necessity of his nature? And in passing, is simplicity always to be preferred to richness and variety? The keynote of Chatham's genius was his conception of grandeur, which ran through the whole gamut of his life, but took on varying forms as it touched on varying objects. It could be lofty

[1] Lecky, III, 489.
[2] Walpole. *Last Journals*, I, 3.

and ennobling when it was concerned with England; it could be
flamboyant and extravagant when concerned with himself. But
at bottom it was always the same—a conception of grandeur;
and it always had one significant feature—that it looked outwards
as well as inwards; it was to give as well as to take. His genius
would have been less than itself if it had failed to project that
grandeur on to his surroundings. It was a Midas touch, with
inevitable disadvantages for the humdrum purposes of life, but
also with a golden content which illumined and enhanced and
enriched the world in which he lived. For the sake of that enrich-
ment, the disadvantages had to be endured; for the outflow of
virtue could not be turned on and off like a tap. The way in which
it worked was not without interest. Chatham was for ever pursuing a two-fold perfection—an ambition to rise to the topmost
heights, and an ambition to shine to the utmost in whatever state
of life he happened to find himself. But there could be no perfection in a vacuum; there must be a fitting frame; and at each
stage of his life it was his ingrained need to create that fitting
frame which forced him to adopt, and absorb into himself, what
he believed to be the characteristics of his role—not affectedly
with the wish to impress, but, under the compulsion of his genius,
to make the most of the passing moment. He did not act a part;
he reacted to his position; and the dignity with which he invested
that position had its effect not only on himself but on the spectators—sometimes indeed for mirth but more generally for
admiration. As Barré said, 'no man ever entered the Earl's closet
who did not feel himself, if possible, braver at his return than when
he went in'. As a member of Parliament Chatham had inevitably
become the Great Commoner, not because he so desired, not
because of affectation and pose, not even because of his eloquence
or his policies, but because of the lustre which he shed on his
position as well as on himself, and which compelled an acknow-
ledgment from the world at large. But it is to be observed that
while the people confined his title exclusively to himself, his object
was to reflect it back on to the Commons. For him the title of Great
Commoner connoted a great House of Commons, the two being
complementary, and he was urgent, in season and out of season,
to raise the Commons—the *milieu* in which he was to shine—up
to the high estate which he had imagined for them and him. So,
when he rose to be Minister, he must be great for England's sake,

and by being great must increase her glory; nothing must be done by him which either in fact or appearance would tarnish her honour or diminish her strength. When he became an Earl, he took the same characteristics to the House of Lords. He was now no longer the Great Commoner, but consciously a Peer of the Realm, and as such he felt all the compulsion of *noblesse oblige*. It was no pose in Chatham; it was natural; it partook of that pride of tradition which sanctions odd customs in public schools, and that *esprit de corps* which welds raw recruits into famous regiments. If Chatham was affected it was under the compulsion of his genius; if he posed it was because of his conception of grandeur. But affectation and pose seem strange bed-fellows for genius and grandeur, and perhaps in this case have been misnamed.

(iii)

The old Adam is deeply implanted in human nature, and beguiles too many men to imagine that in life's evening when their work is done, they can make a success of that seemingly simple occupation, farming. They are deceived; they lose money; and if they are wise, they draw back before they have ploughed up their fortunes as well as their fields. Chatham would no doubt in any case have suffered the usual fate, but his inborn characteristics made it doubly sure. At Burton he was neither the Great Commoner nor the Great Earl, but very easily and very naturally the Great Landowner. He threw himself into the part with his accustomed completeness, and was encouraged by the benefit to his health. His first summer (1771) was 'a summer of more health that I have known these twenty years', and at the end of it had confirmed him in his resolve 'what not to do'. Looking out from his high hill, he saw that the City of London had lost its weight in the political world, and that the narrow views of the Rocking-hams had 'rendered national union on revolution principles impossible'. What in the circumstances was his proper line of conduct? Clearly to remain where he was: 'I do not see that the smallest good can result to the public from my coming up to the meeting of Parliament'.[1]

But he was not to be left in peace. The Dissenters were anxious to introduce a Bill giving them relief from their disabilities. The

[1] Chatham to Shelburne, 10th January 1772. Chatham Corr. IV, 186.

prospects were doubtful, more doubtful than they thought, for
the King had already given orders for their overthrow. It was the
duty of Ministers, he told North, to 'prevent any alterations in so
essential a part of the Constitution as everything that relates to
religion'. Not but what he was willing to bow himself in the
house of Rimmon, for when told that many members feared to
oppose the Bill because they owed their seats to the Dissenters'
vote, he agreed that the Commons might pass it as a measure of
political expediency, leaving it to the Bishops and the Lords 'to
prevent any evil'.[1] Possibly the Dissenters had got wind of this
scheme, for they entreated Chatham to come to their aid. It was a
subject on which he held strong views. Liberty was one and
indivisible, and tyranny the same whatever its disguise. It was
neither good religion nor sound statesmanship to oppress Dissenters, and he therefore agreed to take part in the debate. The Bill, as
the King had suggested, was passed by the Commons and came
to the Lords, like a lamb to the slaughter, on the 18th May (1772).
Chatham spoke in its support out of a profound knowledge and
with deep religious convictions. The Bishops had laid emphasis
on the excellent system of the Church of England and had spoken
of the dissenting ministers as men of close ambition. 'They are so',
Chatham retorted, 'and their ambition is to keep close to the
college of Fishermen, not of cardinals, and to the doctrines of
inspired apostles, not the decrees of interested and aspiring
bishops; they contend for a spiritual creed, and spiritual worship;
we have a Calvinist creed, a Popish liturgy, and an Arminian
clergy'. So much for the vaunted system.[2] But in spite of his efforts
the Bill was thrown out, and Chatham returned to Somerset with
his usual portion of present defeat which the future was to reverse.

He returned the more gladly because London had proved bad
for his health,[3] but alas! he returned to conditions of increasing
embarrassment. The land was taking its toll of his inexperience
and his expansiveness. He had been too successful in the character
of Great Landowner, acquiring fresh fields, enlarging his house to
a size commensurate with his dignity, erecting a column 120 feet
high to the memory of his benefactor, putting up farm buildings
'all arranged in the greatest order and supported by Tuscan

[1] George III to North, 2nd April 1772. Fortescue, II, 334.
[2] Burke's Speech, May 1790. Quoted Chatham Corr. IV, 220 (*n.*).
[3] 'I am far from well, and extremely lame'. Chatham to Shelburne, 18th May
1772. Chatham Corr. IV, 218.

pillars',[1] buying prize cattle, brood mares and 'the most beautiful of sows', and filling his grounds with 'peacocks, dogs, horses and gallinas'.[2] There were widespread plantations in all directions; there was entertaining 'in a very extensive way'. Money was poured out in lavish style, but not on farming as the farmer understands it. Chatham's own contribution was strenuous indeed, but ineffective. He had, as he once assured Lyttelton, 'numberless occupations indispensably requiring me here'.[3] Certainly it would be interesting, and perhaps instructive, to know what exactly those occupations were, for the correspondence that remains does not give much evidence of indispensability. Chatham liked to think of himself as occupying 'a farmer's chimney-corner',[4] and in keeping with the character took to drinking ale, much to Hester's alarm, who thought it would bring on his gout; he even deluded himself with the idea that he was 'tending his flocks or following the plough';[5] but his actual work as a farmer seems to have been mainly the pursuit of health and happiness. 'Papa', young William told his mother, 'continues his four hours' rides every morning, not to mention an airing in the afternoon'.[6] Indeed the Great Farmer's day was mostly spent on horseback, which he represented to his doctor, no doubt with complete conviction, as 'hunting and agriculture'.[7] His system of farm management was financially deplorable, whatever it may have been in other respects, and had at last to be handed over to professionals. Debts were for ever mounting and remained a matter of anxiety to his dying day. His difficulties had many sources—his extravagance, his inexperience as a farmer, the rising cost of living and the consequent depreciation of capital, mistaken advice from his solicitor, Nuthall, on the powers of his trustees, and not least, the irregular payment of his pension. This last misfortune, for which he was not to blame, was inexcusable. Chatham's pension was charged on the West Indian revenues, and had been put in jeopardy by the King who had imposed a prior charge on the fund to give allowances to his brothers. Thereafter Chatham's pension was always in arrears and was about a year in

[1] Dickins and Stanton, p. 430.
[2] Chatham to Hester, 8th April 1772. Chatham Corr. IV, 205.
[3] Chatham to Lyttelton, 22nd July 1772. Phillimore, II, 773.
[4] Chatham to Shelburne, 22nd June 1773. Chatham Corr. IV, 239.
[5] Chatham to Shelburne, 20th October 1773. Chatham Corr. IV, 298.
[6] William to Hester, 9th July 1772. P.R.O., Chatham MSS. G.D. 8-11.
[7] Addington to Hester, 25th January 1772. P.R.O., Chatham MSS. G.D. 8-15.

his debt when he died. Even when it was paid, it was subject to fees and duties which reduced it from three to two thousand pounds. North, who whatever his failings as a statesman was a man of kindly nature, knowing and being grieved at Chatham's difficulties, once asked the King to make up the annuity to an effective £3,000, but the King refused unless and until, in his own words, 'decrepitude or death puts an end to him as a trumpet of sedition'.[1]

Chatham's efforts to help himself displayed little financial acumen and none of that firmness of touch which he showed when speaking for England. He tried to sell Hayes by a kind of Dutch auction, and when that failed went on to a similar failure with Burton. Buyers were scarce at that time of financial *malaise*, and in the end he had to be content with mortgages. The details are obscure and of no great interest. Debt, be it large or small, is the same all the world over—the begetter of discomforts and the mother of makeshifts, a millstone round the neck and a burden on the conscience. Chatham was eased of the sharpest pangs by two women—Hester, who had a far more practical mind for domestic affairs and by degrees took over control, bringing into play what she called 'the oeconomicals';[2] and Molly Hood in whose memory there still lingered the fragrance of those olden days when, as Molly West, she had cherished certain tender thoughts in her heart. She could still, in spite of newer loyalties, call Chatham '*the greatest of all men*',[3] and at her instigation her husband, though he could ill afford it, and her West relations who were well-to-do, lent Chatham large sums of money at a low rate of interest. It is a melancholy thought that the one statesman of the times who above all others had kept himself free from any suspicion of that peculation of public moneys sanctioned by common usage, should in his old age have found himself obliged to impose on the kindness of friends. Their loyalty alone redeemed the situation.

A more cheerful thought is the pleasure and pride which he took in his children. They were a happy and united family; not over-awed by their father's greatness, but with a proper sense of the respect due to him and a firm belief in his wisdom. Having suffered much himself at Eton, he refused to send them to school,

---

[1] George III to North, 9th August 1775. Fortescue, III, 241.
[2] Hester to Chatham, 1st July 1773. Chatham MSS. G.D. 8–9.
[3] Dickins and Stanton, p. 430.

keeping them at home in the charge of a tutor. But lessons were not left only to hirelings; Chatham himself took an active part in their education and found great contentment in the work.[1] About this time, too, he began to make trips to Lyme Regis 'where the sea is nobly beautiful',[2] and where there are 'noble heights round the town'.[3] There he went 'hunting landskips' with young William,[4] or watched the boys bathing, not without the anxiety natural to a crippled onlooker when 'the Nereids were a little more boisterous than becomes nymphs of their quality',[5] or laughed at their flirtations with the Lyme 'misses' and occupied himself with being 'commodious to the ladies for William'.[6] All was conducive to good appetite, sound sleep and returning health. It is a tribute to his frequent visits, and perhaps a reflection of the effect which he invariably made, that the house he occupied though no longer standing, is still remembered as the Great House; and it is perhaps a sidelight on his habitual grandeur that the Great House in his eyes 'wanted just another half to hold us all together'.[7] Yet, great or humble, there was balm at Lyme for the tired old statesman in the interval before the final act.

[1] 'The promise of our dear children does me more good than the finest of pure air'. Chatham to Hester, 8th June 1773. Chatham Corr. IV, 267.
[2] Chatham to Nuthall, 7th October 1772. P.R.O., Chatham MSS.
[3] Chatham to Hood, 11th June 1773. Add. MSS. 35,192.
[4] Chatham to Hester, 20th June 1773. P.R.O., Chatham MSS.
[5] Chatham to Hester, December 1773. P.R.O., Chatham MSS.
[6] Chatham to Hester, 16th June 1773. Chatham Corr. IV, 273.
[7] Chatham to Hester, 11th June 1773. Chatham Corr. IV, 268.

XXII

AMERICA

(i)

THOUGH CHATHAM looked on himself as retired, he was consulted from time to time by Shelburne, especially on Indian and Irish problems. The advice he gave not only displays the breadth and wisdom of his views, but also helps to explain the latent antipathy between himself and Rockingham. Even had there been no personal jealousies, they could never have worked harmoniously together, approaching their problems as they did from entirely different angles—the one legalistic and selfish, the other forward-looking and humanitarian.

In dealing with North's India Bill, Rockingham took his stand on the rights of the Company under their Charter. The fact that their status had entirely altered, and that, more by chance than premeditation, they had turned from a small trading concern into a great territorial power, meant nothing to him; they were not for that reason to be subjected to any fresh control. As they had conquered India, no matter how or by what forces, it was, in his eyes, their possession; it belonged to them with all its inhabitants and all its seemingly boundless wealth. To Chatham such a view was utterly abhorrent. Trade was certainly of the greatest importance, and charters should not be lightly ignored, but they could not overthrow justice and equity. Indian trade, under the Company in its new form, stood on little else than guns and ships and fortresses; it should stand on a system of justice and humanity.[1] The company should draw a clear distinction between their territorial revenues and their trading profits. The former must be used for the public good alone, never for the purpose of paying dividends, and should be apportioned between the state and Company according to the cost incurred by each in defending India and extending her commerce. Nor must the Company use their position to grab for themselves the internal trade of the

[1] Chatham to Shelburne, 22nd January 1773. Chatham Corr. IV, 239.

country; monopolies imposed by force—which today would be called nationalisation—were oppressive and should be abolished for ever. Justice there must be and it should be administered by independent judges appointed on the same basis as in England.[1] These were the standards he applied to North's Bill. It might have been so great and so good; for India, as Chatham wrote, 'teems with iniquities so rank as to smell to earth and heaven. The reformation of them, if pursued in a pure spirit of justice, might exalt the nation and endear the English name through the world'. But it failed in its intention because 'the generous purpose is no sooner conceived in the hearts of the few, but by-ends and sinister interests taint the execution, and power is grasped at, where redress should be the only object'. Some portions of the Bill were laudable, others less so; but Chatham welcomed the attempt at reformation, and only grieved that it should be jeopardised 'by the unhappy misapplication of a respectable sound, *chartered rights*'.[2]

He manifested the same liberal spirit and the same adherence to principle when the Irish Parliament proposed to levy a tax on absentee landlords. Rockingham was up in arms at once. He was himself an absentee landlord who spent the income from large possessions in Ireland on his pursuits in England. His interests must be defended; and the Privy Council must refuse to sanction such a tax. 'We have a right to protection', he declared, 'we have committed no crime; our property is our own; we have a right to spend it where we please'.[3] Chatham's interest in Irish property was not so great or so direct, though it existed. But the problem presented itself to him in a different light. There was a principle involved. It was the 'inherent exclusive right' of the Irish Government to raise supplies in the manner they thought best.[4] It was they who had proposed this particular tax, and no doubt its excessive severity was in part due to a feeling that the product of Irish estates should in the main be spent in Ireland. But the fitness or justice of the tax was a matter for the Irish Parliament, not the English Privy Council. If Rockingham felt aggrieved, he should not seek to overthrow the Bill by the exercise of a veto in England, but by persuading the Irish Parliament to change their mind. 'The power of the purse in the Commons was fundamental and

[1] Chatham to Shelburne, 24th May 1773. Chatham Corr. IV, 264.
[2] Chatham to Shelburne, 17th June 1773. Chatham Corr. IV, 275.
[3] Rockingham to Bessborough, 21st September 1773. Albemarle, II, 228.
[4] Chatham to Shelburne, 24th October 1773. Chatham Corr. IV, 299.

inherent; to translate it from them to the King in Council was to annihilate Parliament'.[1] In short, Chatham's quarrel with Rockingham was a repetition in a new form of their quarrel over the Declaratory Act. Rockingham wished to take away the 'power of the purse' from both the colonial assemblies and the Irish Parliament. Chatham could not admit the right of England, as an outside power, to impose taxes in the one case or disallow them in the other. His views were not adopted, but as it happened the Irish Parliament solved the difficulty by changing their minds and withdrawing the tax.

(ii)

But India and Ireland, important as they were, did not occupy the first place in Chatham's thoughts. That was reserved for a wider picture, with America in the foreground and France looming up behind it. 'America' said Chatham, 'sits heavy upon my mind.'[2] She was, in a sense, his real child; he had given the colonies safety; he had doubled their size. And France was the universal enemy—the enemy who in the past had hurt England by oppressing the colonies, and now threatened to destroy England by subverting them. No one seemed to realise the danger or to care. In his 'meditation by my chimney corner' a feeling of hopelessness was induced by what he called 'the singularity in which I find I stand as to my notions', and his complete inability either to quiet his own forebodings or to impress others with their urgency. 'I grieve', he cried out, 'to find myself constrained by irresistible conviction to set my single opinion against that powerful stream, that bears all down before it'.[3] His grief was the greater because the Empire meant so much to him and so little to others; indeed it seemed to mean nothing at all. England in the eighteenth century was extraordinarily insular. The Scots were still our 'natural enemies'[4] with Bute at their head. The Irish had long been despised and oppressed. Half of England was consumed with envy of the 'Nabobs' for their success as 'fleecers of the East Indies',[5] and half felt their consciences pricked by the stories of

---

[1] Chatham to Shelburne, 4th November 1773. Chatham Corr. IV, 305.
[2] Chatham to Shelburne, 6th March 1774. Chatham Corr. IV, 331.
[3] Chatham to Shelburne, 10th January 1774. Chatham Corr. IV, 319.
[4] Lecky, III, 50.
[5] George III to North, 11th May 1773. Fortescue, II, 483.

tyranny and pillage; but few, if any, felt either pride or responsibility. America had long been ignored politically and had recently proved to be financially expensive. No one, apart from the merchants, was really interested in her, and even the merchants regarded the West Indian Islands as more profitable and so more desirable. Hence that surprising controversy at the time of the Peace of Paris over the relative merits of Guadeloupe and Canada. The idea of Empire was practically non-existent; it had no particular meaning for King, politician or man-in-the-street, except in the sense of a possession—a disregarded and mainly unwanted possession. England was unaware that she was in process of acquiring a vast Empire, which was to become the proudest and most beneficent in the world, and which, in new forms and with wider horizons, is still the world's best hope. Chatham alone looked beyond the narrow confines of England proper; Chatham alone put in a word for the maligned Scots, emphasising that he did not object to Bute because of his nationality but because of his incompetence; Chatham alone had some sympathy with Irish hopes; Chatham, almost alone, understood and supported American aspirations. He did so because of his glowing vision of a great family of nations, the kith and kin of the motherland, free with England's freedom and, under her guidance and suzerainty, growing in wealth and prosperity until at last they would all stand with her 'on the pinnacle of glory, on the very heights of national grandeur'.[1] It was the apotheosis of that conception of grandeur which was immanent in his character and the basis of his genius.

(iii)

America might well sit heavy on Chatham's mind, for there seemed to be a fate overshadowing Anglo-American relations. Peace and quiet could never exist on both sides of the Atlantic simultaneously. After the repeal of the Townshend duties (March 1770), the disturbances in America died down; the non-importation agreement, which had proved oppressive to English merchants and to American consumers alike, was given up, and there was a sudden, copious and delightful influx of English goods: 'the colonists had never seemed so prosperous . . . lands

[1] Chatham Corr. IV, 522 (*n.*).

were increasing in value, roads were being improved, and the
people were in general contented and happy'.[1] But trouble sprang
up in England. Grafton, by creating, at Bedford's behest, a new
department of Secretary of State for America, had in fact, though
not in theory, reimposed that dual administration over the colonies
which Chatham had so wisely abolished. The Secretary for the
Southern Department could not reconcile himself to this diminution of his own importance and managed to find occasions and
excuses for intervening in American affairs. There were constant
'jarrings'—to use the King's word—between the two departments,
which became so frequent and so generally disturbing that
the King seized the opportunity of Hillsborough's resignation
(August 1772), to introduce new arrangements.[2] Ironically,
instead of solving the problem, they had the effect of reviving
duality in theory as well as in fact. North was rightly doubtful
of their efficacy, but, again ironically, it was not the lumbering
procedure of the departments which produced the next flare-up,
but events in America, events which in every case were connected
in one way or another with taxation.

There had been much restlessness in Rhode Island at the
activities of Lieutenant Dudington, who in the revenue cutter
Gaspee, was doing much execution among the smugglers of
Narragansett Bay. On the 9th June 1772, he had the misfortune
to run aground on a shoal not far from Providence. Seizing
occasion by the forelock, the inhabitants of the town poured out
at night on mischief bent; they surprised and captured Dudington,
and burnt his ship. North, on hearing the news, ordered an
enquiry, but nothing came of it owing to deliberate and baffling
lack of evidence. The failure to discover and punish the culprits
was a direct encouragement to the extremists in Boston, where
trouble was always on the verge of boiling over because of the
perennial friction between their Assembly and their Governor,
Hutchinson. Whatever his previous sins may have been, Hutchinson added to them at the end of the year by arranging that his
own salary and that of the judges should in future be paid out of
Crown revenues and not by the Assembly. It was not an unreasonable move in itself, and might well have had Chatham's blessing,[3]

[1] Miller, p. 224.
[2] George III to North, 9th August 1772. Fortescue, II, 378.
[3] Cf. 'I rejoice that America, at least, has a chance to have independent judges'.
Chatham to Shelburne, 17th July 1773. Chatham Corr. IV, 283.

but it seemed in colonial eyes a sinister measure investing Hutchinson with a dangerous independence likely to encourage him in arbitrary ways, and creating a corrupt Bench of judges to uphold and justify him. The Assembly, therefore, retaliated with a remonstrance peremptorily denying the jurisdiction of the English Parliament;[1] and when their fears seemed to be more than justified by the contents of some of Hutchinson's private letters, published without his knowledge or authority (June 1773), they addressed a petition to the King demanding his removal. Both remonstrance and petition were left unanswered and indeed unconsidered. It was in the midst of this largely artificial but none the less acute ferment that the East India Company's tea chests arrived, and were thrown overboard in that riot known as the Boston Tea Party.

The news reached England in January 1774. It aroused such angry feelings that it must be regarded as having been something in the nature of a last straw. For years America had been a source of worry, and the fact that the worry was largely of the Government's own contriving did not make it any the easier to bear. The Government's patience had been wearing thin, and now it snapped. With their patience they discarded caution, moderation and even the most elementary sense of justice. They did not wait to make enquiries; they did not attempt to differentiate between the perpetrators of the outrage and the rest of the inhabitants; they did not ask for redress, nor did they offer any opportunity for defence or excuses. They determined there and then on coercive measures. Franklin, the colony's agent in London, was outrageously bullied by Wedderburn, the Solicitor General, before a sniggering committee of the Privy Council,[2] and deprived of his office as deputy postmaster-general in North America, merely for having presented Boston's petition, which was now, some six months after receipt, suddenly remembered. North, a little reluctantly, but borne on by the general indignation, introduced a series of Bills into Parliament designed to crush Boston once and for all. One Bill ordered the closing of the port until the East India Company had been compensated and the Crown satisfied that Bostonians would in future behave with

---

[1] Walpole. *Last Journals*, I, 188.
[2] 'The favourite part of his discourse was levelled at your Agent, who stood there the butt of his invective ribaldry for near an hour'. Franklin, p. 318.

restraint; another remodelled the Charter of Massachusetts in
favour of the Crown; while a third authorised the Governor
to send for trial in Great Britain persons indicted for capital
offences. Hutchinson was indeed removed, but only to give place
to General Gage, the Commander-in-Chief of the English forces
in America, who was to be the instrument of coercion. By way
of assistance, a fourth Bill authorised him to quarter his troops
on the inhabitants.

(iv)

The Bills were passed almost with acclaim. There were few
people in England, perhaps none, who had any sympathy with
the Americans; their conduct, which had long been wayward,
violent and provocative, had now reached a climax; and in
addition their attitude towards the financial burdens which the
mother country had incurred, largely on their behalf, seemed ungrateful and unreasonable. Yet on the question of finance there
was a marked division of opinion. Broadly speaking there were
three points of view. At one extreme there were the followers
of Grenville who argued, not without logic, that the colonies
should contribute towards the expenses of the Empire from which
they benefited, and that only the English Parliament, situated at
the centre, could apportion those expenses fairly between the
different members. Parliament had the knowledge and the right,
and would be acting unjustly towards all if she did not recover a
fair contribution from each. It was a logical position, though based
on a system of accounting rather than on the then practically
non-existent science of economics; but it ignored sentiment and it
assumed a right of taxation in Parliament which was open to
challenge on many counts. Perhaps more perniciously, it was a
view with particular temptations for a heavily taxed nation.

At the other extreme stood a small group of theorists, headed by
Dr. Tucker, the Dean of Gloucester, who was before long to be
supported by the works of Adam Smith and by a growing number of disciples. They were not much concerned with Parliament's
rights or American grievances, but believed that the colonies, in
their present truculent mood, were neither a political nor a
financial asset. As economists they argued that England would
stand to gain by separating herself totally from her colonies and

then entering into 'alliances of friendship and treaties of commerce with them, as with other sovereign, independent states'.[1] Their view was based on a theory—new at the time and therefore the less acceptable—that trade was governed by the laws of economics, and not by Navigation Acts or the possession of colonies; and that the Americans, if they became independent, would continue to trade with England because it would pay them to do so. These theorists were in advance of their times, but, in common with the followers of Grenville, they ignored sentiment, relying on the abstract economic man as Grenville had relied upon logic. They suffered the usual disadvantages of all innovators, with the added drawback that their theory offered only the negative benefits of an end to squabbling and would, as it seemed, involve England in the loss of power and prestige as well as territories. Nor could they guarantee that colonies which had been pushed out by their mother country, or had broken away in anger, would be in the mood that produces 'alliances of friendship or treaties of commerce'.

Between these two extremes stood the Rockinghams, with Burke for their spokesman. Burke rejected Tucker's political views out of hand, declaring that to suggest giving up the colonies was 'nothing but a little sally of anger, like the frowardness of peevish children; who, when they cannot get all they would have, are resolved to take nothing'.[2] Equally he rejected Grenville's insistence on the payment of taxes, and in doing so seemed to incline toward Tucker's economic views, at least to the extent of assuming that England's proper return from the colonies lay in trade not taxation. 'The complicated system of the colonies', he argued, was 'a commercial monopoly',[3] which by its workings brought over to England the profits of American trade; in that way America 'performed her part to the British revenue'.[4] More interesting than his economic arguments, which were not very clear nor very sustained, was his appeal to sentiment, which in its scope and nature was certainly revealing. Burke's two great speeches on American taxation were splendid in imagery, devastating in criticism and lucid in history, though indeed distinctly jejune in policy. In them he allowed his sentiment full play, but in

---

[1] Tucker. *An Humble Address*, etc., p. 5.
[2] Burke. Speech, 22nd March 1775. Works II, 194.
[3] Burke. *American Taxation*. Works II, 112.
[4] Burke. Speech, 22nd March 1775. Works II, 234.

keeping with his essentially negative character, his sentiments partook more of static nostalgia than of active affection. He looked back to the golden age of the Declaratory Act and admonished Parliament to return to it. 'When', he said, 'you have recovered your old, your strong, your tenable position, then face about—stop short—do nothing more—reason not at all—oppose the ancient policy and practice of the Empire as ramparts against the speculations of innovators on both sides of the question; and you will stand on great, manly and sure ground'.[1] Sentiment he had —and obstinacy. 'If you mean to please any people', he declared, 'you must give them the boon which they ask; not what you may think better for them'. And so in response to American demands he was ready to repeal all the Acts of all the Ministries—except one. 'I am resolved,' he said, 'this day to have nothing at all to do with the question of the right of taxation. . . . The question with me is, not whether you have a right to render your people miserable; but whether it is not in your interest to make them happy'. And from his answer it seems that it was not in England's interest to make Americans happy if that involved denying Parliament's abstract right to levy taxes, or the repeal of Rockingham's Declaratory Act.[2] Not, in short, if it meant jettisoning useless lumber which happened to appeal to Burke.

Standing outside these three groups were two men—Chatham and the King—who mixed their own particular prepossessions into the theories of others, and by so doing came to be protagonists in a battle, literally to the death, over America. They had one thing in common; neither had the least wish to follow Tucker's advice and separate England from her colonies. To the King they were part of his patrimony which belonged to him and which he had no intention of losing, though he did recognise the theoretical possibility.[3] To Chatham they were members of the family group, tied to the mother country by the bonds of blood and kinship; to lop them off would not be the alienation of an outlying field, but the severance of a limb. Probably neither of them gave much thought to the possible proceeds of taxation, neither being skilled in the art of finance, though Chatham through his friends in the City had a fair knowledge of American trade and a shrewd idea of its

---

[1] Burke. *American Taxation*. Works II, 145.
[2] Burke. Speech, 22nd March 1775. Works II, 201/2.
[3] 'Blows must decide whether they are to be subject to this country or independent'. George III to North, 18th November 1774. Fortescue, III, 153.

value. Far more important than any agreement or want of agreement on points of detail, was their general outlook. The King regarded the colonies much as he regarded Wilkes; their rights and wrongs did not interest him; the outstanding fact was that they had flouted his authority, they were rebellious subjects, they must be punished.[1] It was a thousand pities that the King was by nature more touchy than imaginative. By contrast Chatham's imagination was over-exuberant, leading him to sympathise more completely with American views than was altogether justified, and to credit the colonists with feelings of loyalty and generous impulses which probably few of them possessed. Unlike Tucker, he did not rise above the economic views of his age; in his belief the colonies should be a source of wealth to the mother country, and for that reason must at all costs be retained; but he agreed with Burke that the true financial return was to be found in the volume of trade, not in the imposition of duties, and that the direction of trade was a function of the mother country. Yet if circumstances made England complete mistress of what Burke called the 'commercial monopoly' she must take care to use it for the good of the Empire as a whole; the system was not a method of manipulating trade solely for the benefit of England, but of ensuring that the resources of all were so employed that the greatest profit would accrue to all, both collectively and individually. In return for the small measure of subservience which the working of the system involved, the colonies were to be protected and cherished; they were to enjoy all the privileges of Englishmen, and all the benefits of Empire trading. So much for America. But Chatham was oppressed by a further, and a terrifying thought. The King's attitude seemed to him not only contrary to the principles of English justice and English liberty, but a direct incentive to French aggression. Bearing in mind the physical connexion between the colonies and Canada, and remembering the sentiments of revenge which France was known to entertain, Chatham believed that a breach with the colonies would make a renewal of war with France inevitable. In short, everything—the ties of kinship, the requirements of trade, the preservation of peace— all enforced the propriety of a kindly and tolerant policy towards the colonies. 'There', Chatham wrote while the coercive Bills were

[1] Cf. 'They have boldly thrown off the mask . . . this indeed decides the proper plan to be followed'. Memorandum by the King, 1773. Fortescue, III, 47.

passing through Parliament, 'there where I had garnered up my heart; where our strength lay, and our happiest resources presented themselves, it is all changed into danger, weakness, distraction and vulnerability'.[1] In short, while the King thought only of asserting his authority and upholding his idea of honour, Chatham was grieved at the injustice done to his fellow countrymen over the seas and all which that injustice might entail.

[1] Chatham to Shelburne, 6th March 1774. Chatham Corr. IV, 331.

XXIII

TREMBLING ON THE BRINK

(i)

WHILST TROUBLES had been brewing in America, Chatham's
infirmities had been growing upon him, and of both necessity as
well as inclination he had stayed away from Parliament. In his
absence Opposition had sunk into insignificance, and in Chatham's
view, perhaps into uselessness. 'I have long held one opinion,' he
told Shelburne, 'as to the solidity of Lord North's situation; he
serves the Crown more successfully and more sufficiently upon the
whole, than any other man now to be found could do'.[1] Not only
was the Opposition insignificant, but when the coercive bills were
introduced, it became divided against itself and uncertain of
its aims. The Duke of Manchester, feeling that public opinion
favoured harshness, urged the policy of 'remaining spectators,
without throwing any embarrassment in the way of Government',[2]
while Rockingham, anxious to keep in the public eye, preached
the advantage of *occasionally* giving a strong mark of their disapprobation when they thought they could do so with credit to
themselves.[3] To Chatham the times seemed far too dangerous for
any such halting and self-centred councils. He became increasingly
anxious about the Government's proceedings, and so convinced
that 'the fate of Old England was at stake not less than that of the
New' that at last he felt it imperative to intervene. Boston, he
told Shelburne, owed reparation for 'a tumultuous act of a very
criminal nature', but the handling of the matter was 'beset with
dangers of the most complicated and lasting nature', and it was
unlikely that true wisdom would be the issue of 'narrow, short-
sighted councils of state, or over-heated popular debates'.[4] The
Boston Port Bill had gone too far; it should have stopped short
at demanding compensation: to indulge in further severities

[1] Chatham to Shelburne, 6th March 1774. Chatham Corr. IV, 331.
[2] Manchester to Rockingham, 20th April 1774. Albemarle, II, 242.
[3] Rockingham to Manchester, 20th April 1774. Albemarle, II, 244.
[4] Chatham to Shelburne, 20th March 1774. Chatham Corr., IV, 336.

would put all to the hazard; 'America guilty would have submitted; and subsequent lenitives might have restored mutual goodwill and necessary confidence. America disfranchised, and her
charter mutilated, may, I forebode, resist; and the cause become
general on that vast continent'.[1] History is witness how exactly he
foresaw and foretold the course of future events.

In the meantime he struggled up to Hayes in order to be on the
spot, and was there prostrated for a month. It was not until the
third reading of the fourth coercive bill—for quartering soldiers
on the inhabitants of Boston—that he was able to attend the
debates (26th May 1774). The occasion was momentous, for
news had just been received that Louis XV had died a fortnight
earlier and with his death no one knew what line France would
take, whether she would continue her pacific policy, or would
add to England's troubles by supporting the colonies, or even by
declaring war. It was a catastrophe which Chatham had foreseen
and dreaded: 'I little thought once,' he had told Shelburne only
two months earlier, 'I should form daily wishes for the health and
life of his most Christian Majesty. I believe now, that no French
subject of the masculine gender prays so devoutly for the preservation of his days as I do, in my humble village. I consider the
peace as hanging on this single life; that life not worth two years'
purchase, and England undone, if war comes; unless war can
prosper, without sinews or hearts, national credit or the affections
of the people'.[2] With thoughts such as these in his mind, his
speech was a temperate plea for a milder and more forgiving
attitude towards America. The colonists, he urged, were the
freedom-loving sons of freedom-loving fathers; it was natural
for them to react violently when they thought their dear-bought
privileges threatened. Their late conduct was unwarrantable, but
the action taken to bring them back to a sense of their duty had
been harsh and indiscriminate and opposed to sound policy. Nor
had the Americans been without provocation. In their gratitude
for the repeal of the Stamp Act they had shown themselves loyal
and dutiful and would have continued to do so but for the new
tax on tea. Why had it been imposed? What could induce Government 'to dress taxation, that father of American sedition, in the
robes of an East India Director?' Could it be pique at the loss of

---

[1] Chatham to Shelburne, 6th April 1774. Chatham Corr. IV, 341.
[2] Chatham to Shelburne, 6th March 1774. Chatham Corr. IV, 331.

the Stamp Act? Whatever it was, Government would now be well
advised 'to adopt a more gentle method'. Lure the colonists back
to their duty by kindness and affection, and they would prove
children worthy of their sire. Only if they still remained turbulent,
should sterner measures be taken, for the day was not far off when
England would need the assistance of her most distant friends.[1]
To Walpole—and to others—this temperate plea was evidence of
Chatham's desire, not to pour oil on troubled waters, not to
prepare for possible war with France, but to curry favour with the
King! As was usual with Walpole when he failed to penetrate
Chatham's mind, he fell back on his journalistic talents and
contented himself with sarcastic pictures of Chatham's dress and
appearance—sarcastic, and yet in retrospect shot with an almost
intolerable pathos. Chatham, according to Walpole, was 'a com-
edian, even to his dress', and so came to the House with 'his
legs wrapped in black velvet boots, and as if in mourning for the
King of France he leaned on a crutch covered with black likewise'.
Two days later Thomas Walpole found him at Hayes 'sitting up
in bed, with a satin eider-down quilt on his feet'. Thomas reported
the scene to his cousin who recorded it with gusto. Chatham 'wore
a duffel cloak, without arms, bordered with a broad purple lace.
On his head he had a night cap, and over that a hat with a broad
brim flapped all round. It was difficult not to smile at a figure
whose meagre jaws and uncouth habiliments recalled Don
Quixote when he received the Duenna to an audience after he had
been beaten and bruised, and was wrapped up in sere-cloths'.[2]
No doubt it was a strange casket, but it enshrined the spirit of
wisdom.

(ii)

Hard upon the heels of their coercive measures against Massachusetts, the Government produced a Quebec Bill for settling
Canadian affairs. It was introduced into a thin House late in the
session—purposely as the opponents thought, but more probably
because the legislative programme was exceptionally heavy. The
Rockinghams contested each stage hotly, and when it came finally
to the Lords on the 17th June, Chatham, in Walpole's words,
'bitterly arraigned the Bill in every part'.[3] The Bill has been

[1] Speech, 26th May 1774.   [2] Walpole. *Last Journals*, I, 350.
[3] *Ibid.*, 354.

described as statesmanlike, and Chatham's opposition to it as 'one
of the most regrettable acts of his public life'.[1] Yet there may be a
different opinion. True statesmanship does not consist simply in
doing the right thing, but in doing it at the right time and in the
right way; and there can be little doubt that, whatever the merits
of the Bill, it was neither necessary nor desirable to press on with
it at that precise moment. Canada ever since its cession had been
under the rule of governors appointed by virtue of the proclamation of 1763. Their instructions required them, among other
things, to ensure religious freedom and to introduce English
law—this latter requirement being incidentally of doubtful
legality.[2] To the Canadians autocratic government was familiar,
and the wisdom of the two governors hitherto appointed—
Murray and Carleton—had smoothed over difficulties and reconciled them to their new way of life. They were now loyal and for
the most part contented subjects with their own language and
religion and some new benefits from English rule. Their only
remaining grievance was the uncertainty resulting from the
introduction of English civil law, which though more liberal than
its French counterpart, they found difficult to understand and
contrary to many of their cherished customs. They were therefore
anxious that the old system should be restored. Both Murray and
Carleton were sympathetic. As far as they could, on their own
authority, they retained the French procedure and urged the
Government to restore it entirely—as could have been done at
once by a fresh proclamation, had the Government so wished.
The sympathy, however, shown to the Canadians offended the
English immigrants—a body very small in numbers, but important
in trade—who wanted English law and nothing else. Annoyed by
the legal confusion, and egged on by propaganda from the south,
these immigrants not only pressed for English law in its entirety,
but also for a change in the constitution by the appointment of an
Assembly of the usual colonial type, the membership of which
they hoped would be reserved for themselves. The need to
come to a decision on these points of policy had been recognised
in England for years past, and indeed had been the subject of
endless reports. All who had studied the matter had, rightly or
wrongly, been convinced that Canada could not be given an
English constitution; that it must develop on French lines with

---

[1] Robertson, p. 260.   [2] See Wrong, pp. 244-5.

an autocratic government and no Assembly; that Roman Catholicism must be the recognised state religion, and that French civil law must prevail. The Bill had been drawn on these lines and except as regards the last point, merely confirmed existing practice. Certainly the Bill was liberal and no doubt statesmanlike, but it could have been introduced at any time during the past ten years, and having been held up so long could, without undue risk, have been held up a little longer. In pushing on with it now, the Government were not thinking of Canada's welfare, but of the ferment in the colonies and the possibility that France might join in the struggle. They were growing nervous; they wanted to ensure the loyalty of French Canada in the event of trouble, and even to use Canada, as North admitted later, to help in subduing the English colonies if they became recalcitrant.[1] It was largely for this purpose that they extended the boundaries of Canada under the bill to include the Great Lakes together with the vast triangle of land between the Ohio and Mississippi rivers, on which the colonies had long been casting envious eyes. The Government could have shown their statesmanlike qualities in better ways; it would have been wiser for them to ponder over the probable results of the Bill, which in fact had little effect on Canadian loyalty but by exasperating the colonists made the American revolution certain and so hastened instead of delaying the war with France. In short, while the Bill itself was possibly excellent and the underlying policy wise, its introduction at that moment so far from being a statesmanlike action, seems to have been an ill-judged and even a disastrous attempt at what in betting circles would be called hedging.

Chatham was under no delusions. He described the Bill as an essential part of 'the whole system of American oppression',[2] appreciating only too keenly the effect it was likely to have on the colonies and through them on France. That would have been enough to ensure his opposition and also to justify it. But perhaps he had something further in his mind. The bill was based on the assumption that Canada must remain French in language, habit and outlook. As such it would be a constant magnet for France whether or not the colonies were quiescent, a perennial fifth column in the heart of America. Should England's aim be to fence

---

[1] Wrong, p. 254, and Coupland, p. 137.
[2] Chatham to Hood, June 1774. Add. MSS. 35,192.

off an alien and consequently dangerous enclave? Or would it not rather be wiser to absorb it gradually and by degrees into the full stream of Empire, winning its adherence by the proven benefits of English law and liberty? The Canadians would have much to gain, such as Habeas Corpus and Trial by Jury, from which the Act would debar them, and much to give to the common fund. It was an alternative and perhaps a less desirable policy, but its relevance lies not only in the course of historical development, but also in the fact that the Bill had hardly become law before the Government found it necessary, or at least expedient, to send private instructions to the Governor for the issue of ordinances which were 'a drastic departure from the "basis" of French law established by the Quebec Act'.[1] That the Governor, with much heartsearching, ignored those instructions because of the situation in which he found himself, does not detract from the argument. One further point: Chatham's criticism of the establishment of the Roman Catholic church should not be taken as evidence of intolerance. He had cleared himself of any such charge in advance when as Secretary of State in 1759 he had accepted the free exercise of the Roman religion as one of the terms of capitulation; and now by his references to the 'Revolution' and the Coronation Oath, he made it clear that what he had in mind was not the religious but the political aspect of Popery, which would be enhanced by its establishment as the state religion.

(iii)

After the coercive Acts had been passed, Parliament was suddenly dissolved (1st October 1774), six months before the due date. North and the King, believing that their policy might end in war, wanted election troubles to be behind them, even if it meant losing a few seats. As it turned out, their losses were small; undoubtedly the country approved their policy.[2] Sure of Parliament, the King had no qualms; on the contrary he seemed almost to welcome the prospect of a fight with the colonies; 'I am not sorry', he declared, 'that the line of conduct seems now chalked out . . . the New England governments are in a state of

---

[1] Coupland, p. 127.
[2] Cf. 'I am much pleased at the state of the supposed numbers in the new Parliament'. George III to North, 14th November 1774. Fortescue, III, 153.

rebellion; blows must decide whether they are to be subject to this country or independent'.[1] He had no doubts about the issue.

Nor was he far wrong in his diagnosis; the colonies were in a state of rebellion, though as yet suppressed, and perhaps suppressible. But they would flare up before long if they were subjected to many more shocks. News of the coercive measures effectively stopped any tendency they might have had to reproach Boston for its Tea Party, and won universal and active sympathy for Massachusetts. Greatly daring, delegates from twelve of the colonies met in Congress at Philadelphia (October 1774), when they resolved to put an end for the time being to all trade with Great Britain and drew up a series of addresses and petitions which were not the less strong for their temperate language.

News of the Quebec Act put a further strain upon them, perhaps the more intolerable because it was founded in fear. The Americans did not see the Act in the same light as the Canadians. In Canada it had surprisingly little effect. It pleased the Seigneurs, who hoped that the reintroduction of French law would give them back some of their lost prestige; it was not displeasing to the priests, who were glad to have their tithes confirmed by statute; it angered the English immigrants and inclined them to sympathise with the Americans; but it left the great body of the inhabitants, the French peasantry, largely unmoved. They knew little, and cared less, about Acts of Parliament; they were not interested in constitutions; they had no wish to succour their old enemies in the south or to join with them against England; nor did they hanker after the return of the French. They had tasted some of the sweets of liberty and now their only wish was to be left in peace to cultivate their lands. Amid the many disputes raging round them, their motto was 'a plague o' both your houses', and their policy the truly modern one of neutralism.[2]

Unlike the Canadians, the colonists viewed the Act with something akin to panic. Here was the prototype of a colony as the King saw it, a blue-print of the status to which they were all to be reduced. The model was life-size and manifest—a colony without any popular element; a legislature and an executive combined in the same person; a Governor uncontrolled by an Assembly; a

---

[1] George III to North, 18th November 1774. Fortescue, III, 153.
[2] Cf. 'The Quebec Act had slight effect in inducing the Canadians to take up arms against the revolted colonies'. Wrong, p. 259.

z

corrupt or at least corruptible judiciary; the rigour of the law without the benefit of habeas corpus; a system of trials without juries; and, to crown all, Popery as the state religion. It was no colony for free Englishmen; it was a compound for slaves. And it was the ordained end towards which the coercive Acts were the first move. Now, if ever, they must strike for liberty.

(iv)

Chatham spent the recess in collecting news from the colonies. 'Nothing', he declared, 'can be so interesting in the present critical moment as authentic information relating to America'.[1] He sought it in every direction—from friends in the City who had correspondents in America; from the votes and proceedings of Congress which seemed to him to 'hold forth to us the most fair and just opening, for restoring harmony and affectionate intercourse as heretofore',[2] and above all from Franklin, with whom he kept in close touch.[3] Everything confirmed him in his view that America was trembling on the verge of rebellion and that not a moment was to be lost in seeking a settlement. Nor had he any doubt of the proper course to be taken. The colonies could be subdued, but could not be kept loyal, by force of arms. They must be won by affection and retained by confidence. As an earnest of England's intentions, the coercive Acts must be repealed at once; the troops, which had been massed in Boston, withdrawn; and the tea duty dropped. But that by itself was not enough. Taxes had been dropped before, only to be reimposed; promises made, only to be broken. Taxation was at the bottom of all the trouble, and the colonists must be freed from fear of it in the future. The only way of reassuring them was to give up the pretended right, and reaffirm the old doctrine of no taxation without representation. To do that the Declaratory Act must be repealed or appropriately amended. By no other means could the storm be calmed.

He decided to offer his solution to Parliament at the earliest moment, and to give it a better chance, tried to win the support of the Rockinghams. It was not easy because he had two formidable obstacles to overcome, only one of which he realised. He knew, or

---

[1] Chatham to Sayre, 9th July 1774. Almon, II, 379.
[2] Chatham to Sayre, 24th December 1774. Almon, II, 385.
[3] 'He inquired much ... I gave him answers'. Franklin, p. 365.

could guess, that the Rockinghams would put up a stiff fight for their favourite Declaratory Act; but he hoped that the crisis would make them not too unyielding. What he did not know was that the Rockinghams refused to admit that there was any crisis. 'I agree with your lordship entirely', Burke wrote to Rockingham, 'the American and foreign affairs will not come to any crisis . . . during the course of the next session. I have my doubts whether those at least of America, will do it for some years to come'.[1] When, therefore, Chatham made approaches, Burke advised Rockingham to find out what Chatham proposed to do, and if possible fall in with his wishes; but to bear in mind that Chatham had ulterior motives; he imagined the Closet door stood ajar to receive him, and was as ever intoxicated at the thought. Rockingham must therefore be on his guard, and to secure himself from Chatham's manœuvres should 'make no approaches *to* him, but show yourself always approachable *by* him'.[2] As usual Rockingham was to be leader, Chatham the follower—a very troublesome follower because, as Richmond pointed out, he might insist on taking the lead.[3]

No meeting took place until the 8th January 1775, when Chatham called at Rockingham's house, to develop his ideas. Perhaps he did not explain himself clearly; or perhaps Rockingham did not wish to understand; but the upshot was that Rockingham, with his exasperating air of prim morality, more fitted for a schoolmarm than a statesman, rebuked Chatham for suggesting that the Declaratory Act had been the cause of all the trouble.[4] As he showed no sign of weakening and could not, or at least did not, make any alternative suggestion, it is not surprising that Chatham thought further discussion useless; but it is surprising that the Whigs should subsequently have accused him of acting 'without concert or communication with any individual'.[5] Rockingham's negative attitude and North's quiescence left Chatham and the King facing each other squarely. Both were certain that war was coming, and coming soon; but while the King waited for it almost with satisfaction, Chatham was bowed down with despair as he pondered over the sadness and madness of a civil war.

Chatham was too ill to attend the opening of Parliament, where

[1] Burke to Rockingham, 16th September 1774. Corr. I, 233.
[2] Burke to Rockingham, 5th December 1774. Corr. I, 250.
[3] Richmond to Rockingham, 28th January 1775. Albemarle, II, 268.
[4] Rockingham to Burke, 8th January 1775. Albemarle, II, 261.
[5] Burke. Quoted Albemarle, II, 265.

North had matters all his own way and where 'the current ran strongly against the Americans'.[1] But on the 20th January (1775), he was able to open his campaign. His plan involved two stages. On the 20th he pleaded that, as a preliminary to a happy settlement, the troops should be recalled from Boston. They were useless where they were, an army of impotence and contempt, penned up in the town and unable to act; and indeed it was as well that they could not act, for 'the first drop of blood shed in civil and unnatural war might be *immedicabile vulnus*'. The Americans could never be defeated. Their merchants might be crushed, their towns destroyed and their luxuries cut off, but their settlers and backwoodsmen scattered over that vast continent were invincible. What troops could England oppose to their three millions of men? Only a few regiments on the spot and seventeen or eighteen thousand soldiers at home. It was our own violent proceedings which had roused their resistance, and the only way to win them back was to repeal not merely Acts of Parliament, but their fears and resentments. We should have to retract our coercive measures sooner or later. How much better to retract them while we could than when we must. How much more becoming for England to make the first advances towards concord, peace and happiness. It was the path of magnanimity; it was the path of justice, dignity and prudence. On the other side lay every danger and hazard, and at the same time a foreign war hanging over our heads, as France and Spain watched and waited for the maturity of our errors.

He received little support, except from Shelburne and Camden. The Rockinghams havered and wavered and several retired without voting. In the end Chatham's motion was lost by 77 to 18.[2]

Chatham refused to be daunted. The first half of his scheme had gone but on the 1st February he offered the second half, like the depleted Sibylline books. It was a difficult, and in some ways a pathetic, task. Chatham was now an old man, broken in health, and far worse, consumed and eaten up with a dark fear that England's offspring was about to destroy her. Folly, ingratitude and ignorance reigned on every side; misunderstanding flourished. The colonies were riotous, the mother country violent, and both were sharpening their swords. For what? For the sake of *amourpropre* in England; for an empty fear in America. In America the taxes imposed by Grenville and Townshend had created not actual

---

[1] Walpole. *Last Journals*, I, 412.   [2] *Ibid.*, 422.

hardship but the fear of it; while in England the loss of the taxes had touched the country's pride rather than her pocket. America was clamouring for a liberty which in practice she already possessed; and England was standing out for a right which she was afraid to use. Never was a greater flame raised from so small a spark. How was the confusion to be sorted out? How was the tempest to be calmed? What hope had an old and shattered man with no more than a handful of followers, two or three doubtful supporters, and the unwilling and intermittent help of the small Rockingham group, whilst against him stood a solid phalanx—the King, the Government, Parliament and a deluded country. Yet Chatham felt that something must be attempted. England must if possible be persuaded that as she was the greater so she was the better fitted to forgive and to hold out the hand of friendship. If he tried and failed, at least he would have done his duty; at least he would have erected a memorial to his own endeavours to serve and save his country.

He presented his plan to the Lords. It bore the title of 'a provisional Act for settling the troubles in America, and for asserting the supreme legislative authority and superintending power of Great Britain over the colonies'. He did not pretend that it was final; he offered it as 'a basis for averting the dangers which now threatened the British Empire', and 'entreated the assistance of the House to digest the crude materials'. Certainly it offered a basis for compromise. It asserted England's supreme legislative power, especially over all things pertaining to 'navigation and trade throughout the complicated system of British commerce', but in return it recognised Congress, it admitted the right of the colonies to raise their own revenues through the Assemblies, and it called on them to consider in Congress the grant of a free aid towards the service of the national debt. It asserted England's right to keep up a standing army in America, but it reformed the judiciary and it repealed all the coercive measures. Truly a comprehensive and a healing 'basis'. To their everlasting shame, the Lords refused it even a first reading. As the copies which still exist proclaim, it 'was rejected and not suffered to lie upon the table'.

XXIV

THE WAR IN AMERICA

(i)

CHATHAM HAD produced his plan hurriedly because he had been told that 'the doom against America was to be pronounced from the Treasury bench, perhaps in a few hours'. He knew that he was rushing matters and expected to be abused for 'dictatorial assumption',[1] as indeed he was, mainly by the Whigs. The effect of the hurry on top of the effort of the past few months was the same as ever; there was a marked reaction and he went down with gout. At first the attack was 'not yet of the most violent sort, but enough to confine him to bed';[2] and encouraged by occasional signs of improvement to hope for a quick recovery, he kept himself abreast of Parliament's proceedings. They were a curious mixture, first (8th February), a Bill to cut off the colonies from access to the fisheries, and then (20th February), an offer by North to exempt from imperial taxation any colony which undertook to contribute its quota towards the cost of common defence and make provision for its own administration—a proposal which Chatham pronounced to be vague, but welcomed as a sign of relenting on the part of the Government.[3] But the graph of his illness was steadily downwards and by the middle of the year he had sunk once more into his terrible slough of despond, where he lay tortured and despairing, while Hester watched over him with tender vigilance, and struggled unaided with the many cares and worries of growing children and pressing debts. There was a blank in Chatham's life for two and a quarter years (February 1775 to May 1777), broken only by rare and fleeting moments of lucidity. In one of them, thinking that he was near death, he gave Addington his political testament, conjuring him to let the world know that he persevered to the end unshaken in his views on

---

[1] Chatham to Stanhope, 31st January 1775. Chatham Corr. IV, 388.
[2] William to Hester, 5th February 1775. P.R.O., G.D. 8-11.
[3] Chatham to Mahon, 20th February 1775. Chatham Corr. IV, 402.

America, and was persuaded that unless effectual measures were taken for a reconciliation with the colonies, France would in a very few years set her foot on English soil; she was waiting only until we were more deeply embroiled in America, and she could assess how far the colonies could stand against us in their own strength.[1]

Meanwhile events took their course in America. The Government expected war there, in the way that men sometimes wait for a trouble in which they do not altogether believe. The King, however, had no doubts, and in December drew up, in his own handwriting, a list of generals who might be sent out.[2] Gage was not considered good enough to be in chief command in the event of war, and the King chose Amherst in his place; but Amherst, in spite of every inducement, refused the appointment. Perforce Gage was continued, and was bolstered up, possibly against his will and certainly not much to his advantage, by the arrival on the spot of Howe, Burgoyne and Clinton. It was symptomatic of the whole situation that the commander-in-chief when the first blood was shed at Lexington (18th April), and when the first deliberate battle was fought at Bunker Hill (17th June), should not have had the Government's full confidence. About the time that fighting broke out, there arrived in America news of Chatham's plan and North's offer. Both were rejected with scorn, but, as Suffolk told Germain, with malicious and meaningless glee, North's offer was 'not so much reviled by a great deal as Lord Chatham's plan'.[3] It was possible, and quite understandable. Chatham's plan was much wider and more comprehensive than North's offer; it was a whole project of peace; and when it arrived America was in the full flow of bitterness and spoiling for a fight. The time for thinking of peace is not just before or just after the first blow has been struck but when weariness has set in, and there are wounds to be licked. In spite of his hurry, Chatham was too late—or much too early! About this time, too, the colonists were invading Canada, which was saved for future greatness in the British Empire, not by the gratitude of the French Canadians for the Quebec Act, but by their utter indifference to both sides, combined with the dogged determination of Carleton and the

[1] Declaration, July 1776. Chatham Corr. IV, 424.
[2] Fortescue, III, 162.
[3] Suffolk to Germain, 15th June 1775. H.M.C. Stopford-Sackville MSS.

sprinkling of English troops under his command—an epic story little known in this country.

There is no need to give details of the fighting in the next two years, but certain broad facts are relevant. The actual outbreak of war came as a shock.[1] Englishmen have a good conceit of themselves and expect a measure of deference, but they are by nature kindly and tolerant; their wrath is much more easily appeased than aroused; they may resent an injury, but they rarely remember it long, and still more rarely make it a *casus belli*. In their exasperation at the colonists, they were ready to condemn recalcitrant assemblies and put down violent mobs, but their thoughts went no further. They looked on the colonists as rapscallions, troublesome and maybe rebellious, certainly deserving of punishment, but in no sense subjects for a full-blooded war. It was a terrible thing to shoot down one's own countrymen, and not lightly to be undertaken. England entered the war reluctantly; many officers resigned and it was difficult to raise recruits;[2] many politicians felt confused. The Government were as confused as any, and needed stiffening by the King. 'I have no doubt', he assured North, 'but the Nation at large sees the conduct of America in its true light, and I am certain any other conduct but compelling obedience would be ruinous and culpable, therefore no consideration could bring me to swerve from the present path which I think myself in duty bound to follow'.[3] It was a sentiment which he repeated time and again. But many of his Cabinet did not see matters in quite the same light. Amongst others, Grafton, who had begun his political life so fairly under the aegis of Chatham, and during Chatham's illness had fallen so headlong from grace, now saw the error of his ways, and began the return journey—too late—by resigning (October 1775). As previously he had, with the best of intentions, betrayed Chatham, so now, with almost better intentions, he betrayed England. His resignation gave the well-meaning, if feeble, Dartmouth an opportunity to slip into his place, and hand over the conduct of American affairs to Lord George Germain, who, as Lord George Sackville, had failed at Minden, and in Chatham's eyes was not fit to be a Minister.

---

[1] 'The Administration was thunderstruck: spirit began to appear, and bitter invectives were published every day against the governing party'. Walpole. *Last Journals*, I, 465.

[2] Cf. North to George III (?), 14th August 1775. Fortescue, III, 245.

[3] George III to North, 5th July 1775. Fortescue, III, 233.

Germain had some talent as a debater and some reputation as an administrator; but he was obstinate and injudicious; the war under his guidance was more likely to be exacerbated than successful; and indeed his first action was to embitter the colonists by sending German mercenaries against them, and encouraging the use of Indians. To make matters worse, he was not altogether *persona grata* to the King.[1] From the outbreak of the fighting to the time of Chatham's reappearance, though the fortunes of war swayed to and fro, nothing really decisive took place in America. At home, North ploughed doggedly on with his automatic majority and his royal backing, but he was not happy;[2] the Opposition, void of policy and easily discouraged, were inclined to secede from Parliament; and the nation at large was apathetic.[3] Nor was the war conducted with any skill; Germain was no Chatham; his strategy was the old strategy of Queen Anne's day, in reverse and under changed conditions. It was no longer suitable and in any event it lacked the master-touch; there was no kindling of the spirit; there was no co-ordination of the parts; there was insufficient preparation; and there was a bad choice of commanders. Perhaps the best English general in America was Carleton. He had been chosen to lead an invading army from Canada down the Hudson route; but Germain who had an old grudge against him, pushed him out in favour of Burgoyne. The combination of Germain and Burgoyne was in due course to end in the surrender at Saratoga. But that was after Chatham's reappearance. In general, the war was following the usual pre-Chatham course—it was a series of largely uncoordinated incidents, too frequently unsuccessful. The Government consoled themselves as best they could. As Wedderburn admitted ruefully: 'in all undertakings carried on by the arms of this country, the beginning has been unprosperous'.[4] There were, however, two striking differences between this and other wars. In the first place there was no enthusiasm for it in England; and in the second place the hardships of winter in camp without proper arms or supplies were rapidly killing the first enthusiasm of the colonists. Had the

---

[1] See George III to North, 13th December 1776. Fortescue, III, 406.

[2] Cf. 'I would abandon the contest were I not intimately convinced in my own conscience that our cause is just and important'. North to Burgoyne. Quoted Hudleston, pp. 87–8.

[3] 'I am sensible of the shocking indifference and neutrality of a great part of the nation'. Burke to Richmond. Corr. I, 293.

[4] Wedderburn to North. Quoted Hudleston, pp. 88–9.

English generals followed up such victories as they won; had Washington, who alone kept the colonial armies in being, faltered; the war would soon have been over. As it was, when Chatham reappeared, there was a growing weariness on both sides. Now, if ever, was the time for reconciliation.

(ii)

Chatham woke to active life in the spring of 1777. His revival was not welcome to the Whigs. During his illness, every rumour of his return had resulted in an outburst of spleen from Burke. 'Acquainted as I am', he remarked in September 1775, 'with the astonishing changes of Lord Chatham's constitution (whether natural or political), I am surprised to find that he is again perfectly restored. Be it so. He will probably play more tricks, but though I hear that his old friend Wilkes is doing all he can to restore his lost reputation in the City, I hope, if proper means are taken, neither of them will be able, in future, to do so much mischief as formerly'.[1] A month later, he refurbished his animosity: 'Lord Chatham's coming out', he wrote to Rockingham, 'is always a critical thing to your Lordship. But even if he should not attack, as it is possible he may not, would it be right for your Lordship, in a great American affair, to let him and his partisans have the whole field to themselves?'[2] No wonder Rockingham's more level-headed follower, Sir George Savile, bemoaned the fact that the Opposition, small as it was, was 'rendered less respectable than even a Minority need be'.[3] Not that the Rockinghams had either a policy of their own or perseverance. During Chatham's absence they became more and more ineffective and finally for all practical purposes ceased attending Parliament. Their attitude was well summed up by Savile. 'We have fully enough, I conceive, expressed ourselves in Parliament. To do it again and again would be, I think, cheapening ourselves only to disturb that good humour with which the good company is doing mischief'. The only remarkable thing about his sentiment was that he did venture to suggest one last effort as 'a *pièce justificative*, but by no means with the *least* expectation of its having the *least* present effect'.[4]

[1] Burke to Rockingham, 14th September 1775. Corr. I, 286.
[2] Burke to Rockingham, 17th October 1775. Corr. I, 296.
[3] Savile to Priestley, 29th October 1775. H.M.C. Savile Foljambe MSS.
[4] Savile to Rockingham, 15th January 1777. Albemarle, II, 304.

It was impossible for Chatham to take so defeatist an attitude. What held him back from hammering again and again at the Government's door was sheer physical and nervous prostration. He had suffered greatly and was still suffering: 'my poor Lord', said the sad Hester, 'goes on just the contrary of our wishes for him';[1] but by degrees symptoms of improvement appeared. At the end of September (1776), Addington felt the time had come to boost his self-confidence by cutting down the amount of attention he was given; too much, he said, might 'be the means of nourishing and prolonging the hypochondriacal part of the disorder'.[2] The improvement so happily begun continued, and towards the end of May Chatham was able to tell Camden that 'he was enough recovered to hope to be able to crawl to the House of Lords; he means to be there, on Thursday next, in order to move the consideration of the American war'. He asked Camden to summon the House accordingly.[3]

Actually he was unable to come till the Friday (30th May 1777), when he dragged himself into the House, with the aid of a crutch and swathed in flannel. The news of his arrival spread like wildfire, and peers and commoners surged round to see this limping ghost of the past, this haunting legend from the great days of old. It was a sight to wring the heart. Chatham was a pale shadow of his former self, his voice weak and low and to be heard only with difficulty, his fire apparently quenched. But the wisdom and the foresight were as keen, and the patriotism and pride in his country as bright as ever. He had come because he knew that men were momentarily elated with false hopes, springing from a few minor victories, and at the same time were stirred by a useless anger at lost trade and difficulties at home, difficulties that are inseparable from war. He came too because he had learnt that France was financing the colonies, and, more ominous, that American representatives had gone to Paris for purposes that were only too clear. The danger was great; the time was short. There was, he told the House of Lords, only a fleeting moment before France recognised the independence of the colonies and entered into a treaty with them. The moment that happened we must declare war against France, however unready we might be. That

[1] Hester to Captain Hood, 14th June 1776. Add. MSS. 35,192.
[2] Addington to Hester, 29th September 1776. P.R.O.
[3] Chatham to Camden, 26th May 1777. Chatham Corr. IV, 432.

was the prospect facing us, and unless we met it, the country was undone. What prevented us from forestalling the peril by being reconciled to our colonies? We called them rebels, but they were only defending their unquestionable rights. Nor could we in any case conquer them; it was impossible. And in attempting it we were forgetting their importance to us—for trade in times of peace, for support in times of war. We had been the aggressors, and it became us to be the first in offering reparation. He had suggested methods in the past, but conditions were always altering, and always for the worse. The Bill he had tried to introduce in 1775 no longer sufficed, nor was it any use harping, as the Government did, on unconditional submission. We should never obtain it, nor did we deserve it. Let us try instead unconditional redress. A repeal of the laws of which the colonists complained would be the first step. If conciliation took the place of chastisement, the King would be once more enthroned in the hearts of his American subjects and the Lords by contributing to so great, glorious and salutary a work would receive benediction from every part of the British Empire.[1]

But no one was prepared to listen. The Lords rejected his motion, and the King described it as 'highly unseasonable'. 'Like most of the productions of that extraordinary brain', he told North, 'it contains nothing but specious words and malevolence', and went on to explain briefly but clearly the difference between Chatham's standpoint and his own, as seen by himself. Chatham spoke of the Americans as though they were 'poor, mild persons who after unheard of and repeated grievances had no choice but slavery or the sword', whereas to the King it was self-evident that 'the too great lenity of this country increased their pride and encouraged them to rebel'. More interesting because more fundamental in baring his soul, was his final remark: 'thank God the nation does not see the unhappy contest through his mirror; if his sentiments were adopted, I should not esteem my situation in this country as a very dignified one, for the Islands would soon also cast off all obedience'.[2] Kings are alone judges of their own dignity, and so long as dignity was the King's motive, Chatham's fight for sanity, tolerance and the maintaining of the bonds of kinship was doomed to failure. His differences with the King and

[1] Speech, 30th May 1777.
[2] George III to North, 31st May 1777. Fortescue, III, 449.

Government extended not only to the origin of the dispute, but to the immediate prospects. Chatham was convinced that the break with France was a matter of weeks rather than months, and that a military victory over the colonists was impossible. What could we hope to achieve beyond the effective range of our ships? What did we hope to conquer? The map of America? For nothing else was in our power. In contradistinction, North considered it as 'most probable that we shall not during the course of this year have any contest with any European power',[1] while the King gave it as his opinion that 'the Americans will treat before the winter'. In view of this belief he was anxious that the speech at the rising of Parliament should give no encouragement to 'many very good friends' who were under the impression 'that there is some intention rather to plaister up the breach with the colonies than radically to cure the evil'.[2] When, therefore, the House rose on the 6th June, there was little sign of weakening in the official attitude towards the colonies. But individual doubts were rising and Barrington besought the King to be allowed to retire.[3]

(iii)

During the recess, events in England were mainly symptomatic. The King gave way to an exuberant outburst of joy on hearing that Burgoyne had captured Ticonderoga. According to Walpole, he 'ran into the Queen's room crying I have beat them! beat all the Americans',[4] but his jubilation suggests an element of relief rather than a settled expectation of victory. If the King was cock-a-hoop, North was suffering a constant and painful fall in his hopes. The conviction he had expressed in March that the French would not move till the next year at the earliest, had given way by August to a hope that they would remain quiet until anyhow October; and he warned the King that 'we must be ready to meet them at that time wherever they may think proper to attack or insult us',[5] a thought which illuminated for him in alarming fashion our state of unpreparedness. Other Ministers, besides North, were gloomy and depressed. But perhaps in the long run the most

[1] North to George III, 20th March 1777. Fortescue, III, 431.
[2] George III to North, 4th June 1777. Fortescue, III, 450.
[3] Barrington to George III, 5th June 1777. Fortescue, III, 451.
[4] Walpole. *Last Journals*, II, 42.
[5] North to George III, 22nd August 1777. Fortescue, III, 470.

serious event of the recess was an accident trifling in itself.
Chatham, out riding, was thrown from his horse, and the fall
brought back his gout and confined him to bed. It was ominous
that his bodily strength should be steadily failing as the need
for it was rapidly rising. In bed he had time enough to brood
over the darkening scene. 'News from America', he complained,
'is slow. The delay is at least a sort of protraction of our political
existence; for the event, I consider as ruin; be the victory to
whichever host it pleases the Almighty to give it, poor England
will have fallen upon her own sword'.[1] To Addington he wrote
in the same desponding strain: 'Could I be the fortunate instrument of healing the wounds of a distressed country, which stands
upon the perilous edge of a fatal precipice, I should have lived not
in vain; but alas! I see no way of political salvation—*fuit Ilium et
ingens gloria*'.[2] Yet if desponding in private, he had no intention of
despairing in public. He must still while life remained press his
remedies on the King, on the Government, on the country: 'in
the present terrifying crisis, to be silent on the first day of the
session', Hester told an old friend at Chatham's bidding, 'would
be want of duty to the King, and utter insensibility to the public
calamities'.[3]

He had no intention of being silent himself; nor, if he could
help it, should anyone be whose voice might help, and for that
purpose he did his best to whip up a united opposition. But his
prospects were poor. Burke, empty of ideas, was playing the
ostrich: 'I have thought little on business', he told Rockingham,
'and like so very little the general aspect of affairs, that I endeavour
to banish them out of my imagination as much as I can. I have not
read so much as a newspaper for near a month past.'[4] The other
Rockingham leaders were debating the pros and cons of secession,
and the relative merits of negative and active opposition. They
were in no sense fired by the knowledge that Chatham was well
enough to attend and was resolved to speak. Burke indulged in
his usual sneer: 'Lord Chatham's figure had been for some time
exposed to several; the blood of St. Januarius began to liquify. He
was perfectly alive; very full of conversation; nowise communica-
tive; and fully resolved to go down to the House of Lords on the

[1] Chatham to Temple, 24th September 1777. *Grenville Papers*, IV, 573.
[2] Chatham to Addington, 26th September 1777. Chatham Corr. IV, 443.
[3] Hester to Lancelot Brown, 13th November 1777. Chatham Corr. IV, 449.
[4] Burke to Rockingham, September 1777. Albemarle, II, 313.

first day of the session. But I am afraid that the present American news will put as many folds of flannel about him, as there are linen fillets about an Egyptian mummy; but like a true obeyer of the laws, *he* will be buried in woollen'.[1] Not knowing, or, if he knew, ignoring Burke's jibes, Chatham summoned Rockingham and Grafton and other friends and followers to the fight, and managed to endue them with some faint semblance of vigour.

Parliament met on the 20th November (1777). The Speech held out the hope of obtaining, not victory or peace, but an 'important success' in America, and hinted at the possibility of trouble in Europe. It ended by declaring that the King would steadily pursue the measures already adopted for re-establishing constitutional subordination in all parts of the Empire. When the Address had been moved and seconded, Chatham brought up his amendment. His speech was a strong plea for peace while there was yet time, a plea based on solid argument and accompanied by a trenchant indictment of the King's encroachments and the Government's inadequacy, and all couched in the golden eloquence to which Chatham alone held the key. These, he said, were perilous times, which demanded not adulation but truth. It was customary for the Crown to seek Parliament's advice and assistance, but today far from asking advice, the Crown had proclaimed its unalterable determination to pursue measures—the measures that had already brought ruin to our doors. It was a shameful truth that not only the power and strength of this country were being wasted away, but that her well-earned glories, her true honour and dignity were being sacrificed. France had insulted us by encouraging and sustaining America, and she had at that moment ambassadors and representatives of our rebel colonies in Paris. Could our Ministers sustain a more humiliating disgrace? It was a position in which the dignity of nations demanded a decisive conduct: and our Ministers dared not interfere. In such a ruinous and ignominious situation where we could neither act with success nor suffer with honour, we must remonstrate in language strong and loud enough to reach the King's ear through the delusions which surrounded it. The desperate state of our arms abroad was in part known. In three campaigns we had done nothing and suffered much. Howe had been obliged to withdraw from New York; Burgoyne's army had met with reverses and might at that very moment be a total loss.

[1] Burke to Rockingham, 5th November 1777. Corr. I, 357.

What more was to come, we should soon know. But one thing could be known now: we could not conquer America. Swell every expense and every effort, it would be for ever vain and impotent —doubly so from our reliance on mercenaries and the inhuman employment of Indians with their tomahawks and scalping knives. The Address had referred to the American views of independence. No man wished more for the due dependence of America on this country than Chatham did; and the object which all ought to unite in seeking, was to preserve that dependency and not confirm the independency into which the Government's measures were driving them. The attainment of that object was still possible. America was in ill-humour with France on some points that had not entirely answered her expectations. Let us wisely take advantage of the moment for reconciliation. America had a natural leaning towards England, and in spite of recent events a very considerable part of it was still loyal. If we expressed a wise and benevolent disposition to yield to them those immutable rights of nature and those constitutional liberties to which they were equally entitled with ourselves, we should confirm the loyal part and conciliate the adverse. America was not in that state of desperate and contemptible rebellion which this country had been deluded into believing. It recognised its duties as well as its rights and would be content to admit a dependency from which it drew benefits and in which it had a stake.

As to foreign countries, we should not deceive ourselves. Their disposition was not, as the Speech suggested, pacific and friendly. The uniform assistance given by France to America and her extraordinary preparations by land and sea should rouse us to a sense of her real intentions and our own dangers. What could we oppose to the combined force of our enemies? Less than five thousand troops in England and perhaps three thousand in Ireland; and scarcely twenty ships of the line at sea and those badly found.

We could not conciliate America by our present measures, nor subdue her by any measures. What then could we do? If it were a question of supporting a just war to maintain the rights and honour of the country, Chatham would strip the shirt from his back; but this war was unjust in its principle, impracticable in its means, and ruinous in its consequences. He had hoped that the Ministers would have confessed their errors and tried to redeem them; but as they had not, Parliament must interpose. They should recommend to the King an immediate cessation of hostilities and the commencement of a treaty to restore peace and liberty to America, strength and happiness to England, security and permanent prosperity to both countries.[1]

In the course of the debate that followed Suffolk defended the employment of Indians on the ground that 'it was perfectly justifiable to use all the means that God and nature put into our hands'. Chatham leapt indignantly to his feet. 'I do not know', he cried, 'what ideas that Lord may entertain of God and nature; but I know that such abominable principles are equally abhorrent to religion and humanity'; and in a flow of wonderful and moving eloquence he denounced the Government for letting loose 'savage hell-hounds against our brethren and countrymen in America'; and called on each part of the House to stamp Suffolk's doctrine with an indelible stigma of public abhorrence. It was retorted on him that he had himself, in the previous war, authorised the employment of Indians; and in the curious way of debates, this inconsistency, which he at first denied but was finally obliged by Amherst's evidence to admit, was held, not so much to condemn Chatham's previous actions as to justify the present practice. Chatham was of course guilty of both forgetfulness and inconsistency; but neither do away with his argument and both tend to emphasise a ruling passion of his life. His own direct share had been to countenance an existing use of Indians mainly for camp services and scouting; and his attitude is well exemplified in his despatch to Amherst on 'the happy completion of the great work entrusted to your care', in which he expressed thanks to all the troops concerned, including 'His Majesty's faithful Indian allies under Sir William Johnson', and added that 'His Majesty has learnt with sensible pleasure, that, by the good order kept by Sir William Johnson among the Indians, no act of cruelty has stained the lustre of the British arms'.[2] But, whilst Chatham can certainly be absolved from any taint of cruelty, there is no doubt that his burning patriotism always and at all times biased his judgment, even his moral judgment. Scalping Frenchmen would have revolted him, but nothing like so much as scalping Englishmen; and the source of his indignation against Suffolk's doctrine was not

[1] Speech, 20th November 1777.
[2] Pitt to Amherst, 24th October 1760. Kimball, II, 344.

2 A

simply hatred of cruelty in the abstract, but hatred of cruelty towards 'our ancient connexions, friends and relations'.

Chatham's efforts roused the Rockinghams who decided to demand a debate on the state of the nation. They settled on the 2nd February, as a suitable date, and consulted Chatham as to whether they should move for that date to be fixed, or merely give formal notice, or wait the lapse of time.[1] Chatham had no doubt; the public interest must be sustained and the Opposition must show itself united and the Government kept on the stretch. 'I think', he said, 'the *direct right forward* proceeding, the most advisable. I fear that all delay would tend to cool a public already too cold; and that, moreover, *indecision* might create jealousy and stand in the way of returning mutual *confidence* and *reunion*, so necessary to the preservation of the whole; *all must unite* at present, or all must be lost. I grieve that my own health does not enable me to offer much assistance, but such attendance as I can give shall be devoted to the public'.[2] Accordingly on the 2nd December, Richmond moved for an enquiry to be held. He was supported powerfully by Chatham who, giving one of his wide and masterly surveys of our military situation *vis-à-vis* the French, suggested that the enquiry should be extended to cover not only America but the Mediterranean and the state of the navy. In the course of his speech he reminded the House of his successful treatment of the Scottish Jacobites at the outbreak of the Seven Years' War, and asked whether a similar treatment of 'the Whigs and freemen of America whom you call rebels' might not produce a similar effect. 'They would', he declared, 'fight your battles; they would cheerfully bleed for you; they would render you superior to all your foreign enemies; they would bear your arms triumphant to every quarter of the globe'—a prophetic vision of the valour and devotion of other sons of the Empire. And he ended with a warning: 'My Lords, I would have you consider, should this war be pushed to extremities, the possible consequences'.[3]

[1] Rockingham to Chatham, 27th November 1777. Chatham Corr. IV, 457.
[2] Chatham to Rockingham, 27th November 1777. Albemarle, II, 324.
[3] Speech, 2nd December 1777.

XXV

THE END

(i)

RICHMOND'S MOTION was accepted, but even while the debate was proceeding, news was rapidly approaching England which confirmed Chatham's sadly-prophetic fears, and completely altered the situation both at home and in America. It was on the evening of the 2nd December, that despatches arrived from Carleton telling of Burgoyne's surrender with his whole army at Saratoga (12th October 1777). The effect was instantaneous. Englishmen react strongly to disaster, and if the war had been popular or against a foreign country, they would have girded themselves in earnest. As it was, recruiting prospered for a moment in the big cities and ports and in the Highlands.[1] But mingled with the grim resolve and overlying it was a widespread revulsion of feeling and a belief that the Government must fall and the policy change. North partook of that belief; his fortitude broke down, and he entreated the King to accept his resignation. But the King was endowed with a resolution which, if merely obstinate in essence, had yet a touch of royal dignity about it. Though it is said that on receipt of the news he 'fell into agonies',[2] he recovered himself quickly, and turned to the task of upholding his despondent Minister, nerving him to further effort by the suggestion that to resign in a time of difficulty was in fact to abandon his duty. North was reluctantly persuaded to remain in office, half-fearing, but perhaps not wholly expecting, that he was destined to stumble on to further disasters and fresh disgraces.[3] But even the King recognised that Saratoga had altered the whole outlook and advised North that for the present it would be wisest 'to act only on the defensive with the army'.[4] North had very little say in the disposition of the troops but even he could see that the inactive

[1] See e.g. George III to North, 15th December 1777. Fortescue, III, 513.
[2] Walpole. *Last Journals*, II, 80.
[3] North to George III, 4th December 1777. Fortescue, III, 503.
[4] George III to North, 4th December 1777. Fortescue, III, 503.

occupation of a few coast towns would never subdue the colonies, and he began from that moment to turn over in his mind 'a plan for treating with the Americans'.[1]

The Opposition, in the meantime, leapt to the attack like a pack of hounds worrying and snapping at the Ministers. Chatham joined with them, but with this difference, that while the majority were content mainly with personal abuse, he looked more deeply into causes with his profound strategic knowledge. His starting point was that a great catastrophe had occurred, and whether Burgoyne or the Ministers were primarily to blame could not be judged till the facts were known. In order that they might be known he moved for the publication of the orders and instructions sent to Burgoyne. In his speech he declared that the strategy so far as it had transpired at home 'justified him in affirming that the measures were founded in weakness, barbarity and inhumanity'. Further than that, the plan of invading the colonies from Canada, for which he believed the Government were solely responsible, was 'a most wild, uncombined and mad project', and even if it had been successful would have been a wanton waste of blood and treasure. Clearly Chatham had in mind the fact that if troops had to be taken from Montreal to New York, they should have gone, not by a long and difficult land route, but by sea, where as yet our fleet was in complete control, and where we could have exerted the full pressure, and enjoyed the many advantages, of sea power.[2] But there was little good in brooding over the past. Facts must be recognised, and Chatham emphasised once more the pressing need to withdraw our troops entirely as a preliminary to peace. 'Ministers', he summed up, 'had undertaken a rash enterprise, without wisdom to plan or ability to execute'.[3] Evidently in his opinion they must go.

His motion was negatived, and six days later Parliament rose for the Christmas holidays. In moving the adjournment North informed the Commons that on their return he would lay before them a plan for treating with the Americans. The Opposition urged that Parliament should remain in session because of the crisis. Chatham, in the Lords, argued that their presence was necessary, not merely to give advice, but to prevent the Government from

[1] Walpole. *Last Journals*, II, 84.
[2] See Hudleston, p. 226.
[3] Speech, 5th December 1777.

rash acts. In everything they had done, the Ministers had proved themselves weak, ignorant and mistaken. They were totally unworthy of confidence. Now they were speaking of conciliating America, but the men who had plunged the country into its present perilous position were not the men to rescue it; nor could the men who had relied on German bayonets and Indian toma-hawks hope for success as negotiators. The Lords should forgo their pleasures, and spend their time enquiring into the past, providing remedies for the present and preventing evils in the future. France was clearly meditating some immediate and decisive stroke and the question of home defence should therefore be taken at once into earnest consideration. We had stripped England to conquer America, and still had not succeeded and never would. We had no hopes of raising further troops on the Continent; and how in the circumstances could we protect our own Island. All possibilities should be studied and the militia revived.[1] But his pleas were ignored, and Parliament adjourned from the 11th December, to the 20th January, a period big with fate.

(ii)

Chatham's fear that the French were contemplating some decisive stroke was as prophetic as his fear that Burgoyne's army would be lost. Saratoga brought French hesitations to an end. On the 17th December (1777), they told Franklin in Paris that they were ready to acknowledge America as an independent state, and to enter into a treaty of commerce with her, provided that she would agree to make no peace with England which did not involve England's recognition of her independence. Clearly such a treaty, as Chatham had long ago warned, would mean immediate war with France and an end to all hope of reconciliation. Some hints of the possibility, together with the disaster at Saratoga, so shook the Rockingham Whigs that they now gave up the struggle and adopted the idea of forestalling France by making a voluntary offer of independence from this end. Such an idea seemed disas-trous to Chatham; it meant the final overthrow of all he had worked and toiled for throughout his parliamentary career. He had championed the colonies through good report and ill; he had fought France on their behalf more than on England's; and he

[1] Speech, 11th December 1777.

had snatched victory out of disaster and won for them safety and a glorious future. When he had completed his work, by some curious twist of fate all had been thrown into jeopardy for the sake of a trifling revenue—a peppercorn as he called it in angry contempt—a revenue clamped down on the colonies foolishly and as he thought illegally, before they had had time to recover from years of constant war and harrying. He had striven to overcome this folly, and had been foiled, not by declared enemies, but first by members of his own 'cousinhood' and then by so-called allies who were timid and doubting towards himself and strong only in their own conceits and jealousies. And now these same allies were bringing final destruction on his masterpiece; they were overthrowing the monument which he had raised to his own memory and to England's honour. For the first time he felt not only alone but hopeless. 'I wish', he told Shelburne, 'I might be permitted to live and die in my village, rather than sacrifice the little remnant I have left of life to the hopeless labours of controversial speculation in Parliament. If I can avoid it, I mean to come little to Parliament, unless I may be of some service. I know I cannot alter in the point, and if others who have as good a right to judge cannot either, I had better stay away. I shall thereby do less mischief to the public. I will as soon subscribe to *Transubstantiation as to Sovereignty by right in the Colonies*'.[1] Ironically, in this view he was at one with the King: 'I do not think,' the King told North, 'there is a man either bold or mad enough to presume to treat for the Mother Country on such a basis'.[2] Fate, in sardonic humour, was to bring the King and Chatham in one sense ever closer together, though in another ever wider apart. As Chatham retired further into the loneliness of his sad forebodings, the news from France was driving the King to adopt his whole policy. There was in the end to be little difference between them save the gulf of a fixed and unalterable hatred on the part of the King.

(iii)

Throughout the winter North and the King were making tentative approaches to Franklin through the agency of a Moravian preacher, Hutton, but Franklin was not encouraging: 'a

---

[1] Chatham to Shelburne, 18th December 1777. *Macmillan Magazine*, July 1894.
[2] George III to North, 13th January 1778. Fortescue, IV, 14.

peace', he replied, 'you may undoubtedly obtain by dropping all your pretensions to govern us', but no peace would be lasting or profitable unless the affections of the Americans were also re-covered; and no peace could ever be signed with the present Ministers whose hands were red, wet and dropping with blood.[1] If Franklin was cold and aloof, the French were evidently pre-paring for war; but this fact left the King unmoved: 'my mind', he said, 'is perfectly prepared to meet what I should certainly think a very unhappy event, from the consciousness that I have scrupulously attempted to avoid [it], and that without one single grievance France chooses to be the aggressor'.[2] But North could not be so calm. His character was strange and perplexing. He had many excellent qualities, well fitting him to lead the House; nor was he so completely deficient in statesmanship as is often supposed; he saw far more clearly than the King the probable outcome of the policy he was pursuing. But he was afflicted with one extraordinary weakness, which he recognised and deplored, which certainly caused him untold suffering, and which finally brought ruin on himself, his Government and England. He was, for whatever reason, utterly unable to withstand the King. In his presence he was like a rabbit fascinated by a stoat; his resolution disappeared; his convictions were hamstrung. Through this fatal weakness on his part, combined with his skill in handling the House, the King to his abiding joy gained complete control of the Government and complete mastery over policy. But for all that, North's eyes were fully open to the folly of the course he was obliged to pursue. He did not like coercing the colonies; he did not approve of the war; he foresaw the inevitable break with France; but carried along by the sheer will-power of the King, he went forward doggedly hoping for the best. Events, however, were proving too strong. Added to the news from France was a rising uneasiness in England. It showed itself in many quarters. Winchilsea refused an appointment as ambassador; Howe asked to be recalled from America; Germain showed dissatisfaction in the Cabinet. The mounting catalogue of worries became too great, and shortly after Parliament reassembled, North poured out his troubles to the King: 'The anxiety of his mind', he wrote, in the curious *oratio obliqua* he generally adopted, 'for the last two months

[1] Franklin to Hutton, 1st February 1778. Works, p. 416.
[2] George III to North, 7th January 1778. Fortescue, IV, 6.

has deprived Lord North of his memory and understanding'. He had now to fulfil his promise of presenting Parliament with a plan of reconciliation, 'but the former opinions, the consistency, and the pride of his political friends and himself stand in the way of everything that would be effective'. There were several possible plans, but they all had serious drawbacks and so he came to his mournful conclusion: 'Lord North is in such a situation that, whatever he does must be attended with some disgrace, and much misery to himself, and what is worse, perhaps, with some detriment to the public. In this case perhaps a change which might bring into his room some person less pledged than himself might be of advantage to His Majesty's service'.[1] The King's reply was typical of his ruthlessness where North was concerned. Though touchy beyond words about his own honour, he calmly advised North to go back on his promise: 'you will remember', he said, 'that before the recess I strongly advised you not to bind yourself to bring forward a proposition for restoring tranquillity to North America', and now he suggested that North had better put all idea of it out of his mind—not necessarily for ever but certainly for the time being.[2] North had already postponed the matter eleven days; he now with misgiving and at the King's instigation, postponed it a further sixteen. It was during this sterile pause that the treaty between France and the United States was signed in Paris (6th February 1778).

(iv)

The belief that a treaty was either actually or soon to be signed, was growing, and with it came indications of the break-up of the Government. The Chancellor was threatening to resign; and resignations were expected from other quarters. Almost hopefully North wrote to the King: 'There is no doubt but if a change of administration should become requisite, Lord Chatham is of all the Opposition, the person who would be of most service to his Majesty, and probably the least extravagant in his demands'[3]. He was voicing the general wish that Chatham should return once more as the saviour of his country. It was a wish to be heard in

[1] North to George III, 29th January 1778. Fortescue, IV, 26.
[2] George III to North, 31st January 1778. Fortescue, IV, 30.
[3] North to George III, 16th February 1778. Fortescue, IV, 38.

quiet hints and whispers. It was a wish to be heard boldly voiced in Parliament. It was always now present in North's mind. It was the one hope to which people were turning.

Failing to get any satisfactory response from the King, North felt obliged to bring forward his plan of reconciliation. He did so on the 17th February (1778). Under it he proposed to repeal at once the Acts dealing with the Massachusetts Charter and imposing a duty on tea; he promised that no 'internal' taxes should be levied on the colonies, and that any revenue from 'external' taxes should be applied to the public services of the colony; and he appointed Commissioners to negotiate a peace with Congress, giving them full powers to end hostilities and to suspend any or all of the Acts passed since 1763. It was a most ignominious surrender of everything for which the King had been ·fighting. The Government supporters listened with amazement, but had no option but to vote for it. Nor could the Opposition well object. It was passed by both Houses to an accompaniment of sarcasms at which North inwardly winced. But two facts made the plan hopeless. In the first place it did not grant the independence which had been recognised eleven days earlier by the French treaty, and in the second place if there were still a moment of time before that treaty was ratified, Congress would never negotiate with the Ministers responsible for the war. The plan was not workable without a change of ministry.

North received official notice of the signing of the treaty between France and America on the 13th March, and the same day recalled our Ambassador from Paris. From that moment, with the prospect of a French war in front of him, he became importunate in his pleas to the King to be released from office in favour of Chatham. The King with a cynicism that was almost sadistic, gave him leave to approach Chatham, but only with an insulting message, 'you must acquaint him that I shall never address myself to him but through you and on a clear explanation that he is to step forth to support an administration whenever [? where] you are to be the first Lord of the Treasury and Chancellor of the Exchequer'. To make his own position clearer, he added: 'no advantage to this country nor personal danger can ever make me address myself for assistance either to Lord Chatham or any other branch of the Opposition. Honestly I would rather lose the Crown I now wear than bear the ignominy of possessing it under their shackles. I might write volumes if I would state my feeling of my mind. . . . Should Lord Chatham wish to see me before he gives an answer, I shall most certainly refuse'.[1]

On the strength of this extraordinary mandate, North sounded Chatham and found, as he told the King, 'that he wishes to speak to His Majesty in order that his plans may not be misrepresented; that he expects to be a confidential Minister, that he must have the appearance of forming the Ministry, that the most important offices being filled with efficient men, Lord Chatham's desire would be in everything to attend to the wishes of His Majesty'.[2] The King's reply was that these conditions—surely reasonable enough—were 'totally contrary to the only ground upon which I could have accepted the services of that perfidious man'.[3] There followed piteous letters from North and heartless replies from the King, until at last, greatly daring, North resigned. At the King's command, however, he agreed to remain in office till the end of the session, or even beyond, to allow the King time to make other arrangements, and in the meanwhile to keep his resignation a secret. But he emphasised, again and again, that the country, under his guidance, was 'totally unequal to a war with Spain, France and America', and that 'peace with America, and a change in the Ministry are the only steps which can save this country'.[4]

(v)

It may be doubted if the King, in spite of his promise, had any intention of releasing North, but North was comforted by the thought that 'His Majesty begins to think seriously of making some new arrangement'.[5] While North was thus looking forward hopefully to Chatham's third premiership, the Rockinghams were deserting him for the last time. Richmond told him that he intended to propose that the colonies should be given their independence. Chatham, ill and dying, expressed his 'unspeakable concern' at their difference of opinion. He acknowledged his growing despair of being able to bring about a successful and

[1] George III to North, 15th March 1778. Fortescue, IV, 57.
[2] North to George III, 16th March 1778, Fortescue, IV, 59.
[3] George III to North, 16th March 1778. Fortescue, IV, 59.
[4] North to George III, 25th March 1778. Fortescue, IV, 77.
[5] North to George III, 1st April 1778. Fortescue, IV, 92.

honourable issue, but declared that he would try once more, 'before this bad grows worse'.[1]

True to his promise, on the 7th April, he struggled up to town, to strike one last blow for the country of his pride. He entered the House supported on either hand by his son, William, and his son-in-law, Mahon, and with his stately, old-world courtesy bowed to the assembled peers. Moved by a sense of his greatness, and perhaps by some premonition of the end, they stood to do honour to this gaunt, shattered remnant of a man, as he was led rather than walked to his seat, the most famous and the loneliest of them all. He had come to oppose Richmond, that same Richmond who in his first days as a peer had called him an insolent Minister, and directly Richmond had spoken, he rose with an effort, to reply, his face colourless and shrunken, and only his eyes gleaming with something of their old intensity. He stood with difficulty; he spoke with difficulty; his words were barely audible, and at times his mind wandered so that words eluded him altogether. But, as though they were listening to an oracle, the whole House kept breathlessly silent.

There were two great issues that jostled in his mind, and at times became confused—the retention of America, and the menace of France. America came first. He rejoiced, he said, that the grave had not closed upon him and that he was still alive to lift up his voice against the dismemberment of this ancient and most noble monarchy. Pressed down by infirmities, he was little able to assist his country, but while he had sense and memory he would never consent to deprive the King of his fairest inheritance. Then, turning to the menace of France, he declared that a country which had survived Danish depredations, Scottish inroads, the Norman invasion and the Spanish Armada, should never yield to the House of Bourbon. Nor should it halt between two opinions. If peace could not be preserved with honour, war should be begun without hesitation. He was not well informed of the resources of the kingdom, but he trusted it still had sufficient strength to maintain its just rights. 'But', he ended, 'any state is better than despair. Let us at least make one effort; and if we must fall, let us fall like men'.[2] It was the speech of a dying patriot, and when it was finished he sank back exhausted. Richmond answered him 'with

---

[1] Chatham to Richmond, 6th April 1778. Chatham Corr. IV, 518.
[2] Speech, 7th April 1778.

great tenderness', we are told,[1] and we may hope it was so—but with no alteration of his views. Chatham attempted to rise once more, but fell back in a faint. He was carried out of the Chamber, and the Lords adjourned as a mark of respect. As a mark of a different sort, the King when the news came to his ear, wrote to North: 'may not the political exit of Lord Chatham incline you to continue at the head of my affairs'.[2] It is a catastrophic death that brings benefit to no one.

Since that day men have argued whether Chatham's view was right or Richmond's, and the verdict has usually gone against Chatham. Yet two thoughts are perhaps worth pondering. Chatham's view was based on the supposition that he would become the responsible Minister. There was at least the hope that the loyalists in America would have responded to his appeal and overborne the numerically smaller body of extremists; and if that had failed, it is at least likely that Chatham, had he lived and been in office, would have conducted the war against France more skilfully and more successfully, and have been able to exert to better effect the blockade of America which, after his death, nearly brought the colonists down. The second thought is that Richmond's motion, whether right or wrong, was singularly ill-timed. It split the Opposition at a crucial moment, to the King's delight,[3] and was quite useless as there was no prospect of its being adopted. Its main result was to drag Chatham from his sick-bed to the House, and one may believe hasten his death. Had he remained quietly at home, he would have been a potential premier, giving North a chance to go at the end of the session, in which case the course of events would have been so altered that speculation becomes meaningless.

But it was not to be. Chatham had fought his last fight and had lost. He was carried down to Hayes, where he lingered on a few weeks surrounded by the family he loved. On the 11th May, he died. Let Sir Philip Francis speak his epitaph:

'He is dead, and has left nothing in this world that resembles him. He is dead; and the sense, and honour, and character, and understanding of the nation are dead with him'.[4]

---

[1] Walpole. *Last Journals*, II, 160.
[2] George III to North, 8th April 1778. Fortescue, IV, 102.
[3] See George III to North, 2nd February 1778. Fortescue, IV, 33.
[4] Chatham Corr. IV, 177 (*n.*).

BIBLIOGRAPHY

Addresses of the Corporation of the City of London. 1865

Albemarle, Earl of   *Memoirs of the Marquis of Rockingham.* 2 Vols. 1852.

Almon, John   *Anecdotes of the Life of William Pitt.* 3 Vols. 3rd edition. 1793.
History of the Late Minority. 1766.
Review of Lord Bute's Administration.

Annual Register

Anson   *Memoirs of the Duke of Grafton.* 1898.

Ballantyne, A.   *Life of Lord Carteret.* 1887.

Bancroft, George   *History of the American Revolution.* 3 Vols. 1812.

Bedford   *Correspondence of John, Fourth Duke of Bedford.* 3 Vols. 1842–6.

Bridport Papers   British Museum.

British Diplomatic Instructions. Vol. VII. *France*, Part IV, 1745–89. *Camden Third Series.* 1934.

Buckinghamshire, Earl of *Correspondence*, 1762–5. 2 Vols. 1900–2.

Burke, Edmund   *Correspondence.* 2 Vols. 1852.
Works. *World's Classics.* 6 Vols. 1906–7.

Burrows, M.   *Life of Edward, Lord Hawke.* 3rd edition. 1904.

Butler, John   *Serious Considerations on the Measures of the Present Administration.* 1763.

Cambridge Modern History. Vol. VI. 1934.

Carlyle, T.   *Frederick the Great.* 5 Vols. 1903.

Chatham   *Correspondence of William Pitt.* 4 Vols. 1840.
Plan Offered to the House of Lords. 1775.
Speeches. *The Modern Orator.* 1848.
MSS. Public Record Office.

Chatsworth Collection   MSS. at Chatsworth.

Chesterfield, Lord   *Letters.* 3 Vols. 1926.

Clive, Lord   *A Letter to the Proprietors of the East India Stock.* 1764.

Coleridge, E. H.   *Life of Thomas Coutts.* 2 Vols. 1920.

Conduct of a Rt. Hon. Gentleman in resigning the Seals, The. 1761.

Corbett, Sir J.   *England in the Seven Years' War.* 2 Vols. 1907.

Coupland, R.   *The Quebec Act.* 1925.

Cotes, H.   *An Enquiry into the conduct of a late Rt. Hon. Commoner.* 1766.

Devonshire, Duke of   MSS. Diary. Chatsworth Collection.
Dickens and Stanton   *An Eighteenth Century Correspondence.* 1910.
Dodwell, H.   *Dupleix and Clive.* 1920.
Egerton MSS.   British Museum.
Elliot, G. F. S.   *The Border Elliots.* 1907.
Eyck, Erick   *Pitt versus Fox: Father and Son.* 1950.
Fitzmaurice, Lord E.   *Life of William, Earl of Shelburne.* 2 Vols. 1875–6.
Fortescue, Sir J.   *Correspondence of King George the Third.* Vols.
                        1–4. 1927–8.

Franklin, Benjamin.   *Autobiography and Letters.* Edited by John
                        Bigelow.
Fulford, R.   *Glyn's 1753–1953.* 1953.
Gleig, G. R.   *Life of Robert, First Lord Clive.* 1907.
Grant, R.   *History of the East India Company.* 1813.
Grenville   *The Grenville Papers.* 4 Vols. 1852.
Hartshorne, A.   *Memoirs of a Royal Chaplain, 1729–63.* 1905.
H.M.C.   Bathurst MSS.
                        Denbigh MSS.
                        Emly MSS.
                        Lansdowne MSS.
                        Lonsdale MSS.
                        Lothian MSS.
                        Macaulay MSS.
                        Stopford-Sackville MSS.
                        Townshend MSS.
                        Underwood MSS.
                        Various Collections, Vol. VI.
                        Weston MSS.
Hardwicke   Hardwicke Papers. British Museum.
Hervey, Lady   *Letters of Mary Lepel, Lady Hervey.* 1821.
Hudleston, F. J.   *Gentleman Johnny Burgoyne.* 1928.
Ilchester, Earl of   *Henry Fox, First Lord Holland.* 2 Vols. 1920.
Ives, Edward   *A Voyage to India and an Historical Narrative,*
                        etc. 1773.
Jenkinson, Charles   *A Collection of Treaties.* 3 Vols. 1785.
Johnson, Dr.   *The False Alarm.*
                        Thoughts on the late Transaction respecting
                        Falkland's Islands.
Jucker, N. S.   *The Jenkinson Papers, 1760–1766.* 1949.
Junius   *Letters.* 2 Vols. 1907.
Kimball, G. S.   *Correspondence of William Pitt.* 2 Vols. 1842.
Knox, W.   *The Present State of the Nation.* 1768.
Lloyd, Charles   *A True History of a Late Short Administration.*
                        1766.
Lecky, W. E. H.   *History of England in the 18th Century.* 8 Vols.
                        1883.
Long, J. C.   *Mr. Pitt and America's Birthright.* 1940.
Mahon, Lord   *History of England.* 7 Vols. 5th edition. 1858.

Maitland, F. W.   *Constitutional History of England.* 1909.
Malmesbury, Earl of   *Diaries and Correspondence.* 4 Vols. 1845.
                           Letters. 2 Vols. 1870.
Mantoux, Paul   *The Industrial Revolution in the 18th Century.*
                           1948.
Miller, John C.   *The Origins of the American Revolution.* 1946.
Mitchell, A.   Mitchell Papers. British Museum.
Morison, S. E.   *Sources and Documents Illustrating the American
                           Revolution, 1764–1788.* 1923.
Mumby, F. A.   *George III and the American Revolution.* 1930.
Namier, Sir L.   *England in the Age of the American Revolution.*
                           1930.
                           *The Structure of Politics at the Accession of
                           George III.* 1929.
Newcastle, Duke of   *A Narrative, etc.* Letters edited by M. Bateson.
                           1898.
                           Newcastle Papers. British Museum.
Norfolk Contest, The   *A Collection of the most material Papers, etc.* 1768.
Papers relative to the Rupture with Spain. 1762.
Parkes and Merivale   *Memoirs of Sir Philip Francis.* 2 Vols. 1867.
Parkman, F.   *The Conspiracy of Pontiac.* 2 Vols. 1899.
Pemberton, W. B.   *Lord North.* 1938.
Phillimore, R.   *Memoirs and Correspondence of George, Lord
                           Lyttelton.* 2 Vols. 1845.
Plumb, J. H.   *Chatham.* 1953.
Prior, J.   *Life of Burke.* 2 Vols. 1826.
Rashed, Z. E.   *The Peace of Paris, 1761.* 1951.
Robertson, Sir C. Grant   *England under the Hanoverians.* 2nd edition.
                           1912.
Ruffhead, O.   *Considerations of the Present Dangerous Crisis.*
                           1763.
Ruville, A. von   *William Pitt, Earl of Chatham.* 3 Vols. 1907.
Sedgwick, R.   *Letters from George III to Lord Bute, 1756–66.*
                           Edited by R. Sedgwick. 1939.
Select Collection of the most interesting letters, etc. 2 Vols. 2nd edition. 1763.
Sherrard, O. A.   *A Life of John Wilkes.* 1930.
                           Lord Chatham: Pitt and the Seven Years' War.
                           1955.
Taswell-Langmead, T. P.   *English Constitutional History.* 6th edition.
                           1905.
Tucker, Josiah   *An Humble Address, etc.* 2nd edition. 1775.
Tunstall, Brian   *William Pitt, Earl of Chatham.* 1938.
Walpole, H.   *Last Journals.* 2 Vols. 1910.
                           Letters.
                           Memoirs of the Reign of George III. 4 Vols. 1894.
Wilkes, J.   *A Complete Collection of Genuine Papers, etc.* 1767.
                           North Briton. 2 Vols. 1763.
                           MSS. British Museum.

Williams, B.   *The Life of William Pitt, Earl of Chatham.*
                      2 Vols. 1913.
Winstanley, D. A.   *Lord Chatham and the Whig Opposition.* 1912.
                      Personal and Party Government. 1910.
Woodward, W. H.   *A Short History of the Expansion of the British*
                      Empire. 2nd edition. 1907.
Wortley, Stuart   *A Prime Minister and his son.* 1925.
Wright, Thomas   *England under the House of Hanover.* 2 Vols.
                      1848.
Wrong, G. M.   *Canada and the American Revolution.* 1935.

INDEX

DATE DUE

FEB 7 '90